CONTENTS

D0701833

Vertical Tab

The vertical tab on the right-hand margin of each double-page spread is a navigational tool designed to help you find your way around the guide. The top section lists the individual chapters, while the lower section highlights the part of the chapter you are currently reading.

Index

If you would rather play with a minimum of assistance, the guide's comprehensive Index can be used to jump to a topic of interest whenever you need a hint or specific piece of information.

Update

We have taken every step to ensure that the contents of this guide are correct at the time of going to press. However, future updates to Dragon Age II may incorporate attribute adjustments, gameplay balancing and even feature additions that we cannot anticipate at the time of writing.

Foreword

Following the critical success of Dragon Age: Origins, we knew we had something special on our hands: the world of Thedas seemed to resonate with people, drawing them in (and in some cases *back*) to fantasy. Reflecting on it, I think Origins' success was a result of being both different enough to break the mould while still being familiar enough that you could recognize the pieces. It didn't seek to alienate long-time fantasy fans so much as provoke thought: if mages could control people's minds, wouldn't people be terrified of them? Of course!

And so, as a team that I am quite frankly honored to work alongside turned their sights to Dragon Age II, one thing stood out to us: we didn't want to make the sequel everyone expected. Jokingly, we used to pitch that sequel as "two archdemons stapled together to lead a *super Blight*!" Perhaps you can see why we wanted something different.

The guide you hold in your hands — which details one regular person's rise to an extraordinary place in history, with all the twists and turns that entails — is the end result of that team's remarkable hard work and dedication.

Herein, you'll find detailed quest information, strategies for building and deploying your character and companions, tactics to master the new responsive combat mechanics and cross-class combos, and a number of secrets that might have slipped past you otherwise. The team at Piggyback (supported by the tireless efforts of our own Chris Corfe) have taken great pains to ensure this guide is all you need to savor the Champion of Kirkwall's rise to power.

So, as you set out to play through the most significant moments in the life of the man or woman who changed the world, good fortunes and safe travels in the dark days ahead. On behalf of the teams at both BioWare and Piggyback, welcome to Kirkwall. We know you'll do us proud, Champion.

Mike Laidlaw
Lead Designer, Dragon Age II

PRIMER

We understand that you're eager to begin playing straight away, so rest assured that we intend to restrict preamble to a bare minimum. Over the following pages we'll introduce you to the structure employed by this guide (and how you might best use it), offer a concise appraisal of useful game features and functions, and end with an overview of a few essential Dragon Age II concepts.

INTRODUCTION

Before you continue, please take a moment to familiarize yourself with the structure of this guide. Despite the dizzying array of options and opportunities in a single Dragon Age II playthrough, we have attempted to create a guide that doesn't merely offer a prescribed path through the adventure, but also enables you to make your own decisions – to play in the manner that *you* see fit.

WALKTHROUGH

With Dragon Age II defined by its huge number of quests, many of which have short or long-term consequences, a conventional start-to-finish walkthrough would be a sprawling jungle, crawling with bewildering caveats and qualifications. For this reason, we have instead chosen to present what we regard as a rewarding and enjoyable path through BioWare's absorbing and expansive adventure.

In short, you can regard our walkthrough as an "optimal" Dragon Age II playthrough, charting an efficient and rewarding route through all essential main plot missions.

Players who would like to complete optional activities will find page references to the companion Quests chapter, while those who simply wish to see the story through to its conclusion can do just that. Follow our guidance, prompts and suggestions closely, and you'll experience a successful and enjoyable first playthrough.

As a general rule, left-hand pages in the Walkthrough chapter offer concise guidance on what you must accomplish in each main plot quest. Right-hand pages focus on tactics and strategies, feature introductions, analysis and optional tasks.

1

2

QUESTS

This chapter has information on every quest in Dragon Age II, and details the repercussions of all major actions or decisions. During a first run through the game, readers can follow page references from the Walkthrough chapter to complete optional tasks or study alternative solutions to critical main plot quests. On any subsequent playthrough, this chapter can be used for reference as you experiment with different resolutions to the many interlinked stories.

The majority of quests are divided into five categories: main plot, secondary, companion, side quests and (in a few select instances) Premium Content.

- The Quests chapter is split into sections that correspond with Dragon Age II's three-Act structure. Each of these begins with a flowchart that offers a visual representation of how to unlock the core quests in that Act.
- The main plot sections act as an addendum to the Walkthrough chapter, detailing alternative approaches to situations within mandatory quests critical to the main storyline.
- The secondary, companion and side quest sections offer more detailed descriptions and walkthroughs for their respective quests, with guidance tailored to suit the level of assistance most players will need.

STRATEGY & ANALYSIS

Once you are ready to understand the game on a deeper level, the Strategy & Analysis chapter is where we examine the mechanics that underpin the entire Dragon Age II experience.

As most players will want to learn more about certain key game features (such as combat tactics, abilities, or leveling up and associated concepts) during a first playthrough without having the story ruined, we have divided this chapter into two sections: an opening "spoiler light" section, followed by a second part that covers features that are strongly linked to narrative events in Dragon Age II (such as companion relationships). We strongly advise that players leave the latter part well alone until they have finished the story at least once.

INVENTORY

This chapter not only provides details on all preset items in Dragon Age II, but also reveals where to find unique objects (including armor upgrades for companions and Backpack expansions), and a guide to how the "random" item generation system works.

EXTRAS

The Extras chapter is home to reading material only suitable for consumption after completing the game, including story recaps (for both Dragon Age II and predecessor Origins) and a glossary of major events, characters and concepts.

Extras also includes a dedicated guide to all Achievements and Trophies in Dragon Age II. Players who take pride in acquiring such accomplishments should be warned that this is also (alas, unavoidably) packed with story spoilers. We do, however, offer prompts on "missable" accomplishments of this ilk throughout the Walkthrough and Quests chapters.

3 4 5 6 7 8

MAPS

To save you the trouble of scouring every corner of each new environment for collectibles, the Maps chapter reveals the location of every notable container or item you can get. To find a location visited during your current quest, just refer to the tab system of the Maps chapter, or to the guide's Index. Given the sheer number of areas in Dragon Age II, and different permutations of frequently visited locales, grouping all maps together is by far the most practical and user-friendly solution to make them easy to access.

BESTIARY

Dragon Age II features a huge variety of combat situations. This chapter examines each type of enemy, offering information on their abilities, strengths and weaknesses – and how you might adapt your strategies to counter or exploit these to your advantage.

As with the Strategy & Analysis chapter, all spoiler-heavy contents (story-related enemies) appear in the final section of the Bestiary.

INDEX & GLOSSARY

Last (but, given the need for easy reference in a tome this large, by no means least), our comprehensive Index will enable you to find the information you need in an instant. All entries are color-coded to help you to avoid spoiler-heavy sections of the guide until you are ready. We have created a short glossary for those who have yet to play Dragon Age: Origins, or are otherwise unfamiliar with RPG mainstays.

USEFUL FEATURES

ONSCREEN DISPLAY

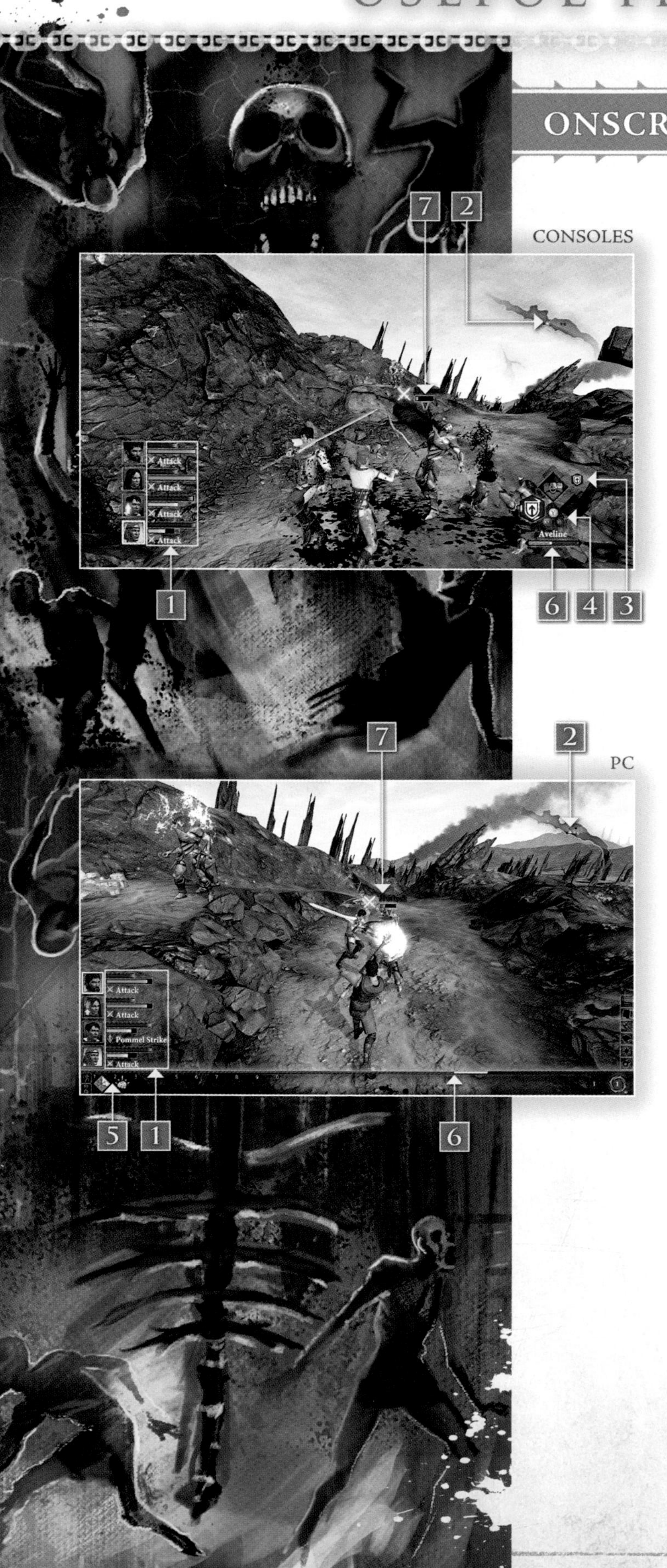

1 **Party Gauges:** These provide information on the status of Hawke and his active companions.

- The box highlight indicates the character currently under your direct control.
- The red bar is the health gauge. When this is exhausted during combat, a character is rendered unconscious and can play no further part until combat ends (or, later in the game, is revived).
- The bar beneath indicates a character's current stamina (yellow) or mana reserves (blue – mages only). This is required to use the majority of abilities acquired during the course of the story.
- During combat, simple descriptions of each party member's actions or reactions will appear beneath the above gauges. You can use these prompts to keep track of companions outside your field of view.
- If a party member is ready to level up, an animated arrow will appear within their portrait window.

2 **Minimap:** This shows an outline view of your current surroundings, including significant points of interactivity. See "Maps" overleaf for further information.

3 **Sustained Abilities & Status Effects:** These icons indicate which status effects or sustained abilities are affecting the currently selected party member. A red hue denotes a harmful status effect inflicted by an opponent; a clockwise fill indicates the time remaining until this effect elapses.

4 **Battle Menu Shortcuts (Xbox 360 & PS3 only):** By default, this display shows the first set of three abilities that can be performed with the Battle Menu Shortcut buttons. Hold the Shortcut button (RT / R2) to both view and activate abilities in the second set.

5 **Quickbar (PC only):** Those playing the PC version can assign up to ten keyboard shortcuts for abilities, and have a further nine mapped to the quickbar for easy access with a mouse. From the Abilities menu, simply drag the talents or spells of your choice to the slots at the bottom of the screen. The quickbar also features shortcuts that correspond to Radial Menu options in the console releases.

6 **XP Gauge:** This bar gives an approximate indication of how far the selected character has to progress until they level up. Sums of XP awarded after battles or from specific feats will appear briefly to the left of this meter.

7 **Current Target:** This icon indicates your current target; the enemy in question will also be surrounded by a fairly subtle highlight and have its name displayed. When you use an activated ability that covers a specific area (rather than an individual opponent), all adversaries within its effect range will be emphasized in this manner. During combat, the allegiance of all participants is denoted by a circle at their feet: red for enemies, yellow for companions and blue for other allies.

RADIAL MENU (XBOX 360 & PS3 ONLY)

Activating the Radial Menu (LT/L2) offers access to a wide range of useful features and functions. It also pauses the action, which provides time to survey the field of combat and formulate strategies. Though you will rarely need to use it for this purpose during the opening few hours of play, you will find that it becomes a common occurrence during many of Dragon Age II's more demanding battles – especially on higher difficulty levels. On PC, most icons from the Radial Menu appear on the quickbar at the bottom of the screen.

The text that follows is a quick introduction to each Radial Menu option. We'll cover these in greater detail in the Walkthrough chapter.

Quick Heal: Instantly applies the most appropriate Health Potion to the character under your direct control. This can be adjusted in the Options menu.

Hold Position: Instructs selected party member(s) to remain in their current location. Very useful if you wish to carefully entice enemies to a specific position, or need to prevent overzealous companions from rushing into ruinous situations during difficult battles.

Activated Spells/Talents: You will reach a point during Act 1 where you acquire more abilities than Battle Menu Shortcuts, which is where this sub-menu becomes much more relevant. It's also useful when you wish to set up commands for party members while the action is paused – for example, to unleash a simultaneous four-pronged assault on a particularly dangerous opponent. Battle Menu Shortcuts can be assigned or customized via this option.

Poisons and Bombs: This enables you to coat weapons with poisons (contributing additional status effects and/or damage), or hurl explosives at your opponents. (Not available until Act 1.)

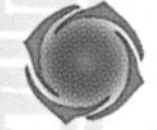
Quick Mana/Quick Stamina: In the same manner as Quick Heal, this instantly applies a Lyrium Potion or Stamina Draught (as applicable) to the character under your control.

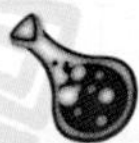
Potions: This sub-menu provides access to all potions in your inventory.

Sustained Spells/Talents: Another sub-menu, used to activate or deactivate "sustained" abilities. We'll return to this later: it's of no great consequence during the Prologue.

Move to Point: This option is used to manually direct selected party member(s) to a specific position. Usually employed in conjunction with Hold Position for precision battle management.

MAPS

The minimap and Map screen are invaluable tools as you navigate Dragon Age II's many locales.

- Press the Map button (BACK/SELECT) to visit the dedicated Map screen.
- Places of interest, points of interactivity and active waypoints are marked by icons. If you are unsure of what a particular symbol on the minimap represents, visit the main Map screen to study the legend. The same icons are used for both the full and truncated map.
- The minimap features animated icons (▲) that direct you to waypoints in active quests (▼). It's sometimes possible to have a few of these active at once. When you visit certain "hub" areas (particularly the major districts of Kirkwall), it's usually sensible to visit the Map screen to identify which one you seek.
- Dragon Age II's maps do not include markers for containers or collectibles... but ours do. Our dedicated Maps chapter begins on page 108.

BUTTON DEFINITIONS

As Xbox 360, PS3 and PC players own different control devices, we generally use the standardized terms presented in the table below to refer to each button or key in many areas of the guide. These should be easy to recognize, but you can return here to refresh your memory at any point.

We also tend to offer slightly more assistance to Xbox 360 and PS3 players in the early sections of the guide as the console versions of Dragon Age II will be played by an audience with wildly varying levels of gaming ability and RPG experience.

XBOX 360	PS3	BUTTON DEFINITION	SUMMARY
L	L	Movement stick	Move the character that is under your direct control. By default, your character will target the closest enemy in the direction faced unless instructed otherwise.
R	R	Camera stick	Used to adjust the game camera.
D-pad	D-pad	Target Select buttons	Used to cycle through points of interactivity while free roaming (companions, containers, et al), or to pick specific targets during combat.
A	⊗	Interact button	Used to confirm decisions and ability usage, initiate conversations, collect loot, open doors and containers, and a host of other interactions. During combat, this triggers your character's low-powered "default" attack.
B	◎	Battle Menu Shortcut buttons (Xbox 360 & PS3 only)	Performs the ability assigned to the relevant Battle Menu Shortcut slot. Also employed to cancel actions or move back one step in the user interface.
Y	△		Performs the ability assigned to the relevant Battle Menu Shortcut slot.
X	◻		Performs the ability assigned to the relevant Battle Menu Shortcut slot. Also employed to skip through lines of dialogue, or entire cutscenes.
LB / RB	L1 / R1	Party Select buttons	Cycle through available party members. Press both Party Select buttons simultaneously to select all party members at once.
LT	L2	Radial Menu button (Xbox 360 & PS3 only)	Brings up the Radial Menu. You must hold this by default; there is an option to change it to an on/off toggle at the Options ⇨ Gameplay options screen.
RT	R2	Shortcut button (Xbox 360 & PS3 only)	Hold to bring the second set of Battle Menu Shortcuts to the fore.
L (click)	L3	Target Lock button	Use this to ensure that all attacks will be directed at the specified target. Automatically disengaged once an enemy has been disabled.
R (click)	R3	Center Camera button	Immediately rotates the camera to face in the same direction as the character under your control.
START	START	Pause Menu button	Opens the pause menu.
BACK	SELECT	Map button	Used to open/close the map screen.

ESSENTIAL GAMEPLAY CONCEPTS

CHOOSING A CLASS

The class you choose at the beginning of Dragon Age II has a significant effect on your play experience. Your gender, however, is a primarily aesthetic concern: with the exception of minor dialogue changes and different opportunities for romantic attachments with companions, there are no specific advantages or drawbacks to either sex.

Mage

Perhaps the most enjoyable class to play, mages can exert greater influence (indeed, control) over combat encounters than their more melee-focused peers thanks to the sheer number of potential options at their disposal. The least robust of the three classes, mages specialize in spells that can be cast at range (particularly magical attacks). Their ability to strike or support from afar is a necessity: they will fall swiftly under a concerted assault, and must always rely on their cohorts to shield them from danger. As a player, you will find that their typical position on the periphery of each battle affords you an excellent tactical overview of proceedings.

If you decide that Hawke will be a mage, it makes sense to shape him or her as a so-called "nuke", focused on debilitating magical assaults and devastating Area of Effect (AoE) attacks. That's not to say that you can't slightly customize this archetype to include less explicitly aggressive abilities. An extra Heal spell, for example, will never go amiss.

Rogue

The overhauled rogue class offers an enormous amount of scope for interesting character builds, and is vastly different from the rogues in Dragon Age: Origins. The core decision with a rogue is whether to favor ranged combat (through archery) or focus on causing havoc as a melee fighter (dual-wielding two daggers). Thereafter, the possibilities are astonishingly broad. The rogue's class-specific talents can enable them to flit around any given battlefield with ease, inflicting targeted harm and disappearing before any reprisals can take place. This gives the game a much more action-oriented, hack 'n' slash feel that some players may prefer.

Rogues also have two unique abilities: they alone can pick locks and detect or disable traps. Having a rogue in your party will increase your ability to accumulate loot of all kinds (from otherwise inaccessible locked chests) and, to a lesser extent, XP (awarded for both lockpicking and disarming traps). That said, this doesn't mean that it's a class that you should feel obliged to adopt: you will recruit two companions who can fulfill this role early in Act 1.

Warrior

The warrior specializes in melee combat only, wielding either a sword and shield or a massive two-handed blade or cudgel. Within this class, there are two fairly distinct archetypes:

- The **"tank"**: a near-essential fixture in any party, this warrior is focused on attracting enemy attention and withstanding terrible punishment at the very heart of any given battle. They are not built to inflict heavy damage, but to survive it. Effectively, they act as a lightning rod for hostiles in range, therefore enabling their cohorts (especially weaker mages) to make decisive attacks without fear of devastating reprisal.

- The **"damage dealer"**: a less robust warrior build focused on abilities that cause greater harm. These can play a decisive role in battles against strong individual enemies, but tend to be less efficient against large groups of stock assailants.

Conclusion

Hawke will usually fight alongside three allies. It's therefore vital to remember that your character is a mechanism in a larger machine, and must possess attributes and aptitudes that complement those of his or her companions. The most practical party build for a balanced first playthrough consists of a warrior who adopts the tank role, a rogue (either ranged or close-quarters), and two mages: one concentrating on raw damage, while the other works in a support/healer capacity.

We recommend using the mage class for your first playthrough: concentrating on raw damage from afar is an ideal way to build a greater appreciation of how Dragon Age II works. Our second choice would be the rogue: these dynamic and daring characters are a lot of fun to play, though they are a little more demanding to control. This may seem to belittle the warrior, but that's not our intention: it's just that this class is arguably a more "technical" choice than the other two in how its abilities must be used for maximum efficiency. The warrior is probably best left for a future playthrough when you have a better understanding of the game and its multifarious mechanics.

Players who wish to consider every available option before committing to a decision can find a complete appraisal of character archetypes and reliable party builds in the Strategy & Analysis chapter.

COMPANIONS

Through the early stages of the adventure, Hawke can encounter individuals who become "companions" during the events of Dragon Age II. Each potential cohort has their own unique personality and a wide assortment of aptitudes and specialties.

- Certain companions are enlisted automatically. Others must be sought out, or acquired by completing a particular quest. We'll let you know whenever this is possible.

- While you can select weapons and accessories for companions, each has a preset one-piece armor suit that cannot be unequipped. This can be improved by finding or purchasing special upgrades.

- Your relationship with each companion is graded on a scale that ranges between "rivalry" and "friendship" (Fig. 1). This shifts constantly as they react to your decisions and dialogue choices while they are in the active party. There is no right or wrong way to approach this feature, though there are certainly ways to manage it to achieve your desired goals. The Quests chapter features tips on which actions will lead to significant levels of approval or disapproval.

- Whenever a new companion is introduced, we offer a quick appraisal of key traits or attitudes that define them. You can use this advice to tailor your dealings with your party members and, perhaps more importantly, your attitude towards other people you meet while they are present. Note that, with exceptions that we will make abundantly clear in due time, a state of high rivalry is not necessarily a bad thing: it's just a different type of relationship.

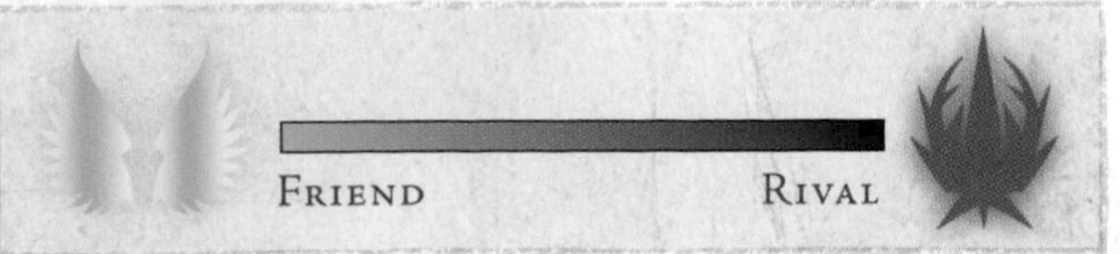

LOOT

Dragon Age II employs a distinctive shimmering effect to highlight certain points of interactivity. In most instances, these are used to highlight sources of loot – such as containers, corpses, furniture or piles of rocks (Fig. 2).

02

Loot can take a variety of forms, though there are broadly three categories: equipment (weapons, armor and accessories), raw currency and junk. The latter exists purely to be sold, often for a modest return, so it can be regarded as essentially coin in a less convenient form. Most pieces of equipment are randomly generated in accordance with Hawke's current level, though you will also encounter many prebuilt items of interest (or resale value).

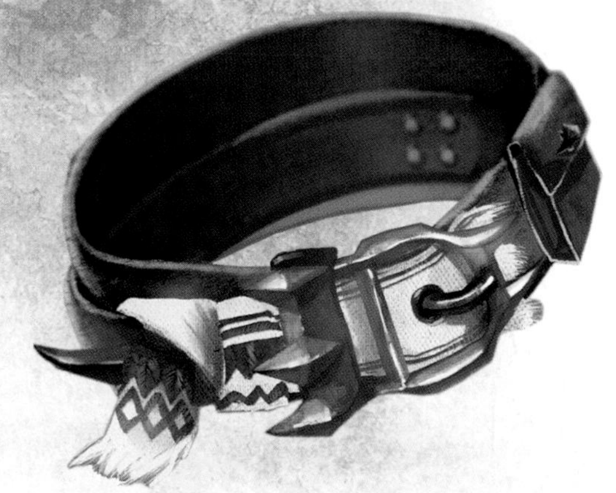

It's impossible to overstate the value of diligent pillaging every last room, path and battlefield. Incremental character growth through attribute increases and talent acquisition is important, granted, but the most reliable way to stay ahead of the difficulty curve is through equipping the finest weapons, armor and accessories that you can find, or your appropriated Sovereigns can buy.

Though collecting everything you can lay your hands on is undoubtedly the path to success, your ability to do so is not unrestricted. All items (with the exception of plot-critical objects, which do not appear on the Inventory screen) have an inherent "weight": one unit per slot of inventory space. In short, this means that both a piece of armor and a stack of seven potions will contribute exactly one point towards your party's collective burden. Your inventory space is initially capped at 50, but you can increase this carrying capacity by purchasing Backpack expansions (each offering additional slots) from select vendors in and around Kirkwall. As a rule, though, it's always a good idea to stop by a vendor to offload surplus items between quests. There's nothing more frustrating than hitting a mother lode of loot while sufficiently far from civilization to preclude a quick selling trip, and realizing that you must leave treasures or destroy existing items due to poor inventory management.

All area maps appear in our dedicated Maps chapter, which begins on page 108. These reveal the location of all notable loot containers (including locked chests) that you can find throughout the game. Your equipment options in the Prologue are rather limited to making use of what you find, but Act 1 introduces countless possibilities. From that point forward, the Inventory chapter will reveal which weapons, armor, accessories and upgrades offer the best perks for your current level – and, in many instances, how much you will need to earn to obtain them.

TERMS AND ABBREVIATIONS

Whenever you encounter an unfamiliar term or abbreviation, our Glossary should provide the explanation you seek. Though we have made every effort to make the guide approachable to players of all backgrounds, readers less versed in RPG terminology and abbreviations can visit this to reveal the meaning of quizzical expressions such as *"Threat"* (the system that governs which party member enemies will target) and *"AoE"* (Area of Effect: used to describe abilities that cover a designated area rather than a specific target).

WALKTHROUGH

Designed to ease players through plot-critical quests on a first playthrough, this chapter charts a direct course through Dragon Age II's main storyline. Readers who wish to plot their own path can use the walkthrough in conjunction with the Quests chapter to experience the adventure in their own unique way.

USER INSTRUCTIONS

BEFORE YOU CONTINUE, TAKE A FEW MOMENTS TO FAMILIARIZE YOURSELF WITH THE STRUCTURE AND SYSTEMS USED THROUGHOUT OUR WALKTHROUGH AND ITS RELATIONSHIP TO THE QUESTS AND MAPS CHAPTERS.

A **Left-Hand Pages – Main Walkthrough:** These offer an "optimal" path through all mandatory quests, taking the most direct possible route through Dragon Age II.

- Each page begins with a "Quest Summary & Map References" section. This is a quick recap of all steps that must be followed in the quests it covers, with useful page references to the Maps chapter.
- The core of the walkthrough is structured in numbered paragraphs. As a rule, each paragraph is dedicated to a specific "main plot" quest. Follow our step-by-step guidance and you'll experience a successful and enjoyable first playthrough.

B **Right-Hand Pages – Additional Information:** These pages cover a wide variety of topics, with a particular focus on subjects related to your progress in the core storyline.

- **Feature Introductions & Analysis:** We offer words of wisdom on new game features and faces as you encounter them and include page references to elsewhere in the guide (particularly the Strategy & Analysis chapter) for those who wish to understand Dragon Age II on a deeper level. We also provide occasional tips to help Achievement and Trophy hunters collect the accolades they crave.
- **Extended Walkthroughs:** For longer or more demanding quests, we offer additional guidance where it matters most – particularly when you face unique opponents.
- **Optional Activities:** To help you to complete all major optional ventures of note, we make recommendations on which ones you really should complete in each Act, with page references to the Quests chapter.

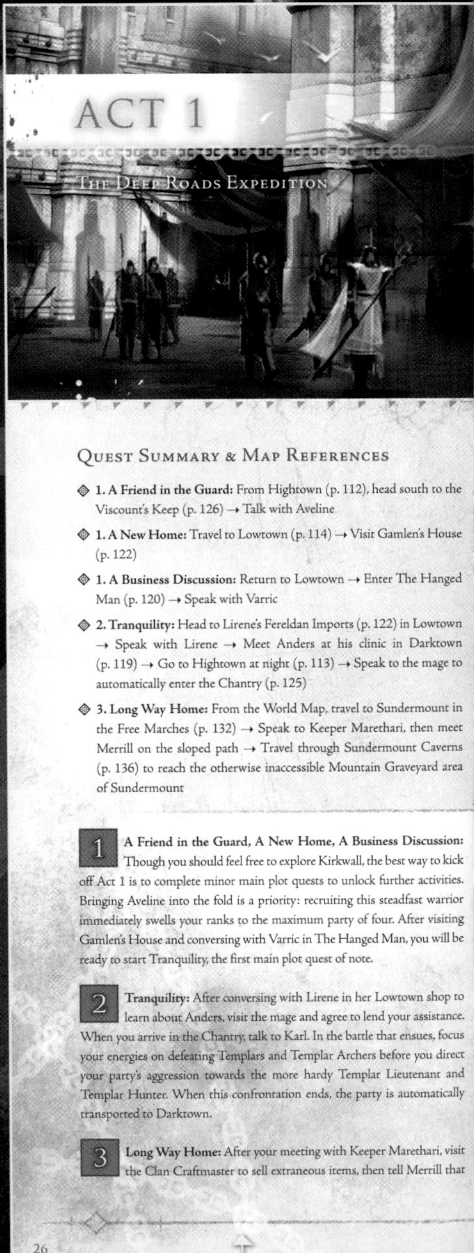

ACT 1

THE DEEP ROADS EXPEDITION

QUEST SUMMARY & MAP REFERENCES

- **1. A Friend in the Guard:** From Hightown (p. 112), head south to the Viscount's Keep (p. 126) → Talk with Aveline
- **1. A New Home:** Travel to Lowtown (p. 114) → Visit Gamlen's House (p. 122)
- **1. A Business Discussion:** Return to Lowtown → Enter The Hanged Man (p. 120) → Speak with Varric
- **2. Tranquility:** Head to Lirene's Fereldan Imports (p. 122) in Lowtown → Speak with Lirene → Meet Anders at his clinic in Darktown (p. 119) → Go to Hightown at night (p. 113) → Speak to the mage to automatically enter the Chantry (p. 125)
- **3. Long Way Home:** From the World Map, travel to Sundermount in the Free Marches (p. 132) → Speak to Keeper Marethari, then meet Merrill on the sloped path → Travel through Sundermount Caverns (p. 136) to reach the otherwise inaccessible Mountain Graveyard area of Sundermount

1 **A Friend in the Guard, A New Home, A Business Discussion:** Though you should feel free to explore Kirkwall, the best way to kick off Act 1 is to complete minor main plot quests to unlock further activities. Bringing Aveline into the fold is a priority: recruiting this steadfast warrior immediately swells your ranks to the maximum party of four. After visiting Gamlen's House and conversing with Varric in The Hanged Man, you will be ready to start Tranquility, the first main plot quest of note.

2 **Tranquility:** After conversing with Lirene in her Lowtown shop to learn about Anders, visit the mage and agree to lend your assistance. When you arrive in the Chantry, talk to Karl. In the battle that ensues, focus your energies on defeating Templars and Templar Archers before you direct your party's aggression towards the more hardy Templar Lieutenant and Templar Hunter. When this confrontation ends, the party is automatically transported to Darktown.

3 **Long Way Home:** After your meeting with Keeper Marethari, visit the Clan Craftmaster to sell extraneous items, then tell Merrill that

26

C Quests Chapter: Whereas the walkthrough offers one path through the game, the Quest chapter adopts a more open approach, enabling you to complete the story in the manner you see fit. This is where you will find all details on branching story paths, the long-term consequences of your choices, and much, *much* more. You can use both chapters in conjunction to reach 100% completion.

D Maps Chapter: All maps in this guide appear in a dedicated chapter. Whenever you need to consult one of them as you follow our walkthrough, simply look up the relevant page reference in the Quest Summary on the left-hand page.

Index & Glossary

With a game as huge as Dragon Age II, page-flicking through the mighty tome in front of you to find details on a quest, a map, a concept or a creature can be a thankless task. This is where our invaluable Index comes in. If you ever need to find information on a specific topic or term, just look it up in the Index.

. The Dalish mage acts as a guest party member for ...est. Though you cannot control her directly, she will ...he sees fit. The journey to the Sundermount Passage ...y battles with undead foes; the presence of bodies on ...ign of trouble ahead.

... Caverns, try to stay close to the entrance when ...more enter the fray from the ceiling as the fight ...econd ambush in close confines (this time featuring ...t before the Mountain Graveyard exit. Don't head ...uring this battle (Fig. 1): doing so will bring further ...rpses, Shades and a dangerous Shadow Warrior) ...hese separately afterwards, claim whatever loot you ...nearby exit.

01

...o trigger a cutscene; your reaction to Merrill's magic ...iendship increments. Once the way forward is clear, ...counter will start. Beginning with Skeleton Archers, ...e such fiends as an Arcane Horror and a Shadow ...ave the latter foe until last: its high endurance will ...t while its weaker cohorts inflict great damage. After ...r (and the resultant conversation), return to the cave ...omatically transported first to the Dalish Camp, then ...cluding conversation with your new companion.

Using the World Map

- All exits marked "Leave Area" will take you to the World Map; those with an area name lead to a connected map.
- The World Map has three pages: Kirkwall (Day), Kirkwall (Night) and the Free Marches. All locations where you can advance active quests are marked by an arrow ( ). New destinations generally appear as you accept quests or make progress in existing ventures. Not all of these are permanent additions to the game world: certain locales disappear completely once you have satisfied all related plot requirements.
- Certain Kirkwall locations are only available during the day or night. Some areas (such as Lowtown, Hightown and the Docks) have unique evening versions of their maps where you will encounter different loot, denizens and quest opportunities.

Gamlen's House

Though Hawke's uncle may not be the most convivial host, this hovel acts as your base of operations during the events of Act 1. Paying a visit will instantly cure any existing injuries and allow you to reselect your party members.

- Interact with the Writing Desk to collect letters sent to Hawke. Though some missives only reflect plot developments (such as the letter that awaits you on first visit from the employer you chose at the end of the Prologue), reading many of these will trigger a quest or unlock the possibility of interaction in the game world. An animated envelope ( ) will appear next to Gamlen's House on the World Map whenever new mail arrives.
- The chest marked Storage can be used to safely stash items for future retrieval. This is extremely useful when you wish to save powerful weapons, armor or accessories until Hawke or his companions meet the usage requirements.
- Bethany or Carver can be found here when not travelling with your party. If you have access to Dog, you have one opportunity to rename him here. Miss it in Act 1, and you have to settle for the default monicker.

Optional Activities

The Birthright companion quest (page 63), unlocked on your first visit to Gamlen's House, is a short but rewarding episode that leads to a collection of significant secondary quests. You can also acquire Bait and Switch (page 57) from the Writing Desk (see Gamlen's House) which can lead to the recruitment of a new companion. If you have access to any of the three Premium Content quests available at launch, you can attend to these short tasks straight away (see page 69).

Lest you forget, the purpose of your Act 1 adventures is to raise capital to join Bartrand's Deep Roads expedition. The funds that you acquire by completing optional quests will provide all the sovereigns you need to accomplish that – and more besides.

Companions

Varric

Varric is arguably the most easygoing of Hawke's companions. You really need to be a *thoroughbred* bastard to invite his regular disapproval.

- He responds well to banter and relaxed humor. Unlike most other companions, Varric isn't defined by a personal crusade or all-pervading belief. He doesn't mind situations where individuals are seeking enrichment in ways that won't necessarily harm others. His silver tongue can be called into action to mediate peaceful solutions in a number of situations.
- Uniquely, Varric has a fixed weapon: Bianca, a crossbow that increases in power as he gains successive levels. Functioning exclusively as an archer, he can offer a potent combination of AoE assaults and debilitating attacks that offer your party an interesting tactical edge. See page 184 for further details.

Anders

First encountered in Dragon Age: Origins – Awakening, Anders is an apostate (a mage who refuses to submit to the Circle of Magi) and an erstwhile Grey Warden.

- Anders is an emotional character. He won't respond well if you reprimand him or if you are anything but committed in potential romantic interactions.
- Anders is inflexibly vociferous in his opposition to the treatment of mages in Kirkwall. That said, he adopts a rather less compassionate stance towards those who dabble in blood magic or involve themselves with demonic entities. Condoning such activities will anger him.
- Unless you intend to have Hawke perform this function, Anders is the companion best suited to the support healer role. See page 184 for more advice on this subject.

27

B

PROLOGUE

The Destruction of Lothering

1 After choosing your character's class (see page 13 for an overview of the available options) and watching the opening cinematics, you'll be plunged straight into combat against darkspawn. You will always automatically target one enemy in the direction faced, but it's worth noting that you can adjust this by moving the Camera stick, or using the Target Select buttons (✥) to cycle through assailants in order. On PC, you have to click on a target to select it. There's relatively little danger in this opening fight, so it's the perfect time to get a feel for the pace of combat.

Follow the onscreen prompts to try out a selection of abilities. Some of these require that you manually select a specific section of the battlefield. Once the targeting system activates (Fig. 1), use the Movement stick to select a suitable group of opponents, then unleash your assault of choice (Ⓐ/⊗ to fire; Ⓑ/◎ to cancel).

2 All characters in Dragon Age II have two forms of attack. The first (and most important) is activated abilities. On PS3 and Xbox 360, these are selected via the Radial Menu or, more commonly, the Battle Menu Shortcuts displayed in the lower right-hand corner of the screen (Fig. 2). Use the Shortcut button to toggle between the two available sets of three. On PC, you can simply use shortcut keys or the quickbar instead.

The second is a basic, standard assault with the equipped weapon, activated with a press of the Interact button (Ⓐ/⊗). If you wish, there is an option in the Options → Gameplay menu that forces your selected character to perform this attack automatically while not following other instructions.

3 Unlike the infinitely replenished standard attack, the use of all activated abilities is governed by the Cooldown mechanism. It's probably during your fight with the Ogre that this system will first become apparent. You cannot perform abilities (or repeat certain actions, such as using a potion) until the grey Cooldown transparency completes a full 360-degree refresh over the icon used to represent an ability or action (Fig. 3). As you will doubtlessly exhaust your stock of abilities before the Ogre and allies are beaten, this marks a solid introduction to Dragon Age II combat in its most rudimentary form. When enemies attack, this entry-level style of play sees you unleash every available activated ability, then switch to the standard attack while you wait for assorted Cooldowns to expire.

01

02

03

CREATING HAWKE

The second stage of the character creation process (following the earlier choice of class) is to pick your character's appearance and name, and select a narrative background that encompasses the events of Dragon Age: Origins. You must also select a difficulty level.

Appearance, Portrait and Name

These three options enable you to personalize your character, and have no bearing on Hawke's capabilities or later development. Though you may not notice on first playthrough, your chosen portrait will actually affect the appearance of Hawke's family members.

If you have access to the Black Emporium Premium Content (see dragonage.com/da2/addons), you can change your character's appearance, portrait and name at a later date.

Events of Dragon Age: Origins

Dragon Age II allows you to import information from a Dragon Age: Origins save file stored on your hard drive. The data interpreted by this feature reflects key decisions made by the Warden (the protagonist of Origins), and can influence your adventures in a number of ways. For example:

- Some Dragon Age II quests are only available if you aligned yourself with particular factions or individuals while playing Origins or its expansions. If, hypothetically, your Warden chose to side with the Dalish elves rather than the werewolves, supported Bhelen instead of Lord Harrowmont in Orzammar, or opted to eliminate Sophia Dryden and spare Avernus in the Warden's Keep downloadable content, you can potentially encounter side quests that reflect later consequences. The reverse, with these three instances, is also true. These are just a handful of examples.
- You will also encounter many ambient references to the world you left behind in your save: from a barman referencing the miraculous recovery of Arl Eamon at Andraste's apparent behest, to story summaries in the Journal that offer a precise appraisal of your adventures.

If you didn't play Dragon Age: Origins, worry not: there is a selection of three preset backgrounds that you can choose from.

- **Hero of Ferelden** represents an optimal playthrough in which the Warden adopted a resolutely noble approach to any given situation. This is the classic "good guy".
- **The Martyr**, as the name suggests, implies a path where the Warden opted to sacrifice himself at the climax of Dragon Age: Origins. This wasn't a Warden who always favored popular or easy decisions, but Ferelden was ultimately a better place for their actions.
- **No Compromise** could be described as the opposite end of the spectrum to Hero of Ferelden. It's not that this permutation of the Warden was necessarily evil, though; merely that this particular hard-bitten bastard strode a less flower-lined path through the moral mazes of Origins.

The Hero of Ferelden preset offers access to more reactive events and side quests than The Martyr or No Compromise, and is the option we would recommend for players who didn't play Dragon Age: Origins.

Difficulty

On a first playthrough, we would suggest that the Normal difficulty level is perfectly pitched for the vast majority of players. Higher settings provide your opponents with improved health, damage output, and attack scores and increase the frequency of special ability usage. You can adjust the difficulty level at any time during play, without penalty, and there really is no shame in dropping down to Casual should you hit a brick wall on a particular quest.

We would advise that all players pay the Nightmare setting a wide berth during their first time through the Dragon Age II story. In addition to the expected array of adjustments that brutally favor your opponents, this mode also activates friendly fire, so your party members can hurt each other with their attacks (particularly the AoE variety). This alteration necessitates an entirely different style of play. Only true Dragon Age masters should even consider it – and, even then, after at least one full playthrough.

Miscellany

- We refer to the main protagonist in Dragon Age II as Hawke throughout the guide. Though he obviously shares this surname with his siblings, this is the neatest way to sidestep the issue of millions of user-created forenames and two potential genders.
- The way in which you approach each conversation can affect how your companions perceive you. Consult page 160 of the Strategy & Analysis chapter to learn about Dragon Age II's dialogue system.

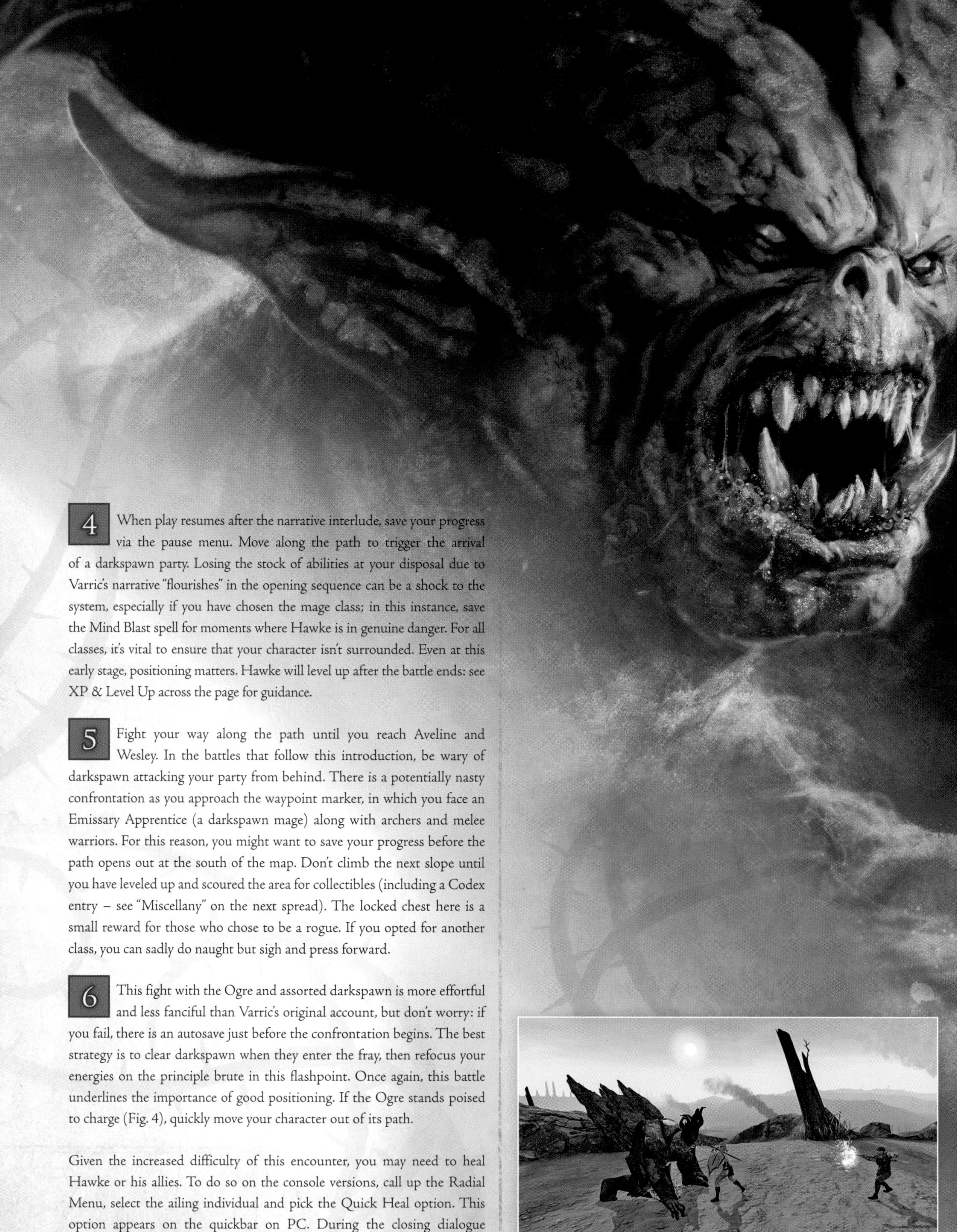

4 When play resumes after the narrative interlude, save your progress via the pause menu. Move along the path to trigger the arrival of a darkspawn party. Losing the stock of abilities at your disposal due to Varric's narrative "flourishes" in the opening sequence can be a shock to the system, especially if you have chosen the mage class; in this instance, save the Mind Blast spell for moments where Hawke is in genuine danger. For all classes, it's vital to ensure that your character isn't surrounded. Even at this early stage, positioning matters. Hawke will level up after the battle ends: see XP & Level Up across the page for guidance.

5 Fight your way along the path until you reach Aveline and Wesley. In the battles that follow this introduction, be wary of darkspawn attacking your party from behind. There is a potentially nasty confrontation as you approach the waypoint marker, in which you face an Emissary Apprentice (a darkspawn mage) along with archers and melee warriors. For this reason, you might want to save your progress before the path opens out at the south of the map. Don't climb the next slope until you have leveled up and scoured the area for collectibles (including a Codex entry – see "Miscellany" on the next spread). The locked chest here is a small reward for those who chose to be a rogue. If you opted for another class, you can sadly do naught but sigh and press forward.

6 This fight with the Ogre and assorted darkspawn is more effortful and less fanciful than Varric's original account, but don't worry: if you fail, there is an autosave just before the confrontation begins. The best strategy is to clear darkspawn when they enter the fray, then refocus your energies on the principle brute in this flashpoint. Once again, this battle underlines the importance of good positioning. If the Ogre stands poised to charge (Fig. 4), quickly move your character out of its path.

Given the increased difficulty of this encounter, you may need to heal Hawke or his allies. To do so on the console versions, call up the Radial Menu, select the ailing individual and pick the Quick Heal option. This option appears on the quickbar on PC. During the closing dialogue sequence, defer to Aveline ( ) during an emotional situation to cement a new friendship.

04

XP & LEVEL UP

Defeating enemies, completing quests and a host of other miscellaneous accomplishments (such as lockpicking and locating Codex entries) all cause Hawke and companions to accumulate experience points (XP). Once total XP reaches a preset threshold (as represented by the bar near the ability shortcuts), a character will level up. This is indicated by an animated arrow ( ) on the relevant portrait in the bottom left-hand corner of the screen.

There are two distinct stages to the level up process. To begin, access the pause menu, then select the Characters option. If you would prefer to have your party members level up automatically, you can use the button command shown at the bottom of this screen to accomplish this instantly. However, we would strongly recommend that you take full responsibility.

Step 1: Attributes

You have three attribute points to spend each time a character levels up. If you are keen to get a feel for the game before you learn more about the intricacies of the leveling system in the Strategy & Analysis chapter, the following short guidelines will suffice for the next few levels:

- **Warrior:** Invest one point in Strength (to increase fortitude and attack power), one in Cunning (to improve defense), and one in Constitution (to increase maximum health and physical resistance).
- **Rogue:** Only applicable for now if you actually chose this class: you don't encounter your first rogue companion until Act 1. We'd suggest that you place two points in Dexterity and one in Cunning.
- **Mage:** Allocate two points to Magic and one to Willpower. This will enhance the raw power of a mage's spells and offer a boost to their mana stocks. An alternative approach would be to put all three points into Magic while the number of abilities at your disposal (and, therefore, average mana expenditure) is low, then redress the Willpower imbalance during a later level-up before frequent mana shortages become an issue.

Step 2: Talents

Raw attributes matter, but it is your choice of talents that makes a character truly unique. There are well over 100 in total, divided into themed "trees", with each character given access to a small selection of these. Talents are unlocked incrementally, and it's easy to lose more minutes than you'd care to admit scouring the assorted trees while choosing a new ability. You only get one talent point for each level, though, so your decisions really matter – and doubly so at this delicate stage in your party's development. We strongly suggest that you turn to page 166 of the Strategy & Analysis chapter to learn which talents might best suit Hawke and his current companions.

COMPANIONS

Carver

A brash and headstrong young man, Carver bristles at the idea of being recognized as Hawke's younger brother rather than being appreciated for his own merits. His best role in the party is as a warrior focused on inflicting heavy damage with two-handed weapons.

- Unlike most other companions, Hawke's relationship with Carver has a preexisting slant towards rivalry from the very start of the game.
- If you want to secure a friendship with Carver, consult him whenever a suitable dialogue option arises, and just generally attempt to make him feel more than a mere passenger on Hawke's journey.
- The city of Kirkwall is in part defined by the tensions that exist between the powerful Order of the Templars and the mages they are charged to keep in line. As a rule, Carver tends to side with the established authorities on this issue.

Bethany

Hawke's sister Bethany is a mage. Sensitive and thoughtful, she is a more approachable soul than the brash Carver – and, therefore, easier to develop a friendship with.

- Bethany will approve if you speak out against or oppose the subjugation of mages. After a lifetime of concealing her natural gifts, she has a keen awareness of their plight.
- Though it's not as apparent as with Carver, Bethany fears that she lives in Hawke's shadow, and will therefore respond favorably if her opinion is sought.
- She will not tolerate ruthless behavior. Callous actions or words in your dealings with the people you meet will swing your relationship with her towards rivalry.

7 Once you arrive at the Gallows in Kirkwall, push through the throng of Fereldans to trigger a cutscene, then head for the waypoint further into the Gallows Courtyard. Ensure that all party members have leveled up and save before you approach Captain Ewald, then defeat the waves of deserters in the ensuing battle. The initial group are ripe for an AoE attack from a suitably capable mage at the start, if you wish. As the affray develops, keep an eye on individual party members to ensure they are not surrounded by opponents as the fight spreads to cover the entire courtyard.

The only way to gain entry to Kirkwall is to follow Gamlen's suggestion to enter indentured servitude with Athenril's smugglers (northernmost waypoint), or Meeran's mercenaries. Jump to 8 if you choose Athenril, or 9 for Meeran, though it's worth reading both: there is an opportunity to gain greater rewards by betraying one of them. After honoring a task for either individual, talk to Gamlen to end the Prologue.

8 Speak to Athenril and agree to attend to the job she offers. On reaching Merchant Cavril, you can resolve the situation in a number of ways:

- To retrieve the money without conflict, speak to Cavril, tell him that Athenril sent you, then call on Aveline to mediate. Open the Merchant's Chest, collect the coins, then return to Athenril.
- The dialogue options "There's no need for violence" or "You need to pay what you owe" both lead to conflict with Cavril's guards. This solution leads to additional XP and the possibility of loot drops.
- Extort money from Cavril (dialogue icon), then collect the sovereigns from the chest after he departs. On your return to Athenril she will be evicted from the Gallows Courtyard. You must now deal with Meeran instead. If you have previously betrayed Meeran (see 9), this option will instead lead to a battle.

9 Speak to Meeran and agree to deal with Friedrich and his men, who can be found in the south of the area. As with Athenril's equivalent task, you can take a handful of different approaches:

- Select "I came to kill you" to begin combat immediately. This is a difficult battle, but there is a simple way to make it easier. As soon as combat begins, highlight all three character portraits at the same time (by pressing both Party Select buttons simultaneously on the console versions, or holding the SHIFT key on PC), then use the Move to Point option (available on the quickbar on PC, and via the Radial Menu on consoles). Select a position next to Captain Ewald at the base of the steps in the main courtyard area. Ewald and his templar allies will then lend their aid during the fight.
- Select "I came to talk" then "Very well" to receive a substantial bribe. Friedrich will depart, but you must still fight his hirelings; use the same tactic outlined above. His absence makes this battle less demanding. Meeran will not take kindly to this course of action, so you must complete Athenril's task to gain entry to the city.
- If you have previously betrayed Athenril, there is no option to negotiate: you must kill Friedrich and his guards.

COMPANIONS

Aveline

For all but players who chose to make her role their own, Aveline will become a staple companion in her specialist capacity as the party's tank.

- As a general rule, try to stay on the right side of the law if you want to keep her friendly, and favor an honest approach in your dealings with others.
- It's easy to assume that Aveline has a very rigid stance on law and order, but that's not the whole picture. She understands that sometimes the letter of the law is less important than its spirit: some people really are better dead than jailed. Needless killing or unwarranted viciousness, however, will offend her immensely.
- Don't shake down or pester people for additional payment. No matter how unthreatening your tone may be, this is something she consistently disapproves of (especially blatant blackmail or intimidation). A little humility will also help you to maintain a cordial relationship: she doesn't like posturing.

Dog

For those who have access to him (visit dragonage.bioware.com for details), this faithful mabari hound can be summoned to act as an ancillary party member.

- If Dog is not present, you can summon him by visiting the Sustained Spells/Talents section of the Radial Menu (or the Abilities menu on PC). He cannot "die" per se, though he will vanish if subjected to extreme punishment by strong enemies.
- Dog acts as a form of "mini-tank", drawing enemy attention away from Hawke and more vital allies. Given that many battles pit you against several foes at once, this service will often come in handy.
- Unlike your companions, the mabari cannot be restrained from leaping into battle with the Move to Point or Hold Position commands whenever precision strategy or discretion are required. In these instances you will find that it makes sense to dismiss him.

QUESTS

The final part of the opening Destruction of Lothering quest is a typical example of the kind of quest that you will encounter in Dragon Age II: there is more than one resolution, which in turn influences a future quest in Act 1, which itself has a "reactive" consequence if you pick a particular path.

Though you can play the vast majority of the main plot quests irrespective of your role-playing decisions, there are many actions that send ripples through Dragon Age II's three main Acts. These can range from unique follow-up quests, to ambient details such as chance encounters with individuals who you may have helped or hindered in the past. This imbues Dragon Age II with an incredible level of replay value. Though this walkthrough must necessarily offer one path through the main story, the Quests chapter details the consequences of all key branching paths and possibilities for every mission you can undertake.

Most quest start points are denoted by an exclamation mark (!) that appears on the main map or minimap. Unless we specify otherwise, it's a good idea to seek out and accept all offers of employment. Refusal may lead to a commission being withdrawn entirely, while you are under no obligation to complete active quests that don't fall into the main plot category.

MISCELLANY

- The Codex, accessed via the Journal option at the pause menu, offers insights and information on the Dragon Age II game world. Though this stock of reading material expands automatically as you explore and interact with the people you meet, some Codex entries are collectible items that can be found in preset locations (Fig. 5). Interacting with these leads to an immediate reward of 50 XP, and a pop-up window that will offer a short text on a particular subject.
- When you use the Inventory screen, activate the Inspect option (see button instructions at the bottom of the display) to easily consider the relative merits of new weapons, armor and accessories.
- Ignoring automatic story milestones, the two potential "missable" Achievements/Trophies in the Prologue are relatively easy to acquire at a later date. You can unlock both "Nefarious" (choose Athenril) and "Mercenary" (choose Meeran) by creating a save file before approaching either prospective employer, then reload afterwards to complete the alternative option.

05

Quest Summary & Map References

- **1. A Friend in the Guard:** From Hightown (p. 112), head south to the Viscount's Keep (p. 126) → Talk with Aveline
- **1. A New Home:** Travel to Lowtown (p. 114) → Visit Gamlen's House (p. 122)
- **1. A Business Discussion:** Return to Lowtown → Enter The Hanged Man (p. 120) → Speak with Varric
- **2. Tranquility:** Head to Lirene's Fereldan Imports (p. 122) in Lowtown → Speak with Lirene → Meet Anders at his clinic in Darktown (p. 119) → Go to Hightown at night (p. 113) → Speak to the mage to automatically enter the Chantry (p. 125)
- **3. Long Way Home:** From the World Map, travel to Sundermount in the Free Marches (p. 132) → Speak to Keeper Marethari, then meet Merrill on the sloped path → Travel through Sundermount Caverns (p. 136) to reach the otherwise inaccessible Mountain Graveyard area of Sundermount

1 **A Friend in the Guard, A New Home, A Business Discussion:** Though you should feel free to explore Kirkwall, the best way to kick off Act 1 is to complete minor main plot quests to unlock further activities. Bringing Aveline into the fold is a priority: recruiting this steadfast warrior immediately swells your ranks to the maximum party of four. After visiting Gamlen's House and conversing with Varric in The Hanged Man, you will be ready to start Tranquility, the first main plot quest of note.

2 **Tranquility:** After conversing with Lirene in her Lowtown shop to learn about Anders, visit the mage and agree to lend your assistance. When you arrive in the Chantry, talk to Karl. In the battle that ensues, focus your energies on defeating Templars and Templar Archers before you direct your party's aggression towards the more hardy Templar Lieutenant and Templar Hunter. When this confrontation ends, the party is automatically transported to Darktown.

3 **Long Way Home:** After your meeting with Keeper Marethari, visit the Clan Craftmaster to sell extraneous items, then tell Merrill that you are ready to set off. The Dalish mage acts as a guest party member for the duration of this quest. Though you cannot control her directly, she will contribute to battles as she sees fit. The journey to the Sundermount Passage entrance is punctuated by battles with undead foes; the presence of bodies on the ground is usually a sign of trouble ahead.

Once in Sundermount Caverns, try to stay close to the entrance when Giant Spiders attack; more enter the fray from the ceiling as the fight progresses. There is a second ambush in close confines (this time featuring Corrupted Spiders) just before the Mountain Graveyard exit. Don't head up the wooden steps during this battle (Fig. 1): doing so will bring further enemies (including Corpses, Shades and a dangerous Shadow Warrior) into the battle. Tackle these separately afterwards, claim whatever loot you can find, then take the nearby exit.

01

Approach the barrier to trigger a cutscene; your reaction to Merrill's magic can lead to rivalry or friendship increments. Once the way forward is clear, a fairly hefty combat encounter will start. Beginning with Skeleton Archers, it will grow to comprise such fiends as an Arcane Horror and a Shadow Warrior. Once again, leave the latter foe until last: its high endurance will enable it to act as a tank while its weaker cohorts inflict great damage. After interacting with the altar (and the resultant conversation), return to the cave entrance. You will be automatically transported first to the Dalish Camp, then to Lowtown for the concluding conversation with your new companion.

USING THE WORLD MAP

- All exits marked "Leave Area" will take you to the World Map; those with an area name lead to a connected map.
- The World Map has three pages: Kirkwall (Day), Kirkwall (Night) and the Free Marches. All locations where you can advance active quests are marked by an arrow ( ). New destinations generally appear as you accept quests or make progress in existing ventures. Not all of these are permanent additions to the game world: certain locales disappear completely once you have satisfied all related plot requirements.
- Certain Kirkwall locations are only available during the day or night. Some areas (such as Lowtown, Hightown and the Docks) have unique evening versions of their maps where you will encounter different loot, denizens and quest opportunities.

GAMLEN'S HOUSE

Though Hawke's uncle may not be the most convivial host, this hovel acts as your base of operations during the events of Act 1. Paying a visit will instantly cure any existing injuries and allow you to reselect your party members.

- Interact with the Writing Desk to collect letters sent to Hawke. Though some missives only reflect plot developments (such as the letter that awaits you on first visit from the employer you chose at the end of the Prologue), reading many of these will trigger a quest or unlock the possibility of interaction in the game world. An animated envelope ( ) will appear next to Gamlen's House on the World Map whenever new mail arrives.
- The chest marked Storage can be used to safely stash items for future retrieval. This is extremely useful when you wish to save powerful weapons, armor or accessories until Hawke or his companions meet the usage requirements.
- Bethany or Carver can be found here when not travelling with your party. If you have access to Dog, you have one opportunity to rename him here. Miss it in Act 1, and you have to settle for the default monicker.

OPTIONAL ACTIVITIES

The Birthright companion quest (page 63), unlocked on your first visit to Gamlen's House, is a short but rewarding episode that leads to a collection of significant secondary quests. You can also acquire Bait and Switch (page 57) from the Writing Desk (see Gamlen's House) which can lead to the recruitment of a new companion. If you have access to any of the three Premium Content quests available at launch, you can attend to these short tasks straight away (see page 69).

Lest you forget, the purpose of your Act 1 adventures is to raise capital to join Bartrand's Deep Roads expedition. The funds that you acquire by completing optional quests will provide all the sovereigns you need to accomplish that – and more besides.

COMPANIONS

VARRIC

Varric is arguably the most easygoing of Hawke's companions. You really need to be a *thoroughbred* bastard to invite his regular disapproval.

- He responds well to banter and relaxed humor. Unlike most other companions, Varric isn't defined by a personal crusade or all-pervading belief. He doesn't mind situations where individuals are seeking enrichment in ways that won't necessarily harm others. His silver tongue can be called into action to mediate peaceful solutions in a number of situations.
- Uniquely, Varric has a fixed weapon: Bianca, a crossbow that increases in power as he gains successive levels. Functioning exclusively as an archer, he can offer a potent combination of AoE assaults and debilitating attacks that offer your party an interesting tactical edge. See page 184 for further details.

ANDERS

First encountered in Dragon Age: Origins – Awakening, Anders is an apostate (a mage who refuses to submit to the Circle of Magi) and an erstwhile Grey Warden.

- Anders is an emotional character. He won't respond well if you reprimand him or if you are anything but committed in potential romantic interactions.
- Anders is inflexibly vociferous in his opposition to the treatment of mages in Kirkwall. That said, he adopts a rather less compassionate stance towards those who dabble in blood magic or involve themselves with demonic entities. Condoning such activities will anger him.
- Unless you intend to have Hawke perform this function, Anders is the companion best suited to the support healer role. See page 184 for more advice on this subject.

Quest Summary & Map References

◈ **4. Wayward Son:** Speak to Arianni (Lowtown's elven alienage – page 114) → Speak to Thrask (Gallows – p. 118) → Meet with Samson (Lowtown, night – p. 113) → Visit the Docks at night (p. 117) → Retrieve the contents of the marked chest at Arthuris's Private Dock (p. 147) → Interrogate Danzig (Darktown) → Travel to the Wounded Coast (p. 134) via a detour to Dead Man's Pass (p. 155) → Free Feynriel in the Slaver Caverns (p. 148) → Return to Arianni in Lowtown

4 **Wayward Son:** This lengthy multi-part quest allows you to resolve situations in different ways, and your decisions will have later repercussions. Our walkthrough here follows the most direct path, but you can consult page 53 of the Quests chapter to learn about alternative solutions. We recommend that you include Aveline and Varric in your party.

After accepting the quest from Arianni, tell Thrask that you wish to help Feynriel, then have Aveline persuade him to accept your aid. The next lead, Samson, requires no special persuasion to reveal the information you seek. Arthuris's Private Dock is your next port of call. Switch to Varric and disarm the traps as soon as you enter the main room. Most of the enemies who attack here fall with little encouragement, though the Marine Enforcer is a more demanding adversary; save him until last, then immobilize him by any means at your disposal. The battle with Captain Reiner and the Abomination is much more challenging. AoE attacks work well within the tight confines of the room where it begins, but Reiner is a slippery foe. If you struggle with this fight, try manually directing your party to the main room and draw opponents to your position gradually. Collect Thrask's Letter from the remains of the Abomination (to start a secondary quest) and the Hideout Location Map from the marked chest, then leave via the area entrance.

Drop into Darktown and confront Danzig. His initial group of slaver allies can be disabled with a couple of simultaneous AoE attacks, but the reinforcements that arrive are made of sterner stuff. The Slaver Mage is a particular danger. Manually positioning your party at the top of the steps is a tactical approach that works well (Fig. 2). Loot Danzig's remains for the Map to the Wounded Coast, then set out for that location. You will be waylaid at Dead Man's Pass during this journey; lend aid to Javaris to begin the Blackpowder Promise quest. Be sure to collect all items on this map (you cannot return here later), then continue on to your original destination. Take the south path to reach the Slaver Caverns. If you encounter a Dalish Assassin on the way there, turn to page 107 for further details.

02

Inside the cavern you will encounter a group of slavers – again pay special attention to the Slaver Mage. When you meet Varian, the quickest and easiest solution is to immediately call on Varric to negotiate on your behalf, then resolve the flashpoint peacefully. The final step is to choose whether to send Feynriel to the Circle or (his preference) the Dalish Camp. For the purposes of this walkthrough (and related quests), we suggest you pick the latter resolution. Take the northernmost exit to return to the Wounded Coast. You must relay the news of her son's whereabouts to Arianni to complete the quest, though you can leave this final task until later if you would rather complete Blackpowder Promise (covered overleaf) while in the vicinity.

MERRILL

If you did not choose the mage class for Hawke, you may find that Merrill represents your party's best choice for destructive magical damage. For advice on possible developmental paths for the Dalish mage, turn to page 185.

- As with Anders and Bethany, Merrill will disapprove if you condone or facilitate the oppression of mages.
- Ruthless behavior upsets her. Merrill is a pure-hearted creature, despite her propensity for consorting with demons, so those who favor a "might makes right" approach to interactions with others will struggle to maintain a harmonious friendship.
- Merrill does not cope well with criticism or condemnation. To establish and nurture a friendship (or, for that matter, romance), take an interest in her views and offer support whenever you can.

MERCHANTS

Kirkwall's principle shopping districts are situated in Lowtown and Hightown during daylight hours, but you will also find individual merchants in other areas. To spend your coins in the most efficient way, digest the following collection of useful tips – and then study the Inventory chapter for more in-depth guidance.

- Though equipment can vary wildly in value between merchants and even between objects with ostensibly similar stats, all vendors offer the same level of reimbursement for the goods that you sell.
- Before you buy anything for a party member, be sure to check attribute and level requirements beforehand. You should also study the star ratings for such items, which indicate how effective a wearable object is for your current level: three is good, five exceptional.
- The majority of weapons, armor and accessories available in stores are "generated" items, randomly chosen from preset categories and scaled to your current level. These are often no better than objects you find on your travels. The best strategy for building a powerful party is to save for hard-coded "unique" items that offer proven long-term benefits: see the Inventory chapter on page 194 for further details.
- On the Normal and Hard difficulty levels, equipment found or offered as quest rewards should be more than sufficient during Act 1.

OPTIONAL ACTIVITIES

- The Wayward Son quest marks your first extended visits to Lowtown and the Docks in the evening, so you may wish to read up on the gangs that inhabit these areas (and, for that matter, Hightown). See page 65.
- Complete the Fools Rush In secondary quest to recruit Isabela (see page 59). This optional companion has an intriguing role to play in major events of Act 2 but will be lost forever if you fail to approach her before you reach the Deep Roads.
- While some companion quests are extensive undertakings, others are simply short cutscenes and dialogue sequences that serve to further both the story and your relationship with the individual in question. Always approach these carefully – and especially so if you intend to unlock the "Great Minds Think Alike" Achievement/Trophy (see page 242).

Quest Summary & Map References

- **5. Blackpowder Promise:** Travel to the Wounded Coast after meeting Javaris → Enter the Tal-Vashoth Cavern (p. 148) → Visit the Qunari Compound (Docks – page 116)
- **6. Shepherding Wolves:** Aid Sister Petrice in Lowtown (Night), then head to her safehouse to the north → Travel through the Undercity Warrens (p. 143) to reach the Vimmark Mountain Pass (p. 153) → Return to Sister Petrice

5 **Blackpowder Promise:** At the Wounded Coast, a lone Tal-Vashoth will warn of others of his kind on the path ahead before departing. Fight your way north from this position. The Tal-Vashoth have a moderate resistance to fire and electricity but are extremely susceptible to attacks imbued with cold and nature elements (including staves used by your mages – see Maximizing Damage). Use this knowledge to cut their ambushes short, then enter the cave.

The first battle inside the Tal-Vashoth Cavern is fairly uneventful, but the encounter that follows proves rather more demanding. Try ordering your party to hold at the bottom of the steps, then entice enemies to your position. If you can create a bottleneck centered on Aveline, a mage armed with Cone of Cold (in addition to other AoE attacks) can make a commanding contribution here.

Tactics of a very similar ilk work well for the final confrontation, where the open floor space of the cavern (not to mention waves of reinforcements) puts your party at a distinct disadvantage. It's advisable, then, to order your party to hold just inside the first wood-lined enclosure (or even the earlier cavern), then draw your opponents to you (Fig. 3). The Tal-Vashoth Leader provides a boost to all his allies while he still breathes (unless briefly incapacitated), so he's naturally a priority target; a micromanaged assault by all party members can topple him reasonably quickly. Potentially most dangerous of all, though, is the Tal-Vashoth Saarebas (a mage). He can cause enormous problems if ignored (especially if your party is concentrated in a small area), so deal with this foe the instant you set eyes on him.

03

6 **Shepherding Wolves:** This quest is entirely straightforward until Sister Petrice makes her offer – just make sure you take a stock of potions to restore health, mana and stamina. The first half of the Undercity Warrens is populated by assorted spiders; note that the poisonous variety can attack from range. The Undercity Thugs fought after the cutscene assail your party in two waves, but both will perish rapidly with a quick succession of Area of Effect attacks.

At the Vimmark Mountain Pass, a confrontation with Arvaarad and his fellows is unavoidable. Due to the additional rewards it brings, we suggest refusing to hand the Tal-Vashoth Saarebas to the Qunari. As a commander (see page 222) he provides a stat boost to his peers, but focusing on him alone from the start would be ruinous. You first need to reduce the numbers ranged against you, and fast. Pause the action and direct a succession of big-hitting spells (Walking Bomb could be interesting) and abilities at the pack before they separate. Additional enemies will appear as the battle progresses; at this stage, it's a good idea to finish off Arvaarad if he's sufficiently injured. With a little astute micromanagement and timely application of potions, this is a tough but satisfying confrontation. Return to Sister Petrice to bring this episode to a close.

MAXIMIZING DAMAGE

Most assailants in Dragon Age II have fixed resistances and vulnerabilities. Acquiring a basic understanding of how these affect combat encounters can enable you to formulate more effective strategies against each enemy type. As this feature is examined in far greater depth in the Strategy & Analysis chapter (with individual strengths and weaknesses revealed in the Bestiary), the following introductory guidelines are merely designed to whet your appetite for further reading.

- Broadly speaking, enemies can possess some form of resistance or susceptibility to physical or magical damage. This explains why an opponent might wither under an arcane barrage yet stand tall in the face of whirling blades and whistling arrows.
- There are five distinct "elements" in Dragon Age II:

FIRE	COLD	ELECTRICITY	SPIRIT	NATURE

Enemies can possess a resistance to elements graded on a scale of one (light resistance) to five (immunity) or a two-level susceptibility: vulnerable and highly vulnerable. If an enemy has neither, elemental attacks will cause standard damage.

- The most obvious way to inflict elemental damage is through spells, but weapon attacks can also be imbued with the five elements. Staves almost always cause one specific type of elemental damage, though this is less common in other weapons (which tend to inflict purely physical harm).

Let's use a very simple example: the Rage Demon. As its body is a mass of flame, you might (correctly) assume that it possesses some degree of resistance to fire but continue to use such attacks regardless of that fact. However, it actually has a blanket immunity to fire attacks: you might as well be proffering pleasantries. Cold, by obvious contrast, is profoundly effective.

In difficult battles, pausing the action and directing all party members manually – even in short bursts – enables you to exploit weaknesses such as these and minimize wasteful assaults. Furthermore, if a party member is wielding a weapon that inflicts elemental damage, it makes sense to carry at least one backup to avoid situations where their default attack is mitigated by a resistance. On higher difficulty levels, you might even consider having a range of different elemental weapons (particularly staves) to exploit vulnerabilities in any given situation.

MISCELLANY

- In addition to scouring areas for interesting loot, you should always keep an eye open for crafting resources. Collecting these will enable you to create runes, potions, bombs and poisons – all of which can make your party stronger in battle. You also receive 200 XP per resource found. Consult the Maps chapter to learn where ingredients can be found.

- All locked chests in Act 1 are of Standard grade at maximum, which requires 20 in Cunning to unlock. If you have a rogue as a permanent fixture in your party, there's profit to be had by boosting this attribute at a fairly early stage. Complex chests that require 30 Cunning appear from the start of Act 2, so you may also wish to begin investing attribute points in anticipation of this.

- In the Xbox 360 and PS3 versions of Dragon Age II, there is a useful trick that you can employ to detect points of interactivity (especially sources of loot) in your immediate vicinity. Activate the Radial Menu and use the Camera stick to scour the environment. If there's anything of note to investigate within range, a text description will appear above it (Fig. 4). Note that this only works with points of interactivity on your current elevation. For the PC version, press the TAB key to achieve the same result.

04

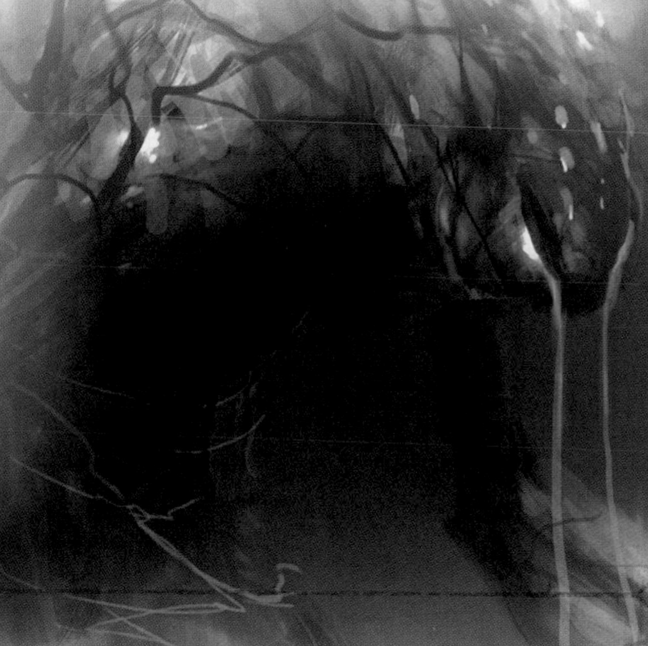

Quest Summary & Map References

- **7. Act of Mercy:** Accept the quest via a letter on Gamlen's desk → Speak to Thrask in the Wounded Coast Approach area (p. 154) → Speak to Grace in the Runaway's Cavern (p. 148), then leave
- **8. Enemies Among Us:** Accept the quest from Macha in Hightown → Speak to Templar Recruit Hugh in the Gallows → Travel to Wilmod's Camp (p. 155) in the Free Marches → Head to The Blooming Rose (p. 123) via the entrance in Hightown; speak with Viveka and Idunna in turn → Journey to Darktown and enter the Sanctuary (p. 143) → Talk with Keran, then return to the Gallows

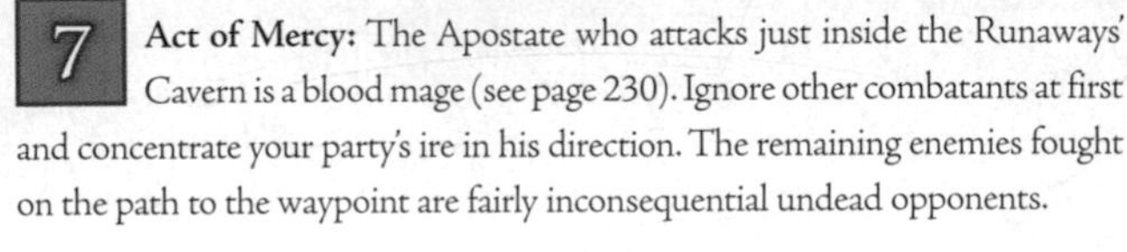

7 **Act of Mercy:** The Apostate who attacks just inside the Runaways' Cavern is a blood mage (see page 230). Ignore other combatants at first and concentrate your party's ire in his direction. The remaining enemies fought on the path to the waypoint are fairly inconsequential undead opponents.

The confrontation with Decimus includes yet more undead and a handful of Apostates. Deal with the blood mage leader first: his ability to drain health from your party members can annihilate the weaker ones within seconds. Consider using the Move to Point command as the battle begins to position your party on the high ground at the east side of the chamber.

When Grace steps forward at the end of the fight, pledge to help the mages escape, then promise to lie to Thrask. Return to the entrance (there are two further confrontations with undead on the journey back) and leave the cavern. With Varric in your party you can resolve the situation outside without bloodshed, but there's greater reward to be had by fighting Ser Karras: choose the "I'm a friend of the mages" dialogue option. This battle sees your party assailed from both sides. Manually position your party further along the path (either direction will suffice) to deny your opponents this advantage. Pay attention to the Templar Hunter. As with all assassin-type opponents (see page 222), he will sneak beyond your front lines and attack your weaker party members.

8 **Enemies Among Us:** After the short cutscene at Wilmod's Camp, your party will be attacked by the hideously mutated Wilmod and waves of Abominations. The last opponent to spawn into the fray is a Rage Demon. This dangerous, fast-moving Fade creature belongs to the assassin archetype, and will cause havoc if ignored. Use cold-based spells (and, if available, suitably frosty weapons) to rapidly cool its ardor for murder.

Ensure that your party includes at least one mage before you travel to The Blooming Rose. In the conversation with Idunna, select "You can't control me" if Hawke is a mage, or otherwise call on Anders, Merrill or Bethany to intervene. Question her, then choose to send her to the templars; you will benefit from this merciful decision later in Act 2 (see page 88, Forbidden Knowledge).

Inside the Sanctuary, fight the Shades and Abominations from the small set of steps close to the entrance. This reduces their opportunities to flank your party, and forces them into a tight group ripe for AoE devastation. Once again, a Rage Demon will appear late in the fight; use the same strategy as before. The two following battles will almost certainly pass without any cause for concern, but be sure to prepare and save as you near the waypoint.

Tarohne begins the battle at the centre of a pack of blood mages, so this is a good moment to pause and stack up a barrage of AoE attacks before they can separate. An intimidating wave of Abominations will swarm your position, so try to keep your party members concentrated in the east side of the room until these are defeated. You will come under fire from Tarohne and a Desire Demon (see page 231) – use potions or healing spells as required and leave these two adversaries until last. Speak to Keran, then meet with Cullen in the Gallows and insist that the young templar is fit to continue in his role (choose "Keran's fine", or "Keran should keep his status") to bring about a happy ending.

OPTIONAL ACTIVITIES

If you have been following our walkthrough, completing Enemies Among Us will finally allow you to begin the Deep Roads Expedition. Before you rush to speak with Bartrand, we strongly suggest that you use the Quests chapter to identify optional activities that you may have missed – particularly secondary and companion quests. Failing to complete many of these will preclude the possibility of playing follow-up quests in Act 2, or an assortment of reactive events, as revealed in the following table.

Quest	Page	Notes
Birthright	63	Short but profitable jaunt. It offers great rewards, and it's the gateway to many other secondary quests.
Bait and Switch	57	Only way to recruit Fenris. Miss it, and you lose him forever.
The Way it Should Be	62	Aveline's companion quest for Act 1. If you don't complete it, you cannot play her character-specific Act 3 quest.
The Bone Pit	58	Has a short reactive quest in Act 1, but opens up four further quests in Act 2 – all of which are otherwise unavailable. It's a highly profitable secondary quest strand.
Magistrate's Orders	56	This profitable quest leads to reactive events in later Acts.
Loose Ends	59	A short quest that follows up on your choice of employer in the Prologue.
The Unbidden Rescue	61	A mostly self-contained quest (with a tiny reactive detail in Act 2), but a great source of XP.
Herbalist's Tasks	61	This collection quest has a linked equivalent in Act 2; fail to complete both, and you'll miss out on both Solitivus's extra inventory in his shop and a unique reward in Act 3.
Fools Rush In	59	Required to unlock Isabela; if you don't complete it, you can't recruit her to your party.
Finders Keepers	60	Another self-contained quest with good rewards. Also unlocks a special merchant.
The First Sacrifice	62	Foreshadows two main plot quests in Act 2.
Night Lies, Pier Pressure & Sharp Little Pinpricks	68	This trio of side quests sees you clear Hightown, Lowtown and the Docks of the gangs that roam their streets at night. Each Act has three of these.

Completing main plot quests only, ignoring all other opportunities, will raise in the region of 35 to 45 sovereigns (depending on how diligent you are in collecting loot), and leave your party at approximately level 7 when you depart for the Deep Roads. Finishing all potential quests, however, will see you amass from 85 to 100 sovereigns, and reach level 11 – not to mention potential earnings and XP from later follow-up quests.

ESSENTIAL PURCHASES

There are certain valuable items that can only be purchased during Act 1. Refer to the following table for details on where they can be found.

Merchant	Location	Item(s)
Hubert's Fine Goods	Hightown Market	Tome of Technique
Robes by Jean Luc	Hightown Market	Backpack
Armor Merchant	Lowtown	Underpadding – Guardsman Pattern (Aveline armor upgrade)
Apparel Shop	Lowtown Bazaar	Inscribed Leather Harness (Varric armor upgrade), Backpack

ACHIEVEMENTS & TROPHIES

- If you would like to unlock the "Exorcist" Achievement/Trophy, you must spare Idunna when you meet her in The Blooming Rose during the Enemies Among Us quest. See page 52 for details.
- Those who wish to unlock "Supplier" (find all crafting resources), "Master Craftsman" (create all items within a specific crafting category) and "I Got Your Back" (upgrade a companion's armor to its maximum level) should ensure that they have collected or purchased all relevant items before they leave for the Deep Roads. Consult the Inventory chapter for further details.
- Collect the "History of the Chantry: Chapter 1" from the Chantry before you complete the Act. The related accomplishment (Chantry Historian) is unlocked when you find the remaining three chapters later in the game.

Quest Summary & Map References

- **9. Friends in Low Places (optional):** Accept the letter at the Writing Desk → Meet Dougal Gavorn in Lowtown (Night)
- **10/11. The Deep Roads Expedition:** Complete all main plot missions (with the possible exception of Friends in Low Places – see below) → Speak to Bartrand in Hightown → Travel through the Deep Roads (p. 128), the Primeval Ruins (p. 130) and the Ancient Crypt (p. 131)

9 **Friends in Low Places:** If you cannot possibly raise sufficient funds to pay Bartrand the required 50 sovereigns, this is your only opportunity to begin the Deep Roads Expedition. Accept Dougal's offer, and he will supply the necessary funds – but at the cost of reduced profits and further repercussions in Act 2. See page 55 for more information.

10 **The Deep Roads Expedition:** Before you go any further, ensure that you have read the Optional Activities section on the previous page.

It should go without saying that a little advance preparation will make this quest far easier. A good stock of potions and injury kits, for example, will be of obvious benefit, especially on higher difficulty levels or if you do not intend to include a dedicated healer in your party. Weapons that inflict nature or spirit damage will make their users more efficient against the darkspawn you face. Note that Varric is locked into the party for the duration of this quest, but this isn't a problem: we'd actually recommend a group consisting of three ranged fighters and a single tank.

After delivering the Grey Warden maps and 50 sovereigns to Bartrand, speak to the dwarf again and confirm that you are ready to depart. If you would like to know exactly why (and do not mind spoilers), refer to the Quests chapter (see page 55).

05

Agree to find Sandal when Bodahn asks, then fight your way through groups of darkspawn until you reach the waypoint. Watch out for Darkspawn Emissaries; they have the capacity to turn a simple encounter into something more fraught if you fail to notice their malignant presence. On the east side of the map, not far from Sandal's position, you will notice a dead-end to the south (Fig. 5). Though optional, you can fight a huge group of spiders here, followed by an encounter with a Monstrous Spider. Attacks that cause electricity damage will work well, and there's a good haul of loot to collect by way of recompense.

After you catch up with Sandal, continue north. You will encounter a small collection of darkspawn as you walk alongside the dwarven statues but it's the larger group that appears behind your party that will cause problems. Be quick to run to the aid of your ranged fighters, or move them manually. The same ambush strategy is employed in the subsequent combat encounter. As you pass through the door to the west, an Ogre attacks: you can use the Move to Point command to help party members avoid its initial charge.

ANCIENT ROCK WRAITH

- This opponent possesses a vast array of resistances and immunities, and its health bar will take a long time to whittle away.
- The Ancient Rock Wraith will regularly teleport around the battleground. Pay attention to the position of your weaker cohorts when this occurs, and be ready to move them manually if required.
- Whenever your opponent hovers in the center of the area, seek immediate refuge behind one of the pillars to avoid the ensuing attack. Your party members will dutifully follow. Once the spectacular assault ends, the Ancient Rock Wraith is temporarily disabled and becomes far more susceptible to your attacks, but he is joined by a group of Profane. Micromanage your party for the duration of these moments, dedicating three to pummeling the Rock Wraith, while a fourth attends to the Profane.
- For more information on this powerful opponent, turn to page 233 of the Bestiary chapter.

11 **The Deep Roads Expedition (continued):** In the far east of the map, your party will face a Dragon supported by waves of Dragonlings. Both are immune to fire attacks; exploit their cold vulnerability to cause maximum harm. Have your tank occupy the larger beast while other party members attack from distance, only breaking to deal with Dragonlings as they appear. Once the confrontation is over, approach the exit to be transported to the Primeval Ruins. You can enchant weapons or armor here, or shop with Bodahn, though he has little to sell. It's more an opportunity to offload items that you don't need.

Follow the path leading east to trigger a conversation and, following that, a fight with Shades and a Stone Golem: a foe with high endurance and a resistance to nature damage, but a weakness to cold and electricity. Take the Primeval Thaig exit to reach the Ancient Crypt area. Approach the Lyrium on its pedestal and, once the cinematic ends, head south. The door to the east contains a collection of chests, but is guarded by another Stone Golem and an army of Shades that are replenished at alarmingly frequent intervals. The most effective strategy here is to move everyone back to the northern corridor. Within the confines of the room, there's really no way to protect your weaker party members.

There are more Shades further south and, at the bottom of the steps, a new opponent: the Profane. These are susceptible to spirit and cold damage and have a moderate resistance to electricity. You'll encounter two more groups of these enemies as the path turns east. After the second, a Hunger Demon occupying the body of a Profane will intervene. For the best possible return in XP and loot, refuse its offer and fight the ensuing horde of Profane and Shades (and, subsequently, another multitude of the same in the corridor to the east). Stop and prepare your party as you reach the stone steps: a very unique opponent awaits. When the battle ends, loot the chests for treasure and return to Kirkwall.

ACT 2

Demands of the Qun

Quest Summary & Map References

◈ **1. Finding Home/Profit and Loss:** Visit Hawke Estate in Hightown

◈ **2. Blackpowder Courtesy:** Enter the Qunari Compound in the Docks during the day (p. 116). → Travel to Darktown (p. 119) and speak with the Coterie Barker → Enter Smuggler's Cut (p. 139) via the nearby entrance, then take the exit to reach the Outside Smuggler's Cut map (p. 153) → Travel to the Side Alley (p. 145) in Kirkwall → Report to the Arishok and Viscount Dumar

1 **Finding Home/Profit and Loss:** Act 2 begins with an intriguing audience with the ruler of Kirkwall. Use the "Gather your Party" station by the door to assemble your favored companions before you leave. Outside, Bodahn will rush to greet you. The main subject of this conversation is determined by how you funded your participation in the Deep Roads adventure. If you paid Bartrand, the Finding Home quest is triggered. If you accepted Dougal's offer of a loan, Profit and Loss begins instead. Both are completed by simply entering the Hawke Estate at the bottom of the steps. Finding Home ends at this point, but Profit and Loss has some interesting repercussions – see page 72.

2 **Blackpowder Courtesy:** Opponents belonging to the Carta await you in Smuggler's Cut. These have a high resistance to magic but are susceptible to cold attacks. Thugs are generic, melee-focused troopers, but the Assassins – as ever – necessitate special measures. After defeating the first band, visit the dead-end path to the west to fight a small group of spiders, then continue north. The second Carta battle is rather more substantial than the first. Take up position at the bottom of the wooden steps, and try not to let your party members spread out. Later fights add Mercenary Archers who have moderate resistance to cold, but quail in the face of nature attacks. Loot the area southwest of the northern exit (especially the chest close to the door – see page 72), then leave.

01

Outside, kill the assorted mercenaries and speak to Javaris. Ensure that your party is suitably prepared for battle, then set off for the Side Alley. Collect the Steel Latch from the ground (Fig. 1), then interact with the barrel directly ahead to stop it from spewing its poison into the air. This triggers a confrontation in which you kill successive waves of mercenaries to obtain further Steel Latches (marked by plot waypoint arrows) that you can use to close each barrel in turn. Each group of enemies features a notable opponent (a commander or an Assassin) before you confront a final wave led by the Elven Fanatic.

COMPANION RELATIONSHIPS

As Act 2 is a fairly critical point in Hawke's relationship with certain companions, this seems a good time to steer you in the direction of related advice elsewhere in the guide.

- The most reliable way to develop friendships and rivalries is to make certain key dialogue choices during companion quests: see page 81. Some of these can change an individual's opinion of Hawke quite spectacularly, with follow-up conversations offering further opportunities for friendship or rivalry gains.
- You can find or purchase gifts for companions during the events of this Act. These offer friendship or rivalry increases – and, of course, another welcome opportunity to interact with your travelling partners. See page 86.
- Advancing a friendship or rivalry beyond 50% completion (in addition to other conditions – such as completing a companion quest) can trigger a special "mid-stage relationship" dialogue. A Journal entry will appear when these have been unlocked. You can learn more about these on page 86.
- Without wanting to be specific, you will *definitely* benefit from nurturing a healthy friendship or rivalry with Isabela during Act 2.

ESSENTIAL PURCHASES

For those seeking to invest riches accumulated during Act 1, Act 2 offers a completely new set of tempting merchant inventories. Before you begin considering the merits of expensive weapons, armor and accessories, though, we strongly advise that you make the following purchases beforehand. Once again, these valuable upgrades are only available until you begin Demands of the Qun, the closing quest of this Act.

Merchant	Location	Item(s)
Trinkets Emporium	Lowtown	Greater Tome of the Mortal Vessel, Signet Ring (a gift for Varric)
Apparel Shop	Lowtown	Rigid Boning (companion armor upgrade for Isabela)
Lirene's Fereldan Imports	Lowtown	Armor Struts (companion armor upgrade for Anders)
Armor Shop	Lowtown	Impact Plating – Guardsman Pattern (companion armor upgrade for Aveline)
Olaf's Armory	Hightown	Reinforced Bracers (companion armor upgrade for Sebastian)
Robes by Jean Luc	Hightown	Supportive Corselet, Samite Lining and Tevinter Spirit Symbol (companion armor upgrades for Isabela, Merrill and Fenris)
Armor Shop	Gallows Courtyard	Enhanced Articulation (companion armor upgrade for Sebastian)
Mage Goods	Gallows Courtyard	Backpack, Lyrium Weave (companion armor upgrade for Anders)
Shady Merchandise	Docks	Coat Lining with Concealed Pockets, Lyrium Scales (companion armor upgrades for Varric and Fenris)
Ilen's Crafts	Sundermount	Tome of Technique, Carved Ironwood Buttons (companion armor upgrade for Merrill)

*See dragonage.com/da2/addons for further details on this Premium Content.

MISCELLANY

- Hawke Estate fulfils the same function as Gamlen's House in Act 1. The Writing Desk and Storage chest are located here, but you can now also apply Runes to weapons and armor via the Enchantment Apparatus.
- On a related note, Act 2 marks the point at which crafting can offer distinct advantages. As you find more resources and recipes, employing new potions, bombs, poisons and runes can give your party a greater edge in combat encounters. There are many benefits to be had from dabbling in this system. For example, restorative brews acquired through crafting are treated as entirely separate to store-bought potions, and therefore have their own Cooldown timers. You can find more in-depth analysis on crafting on page 213 of the Inventory chapter.
- Chests and traps are upgraded for Act 2, with "complex" varieties (requiring that your rogue have minimum 30 Cunning) appearing regularly from the start, and a handful with top-tier "master" locks. On a completionist playthrough, you may wish to invest points in this Attribute category throughout this Act and seek out items that offer a bonus to lockpicking.

Quest Summary & Map References

- **3. Offered and Lost:** Speak to Seneschal Bran in the Viscount's Keep (p. 126) → Visit The Hanged Man at night (p. 121) → Enter the Chantry (p. 125) → Travel to Ser Varnell's Refuge (p. 143)
- **4. Prime Suspect:** Accept the letter from the Writing Desk → Speak to Emeric in the Gallows (p. 118) → Travel to Hightown at night (p. 113) and enter DuPuis Estate (p. 152) → Return to the Gallows and speak with Moira → Visit the Blind Alley at night (p. 145)
- **5. All That Remains:** Enter Hawke Estate → Speak to Gascard in Darktown → Ask him to perform the ritual to reach the Dark Foundry (p. 144) → Use the Hidden Trapdoor to enter The Killer's Lair (p. 143)

3 **Offered and Lost:** This is a short quest, but one with interesting opportunities – see page 72 for a complete appraisal. Ensure that you have Aveline in your party when you reach The Hanged Man. Approach Orwald the Braggart and have the guard-captain question him. When you arrive at Ser Varnell's Refuge (by way of Petrice), choose to attack Ser Varnell. Clear the area of Fanatics with an AoE barrage before you focus on the templar, then turn and brace for a second wave of devout assailants attacking from the rear. In the aftermath, advise the viscount to return the Qunari bodies to the Arishok in their existing state. Collect all loot in the area (especially the Shield of the Knight Herself from the crate to the right of the southeast exit – see page 72), then leave the area.

4 **Prime Suspect:** If you have yet to complete the Ladies' Lights Out side quest, you will encounter members of the Invisible Sisters gang en route to DuPuis Estate – see page 91 for details. On entering the mansion, your party will be assailed by Shades. Electricity and nature attacks work very well, but they're immune to the spirit element. Speak to Gascard at the waypoint and offer to help him.

At the Blind Alley, there is a small army of Shades and a Desire Demon who shares the same elemental resistance and vulnerabilities as her cohorts. She also continually heals her allies (unless temporarily incapacitated), so target her first. When Moira arrives, answer "I don't think so" when she asks if Hawke believes Gascard to be the killer. This allows him to return for the next quest, All That Remains.

5 **All That Remains:** Even though the quest marker directs you to Lowtown (Night), seeking Gascard's assistance in Darktown instead leads to a more interesting conclusion to this storyline. Agree to his suggestion that he perform a blood magic ritual to locate Leandra and the party will be transported instantly to the Dark Foundry. Loot the area, then go through the Hidden Trapdoor.

Inside the Killer's Lair the party will be attacked by numerous Shades and a Rage Demon. You can use the staircase in front of the area entrance to create a choke point for AoE attacks. Smart positioning can also be of service when you reach the northwest room, where further Shades, a selection of Corpses, Abominations and another Rage Demon attack. These arrive in waves, so retreating to the upper level may be prudent on higher difficulty settings (Fig. 2).

02

After the conversation with Quentin, you will face three separate Desire Demons in turn, each supported by Shades, Corpses and Abominations. The Desire Demons gradually replenish the health of their allies, so concentrate your fire on them; if possible, keep them in an incapacitated state to stall their regenerative powers. With the arrival of a fourth and final Desire Demon, Quentin will enter the fray. As a blood mage, he's vulnerable to spirit damage, but still incredibly dangerous. You should either micromanage the fight to keep him disabled until the final Desire Demon falls, or target him first with a barrage of your most witheringly potent attacks.

OPTIONAL ACTIVITIES

Act 2 is shorter than Act 1 in terms of mandatory main plot quests, but offers a rich wealth of other activities. These include some fairly sizable (and commensurately rewarding) companion and secondary quests. There are also plenty of short yet satisfying side quests, many of which act as follow-ups to the events of the first Act.

As with Act 1, the following table details optional quests that we would deem as being essential to a good Act 2 playthrough. The companion quests are particularly important: failing to complete these can have some major repercussions, and cause you to miss out on future opportunities.

Quest	Page	Notes
Repentance*	81	Unlocks Sebastian as a companion.
The Long Road	82	This results in many far-reaching effects for Aveline. Take Isabela along for extra conflict and interesting dialogue.
Dissent	82	A relatively short but decisive step in the development of Anders. Those seeking to enjoy everything related to the core Dragon Age II narrative will find that this contributes a great deal.
Mirror Image	83	Merrill's companion quest is a great source of loot. It's also an essential venture for Achievement and Trophy hunters: it unlocks "That Thing Has Legs".
Family Matter	84	This develops Varric's personal story. It's worth it just for the fun that BioWare's writers have with the *in medias res* narrative technique: we defy you not to snigger.
A Bitter Pill	85	Failure to complete this means that you can't play Fenris's companion quest in Act 3.
Night Terrors	76	In addition to more customary rewards, this distinctive quest offers opportunities to earn bonus attribute points or a free Talent.
Herbalist's Tasks	78	There are three further ingredients to obtain for Solivitus; complete this, and a special reward awaits you in Act 3.
Raiders on the Cliffs	79	A short, action-oriented quest based in the Wounded Coast area. Take Aveline along for additional drama in the opening cutscene.
Inside Job	79	Following on from The Bone Pit, this profitable secondary quest unlocks three separate smaller quests on completion.
Forbidden Knowledge	88	If you spared Idunna during the events of Enemies Among Us, this is your reward. Though listed as a side quest, it actually eclipses many main plot missions in terms of size, difficulty and potential loot.
Hometown Breed, The Lowdown & Ladies' Lights Out	91	There are three more gangs to clear from the streets of Hightown, Lowtown and the Docks.

*See dragonage.com/da2/addons for further details on this Premium Content.

ACHIEVEMENTS & TROPHIES

- To unlock the Chantry Historian Achievement/Trophy, collect the History of the Chantry: Chapter 2 from the Chantry at any time during Act 2, and pick up Chapter 3 from the same location during the Following the Qun quest. The final installment is found in Act 3. You should also purchase all companion armor upgrades to work towards the unlocking of "I Got Your Back".
- If you would like to unlock the "Weapon Master" accomplishment, now would be a good time to plan ahead. Our suggestion would be to max out a weapon-specific talent tree (Weapon and Shield, Two-Handed, Dual Weapon or Archery) for one of your less favored companions.
- See page 88 to learn about the "Exorcist" Achievement, and page 88 for advice on gaining the Arishok's respect to unlock "A Worthy Rival".

Quest Summary & Map References

- **6. Following the Qun:** Read the letter at the Writing Desk → Speak with Viscount Dumar at the Viscount's Keep → Visit the Qunari Compound, by route of an ambush at the Winding Alley (p. 141) and speak to the Arishok → Travel to the Chantry at night (p. 125)
- **7. To Catch a Thief:** Speak to Isabela at Hawke Estate → Travel to Lowtown at night (p. 115) → Enter the Lost-End Foundry (p. 144) → After leaving, collect Isabela's Letter in the Foundry District outside
- **8. Demands of the Qun:** Enter the Qunari Compound → Fight your way through Lowtown (p. 114) to the marked exit that leads to Hightown (p. 112) → Gain entrance to the Viscount's Keep (p. 126)

6 **Following the Qun:** See page 74 for more details on this story-oriented quest. The ambush in the Winding Alley and the Righteous Mob enemies at the Chantry are mere cannon fodder to a well-equipped party, though the Mob Leader is made of sterner stuff. Deal with the former first, and their ringleader will soon perish once isolated.

7 **To Catch a Thief:** This quest is only available if you recruited Isabela during Act 1; if not, jump straight to 8. With both Aveline and the rogue requesting your assistance, pledge to help Isabela first. Ensure that she is in your party when you leave Hawke Estate. A group of Qunari awaits your arrival as you approach the Foundry District. The Sten is the most dangerous in this group, but you should find that the small battleground lends itself to a rapid resolution with an AoE barrage. Take out the fighters employing ranged assaults first: your party members will struggle to perform if they are constantly reeling from projectile impacts.

Inside the Lost-End Foundry, concentrate on the Tevinter Mages and Tevinter Enchanter before you turn to the Qunari – and, ideally, use attacks that will impede the mobility of all opponents (such as Cone of Cold) from the very outset. The Qunari Sten is a commander who continually heals his allies, so you should dispatch him once the mages have been disabled. Fighting with only three party members can be a shock to the system, especially once enemy reinforcements arrive. Destroy the Saarebas the moment he appears or disable him while you eliminate lesser foes. If you find the battle too challenging, try moving the party into the entrance room and use the doorway to create a bottleneck.

Before you leave the area, visit the northeast room to collect the Lambswool Insoles – a companion armor upgrade for your erstwhile rogue. Outside, examine Wall-Eyed Sam's corpse to find a letter from Isabela.

8 **Demands of the Qun:** This quest marks the point of no return for Act 2, so be sure that you are satisfied with your progression in other adventures: see Optional Activities on the previous spread for further advice. Any weapons (particularly staves) that inflict cold or nature damage will be of benefit during the forthcoming battles; you should also invest in a range of potions if your stocks are low.

Inside the Qunari Compound, telling the truth remains (as ever) the best policy when you address the Arishok. When play resumes in Lowtown, there is a sizable battle party lying in wait at the top of the steps. Deal with the Saarebas, spear-throwing Ashaad and melee-focused Karashok in that order. A good tactic is to get your party to hold position approximately halfway down the steps, then lure the Qunari to you (Fig. 3). You should be wary of an additional band of Karashok that arrive from behind, but making a stand here definitely makes the battle easier.

03

Further along the path through the district, you will encounter Grey Wardens and a Qunari battle group similar to the one that you faced moments earlier. This time, pay special attention to the Saarebas and Ashaad on the raised areas. At the area exit, Elven Supporters join the Qunari for another showdown, with the latter bolstered by the presence of a Sten. Kill the weaker archers first, then concentrate fire on the commander while your tank occupies the assembled Karashok. A second wave of opponents will attack from the rear, so be ready to intervene if your ranged fighters are swarmed.

When you reach Hightown, slay the Saarebas when he arrives, and impede the Sten in some fashion while you bring the Ashaad under control. In the northeast area, most of the warring Carta Thugs and Karashok can be slain with a blanket of AoE attacks, though watch out for the Carta Assassin that joins in later. With the last fight south of the Viscount's Keep, consider pulling your party back into the previous area to break the battle up into more manageable segments.

In the conversation with Meredith and Orsino, you have a choice between accepting a distraction to gain instant access to the Viscount's Keep, or fighting your way through the amassed Qunari. Your decision rests on whether you wish to gain the additional XP that a fight entails. Inside the Keep, occupying one of the upper balconies and drawing your opponents to your position will make the battle rather less chaotic.

THE ARISHOK

There are a number of different resolutions to Demands of the Qun, all dependant on your current party, your relationship with Isabela, and your previous dealings with the Arishok. These final tips will be of assistance in the most likely outcome (a fight with the Qunari leader and his warriors), but you can find guidance for all eventualities on page 75.

- First things first: slay the Saarebas immediately. He usually starts the battle on the upper level, but can teleport around the area at will.
- The Arishok heals his cohorts throughout, so your second objective should be to keep him incapacitated at all times. If this entails step-by-step micromanagement, so be it – left unchecked, he will cause any party member problems. His ability to stab a victim and raise them aloft on his sword makes him an effective "tank-buster". As your favored meat shield will lose the attention of all enemies that surround them during this process, this can lead to disastrous consequences for your weaker mages. Use any and every ability at your disposal to becalm his fury, no matter how briefly they may hold him.
- Try to keep your party members in one area (preferably elevated) and not far from your tank. You will lose control of this confrontation if you have companions fighting on both the upper and lower levels of this battleground.

ACT 3

The Last Straw

Quest Summary & Map References

- **1. On The Loose:** Accept the letter from the Writing Desk at Hawke Estate → Travel to the Gallows and enter the Templar Hall (p. 156) to speak with Meredith → Speak to Elsa to learn about each apostate, then head to Hightown at night (p. 113) and enter the De Launcet Mansion (p. 150) → Visit The Hanged Man during the day (p. 120) and speak to Emile → Travel to Lowtown (p. 114) and speak with Nyssa, then leave and return to the area at night (p. 115) → Visit Darktown (p. 119) to speak with Walter, then enter the Sewer Passage → Return to Meredith in the Templar Hall

- **2. Best Served Cold:** Accept the letter from the Writing Desk then visit Orsino in the Templar Hall → Travel to Hightown (Night) and collect the Conspirator's Notes from the body of the Templar Lieutenant → Continue on to the Docks at night (p. 117) and enter the Secret Meeting Place (p. 147) → Visit the Wounded Coast (p. 134) and approach the Ruins → Return to the Templar Hall to speak with Orsino

1 **Note:** We would suggest (and will henceforth assume) that you side with Orsino in the dialogue that takes place at the start of Act 3 as supporting the mages makes things slightly easier later on. If you wish to pick a different path, the Quests chapter will – as ever – be your guide to all options and their consequences.

On The Loose: After speaking with Elsa, you must track down each of the three mages in turn.

To locate **Emile**, speak to Comtesse de Launcet in her Hightown mansion. Feel free to rifle through the building after the dialogue ends. There is an ambush by Blood Mages and Apostate Mages when you leave so be ready to attack with full fury before they can unleash any spells. At The Hanged Man, convince Emile to return to the Circle – though you may permit him a small kindness if you wish.

After interviewing Nyssa, your meeting with **Huon** is less whimsical than the first apostate. This Blood Mage will summon Shades as support, but these are of no consequence: just hammer the twisted elf with everything your party can direct his way.

Once the conversation with Walter reveals the location of **Evelina**, fight your way through Shades and Rage Demons to reach the east side of the Sewer Passage. The mage takes on the form of an Abomination at first but can transform into other demonic forms as the battle progresses. Lay down suppressing AoE attacks, then concentrate your fire on Evelina. When the battle ends, open the chest next to the exit, then return to Meredith.

2 **Best Served Cold:** The battle in Hightown pits you against templars and Circle Mages. As always, it pays to deal with the latter first. There are additional mages among the waves of reinforcements, so keep a watchful eye for these. After collecting the Conspirator's Notes, head for the Secret Meeting Place. The battle that takes place here is an expanded version of the earlier conflict, with the addition of an Enchanter (your priority target) and Templar Hunters. In this fight, concentrate on the weaker foes first to reduce the numbers against you. Leave those with larger health gauges until last. The area is also packed with traps: after the Enchanter falls at the start, consider a brief rush with your most cunning rogue to disarm those in your vicinity. Speak to Keran when the battle ends, then tell him to leave. Be sure to explore the area for loot before you do the same.

At the Wounded Coast, follow the path south from the entrance. When you reach the path that leads to the ruins waypoint, there is a brief battle with templars, mages and corpses before you encounter Samson. No matter what you say to Samson or Thrask, conflict is inevitable.

Grace is by far the most dangerous opponent in this battle. Attack her exclusively until her health is diminished, at which point she transforms into a Pride Abomination. No matter which strategy you opt for (and we would suggest a mages > lesser enemies > Pride Abomination > Lieutenant > Hunter priority order), it's vital that you position your weaker ranged fighters far from the main melee. If you really struggle in this fight, try moving your party far to the north at the outbreak of hostilities. With a little micromanagement, this will enable you to engage each wave in your own time.

TACTICS: FURTHER READING

Even on the default Normal difficulty level, Act 3 presents a more challenging range of opponents than anything you have faced before. Some battles can be pitilessly difficult unless you take a more strategic approach to combat.

- How is your "kiting"? Would you know how to lure enemies to a narrow corridor and employ Aveline as a bulwark? If either question engendered a sense of incomprehension (polite or otherwise), our Combat Strategy section will introduce and explain both (highly useful) tricks – and much more (see page 179).
- Party composition really matters in Act 3. If you dive into certain quests without a dedicated tank to draw enemy attention or a healer to patch up wounds, you may find certain battles hard to cope with (see page 177).
- If you are not using cross-class combos, you are missing out on the best way to inflict catastrophic damage on Act 3's most deadly opponents (see page 174). Even if you are reluctant to micromanage battles, it's still easy to automate the process with the in-game Tactics system (see page 177).

OPTIONAL ACTIVITIES

Dragon Age II's final Act may only feature three mandatory main plot quests, but there are still many other adventures to enjoy before you drive purposefully towards its dramatic conclusion.

Quest	Page	Notes
Alone, Justice, Haunted, Favor and Fault, A New Path, No Rest for the Wicked, Faith	99	A must for those who have dedicated time to similar ventures so far. Not only do most of them offer notable rewards, they are also essential if you wish to reach the final stage in each relationship, particularly romances (see page 161 for details).
Mine Massacre	97	This offers an acid test of your party's survival prospects. The loot is spectacular, too.
A Murder of Crows	98	Featuring a cameo from a familiar face, this quest is a must for Dragon Age: Origins players.
Gamlen's Greatest Treasure	96	If you have been wondering what might become of Hawke's uncle, this is your chance to determine his future.
The Awiergan Scrolls: Pride Unbound	105	This side quest pits Hawke and his cohorts against an enormously powerful opponent at its conclusion.
Reining it In, Red Run Streets and Kind of Want	106	If you have been diligently clearing the streets of Kirkwall in each Act, the last three gangs await – as does your final prize.

RECOMMENDED PURCHASES

Unlike previous Acts, there are no companion armor upgrades or gifts to purchase. There is, however, one final Backpack that you can pick up from Robes by Jean Luc in Hightown, while the nearby Korval's Blades sells an Arcane Tome of the Mortal Vessel.

If you have plenty of sovereigns to spare, the start of Act 3 is an opportune time to invest in some remarkable items that appear in the updated merchant inventories. Some items, especially those sold by the less accessible vendors, have incredible attributes… but with a truly awe-inspiring price tag to match. Study the Inventory chapter to find these "aspirational" purchases or, for those on a budget, affordable equipment with bargain buffs. You can also find a selection of role-specific equipment suggestions in the Character Roles section of the Strategy & Analysis chapter (see page 175).

ACHIEVEMENTS & TROPHIES

If you have been diligently collecting all Achievements and Trophies to date, we would suggest that you create a new save file at the start of Act 3 and a second just before you begin The Last Straw. Keep these safe and you'll be able to return to complete any that remain (including optional feats linked to siding with the templars) at your leisure.

Quest Summary & Map References

3. The Last Straw: Accept the letter at the Writing Desk → Travel to the Gallows; on arrival, there is an automatic transition to Hightown (p. 112) → Leave via the sole exit to reach the Docks at night (p. 117) → Continue forward to the Gallows → From the Gallows Dungeon, make your way to the Templar Hall (p. 156) → Proceed to the Gallows Courtyard (p. 118)

3 **The Last Straw:** Take the time to wrap up any other quests or general activities that you wish to complete as The Last Straw marks the point of no return for the Dragon Age II storyline. Our walkthrough here follows one specific path, but rest assured that we cover all possible permutations in the Quests chapter. Before you begin, ensure that you have a full stock of potions and all other items (such as Mythal's Favor and Fel Grenades) that might be of benefit in the demanding battles that lie ahead.

In the face-off between Orsino and Meredith, side with the mages, then confirm your decision with "I've already made my choice". Depending on the state of your relationship with Fenris and Aveline, one of the two may refuse to follow you from this point forward. Hawke is technically alone but supported by numerous allies in the brief battle that follows. The choice of what to do with Anders is a momentous decision… but if he is your primary party healer, it definitely makes sense to spare his life and ask him to join you for the conflict that lies ahead. This will, however, lead to Sebastian's immediate departure if you count him among your ranks.

After picking your party, proceed through the streets of **Lowtown** until you encounter a mage cornered by templars. You can stand back and watch the initial part of this battle unfold from a safe distance, perhaps contributing long-range AoE attacks to the fracas, but your complete involvement is assured with the arrival of additional Fade creatures. Unless they actively engage your party members, you will benefit by leaving the templars (especially the Lieutenant) alone: these will distract the more numerous Shades and Rage Demons, which will work in your favor. A mage with Mind Blast could make use of that talent to potentially redirect templar aggression whenever possible.

The next fight is against a Desire Demon and an army of Abominations, with the following confrontation plunging you into a pitched brawl between templars and mages allied to your cause. Making a stand at the top of the steps will subject you to assault from both sides, so you may wish to move down the slope and draw templars to your position.

On arrival at the **Docks**, a Blood Mage summons a daunting collection of Shades before attacking with typical venom. Smite this particular foe with everything you have, then use AoE attacks to weaken the numerous swarming hostiles as the Pride Demon enters the fray. Turn to page 231 to learn more about this beast's strengths and weaknesses. The most important tips we can offer are to move away whenever it stands poised to charge or if you notice the blue AoE radius that appears prior to its Crushing Prison-style attack.

At the **Gallows Courtyard**, there is an opportunity to persuade lost party members to return to the fold. Inside the Gallows Prison, you can take a moment to speak with your companions before asking Orsino to advance. Save your progress before you do so (we would recommend that you use a new slot), then make your final party selection. When the templars attack, run forward to engage them on the bridge area. Creating a bottleneck here will concentrate the battle in a confined space, which is beneficial with so many allies fighting alongside you. See the page to your right for information on the battle with Orsino.

There are three simultaneous Rage Demons and even more Shades just inside the **Templar Hall**. Beyond the door, however, is the welcome sight of Sandal and his improvised store. Buy as many potions as you need, offload junk, then move on. Head south to fight a massive group of templars. Another multi-wave attack awaits you in the central area; in the last part of this fight, Aveline or Fenris may confront Hawke. When the dust settles, leave via the area exit to reach the final showdown with Meredith.

ORSINO

- There are three stages to this fight. In the first, Orsino is weak and highly susceptible to spells with incapacitating side effects (such as Winter's Grasp and Petrify).
- Once you pass a certain damage threshold, the "head" of the abomination will leave the body and attack as a separate entity. You will also face a certain number of undead opponents. Try to gather these together and lay down AoE attacks to kill them swiftly, but don't lose sight of your main target.
- In the final stage, Orsino is restored to his full form – albeit briefly. One of his first actions is to rip off his own arm, then use it as a crude but devastating cudgel. He also regularly employs a Blood Drain attack, which freezes his victims in place as the creature feasts on their essence. Your opponent also has greater resistance to spells that impede his mobility during this concluding part of the battle, though that doesn't mean that you shouldn't still employ them for the brief respite they could offer. Preventative maintenance is vital in this final slog. Try to heal early and ensure that party members' mana and stamina gauges are topped up with tinctures before they are exhausted. For more information on Orsino see page 239.

FINAL BATTLE

- Fighting Meredith is much easier if you focus on survival first. With non-party companions and other allies offering assistance, your priority should be to keep health, mana and stamina gauges topped up at all times. If Meredith takes a particular interest in a weaker mage or rogue, try using manual control to move them out of her path.
- Once again, this is a multi-stage battle. After you deplete her health gauge to a set level, Meredith will bring a Gate Guardian to life. The Gate Guardian employs a nasty spinning attack that hits all opponents within a circular radius, though its movement speed is ponderous. To give your party a little respite, try pulling all melee and ranged fighters back to a safe distance, order everyone to hold position, then wear down its health gauge from range.
- After the subsequent bout with Meredith, she will summon a second Gate Guardian; this one is slightly more resilient than the first. Complicating matters greatly, you will face the smaller and weaker Slave Statues. These are also slow-moving (occasional charges notwithstanding), so the major challenge here is exercising effective crowd control.
- In the penultimate part of the battle, Meredith rejoins the fray while the seemingly never-ending Slave Statues continue their assault. Use your party's AoE attacks to keep these under control. Ensure that your weaker ranged fighters maintain a safe distance from the main fracas as the knight-commander now employs a new Energy Burst attack.
- Diminished yet still unbowed, Meredith's next trick is to reanimate both Gate Guardians in a new form. These scuttling monstrosities use short-range flame attacks and fireballs with a homing capacity. This is a dangerous point in the fight, as both may target mages who have managed to stay out of harm's way so far. Focus your attention on one at a time and the immediate peril should subside when the first falls.

With this last gambit successfully dismissed, just wear down the final slivers of Meredith's health gauge. With each successive monologue, her demise grows ever closer.

QUESTS

This chapter covers every unique quest in Dragon Age II, with easy-to-follow advice on what you can accomplish and, over the course of the story, what the consequences of your actions will be. Designed for easy (and, where possible, spoiler-free) reference during your first time through the game, it's also tailor-made for later playthroughs where you might choose to take an entirely different path...

IMPORTANT NOTE: While we have taken steps to minimize story revelations, it should go without saying that casual browsing of the pages that follow may result in **spoilers**.

ACT 1

COMPLETION ROADMAP

If you do not wish to follow the path set out in the Walkthrough chapter, use this diagram to plan your route through Act 1. This reveals the unlock order for all main plot, secondary and companion quests. Over the pages that follow we provide fact sheets for all of these ventures, plus guidance for smaller side quests (which usually have their own unique unlock conditions).

Legend

- Main Plot Quest
- Secondary Quest
- Companion Quest
- Premium Content Quest
- Act Opening/ Finishing Quest

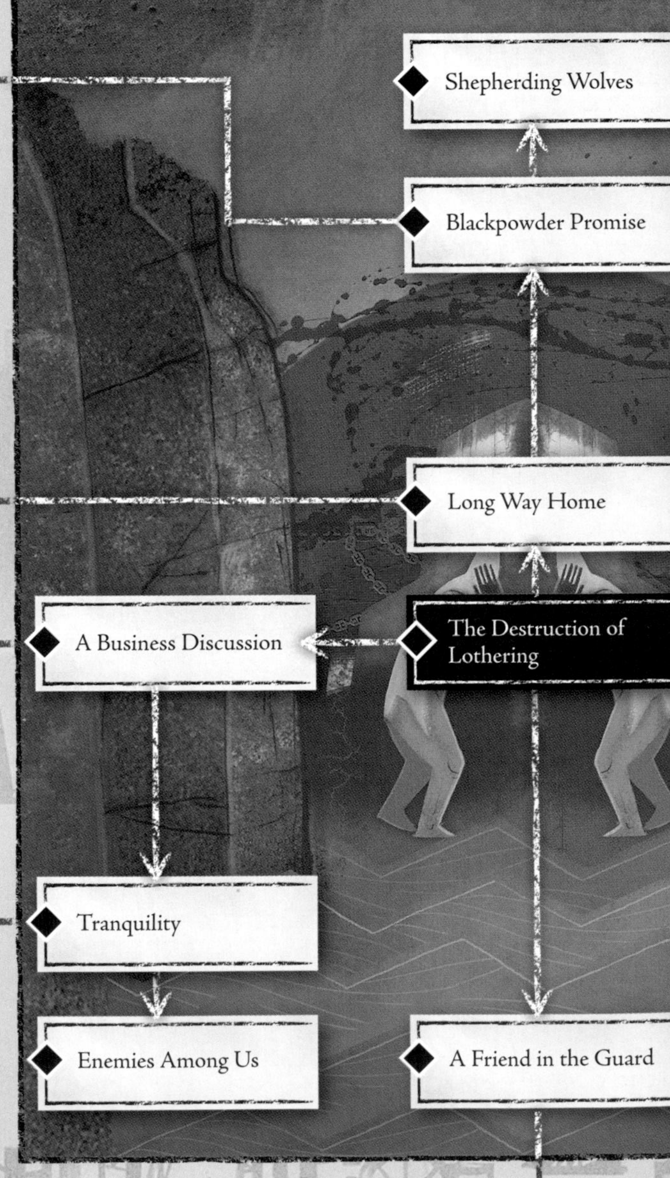

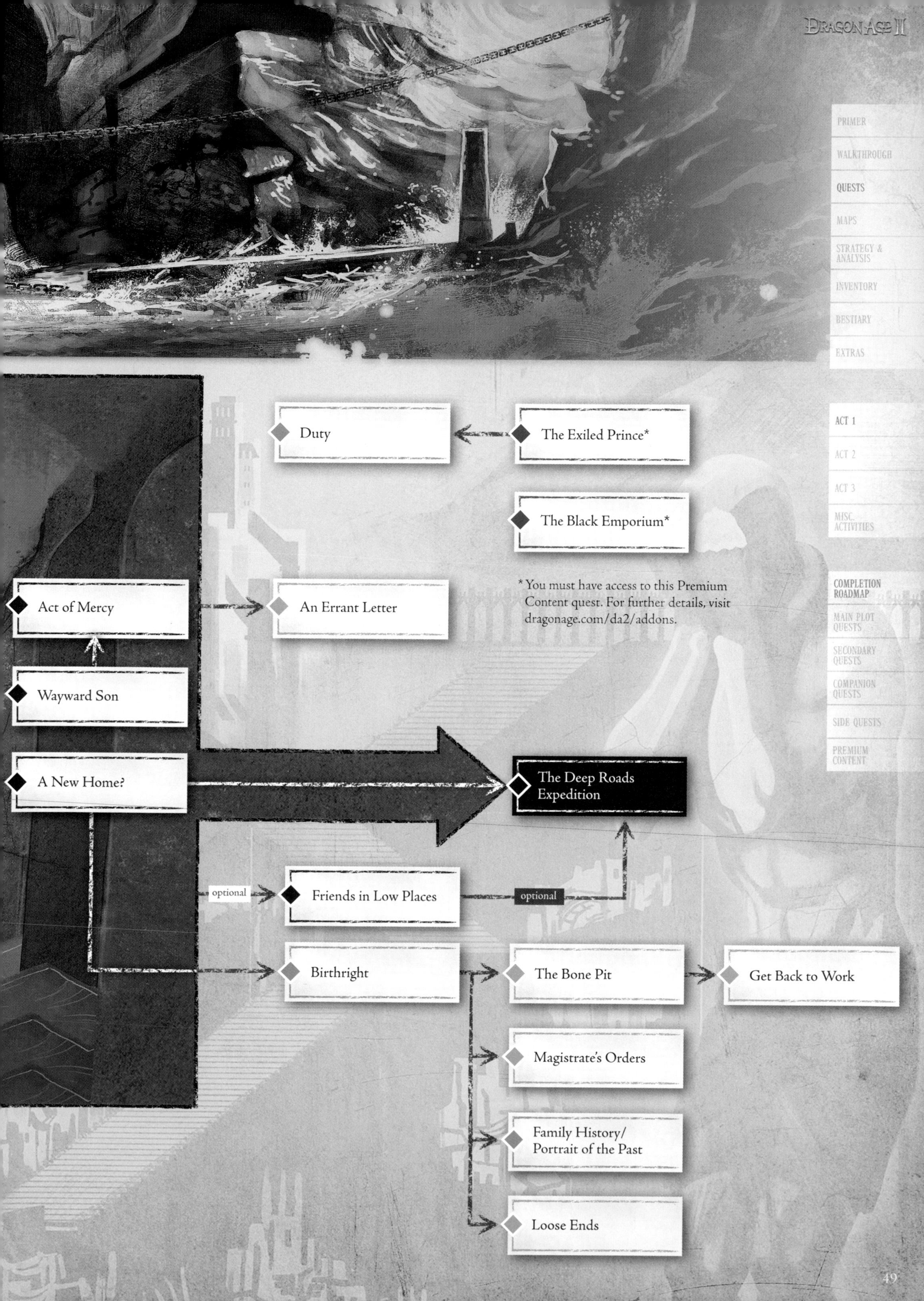

* You must have access to this Premium Content quest. For further details, visit dragonage.com/da2/addons.

MAIN PLOT QUESTS

Prologue: The Destruction of Lothering

Loot and Reward:

Start Location:

Blightlands (Prologue)

Note: Though not a part of Act 1, completing **The Destruction of Lothering** (and, therefore, the Prologue) has a few long-term repercussions.

Consequences:

- If you choose the mage class, Bethany will die in the confrontation with the second Ogre; opt for a rogue or warrior, and Carver will fall instead.
- The decision to work for the smugglers or mercenaries (see page 24) has an impact on the **Loose Ends** Act 1 secondary quest, in addition to an assortment of comments from people you meet that will acknowledge your choice.
- The most profitable way to end the Prologue is to speak to Meeran first, accept Friedrich's bribe and fight his hired goons (thus betraying the mercenaries), then complete Athenril's task with a dialogue selection that leads to a battle with Cavril's guards. In this instance, Meeran will return in Act 1 seeking revenge.

Companion Guidance:

For the best possible start to a friendship with Aveline, defer to her judgment when the question of how to end Wesley's pain is raised. Performing the act of mercy yourself will result in a medium rivalry increase.

A Business Discussion

Loot and Reward:

Start Location:

The Hanged Man (available from start of Act 1)

Requirements:

Enter The Hanged Man (ideally during the day) and speak with Varric.

Consequences:

This short conversation unlocks the **Tranquility** main plot quest – and, if you are amenable, an easy friendship boost with Varric. It also unlocks the Rumor section in the Current Quests page of the Journal. Before you leave The Hanged Man, you may wish to loot the chest in the room south of Varric's quarters to begin the **Shawl of Dalesdottir** side quest. This is only available during daylight hours.

A New Home?

Loot and Reward: 

Start Location:

Lowtown (available from start of Act 1)

Requirements:

Visit Gamlen's House in Lowtown: the quest is completed as soon as you enter.

Consequences:

The **Birthright** companion quest is unlocked on arrival. You can also interact with the Writing Desk to begin the **Bait and Switch** companion quest and receive a letter from the employer you chose at the conclusion of the Prologue. If you have access to Premium Content, you can attend to **The Black Emporium** quest here – see page 71 for further details.

A Friend in the Guard

Loot and Reward: 

Start Location:

Viscount's Keep (available from the start of Act 1)

Requirements:

Visit Aveline in the barracks at the Viscount's Keep.

Consequences:

- Formally unlocks Aveline as a companion. Unless you have chosen the warrior class and intend to act as your party's tank, Aveline's qualities as a magnet for enemy attention makes this trip a necessity at the start of Act 1.
- Agree to help Aveline during this conversation to unlock **The Way It Should Be**.

Long Way Home

Loot and Reward: 

Start Location:

Blightlands (Prologue)

Requirements:

Begins automatically during your encounter with Flemeth midway through the Prologue.

Walkthrough:

- Though some players may be keen to acquire Merrill at an early stage of Act 1, it's probably better to wait until you have gained a few levels before you visit Sundermount. The battle on top of the mountain can be rather tough until your party members have built up a sufficient range of skills (particularly AoE attacks for mages).
- After the confrontation at the altar, you can optionally continue to the top of Sundermount to fight additional battles and collect further loot before returning to the Dalish Camp. As Merrill functions as a bonus "guest" party member (for which, read: extra firepower) until the quest is completed, this is probably the best time to do so.

Consequences:

Completing **Long Way Home** unlocks Merrill as a companion and makes it possible to begin the **Unbidden Rescue**, **Welcome Home**, **Herbalist's Tasks**, **Wayward Son** and **Blackpowder Promise** quests.

Companion Guidance:

Being a blood mage, Merrill is a figure that a number of potential party members (especially Anders, Fenris, Carver and, to a lesser extent, Isabela) may find cause to object to. This is particularly pertinent when she makes use of her dark craft, as is the case with the magical barrier beyond the Sundermount Caverns. Save before you approach it; you may wish to fine-tune your subsequent dialogue choices to reduce the impact on your developing friendships and rivalries.

Tranquility

Loot and Reward: 

Start Location:

The Hanged Man

Requirements:

Complete the **A Business Discussion** main plot quest.

Note: Those seeking maximum XP gain should refrain from revealing Hawke's Fereldan origins (either through an intervention by Bethany or Carver, or the diplomacy option) when confronted by the refugee mob outside Lirene's Fereldan Imports.

Consequences:

Completing this quest secures the services of Anders as a companion, fulfills the second key requirement for the **Deep Roads Expedition** and unlocks other plotlines that you can start elsewhere (including **The First Sacrifice**, **Questions and Answers**, **Talk to Anders** and **Enemies Among Us**). It's a relatively short quest, so we would recommend that you deal with it at an early stage in Act 1.

Companion Guidance:

Sympathize with and encourage Anders after his startling transformation to nurture a burgeoning friendship. It's worth mentioning that he will deliver the Grey Warden maps (and become a companion) irrespective of how conciliatory or damning your reaction is.

Blackpowder Promise

Loot and Reward: 

Start Location:

Dead Man's Pass

Requirements:

- Complete **Long Way Home**.
- Your journey through the Free Marches (usually to Sundermount or the Wounded Coast) will be interrupted by a detour to an area where a dwarven merchant, Javaris, is under attack. The quest begins during the conversation that takes place in the battle's aftermath.

Walkthrough:

- The brief visit to the **Dead Man's Pass** map (where you meet Javaris) is your only opportunity to collect the Caste Treatise item for the **Caste Treatise and House Accounting** side quest.
- At the Wounded Coast, a Tal-Vashoth warrior will greet the party as they reach the path leading north to the quest's waypoint marker. You can gain his assistance in the final battle if you have been playing an "aggressive" version of Hawke by selecting red icon choices for most dialogue opportunities. If this is the case, a bonus conversational option will appear: "You can prove you are better". Select this to secure his future support.
- After the quest ends, you can converse with the Arishok again to learn more about the Qunari in the city and related topics.

Consequences:

- Unlocks the **Shepherding Wolves** and **Nice Crime You Have Around Here** quests.
- If you persuade the lone Tal-Vashoth to assist your party, he will appear in The Hanged Man during Act 3 under the name of Maraas.

Shepherding Wolves

Loot and Reward: ☆☆☆★★

Start Location:

Lowtown (Night)

Requirements:

- Complete **Blackpowder Promise**.
- Approach Sister Petrice in Lowtown at night.

Walkthrough Addendum:

- You encounter a fair number of traps in this quest, so you may wish to take a rogue along to gain XP by disarming them all.
- If you admit that you have a mage in your party when you encounter the Qunari group, Arvaarad and his cohorts will attack immediately.
- Both final decisions lead to combat, but with differing narrative conclusions. Refusing to hand the Saarebas over leads to an extended dialogue with the Qunari mage in the battle's aftermath, an additional reward, and a side quest in Act 2.

Consequences:

- If you return to speak to the Arishok before the end of Act 1, you can use the unique "I killed some of your qunari" line to access additional dialogue in which you discuss the conclusion of this quest. Boldly admitting this feat of arms will increase the Arishok's respect for Hawke – a step that will be of benefit later in the story.

Companion Guidance:

Handing over the Saarebas will meet with disapproval from certain party members (particularly Bethany and Anders) while defending him will lead to friendship increases for all but Varric, Fenris and Isabela.

Enemies Among Us

Loot and Reward: ☆☆☆★★

Start Location:

Hightown (Day)

Requirements:

- Complete the **Tranquility** main plot quest.
- Speak to Macha in front of the Chanter's Board.

Walkthrough Addendum:

- Unique dialogue options appear during your conversation with Idunna at The Blooming Rose if there is a mage in the party. These can be employed to resist her blood magic-augmented wiles.
- If Anders or Merrill are in your party, a special dialogue option appears where either one can instantly establish if Keran is possessed or not when you meet him in the Sanctuary. If Carver is present, he has a special reaction to this situation.
- Collect the Grimoire of the Apprentice from a container close to the Sanctuary area exit to start the side quest of the same name. This is your only opportunity to do so.
- When you travel to Cullen at the conclusion of the quest, you can support Keran (either through a standard dialogue choice or a special option if Anders or Merrill declared him clear of possession) or condemn him.

Consequences:

- If Keran is expelled from the Templar Order, the quest **A Debt in the Family** will be available in Act 2. If he retains his position, **How to Frame a Templar** is given instead.
- If you spare Idunna, you will receive a letter from her at the start of Act 2. This unlocks **Forbidden Knowledge**, a side quest that you can also obtain by other means.

Companion Guidance:

Call on Bethany or Anders to help you during the confrontation with Idunna for a healthy friendship boost with the mage in question.

Wayward Son

Loot and Reward: 

Start Location:

Lowtown (Day)

Requirements:

- Complete the **Long Way Home** main plot quest.
- Speak to Arianni in the Elven Alienage.

Walkthrough:

- Hawke can actually investigate both leads given by Arianni. Speak to Thrask in the Gallows Courtyard first. You can use a diplomacy option (if possible) to learn the location of Samson or, if Aveline is in your party, call on her to convince the templar that the city guard can be of service in locating Feynriel. If you make enquiries about Vincento while speaking with Thrask, you can learn that he is due to be arrested by the city guard. This opens up an additional dialogue path when (or if) you reach Feynriel's father.
- Vincento runs a stall in Lowtown's bazaar. You can try to intimidate him, call on Bethany (if present) to convince him of your good intentions with a display of magic or, as a mage, perform the same feat yourself. If you have previously learned that Vincento is due to be arrested, you can inform him of that fact to discover Samson's location.
- Collect Thrask's Letter from the Abomination in Arthuris's Private Dock to begin the **An Errant Letter** secondary quest.
- If Fenris is in your party when you confront Danzig in Darktown, you have the option of letting him loose on the slaver for a non-violent solution... unless, that is, you decide to have the elf execute him once you secure the information you need. Sister Plinth's Remains are located in this area, so be sure to collect them to begin a side quest entitled **The Remains of Sister Plinth**.
- You can resolve the stand-off in the Slaver Caverns in one of four ways:
  - If you have Varric in your party you can call on him to fast-talk Varian, who will surrender both prisoner and purse before leaving without further hostilities. This is by far the most profitable resolution, but it comes at the expense of sacrificing potential XP gain.
  - Buy Feynriel from Varian: unlikely, but an option nonetheless.
  - Fight the slavers: a tough (but not insurmountable) confrontation.
  - Rogue characters can also choose an option where they kill Varian with a single knife, removing him from the conflict that ensues.
- You can choose to send Feynriel to the Dalish (his preference) or to the Circle. This has later repercussions.

Consequences:

- This unlocks the **Act of Mercy** quest.
- If you send Feynriel to the Dalish, speak with the Keeper in her Sundermount camp later in the Act for a reactive event. This also triggers a potential combat encounter (with no Journal entry) at Sundermount at the start of Act 2. If you send Feynriel to the Circle, you can see him in the Gallows Courtyard later in Act 1; you will also be able to obtain the **Elves at Large** quest from the Chanter's Board in Act 2.
- Arianni's reaction at the end of the quest also reflects your decision (she would prefer that her boy be sent to the Circle); it is referenced in the Act 2 quest, **Night Terrors**.

Companion Guidance:

- Sending Feynriel to the Circle will seriously displease Anders and Bethany, but is met with approval from Fenris and Aveline. Offering to speak to the Dalish Keeper on his behalf, by contrast, will have the opposite effect.
- Allowing the boy to choose for himself will lead to friendship increases across the board with the exception of Aveline (low rivalry) and Fenris (moderate rivalry).

Act of Mercy

Loot and Reward: 

Start Location:

Gamlen's House

Requirements:

- Complete Wayward Son.
- Accept the quest via the Writing Desk.

Walkthrough Addendum:

- If you blackmailed Thrask in the An Errant Letter quest, certain aspects of your conversation will reflect this.
- Your dialogue choices when speaking with Grace (after slaying Decimus) play a part in determining how the quest will end.
  - If you refuse to help, the apostates will leave the caves voluntarily – but only after Grace threatens to expose any mages in your current party (including Hawke). Certain party members have unique reactions to this. You must fight undead opponents on the return journey to the Wounded Coast Approach. This option potentially enables you to avoid conflict with Karras and his templars outside the cave.
  - If you promise to lie to Thrask, the apostates remain in the caves. Again, you fight undead opponents as you travel back to the entrance and may be able to avoid a violent denouement.
  - If you pledge assistance and agree to kill Thrask, you will instead fight groups of templars en route to a mandatory confrontation with Karras.
- Once outside, you can make a final decision on the fate of Grace and her companions. Thrask fights alongside the party in all eventualities that result in conflict.
  - If you refused to help the mages, Grace will attempt one last appeal to Hawke. Relent, and you must fight Karras and his cohorts; remain resolute, and the mages are led away by the templars to a life in the Circle.
  - If you chose to help the mages and agreed to kill Thrask, events will force a battle, and the oblivious templar fighting on your side.
  - If you agreed to help Grace by lying to Thrask, players who have predominately selected humorous dialogue options have a "bonus" line to use with Karras: "I'm your best friend". Varric's silver tongue can be employed to send the templars away without combat if he is in your party.
- A conclusion where Karras is killed is by far the most profitable outcome in terms of rewards.

Consequences:

- If Karras is killed, a quest entitled The Midnight Meeting will occur in Act 2.
- If the mages are returned to the Circle, you can obtain the Bounty Hunter quest from the Chanter's Board in Act 2.
- If the mages go free, the Search and Rescue quest can be obtained during Act 2. You may also encounter Grace and her companions in Kirkwall in the Gallows Courtyard during the same Act. This is just a small reactive event – there are no rewards.

Companion Guidance:

- After killing Decimus, pick the "I'm sorry" response while speaking to Grace to win Merrill's favor.
- If you agree to kill Thrask, you receive a mild friendship boost from Anders, no reaction from Bethany, and rivalry from the rest of your party members, particularly so from Aveline. If you're keen to get along with your cohorts, the best approach is to pledge to assist the mages but not at the cost of Thrask's life (low friendship boost or no reaction) or by lying to Thrask (no reaction or friendship boosts with the exception of Fenris).
- If you tell Grace that you intend to turn the mages over to the templars, Bethany, Merrill and Anders will strongly disapprove. Aveline, Carver and Fenris will approve. Outside the cave, ignoring Grace's final attempt at supplication leads to rivalry increases with Anders and Bethany and friendship boosts for Carver and Fenris; should you have a change of heart, the order is reversed.

Friends in Low Places

Loot and Reward: 

Start Location:

Gamlen's House

Requirements:

- To trigger **Friends in Low Places**, you need to complete at least 50% of the Act 1 quests and must not have delivered the 50 sovereigns investment to Bartrand to fulfill the **Deep Roads Expedition** plot requirement.
- The quest begins when you read the letter delivered to the Writing Desk. Travel to Lowtown at night to speak with its author, Dougal, and consider his proposal to fund your party's involvement in the **Deep Roads Expedition** in return for a repayment of 100 sovereigns at the start of Act 2.

Consequences:

- If Dougal fronts the money for Bartrand, the **Profit and Loss** reactive quest will begin at the start of Act 2.
- This quest is primarily designed to address the issue of players amassing a small fortune during Act 1, then opting to spend it all on equipment and consumables. If it becomes effectively impossible for Hawke to pay Bartrand, Dougal's offer is the only way to advance the plot beyond Act 1.
- Due to the slight reduction in profits from the Deep Roads expedition, you should only accept his offer if you have a burning desire to see the events that transpire (and to obtain the fairly minor resultant XP gain) or if you wish to speed through Act 1 in the shortest possible time.

The Deep Roads Expedition

Loot and Reward: 

Start Location:

Hightown

Requirements:

- Complete the following quests: **A Friend in the Guard**, **Tranquility**, **Enemies Among Us**, **Wayward Son**, **Long Way Home**, **Act of Mercy**, **Blackpowder Promise** and **Shepherding Wolves**.
- Pay Bartrand 50 sovereigns (or, alternatively, accept Dougal's offer in **Friends in Low Places**) and deliver the maps acquired from Anders at the end of **Tranquility**, then agree to depart for the Deep Roads.

Walkthrough Addendum:

- If you attempt to start the expedition and have yet to complete core story quests, party members will comment on outstanding plotlines that must be seen to their conclusion before you can depart. Be sure that you are satisfied with your Act 1 accomplishments before you leave.
- Speak to Bodahn and agree to locate Sandal. You'll encounter him on the path forward regardless, and the additional XP makes this mildly heroic gesture worthwhile.
- For maximum reward, refuse the Hunger Demon's proposal. Accepting his offer enables you to skip further battles with the Profane (which might seem an attractive option for a party struggling with the brutality of a Nightmare playthrough) but ultimately results in a reduced haul of both XP and loot.

Consequences:

- If you choose to take Bethany or Carver into the Deep Roads, Hawke's surviving sibling will suddenly manifest the symptoms of the Blight at the conclusion of the quest.
  - If Anders is present, he will suggest that Bethany/Carver join the Grey Wardens. Refuse this ("We're not doing that."), and the results will be grave. Agree, and they depart to undertake the Joining ritual.
  - If Anders is not in the party, an act of mercy is your sole option.
- If you leave Bethany or Carver behind, you will return home from the Deep Roads to discover that:
  - Bethany is poised to join the Circle.
  - Carver has resolved to join the templars.
- Irrespective of the outcome, Bethany or Carver permanently leave the party at this stage. If they joined the templars, Circle or Grey Wardens, you will encounter them during pivotal moments during Act 2 and Act 3. From a narrative perspective, taking a sibling into the Deep Roads without Anders at your side is the least attractive option of all. It's a path best saved, perhaps, until you wish to sate your curiosity in a future playthrough.

Companion Guidance:

If you bargain with the Hunger Demon, Anders will severely disapprove; Aveline and Fenris will express mild disapproval.

Magistrate's Orders

Loot and Reward: ☆☆☆★★

Start Location:

Hightown (Day)

Requirements:

- Complete the Birthright companion quest.
- Speak to Magistrate Vanard in Hightown (he's located close to the Chanter's Board) and agree to apprehend the escaped criminal.

Walkthrough:

- Travel to the Abandoned Ruins in the Free Marches. Approach the group of guards at the center of the area to trigger a cutscene. When Elren pleads with Hawke to exact murderous justice, pick the conversational options that suit your play style – it's not a decision that you have to make straight away.
- Enter the Ruined Passage map via the cave. You'll encounter a variety of enemies here, predominately Giant Spiders but with an increasing number of Fade denizens later on. Be sure to collect all loot dropped by the arachnids, as one of them surrenders the Spider's Silk Gland item required for the Herbalist's Tasks quest. A word of warning: the chest in the northeast room has a trap in front of it, and plundering its contents will fill the room with eight-legged antagonists.
- Access the central room via the north entrance. This begins as a straightforward battle against Spiders but becomes rather more complicated as Fade creatures enter the fray. If you experience difficulties, consider pulling your party back into the previous area at the start of the fight. This may enable you to draw enemies out in small but manageable groups.
- Head through the south exit and continue until you meet Lia, Elren's daughter. After a brief battle (be wary of the enemies spawning behind your party), you'll reach Kelder in the next room. See the Consequences section for details on how killing him or taking him alive will affect events in the near and distant future.
- If you chose to kill Kelder, you can exit the map immediately via the door to the south. If you opt to spare him, Kelder will flee further into the ruins. You'll need to give chase (and fight additional enemies) before you can arrest him.
- Return to Magistrate Vanard to bring the quest to its conclusion.

Consequences:

- If you spare Kelder, Elren will offer no reward. Magistrate Vanard will pay Hawke for fulfilling his requests to the letter. You can extort further coin by raising the issue of Kelder's parentage though Aveline, if present, will react with a boost to rivalry if you do so.
- If you choose to kill Kelder, Elren will reward the player; Vanard, by contrast, will leave in disgust when you report in to end the quest. This leads to a reactive event later in the story.

Bait and Switch

Loot and Reward: 

Start Location:

Gamlen's House

Requirements:

- Complete **A Business Discussion**.
- Read the **Bait and Switch** letter at the Writing Desk in Gamlen's House.

Walkthrough:

- Travel to Lowtown at night to meet Anso the Contact, then head to the Abandoned House entrance in the northeast area of the map. If you have yet to complete the **Sharp Little Pinpricks** side quest, you will encounter the hostile Sharps Highwaymen here. Don't attempt to avoid these: killing them now will save time later, and it's a good source of XP.
- Inside the Abandoned House, open the south door and kill all hostiles; further groups will spawn as the battle progresses, so be ready to move your ranged party members out of harm's way. The Street Thugs aren't tough but could trouble a low-level mage in numbers. Open the Smuggler's Cargo chest, then leave.
- After the cutscene, the Tevinter forces will attack. The initial group will receive reinforcements, so try not to allow your party to become too spread out. Approach the steps to the west to be introduced to Fenris. Agree to help him during the dialogue that ensues, then travel to Hightown at night.
- Meet Fenris in the Hightown Estates area, then enter Danarius's Manor. The elf will be locked into the party for the next section of the quest. He should also be primed to level up, so spend any available Ability Points immediately.
- Fight your way through numerous Shades (and at least one Rage Demon – a hardy opponent who should be regarded as a priority target) until you reach a room in the northeast corner of the manor. Kill the enemies here and search loot piles to obtain the Magister's Key. Return to the large room with two staircases that lead to a mezzanine level, then save your progress and prepare your party for battle.
- Unlock the Magister's Chambers to trigger the appearance of an Arcane Horror. This enemy type might cause low-level parties a few problems, especially when further opponents join the fray, so you may wish to micromanage the fight (and use manual party movement, perhaps, to seek refuge in the adjoining rooms) if your first attempt ends ignominiously.
- Fenris will leave the party at this point. Ensure that you have collected everything of note, then return to Hightown. After the automatic conversation with Fenris ends, the quest draws to a close.

Consequences:

If you refuse to help Fenris in your first meeting, neglect to enlist him at the end of the quest or simply leave him standing outside Danarius's Manor when you depart Kirkwall for the **Deep Roads Expedition**, you will permanently lose the option to recruit him and undertake his future companion quests.

Companion Guidance:

Fenris has a deeply ingrained distrust of mages, so a Hawke versed in the arcane arts will need to think fast in the conversation that takes place at the end of the quest. If you wish to at least partially placate him, choose the "Survival" or "Nothing" dialogue options when challenged for low rivalry points. If you wish to antagonize him, "Is this a problem?" and "Power" lead to medium and large rivalry points respectively; select them in that order for maximum effect. There is an autosave just before the dialogue occurs, so you can refine your approach if your first attempt does not go to plan.

Fenris

Though his Lyrium-infused body may initially suggest that he is a brittle yet powerful mage, the troubled Fenris is a warrior tailor-made for diving into danger. As a practitioner of the art of wielding two-handed weapons, he's perhaps better suited as a favored companion during playthroughs in which you choose a less conventional party build.

- The events of **Bait and Switch** should have provided most players with sufficient insight to appreciate that Fenris does not feel comfortable with magic or its practitioners. Though you will find instances where he will accept that mages might, *in principle*, be suffered if heavily monitored and controlled, he'll generally object to any action or statement that explicitly favors them or their disputed rights to freedom in Kirkwall. He also disapproves of deals with demons of any kind.
- With the rather obvious exception of mages or magical creatures, Fenris appreciates an honorable approach to transactions with the individuals you meet on your adventures. That said, he's also suitably well-versed in the practicalities of survival: more than any other party member, he understands the verity of the phrase "do or die".
- A tortured soul, Fenris can derive a modicum of solace from physical intimacy... but don't expect him to respond favorably to declarations of love or need in the short term. As with Isabela, flirting and casual enjoyment will work best if you crave his attention or affections for the immediate future. Dismissive or cruel responses will lead to large rivalrly increases and, most likely, preclude a future entanglement of limbs.

The Bone Pit

Loot and Reward: 

Start Location:

Gamlen's House

Requirements:

- Complete the Birthright companion quest.
- Read the letter entitled "The Bone Pit" at the Writing Desk in Gamlen's House.

Walkthrough:

- Visit Hubert in Hightown Market during the day, then accept his offer of employment. Note that weapons and spells that cause cold damage will be of benefit on this quest. You should also stock up on potions.
- Travel to The Bone Pit in the Free Marches. Interact with the skeleton just south of the area entrance to collect "Bearded Beast" Arintal's Remains (to start the related side quest), then continue into the main mining camp to engage groups of Looters. Explore the area for collectibles if you wish, then enter the Bone Pit Mines.
- The mines are populated by Dragonlings, with Dragons contributing additional peril on a couple of occasions.
- Approximately midway through the map, en route to the southern waypoint, you'll encounter a sack containing the Eustice's Pommel collectible. This begins the side quest of the same name. You should find it before your fleeting encounter with a surviving miner.
- Prepare your party and save before you take the Bone Pit Ledge exit at the waypoint marker. See page 227 for more information on the Mature Dragon that attacks when you emerge into the daylight. Try to keep your weaker ranged fighters clear of its attacks, and you'll eventually grind this battle to a successful conclusion.
- In addition to other loot, the Mature Dragon drops the Dragon Fang, an item required for the Herbalist's Tasks. You can collect it even if you have yet to speak to Solivitus and start his quest as it's safely stored until the time comes to hand it over.
- Return to Hightown and report to Hubert.

Consequences:

- On completion of the quest, Get Back to Work begins immediately.
- If you choose not to complete The Bone Pit before travelling to the Deep Roads, Hawke cannot become a partner in Hubert's business. You will miss out on the Get Back to Work quest, and four other secondary quests related to the mine in Act 2 (Inside Job being the most noteworthy of these).

Companion Guidance:

Aveline will object (mild rivalry boost) if you attempt to push for additional payment; Varric, by contrast, will react with a mild friendship boost. Interestingly, an attempt to rebuff Hubert's commercial advances causes him to assume that Hawke is playing hardball, which leads to both extra recompense and mild approval from Aveline.

Get Back to Work

Loot and Reward: 

Requirements:

Begins immediately on completion of The Bone Pit.

Walkthrough:

Speak to Jansen in Lowtown during the day. You can attempt to charm or intimidate the drunken miners into returning to gainful employ, or you can offer them a raise. There is no difference either way.

Loose Ends

Loot and Reward: 

Start Location:

Gamlen's House

Requirements:

- Complete **Birthright**.
- Read the letter entitled Loose Ends at the Writing Desk in Gamlen's House.
- Your choice of "sponsor" during the party's attempts to enter Kirkwall in the Prologue determines who writes the letter. If Hawke spent a year in the service of Athenril, consult the Smuggler Walkthrough; if you instead opted for indentured servitude with Meeran, refer to the Mercenary Walkthrough. These plot strands are mutually exclusive: you can only complete one during the course of a single playthrough.

Smuggler Walkthrough:

- Speak to Athenril outside The Blooming Rose in Hightown.
- Travel to the Docks and save Pryce from the Coterie thugs.
- Decide whether to send the boy away with the goods to start a new life or to complete your orders as prescribed.
- Return to Athenril in Hightown.

Mercenary Walkthrough:

- Speak to Meeran close to The Hanged Man in Lowtown.
- Enter the fray as Gustav fights the nobleman's guards, then speak to Meeran's lackey when the battle ends.
- Listen to Harimann's interjection and choose whether to carry out the assassination.
- Return to Meeran in Lowtown.

Consequences:

If you betray Athenril or Meeran, they may return in search of revenge later in the Act.

Companion Guidance:

If you choose to allow Pryce to abscond with Athenril's goods, most potential party members (particularly Hawke's siblings) will approve. Aveline will purse her lips if you take them back.

Fools Rush In

Loot and Reward: 

Start Location:

The Hanged Man

Requirements:

Complete the **Tranquility** main plot quest.

Walkthrough:

- A cutscene will introduce Isabela when you travel to The Hanged Man to complete the short **Questions and Answers** companion quest. Speak to her at the bar and agree to assist her.
- Head to Hightown at night to meet with Isabela. After the ambush ends, collect Hayder's Letter from a nearby corpse. Follow Isabela to the Chantry and brace yourself for another assault when you reach the courtyard.
- After a third and final battle inside the Chantry (we suggest that you concentrate on Hayder's henchmen before you begin whittling away at his huge health gauge), you have the opportunity to learn more about Isabela. Once the dialogue ends, she joins Hawke's growing circle of companions.

Consequences:

Completing **Fools Rush In** is the only way to acquire Isabela as a companion and unlocks both **Isabela's Contact** and **Finders Keepers**. If you choose not to undertake this quest before the party embarks on the **Deep Roads Expedition**, you cannot acquire her services. This would be a shame, as she potentially has a significant role to play in the events of Act 2.

Isabela

Some players may recall meeting Isabela in a brothel during the events of Dragon Age: Origins, where she could introduce the Warden to the Duelist specialization… among other things.

- Early impressions matter with Isabela, so don't attempt to antagonize or entertain her without considering where you'd like your relationship to go. Once set on a path towards friendship or rivalry, even major events – such as the giving of gifts or rendering invaluable aid – will often solidify her existing feelings. For example: a simple off-the-cuff comment to a friendly Isabela could have a positive outcome, while exactly the same sentence would exacerbate a growing rivalry.
- Play as a paragon of virtue, eager to assist or sympathize with everyone you meet, and you may find it more difficult to maintain a state of friendship with Isabela. The succession of low rivalry increases that you'll experience as an aspirant saint may shape your interactions in a more combative direction. A witty or wry approach to all dialogue choices will definitely work in your favor if you're keen to establish yourself as a kindred spirit.
- If you wish to retain Isabela's services in the long term, try to develop a strong rivalry or friendship with her from a very early stage. Flirting (and where it might lead) can definitely help with this.

Finders Keepers

Loot and Reward: 

Start Location:

The Hanged Man

Requirements:

- Complete **Fools Rush In**.
- Speak to Martin in his room at The Hanged Man and agree to help.

Walkthrough Addendum:

- Travel to the Docks during the day and head to the waypoint marker. Speak to the Longshoreman, then Harbormaster Liam. After being brusquely dismissed by the latter, you'll instead deal with his assistant, Aden. There are three ways to obtain the location of Martin's cargo. The most immediate solutions are to bribe Aden (for two Sovereigns) or attempt to threaten him.
- For a relatively circuitous but slightly more rewarding solution, refuse to pay Aden, leave the Docks and return to the "office" area at night. Kill the Mabari guard dogs, then collect the Dockside Redirect from the table.
- Whichever approach you chose, Woodrow's Warehouse is now marked on the Docks map. Travel there during the day and get rid of the guards to reach the Warehouse entrance. At night there is one sleeping guard. You can sneak past if you pay him a wide berth.
- The Warehouse is filled with Raider enemies, with the Reavers and Assassins worthy of your respect. When you enter the main room, you may benefit from ordering your party to hold position at the top of the ramp, then walk down to trigger the conflict and quickly return. This can enable you to reduce the number of enemies you fight at once and avoid being flanked.
- There are traps in this area, so have a rogue lead the way if you have one in your party.
- Empty the chest at the waypoint marker, then head back to the entrance. You face a further group of Raiders as you leave, so be prepared.
- When you return to Martin, you can refuse to be a part of his scheme, freely divulge the location of his cargo, or offer the information at a price (with an obvious rivalry reaction from Aveline if present).

Consequences:

If you reveal the location of the cargo, Martin will enter into business and offer Hawke his services as a poison vendor. His shop can be accessed via his room at The Hanged Man for the rest of the game. •

An Errant Letter

Loot and Reward: 

Start Location:

Arthuris's Private Dock

Requirements:

- Start the **Wayward Son** main plot quest.
- When you kill the Abomination, loot Thrask's Letter from its body.

Walkthrough:

You simply need to return the letter to Thrask in the Gallows Courtyard. Your choices in the conversation with the templar do have an effect on your future dealings with him, however.

Consequences:

If you decide to extort money from Thrask (he pays five sovereigns), his demeanor will be different when you encounter him in the Act of Mercy quest. A more considerate approach leads to a nominal XP gain (unavailable if you opt for blackmail) but no monetary reward.

Companion Guidance:

Expect a smattering of disapproval (particularly from Aveline) if you blackmail Thrask, but friendship boosts (with Fenris an uncompromising exception) if you decide to hand over the letter and spare the templar the gruesome truth of his daughter's fate.

Herbalist's Tasks

Loot and Reward: 

Start Location:

Gallows Courtyard

Requirements:

- Complete the Long Way Home main plot quest.
- Speak with Solivitus and agree to find the ingredients he seeks.

Walkthrough:

- The Spider's Silk Gland is obtained during the Magistrate's Orders quest: one of the outsized arachnids you fight in the Ruined Passage will relinquish it as loot even if you have yet to start Herbalist's Tasks. Note that the Abandoned Ruins (Free Marches entrance point) and Ruined Passage (sub-area) locations are inaccessible once Magistrate's Orders has been completed. If you neglected to diligently loot spider remains before you left, you're sadly out of luck.
- The Dragon Fang is obtained by completing The Bone Pit and looting its final boss before you leave the mines.
- To obtain Ironbark, speak to Master Ilen in the Dalish Camp at Sundermount. This will unlock the Ironwood Clearing area on the Free Marches map. Clear the vicinity of Hurlocks and fell the Ogre that follows. Once all adversaries have fallen, a waypoint will appear to mark the location of the Pure Ironbark.
- Return to Solivitus to receive payment. Herbalist's Tasks does not technically end here so will remain in your Current Quests log. There's nothing more that you can accomplish in Act 1, though.

Consequences:

If you collect and return the three specified ingredients before the end of Act 1, Solivitus's shop will have an upgraded inventory in Act 2.

The Unbidden Rescue

Loot and Reward: 

Start Location:

Variable

Requirements:

- Complete the Long Way Home main plot quest.
- Start the quest by finding a flyer posted in the city (there's one in Hightown Square, for example, affixed to a pillar) or by approaching Viscount Dumar's chambers in the Viscount's Keep.

Walkthrough:

- A cutscene will begin as you approach Viscount Dumar's office. Speak to Seneschal Bran, then head to the southernmost area of the Wounded Coast.
- The competing Winters party has found Saemus, but he has no desire to return to Kirkwall with them. No matter what you say in the dialogue that ensues on arrival, combat is unavoidable.
- After defeating Ginnis and the initial group of Mercenaries, your party will be assailed by successive waves of reinforcements. The numbers can be quite significant in places. If you experience difficulties, try ordering your party to hold position by the cliff edge and lure small groups of opponents to their location.
- Once the battle ends, select the "Wait here while I look around" option during the conversation with Saemus to pick up loot before you return to Kirkwall. Collect the Redblossom Salve from the red crate in this area to begin the Redblossom Special side quest.
- Return to Saemus and choose to go back to Kirkwall to end the quest.

Consequences:

- Successfully completing this quest will cause Saemus to regard Hawke as a friend when encountered in Act 2.
- If you leave Saemus to be captured by the Winters after accepting the quest, he is returned to the Viscount's Keep alive and unharmed at the start of Act 2. This leads to slight reactive adjustments in dialogue with both Saemus and the viscount later in the story.

The First Sacrifice

Loot and Reward: 

Start Location:

Hightown

Requirements:

- Complete Tranquility.
- Read the "Reward Offered!" poster on a pillar in Hightown Market.
- Speak with Ghyslain de Carrac in Hightown Market during the day.

Walkthrough:

- After accepting the quest from Ghyslain, visit The Blooming Rose to speak with Jethann and learn that a templar named Emeric has also enquired about Ninette's whereabouts.
- Travel to Darktown and enter the Emeric's Investigation area. Fight off the assortment of thugs, then converse with the templar.
- Travel to the Dark Foundry in Lowtown. After a big battle against Shades, Abominations and a Desire Demon, loot the Sack of Bones upstairs to obtain Ninette's Ring and some human remains.
- Show the remains to Emeric in the Gallows, then return to Ghyslain in Hightown to end the quest.
- Simply give the ring to Ghyslain to claim the maximum possible reward. If you instead reveal the grizzly details of Ninette's demise, he will panic.

COMPANION QUESTS

Duty

Loot and Reward: 

Start Location:

Hightown

Requirements:

- You must have access to the Premium Content entitled The Exiled Prince and have completed the quest of the same name.
- Unlike many other companion quests, this can be completed during Act 1 or Act 2.

Walkthrough:

- The Flint Company Mercenary groups can be found in the Docks at night, close to the main Sundermount entrance, and in the northeast corner of the Wounded Coast. We would suggest that you deal with them when other quests lead you to these locations.
- Once all three groups have been defeated, return to the Chantry and speak with Sebastian to complete the quest.

Consequences:

Completing Duty leads to the Repentance companion quest, which is available from the start of Act 2. If you have already reached Act 2, Repentance should be playable immediately.

The Way It Should Be

Loot and Reward: 

Start Location:

Viscount's Keep

Requirements:

- Complete the A Friend in the Guard main plot quest by visiting Aveline in the Viscount's Keep barracks.
- Aveline must be in your party when you visit the Sundermount Ambush Site location and for all subsequent stages of this quest.

Walkthrough:

- On arrival at the Sundermount Ambush Site, fight your way through Raiders until you reach the southwest corner of the map. This area cannot be accessed again once you leave, so you may wish to be thorough in collecting loot (there is a crafting ingredient here).
- When the main ambush begins, try to draw enemies to your party's position: there are traps situated around the rocks. Once all hostiles have been disabled, leave the area and return to the Viscount's Keep barracks. Interact with the marked door, then check the duty roster.
- Travel to Lowtown at night. On arrival at the waypoint, kill Guardsman Donnic's attackers; be mindful of additional foes that arrive at the alley entrance. Finally, return to the Viscount's Keep for the quest's closing cutscenes.

Consequences:

If you do not complete The Way It Should Be before you leave for the Deep Roads Expedition (and, therefore, the conclusion of Act 1), Aveline's Act 3 companion quest (Favor and Fault) will not take place.

Birthright

Loot and Reward: 

Start Location:

Gamlen's House

Requirements:

Complete the A New Home? main plot quest by visiting Gamlen's hovel in Lowtown for the first time.

Walkthrough:

- Talk to Mother in Gamlen's House, then speak with Bethany or Carver as applicable.
- Travel to Darktown, then head to the Amell Estate Cellar. Hawke's surviving sibling is locked into the party once you enter.
- If Carver is present, visit the store room area to loot the chest for Tobrius's Documents or, with Bethany at your side, the Portrait of Your Mother item. This begins a companion quest related to your sibling: see Consequences. You must collect either item before you depart as it isn't possible to return at a later date.
- This quest may be your first encounter with the Assassin and Mage enemy types. See pages 223 and 230 of the Bestiary chapter for more information on these adversaries.
- Collect the Vault Key from the Master Slaver's remains after the battle in the anteroom, then enter the estate vault to pick up Grandfather Amell's Will and Testament from the chest. If you haven't fully reconnoitered the area for loot, decline your sibling's suggestion that you leave immediately: doing so will automatically transport you to Gamlen's House, and there's no way to return here.
- The chest also contains the Fereldan Girded Plating companion armor upgrade for Carver or the Heirloom Amell Protective Sigils equivalent for Bethany.

Consequences:

- Completing this quest and looting the chests in the store room unlocks **Family History** if Carver is alive or **Portrait of the Past** if Bethany survived the Prologue. You can have conversations that reflect on the quest's conclusion with each family member in Gamlen's House afterwards.
- The conclusion of this quest also triggers Magistrate Vanard's appearance in Hightown (he provides the **Magistrate's Orders** secondary quest), and a letter at Gamlen's House that leads to **The Bone Pit**: a venture with profitable follow-up quests in Act 1 and (predominately) Act 2.

Family History

Loot and Reward: 

Start Location:

Amell Estate Cellar (during Birthright quest only)

Requirements:

- Carver must have survived the Prologue.
- The Tobrius's Documents item was collected from a chest in the Amell Family Cellar storeroom during the **Birthright** quest.

Walkthrough:

- Travel to the Gallows and speak with Tobrius.
- Return to Gamlen's House to speak to Carver. Your dialogue choices govern his reaction, but a pleasant tone should yield a sizable shift towards friendship.

Portrait of the Past

Loot and Reward:

Start Location:

Amell Estate Cellar (during Birthright quest only)

Requirements:

- Bethany must have survived the Prologue.
- The Portrait of Your Mother item was collected from a chest in the Amell Family Cellar storeroom during the **Birthright** quest.

Walkthrough:

Visit Bethany at Gamlen's House after having collected the Portrait of Your Mother during the **Birthright** quest. Speak to her, and Hawke will offer it as a gift for a high boost to friendship.

Questions and Answers

Loot and Reward: 

Requirements:

- Begins automatically on completion of the **Tranquility** main plot quest.
- Travel to The Hanged Man during the day. The quest ends once you have conversed with Varric. Speak to Isabela at the bar before you leave to begin the **Fools Rush In** quest.

Isabela's Contact

Loot and Reward: 

Requirements:

- Begins automatically on completion of Fools Rush In.
- Travel to The Hanged Man and speak with Isabela; as is her wont, you'll find her propping up the bar. This short conversation formally unlocks the Finders Keepers secondary quest.

Talk to Anders

Loot and Reward: 

Start Location:

Darktown

Requirements:

Complete Tranquility and return to Darktown to visit Anders.

Walkthrough:

- If Anders is in your current party, you'll still need to enter his clinic in the north of the map to initiate dialogue.
- This is a simple conversation, but it provides the first opportunity to establish a friendship or rivalry and take the initial steps on the road to forging a more intimate relationship with the troublous mage.

Companion Guidance:

- The first aggressive option ("Don't do it again") precludes future relationship opportunities and leads to a high rivalry increase. In general, rebuffing his advances (or otherwise disregarding his feelings) in a cruel or dismissive way will have a similar effect.
- For the highest possible friendship boost with Anders, pick:
  - "It happens a lot."
  - "You did the right thing."
  - When he asks if he is making you uncomfortable: "No".
  - Male characters only should follow that with: "I'm sorry".

Welcome Home

Loot and Reward: 

Requirements:

- Complete the Long Way Home main plot quest.
- Visit Merrill's Home – it's in Lowtown's Elven Alienage district – and speak with her there. As with other such follow-up conversations, the quest ends once the dialogue is over.

Nice Crime You Have Around Here

Loot and Reward: 

Requirements:

To obtain this mini-quest (actually just a simple but amusing conversation with Merrill at her home in Lowtown), you must fulfill at least one of the following conditions:

- Give Solivitus any of the three ingredients required for the Herbalist's Tasks secondary quest.
- Complete Blackpowder Promise, Wayward Son or The Unbidden Rescue.

Fenris Recruited

Loot and Reward: 

Requirements:

- Starts on completion of the Bait and Switch secondary quest if you choose to enlist Fenris.
- Visit Fenris's Mansion (previously Danarius's Manor) and speak with the elf to complete the quest. Ideally, you should do this immediately after the conclusion of Bait and Switch, which leaves you standing right outside his front door. This conversation provides the first opportunity to establish a sexual relationship with Fenris through flirting or to quell the flickering embers of romance before they ever burst into flames.

SIDE QUESTS

PRIMER
WALKTHROUGH
QUESTS
MAPS
STRATEGY & ANALYSIS
INVENTORY
BESTIARY
EXTRAS
ACT 1
ACT 2
ACT 3
MISC. ACTIVITIES
COMPLETION ROADMAP
MAIN PLOT QUESTS
SECONDARY QUESTS
COMPANION QUESTS
SIDE QUESTS
PREMIUM CONTENT

"Find and Deliver" Side Quests

Name	Start Location	Requirements
Bottled Scar 5:34 Exalted	Viscount's Keep	• Find the Bottled Scar 5:34 Exalted collectible in the unlocked northwest office in the Viscount's Keep. • Deliver it to the Elven Vintner in Lowtown to claim your reward.
Shawl of Dalesdottir	The Hanged Man	• Loot the chest in the room south of Varric's quarters in The Hanged Man during daylight hours. • Deliver the shawl to Mais Dalesdottir in The Blooming Rose. • You can also collect the Stone Toe during your stay at The Blooming Rose to begin **The Paragon's Toe.**
The Remains of Sister Plinth	Darktown (Day)	• Collect the Sister Plinth's Remains item from southeast Darktown. (There's actually no need to make a special journey – you'll visit this general locale during the mandatory **Wayward Son** main plot quest.) • Deliver it to Brother Plinth the Archivist in the Chantry. Collect the Locks of the Golden Fool tome from the table in the north of the map to begin the side quest of the same name.
The Paragon's Toe	The Blooming Rose	• Collect the Stone Toe item from The Blooming Rose. It's inside a crate partially concealed beside a wardrobe in the northeast room. • Deliver the item to the New Surfacer in Lowtown's bazaar.
Locks of the Golden Fool	The Chantry	• Collect the Locks of the Golden Fool tome from the table in the north of the map. It will only appear during the daytime. • Deliver it to the Elven Radicalist on the west side of Darktown.
Remains of the Outlaw "Half-Braid" Silsam	Disused Passage (Docks)	• Collect "Half-Braid" Silsam's Remains from a small room in the south of the Disused Passage area. You can reach this location via one of two sewer entrances in the Docks area during night hours (one in the northwest "office" visited during **Finders Keepers**, a second in the far west of the district). • Interact with Eb Silsam in Sundermount's Dalish Camp to claim your reward.
Map of Occupied Kirkwall	Sundermount	• Collect the Map of Occupied Kirkwall item from a crate in the Dalish Camp. It's to the left of the Clan Craftsmaster. • Take the map to Record Keeper Teryn in the Gallows Courtyard.
The Seal of House Talwain	Sundermount Caverns	• Collect the Seal of House Talwain item from a crate directly south of the Mountain Graveyard exit. You will pass it during the **Long Way Home** main plot quest. • Deliver the seal to Sareth Talwain in Hightown Market.
Caste Treatise and House Accounting	Dead Man's Pass	• You will meet a dwarf, Javaris Tintop, during a scripted encounter while travelling between locations during Act 1. This will only occur after you complete **Long Way Home.** Javaris is the source of the **Blackpowder Promise** main plot quest. This brief and irreproducible visit to the Dead Man's Pass map is your only opportunity to collect the Caste Treatise item. • Deliver the Caste Treatise to the Traditionalist Envoy in northeast Hightown.
Remains of the Outlaw "Bearded Beast"	The Bone Pit	• Unlock **The Bone Pit** secondary quest. • Collect "Bearded Beast" Arintal's Remains from The Bone Pit – they're just south of the area entrance. • Deliver them to Arintal the Lesser in the Docks.
Eustice's Pommel	Bone Pit Mines	• Unlock **The Bone Pit** secondary quest. • Collect Eustice's Pommel from a sack situated approximately midway through the winding tunnels if you are travelling to the south exit. • Deliver the item to Guardsman Eustice in the Viscount's Keep barracks.
Redblossom Special	The Wounded Coast	• Collect the Redblossom Salve from a red crate in the southernmost area of the Wounded Coast. • Deliver it to Dalian Shaw in Darktown.
Grimoire of the Apprentice	Sanctuary	• Start the Enemies Among Us main plot quest, and play through until you reach the Sanctuary. The Grimoire of the Apprentice collectible can be found close to the area exit. Be sure to pick it up before you return to Darktown: this location cannot be revisited. • Deliver the book to Bonwald in Lowtown's bazaar.

In Act 1, all "find and deliver" side quests lead to a reward of 50 silver and 250 XP.

The Conspirators

Loot and Reward: 

Start Location:

Lowtown (Day)

Requirements:

Available if you import a save file in which the Silver Order was formed and your character chose to save Vigil's Keep in Dragon Age: Origins – Awakening.

Walkthrough:

- Speak to Sergeant Joanna, who is situated close to The Hanged Man, to accept the task of slaying Amaranthine conspirators. If you start this quest on your first visit to Lowtown, you can fulfill the requirements of her commission while completing other objectives.
- The four groups are located in Hightown, The Blooming Rose (accessed via Hightown), the Docks and the west side of Sundermount. After clearing all four, return to Sergeant Joanna in Lowtown to turn in the quest.

Terror on the Coast

Loot and Reward: 

Start Location:

The Wounded Coast

Requirements:

- Only appears if you are using an imported Dragon Age: Origins save file where you played the Warden's Keep expansion and chose to spare Sophia Dryden.
- Walk along the path leading west from the main Wounded Coast entrance. The quest will begin as you fight the Giant Spiders.

Walkthrough:

- Sophia Dryden can be found further west from the quest start location. Prepare your party before you approach her: she's supported by Mabari and Apostate Mages.
- Given that it's a short walk from the quest start point to its bloody conclusion, the rewards are rather fine: Dryden relinquishes the Robe of Hidden Pockets (an interesting armor choice for mages) and a reasonable sum of coin.

Dark Epiphany

Loot and Reward: 

Start Location:

The Wounded Coast

Requirements:

- Only appears if you are using an imported Dragon Age: Origins save file where you played the Warden's Keep expansion and chose to spare Avernus.
- Walk along the path leading west from the main Wounded Coast entrance until you are attacked by Bandits close to a camp site. Loot the Dead Messenger to begin the quest.

Walkthrough:

- Use the Avernus's Experimental Draught potion immediately: this welcome bonus grants two free attribute points.
- As you leave the camp site, additional Bandits will attack. You may wish to save after collecting the Grey Warden Documents.
- Visit Lowtown during the day to find the dead drop, where Mercenaries await your arrival. Defeat them (watch out for attacks from behind), then interact with the marked barrel.
- Travel to Gamlen's House and read the letter at the Writing Desk to complete the quest.

Secret Rendezvous

Loot and Reward: 

Start Location:

The Hanged Man (Night)

Requirements:

- Only available if you are playing Dragon Age II with an imported save file in which you chose to save Amaranthine in Dragon Age: Origins – Awakening or if you opted for the Hero of Ferelden or The Martyr background options during initial character creation.
- Complete the Fools Rush In secondary quest.
- Speak to the Suspicious Lady in The Hanged Man at night.

Walkthrough:

- Travel to the Docks at night and head for the Warehouse district.
- To obtain the bonus for eavesdropping on the meeting, stand on the steps above and wait for the conversation to end. You should be automatically detected at this point.
- Kill all hostiles in the area; you may find it useful to order your party to hold at the top of the steps as this will force your opponents to come to your position and reduce the risk of being surrounded.
- Return to The Hanged Man at night and report to the Suspicious Lady.

Last Of His Line

Loot and Reward: 

Start Location:

Docks (Day)

Requirements:

You must have imported a Dragon Age: Origins save where Bhelen was crowned king of Orzammar or, alternatively, selected The Martyr as your background option during the character creation process.

Walkthrough:

- Agree to help Harrowmont on the east side of the Docks, then approach the Carta Lieutenant at the top of the steps. He will make a counter-offer: kill the lord in return for a larger reward. This offers a better short-term gain, but lower overall profit: see Consequences. If you agree to side with the Carta, simply return and attack Harrowmont. After he and his Dwarven Bodyguards are dead, return to the Lieutenant to receive your payment.
- If you refuse the offer, the Carta representatives will attack immediately. They will be reinforced partway through the battle, but this is nothing you can't handle. Travel to the west side of the Docks and kill all Carta groups that you encounter, then return to Harrowmont.

Consequences:

- Choosing to side with the Carta will pay three sovereigns as opposed to Harrowmont's one, but the exiled noble will keep his promise to deliver additional coin to Hawke at a later date (you will receive five sovereigns and a piece of armor with a letter at the start of Act 2). Fighting on Renvil's behalf will also lead to a higher XP gain.

Changing One's Nature

Loot and Reward: 

Start Location:

Sundermount

Requirements:

- You must have imported a Dragon Age: Origins save where you chose to side with the werewolves during the Nature of the Beast quest or, alternatively, selected No Compromise as your background option during the character creation process.
- Speak to Clara at the Dalish Camp.

Walkthrough:

- It makes sense to complete this quest at the same time as Long Way Home, which leads you to the northern area of Sundermount. After collecting all four items, return to Clara to receive payment.
- The chest containing Purified Deathroot is directly opposite Clara.
- The Alchemically Sealed Flask is on the far west side of Sundermount in a ruined building, just north of the area exit.
- The Twice-Distilled Quicksilver is hidden behind a wall just south of the Sundermount Caverns entrance.
- The Ebon Rathleek chest is in plain view east of the Elven Graveyard, on the other side of Sundermount Caverns.

Miracle Makers

Loot and Reward: 

Start Location:

Lowtown

Requirements:

- You must have imported a Dragon Age: Origins save where you chose to reveal the existence of Andraste's ashes during the Urn of Sacred Ashes quest or, alternatively, selected The Martyr as your background option during the character creation process.
- Visit Lowtown and find a crowd gathered around a salesman in the bazaar. Wait for a while, and a guardsman will arrive to break up the mob. Speak to Sergeant Melindra to begin the quest.

Walkthrough:

- Head for the waypoint and speak to the individual named simply as "Swindler". This will initiate combat. The ringleader is an Assassin, but all other enemies are easily silenced Carta Thugs.
- Once all enemies have been killed, return to Sergeant Melindra to complete the quest.

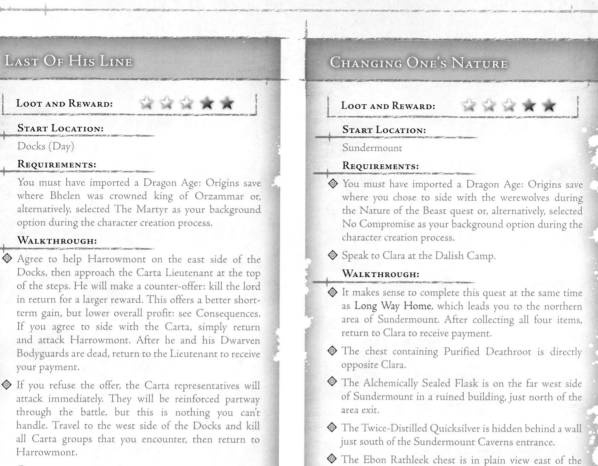

Gangs

Visiting Hightown, Lowtown or the Docks at night will lead to combat with groups of assailants. Though these skirmishes may seem random at first, they are actually an integral part of a major set of side quests in which Hawke and cohorts can strike a decisive blow to Kirkwall's criminal underworld.

- Gangs encountered on the streets usually consist of a mixture of ranged and melee fighters. The initial group is always bolstered by reinforcements, often arriving from two directions simultaneously. Try to identify defensible positions and lure your opponents to you. Above all else, ensure that your ranged fighters are not surrounded as new adversaries enter the fray.
- You may need to visit the area on more than one occasion to kill a sufficient number of gang members. When you pass the required threshold, a pop-up message will mark the formal beginning of the side quest. A Journal entry will appear, and the faction hideout will be marked on the map. Refer to the appropriate side quest entry for further details.
- After killing your first gang leader and leaving their base, your party will be approached by a stranger who promises rewards for your continued efforts in ridding Kirkwall of organized crime. You can visit this individual in The Hanged Man to claim your payment after each gang has been neutralized.
- New gangs will appear during Act 2 and Act 3: same locales, same time, but different opponents. You must defeat all nine across the three Acts to claim the optimum reward.

Pier Pressure

Loot and Reward: 

Start Location:

Docks (Night)

Requirements:

Visit the Docks at night and kill the gangs of Redwater Raiders that appear until the quest is awarded in a pop-up message.

Walkthrough:

- Once the side quest has been awarded, head to the Warehouse entrance in the southwest of the Docks.
- The Redwater Teeth gang is led by a miscreant named Leech: a blood mage. Make him your absolute priority in this fight, practically ignoring all other opponents until he falls. Depending on your difficulty setting, you may need to micromanage this battle very carefully, using a considered sequence of debilitating attacks (to prevent or curtail his most damaging assaults), high-impact single target Talents and Spells for maximum health drain, and showers of AoE attacks that also encompass Leech should his cohorts arrive in numbers. See page 230 for more advice on fighting the blood mage enemy type.
- Further enemies will spawn during the battle, so you may wish to move everyone to the top of the slope (or, safer still, the room beyond it) once Leech has been dispatched in order to reduce the number of foes you face simultaneously.

Night Lies

Loot and Reward: 

Start Location:

Hightown (Night)

Requirements:

Visit Hightown at night and kill the groups of enemies known as Guardsman Pretenders until the quest is awarded in a pop-up message.

Walkthrough:

- The Shallowguard Base is accessed via the marked entrance in northeast Hightown.
- As further Shallowguard opponents arrive via the main entrance once the battle begins, you may profit by manually stationing your party on the upper level of the main room before or after you engage "Captain" Qerth.

Sharp Little Pinpricks

Loot and Reward: 

Start Location:

Lowtown (Night)

Requirements:

Visit Lowtown at night and kill the gangs of Sharps Highwaymen that appear until the quest is awarded in a pop-up message.

Walkthrough:

- Enter the Sharps base via the entrance marked Hovel on the east side of Lowtown.
- This fight involves fewer enemies than you have seen in other gang-related quests, but takes place in a very confined space. Use this to your advantage. Ignacio Strand is an Assassin, so intelligent use of AoE attacks will enable you to keep him in plain view.

PREMIUM CONTENT

The Exiled Prince

Loot and Reward: 

Start Location:

Hightown

Requirements:

You must have access to this Premium Content quest. For further details, visit dragonage.com/da2/addons.

Walkthrough:

This is less "quest" per se and more of a formal introduction to Sebastian. Approach the waypoint marker close to the Chantry in Hightown to trigger a cutscene. Once this ends, approach the Chanter's Board and accept the Duty companion quest to wrap up The Exiled Prince.

Consequences:

Unlocks Sebastian Vael as a potential companion in Act 2 and his related quests. The first of these, Duty, is available immediately.

The Black Emporium

Loot and Reward: 

Requirements:

- You must have access to this Premium Content quest. For further details, visit dragonage.com/da2/addons.
- Read the letter at Gamlen's House to receive a formal invitation to the Black Emporium.

Walkthrough:

- Simply enter the Black Emporium via the main Kirkwall map to complete this quest. Again, like The Exiled Prince, it's merely an exercise in guiding you to a particular location.
- The Black Emporium features several Codex entries, two shops that contain interesting items (many of which will be wildly beyond your financial reach) and, of greater import on your first visit, a collectible marked Discarded Weapons and Armor. This contains free equipment that will give your character a considerable boost during the early stages of Act 1. We suggest that you outfit Hawke with items suitable for your chosen class, keep weapons that you don't need for companions (future or present), then sell unneeded armor at one of the stores to generate funds.
- The Mirror of Transformation can be used to change Hawke's appearance, thumbnail portrait or name. Using it may cause your character to remove their current headgear, so be sure to reequip it before you head out.

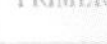

ACT 2

COMPLETION ROADMAP

This diagram will help you plan your route through Act 2 by revealing the unlock progression for all main plot, secondary and companion quests. You will find fact sheets for all of these ventures over the pages that follow, plus guidance for smaller side quests (which usually have their own unique unlock conditions).

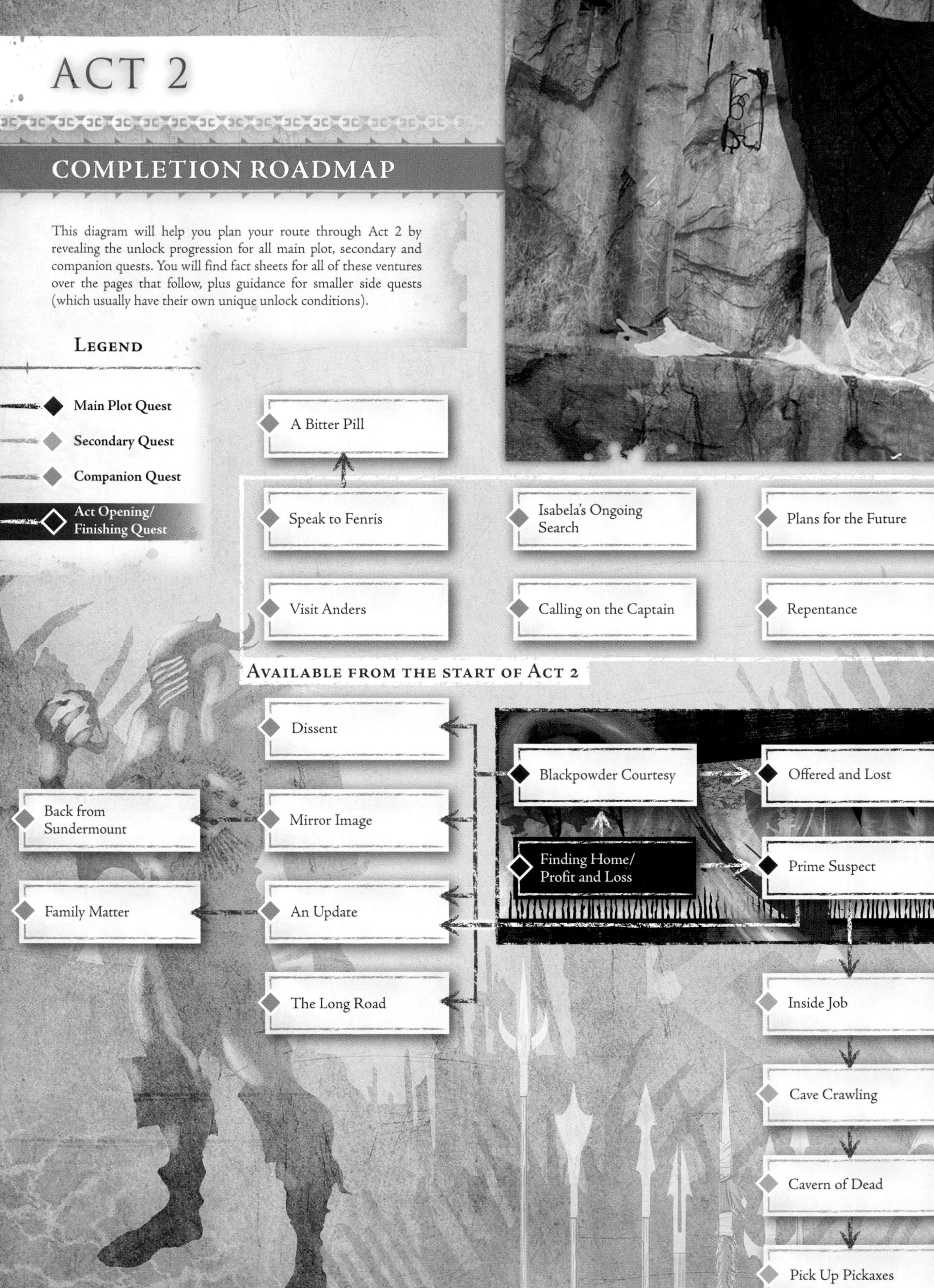

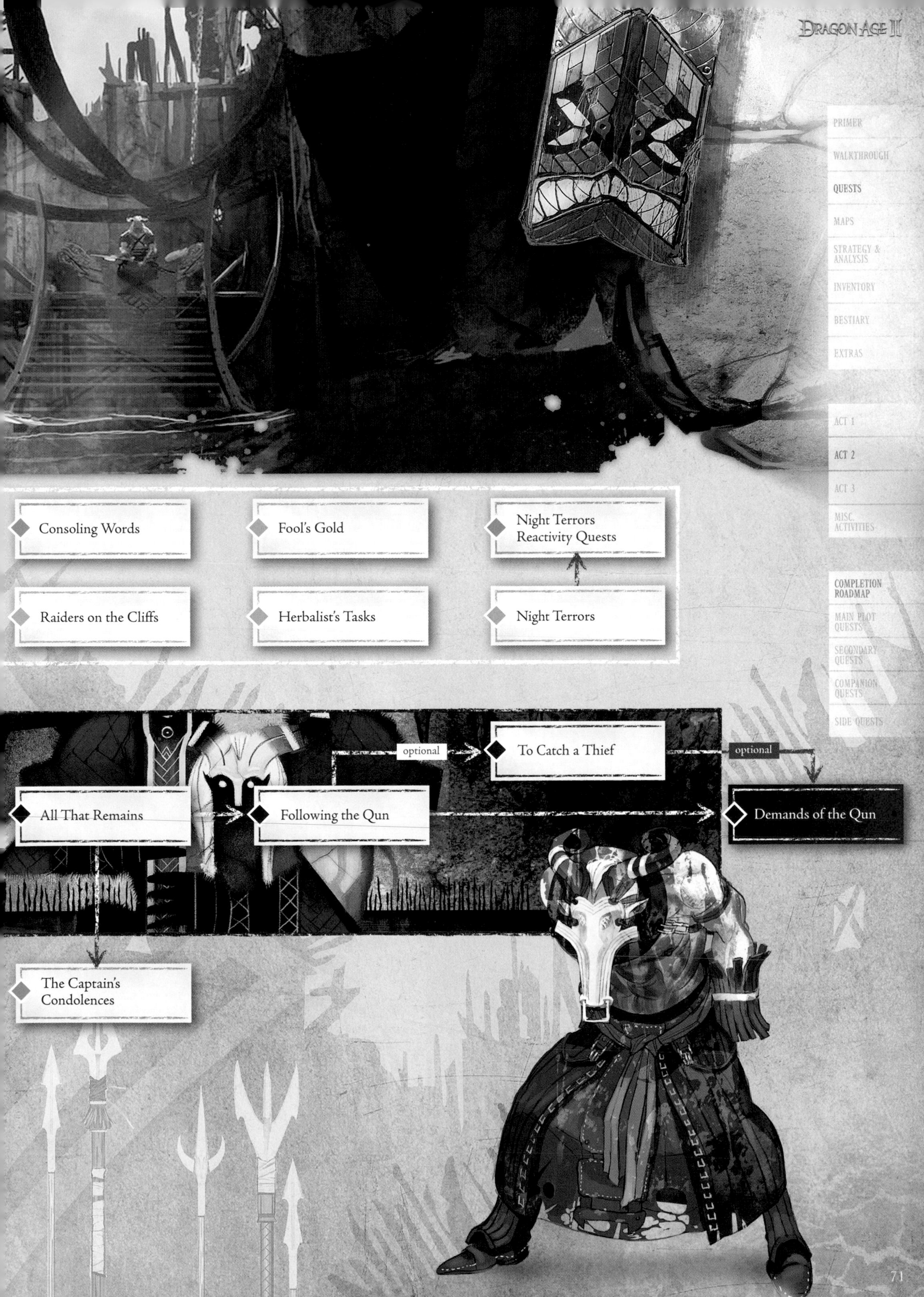
Consoling Words
Fool's Gold
Night Terrors Reactivity Quests
Raiders on the Cliffs
Herbalist's Tasks
Night Terrors
optional
To Catch a Thief
optional
All That Remains
Following the Qun
Demands of the Qun
The Captain's Condolences

MAIN PLOT QUESTS

Finding Home

Loot and Reward: ★★★★★

Start Location:

Hightown

Note: Only activated if Hawke paid Bartrand in full for his part in the Deep Roads Expedition. Unlocks Blackpowder Courtesy and Prime Suspect on completion.

Profit and Loss

Loot and Reward: 

Start Location:

Hightown

Consequences:

- If you accepted Dougal's loan in the Friends in Low Places quest, he returns here in an attempt to extort additional payment from Hawke. This replaces Finding Home as the opening "quest" of Act 2 and unlocks Blackpowder Courtesy and Prime Suspect on completion.
- If you scoff at Dougal's attempt at intimidation and send him packing (and you inevitably will), he will later ambush Hawke in a random encounter during your travels through Kirkwall.

Blackpowder Courtesy

Loot and Reward: 

Start Location:

Qunari Compound in the Docks

Note: Don't forget to collect the Ship in a Bottle from a chest near the north exit in Smuggler's Cut. This is a gift for Isabela – see page 86.

Consequences:

- Unlocks the Offered and Lost main plot quest, and the Dissent, Mirror Image, An Update and The Long Road companion quests.
- Certain actions in the Blackpowder Courtesy, Offered and Lost and Following the Qun quests can increase or reduce the Arishok's respect for Hawke. These actions are flagged throughout this chapter. Gaining a sufficient level of respect has an effect on the climax of Act 2, and will also unlock a reactive side quest in Act 3.

Companion Guidance:

Both Aveline and Sebastian will disapprove if you choose to kill the hapless Javaris.

Offered and Lost

Loot and Reward: 

Requirements:

Complete Blackpowder Courtesy.

Walkthrough Addendum:

- After speaking with Seneschal Bran, you can make an optional visit to the Arishok to inform him that the Qunari delegates have disappeared. He deeply respects this decision.
- There are a few potential outcomes to the meeting with Orwald the Braggart in The Hanged Man:
  - If you have Aveline in your party, you can call on her to resolve the situation without bloodshed (and gain a medium friendship boost).
  - Choose to question Orwald yourself, and a fight will start. Having Aveline, Varric or Isabela in your party will reduce the number of opponents you face: their faces are well known at the inn, and so fewer patrons will be foolish enough to join the melee.
  - If Isabela is not in your current party and is propping up the bar, she will join the fight as soon as it breaks out.
- If the Forbidden Knowledge side quest is active, an Evil Tome can be found in the south area of the Chantry. Refer to page 88 to learn more about the Tomes before you interact with it.
- You can only fight the Qunari at Ser Varnell's Refuge if you have been playing as an "aggressive" Hawke (see page 160) and pick the "Here's your proof" bonus dialogue line. This path influences your future options in Following the Qun.
- In the conversation with Viscount Dumar, select the "Do not hide it. He'll know" response to gain maximum respect from the Arishok when you return to him. Burning the bodies, however, leads to an optional side quest – see Consequences.
- Collect the Shield of the Knight Herself from the crate in the southeast of the map. This is a gift for Aveline, and will begin the companion quest of the same name.

Consequences:

- Only fighting the Qunari (rather than Ser Varnell) will enable you to side with the fanatics who so revile them later in the Act.
- There are optional follow-up conversations to be had with Petrice and the Arishok if you visit the Chantry or Qunari Compound after the quest ends. The meeting with the Arishok can feature optional reactions based on your earlier decisions.
  - If you sided with Varnell, attempting to lie to the Arishok when he asks about the fate of the soldiers he sent to find the delegates will disappoint him. The bald truth, by contrast, will increase his respect for Hawke.
  - If you advised the viscount to burn the bodies of the delegates, the Qunari leader will have specific words to say on this subject. Only returning the delegates in a state that does nothing to conceal the tortures they endured (and doing nothing to deny this salient fact) will engender his respect.
- Choosing to burn the bodies before they are sent to the Qunari unlocks a side quest called The Fixer in Act 3.

Prime Suspect

Loot and Reward: ★★★★★

Start Location:

Hawke Estate

Requirements:

- Complete **Finding Home/Profit and Loss.**
- Accept the letter from the Writing Desk.

Walkthrough Addendum:

- Aveline makes a sizable contribution to the opening conversation with Emeric if included in your party.
- The DuPuis Estate features a collection of plot "clues", some of which are Codex entries. If Merrill or Anders are present as you explore, they will offer an insight on the Vials of Blood that you find.
- When you meet Gascard, there are two paths you can choose from.
  - If you offer to help, he can potentially play a rather significant role in the **All That Remains** quest.
  - If you refuse to believe his explanation, you will be forced to kill him.
- When Moira asks if Gascard is responsible for Emeric's death, confirming her suspicions will forestall his involvement in **All That Remains.** Selecting "I don't think so" is the best choice in terms of story development.

Consequences:

Unlocks **Inside Job**, **An Update** and (with **Offered and Lost** completed at a prior date) the **All That Remains** main plot quest.

All That Remains

Loot and Reward: ★★★★★

Requirements:

Complete **Prime Suspect** and **Offered and Lost.**

Walkthrough Addendum:

- You can optionally report Leandra's disappearance to Moira in the Gallows, though doing so has no lasting effect.
- There are two ways to gain entrance to the Dark Foundry:
  - If Gascard is alive, you can find him in Darktown. Tell him to perform the ritual. Perhaps reflecting the gravity of the situation, companions who usually respond badly to blood magic will let this one instance pass without comment or consequence. After the instant transition to the Dark Foundry, Gascard will accompany your party through the area.
  - An alternative solution (and the only available path if Gascard was killed during **Prime Suspect**, or hunted by a vengeful Moira in its aftermath) is to meet Gamlen in Lowtown at night. Speak to the Urchin and either pay or intimidate him to obtain information. Follow the blood trail to the Dark Foundry entrance.
- If Gascard is with you in the Killer's Lair for the meeting with Quentin, there are three possible outcomes:
  - If Varric is in your party, he has a *very* interesting reaction.
  - Without Varric, you can attempt to persuade Gascard to turn away from his current path via a diplomacy option. If successful, he will fight alongside you in the battle with Quentin. Having this blood mage on your side should make the confrontation easier.
  - If Gascard feels disinclined to assist Hawke, he will join Quentin for the final battle. In this instance, target him immediately with everything your party has: you do not want him alive when the first Desire Demon spawns.

Consequences:

- Unlocks **Following the Qun** on completion, and **The Captain's Condolences** companion quest.
- Gascard can be found in the south of Darktown if he survived the quest. You can opt to let him go (via a little light retribution from Aveline if present) or exact instant revenge. There is a reward at the start of Act 3 if you spare him.

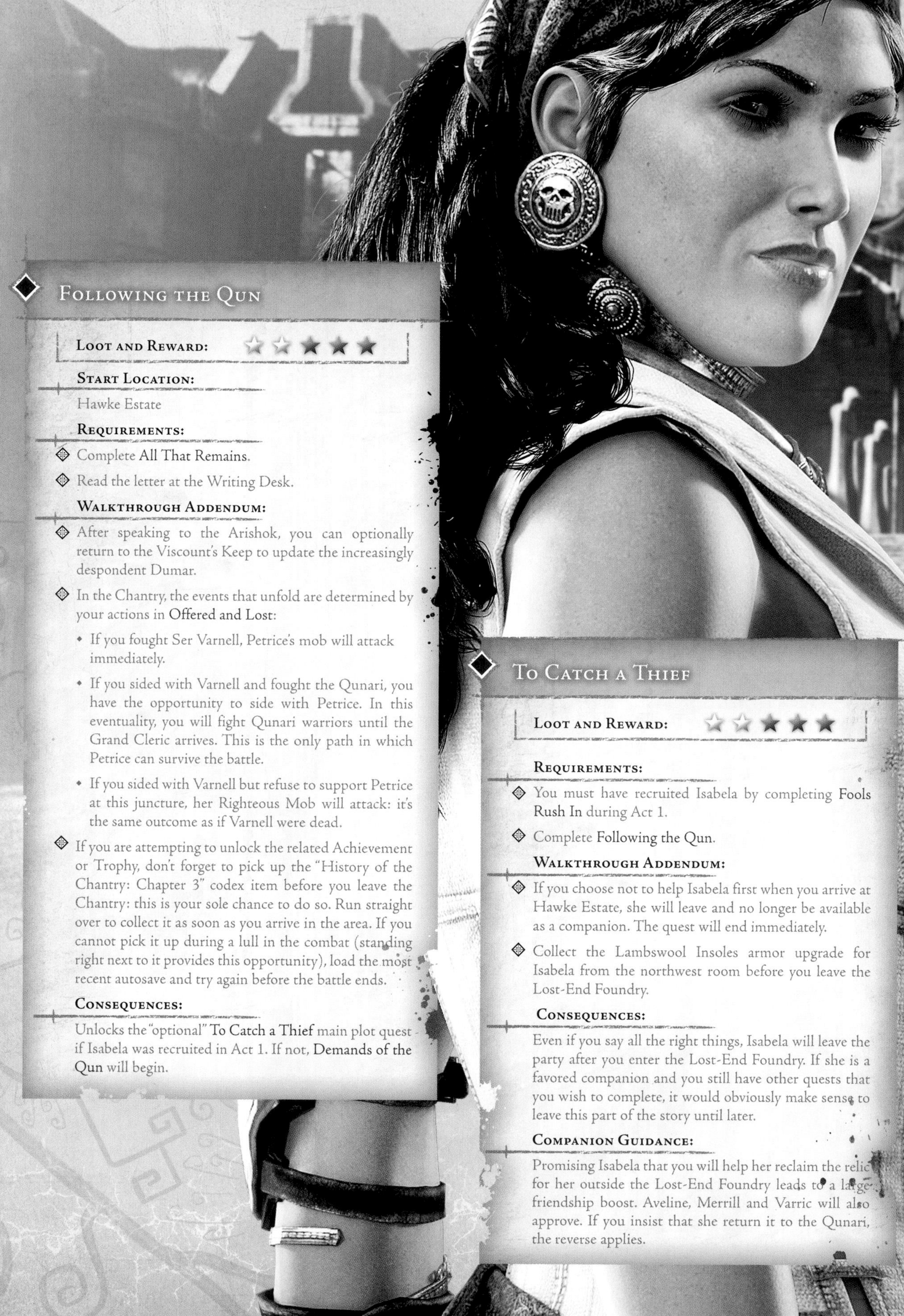

Following the Qun

Loot and Reward: ☆☆★★★

Start Location:

Hawke Estate

Requirements:

- Complete All That Remains.
- Read the letter at the Writing Desk.

Walkthrough Addendum:

- After speaking to the Arishok, you can optionally return to the Viscount's Keep to update the increasingly despondent Dumar.
- In the Chantry, the events that unfold are determined by your actions in Offered and Lost:
  - If you fought Ser Varnell, Petrice's mob will attack immediately.
  - If you sided with Varnell and fought the Qunari, you have the opportunity to side with Petrice. In this eventuality, you will fight Qunari warriors until the Grand Cleric arrives. This is the only path in which Petrice can survive the battle.
  - If you sided with Varnell but refuse to support Petrice at this juncture, her Righteous Mob will attack: it's the same outcome as if Varnell were dead.
- If you are attempting to unlock the related Achievement or Trophy, don't forget to pick up the "History of the Chantry: Chapter 3" codex item before you leave the Chantry: this is your sole chance to do so. Run straight over to collect it as soon as you arrive in the area. If you cannot pick it up during a lull in the combat (standing right next to it provides this opportunity), load the most recent autosave and try again before the battle ends.

Consequences:

Unlocks the "optional" To Catch a Thief main plot quest if Isabela was recruited in Act 1. If not, Demands of the Qun will begin.

To Catch a Thief

Loot and Reward: ☆☆★★★

Requirements:

- You must have recruited Isabela by completing Fools Rush In during Act 1.
- Complete Following the Qun.

Walkthrough Addendum:

- If you choose not to help Isabela first when you arrive at Hawke Estate, she will leave and no longer be available as a companion. The quest will end immediately.
- Collect the Lambswool Insoles armor upgrade for Isabela from the northwest room before you leave the Lost-End Foundry.

Consequences:

Even if you say all the right things, Isabela will leave the party after you enter the Lost-End Foundry. If she is a favored companion and you still have other quests that you wish to complete, it would obviously make sense to leave this part of the story until later.

Companion Guidance:

Promising Isabela that you will help her reclaim the relic for her outside the Lost-End Foundry leads to a large friendship boost. Aveline, Merrill and Varric will also approve. If you insist that she return it to the Qunari, the reverse applies.

Demands of the Qun

Loot and Reward: 

Requirements:

Finish **To Catch a Thief**; if Isabela was not recruited in Act 1, completing **Following the Qun** will suffice.

Walkthrough Addendum:

- A reminder: entering the Qunari Compound really is the point of no return for Act 2. If you have anything else you wish to attend to, do so beforehand.
- On arrival in Lowtown, the Change Party screen will appear. This is your last opportunity to select your party for the rest of the Act. If you have not sought to gain the Arishok's respect up to this point, including Fenris in the party is the only way to engineer one of the three possible resolutions.
- You will encounter a party of Grey Wardens while travelling through Lowtown. If you are using an imported save game or preset world background where Alistair remained a Warden in Dragon Age: Origins, he will be the leader of this party; if not, Stroud will greet you. If Hawke's surviving sibling joined the Grey Wardens at the conclusion of the **Deep Roads Expedition**, you will also meet them here.
- Rather than going straight for the marked exit in Lowtown, continue south to fight against an army of Looters. The majority of these are pitifully weak, but the Coterie Rogue (an Assassin) that joins partway through the battle is a more noteworthy threat.
- If Bethany joined the Circle, or Carver signed up with the templars, you will cross paths with them in Hightown.
- When you approach the Viscount's Keep, you have a choice on how to gain entrance:
  - If you accept the offer of a distraction, you are transported to the Keep without further conflict.
  - If you choose to fight, there is an additional battle with the Qunari warriors assembled in front of the entrance.
- The Arishok's address to the terrified nobility is where things *really* become interesting. After the brief aside where you fight the Qunari, there are two possibilities: either Isabela makes a timely return to the fold (which is only possible if you have completed her mid-stage relationship quest: see page 86), or she remains conspicuously absent.
- If Isabela returns, you have two options: defend her, or hand her to the Arishok.
  - If you choose to stand by the wayward rogue, you must confront the Arishok – either in a duel, or alongside his Qunari.
  - Allowing the Arishok to take Isabela back to his homeland enables you to end this Act without further violence... but at the expense of losing her as a companion.
- If Isabela is not present, or if you opt to defend her, you can resolve the situation in one of two ways.
  - If you have gained the Arishok's respect, select the "On the battlefield" option when he asks how Hawke would resolve the conflict, to begin a one-on-one duel.
  - All other dialogue options lead to a more conventional fight against the Arishok and his entourage. However, if Fenris is present, he will put forward a case for a duel. Accept this, and you can battle the Qunari leader alone; refusal leads to the more conventional brawl.
- If you choose the duel, note that this is by far the most difficult conclusion to the Act. Make gradual use of abilities or spells that might incapacitate the Arishok throughout the battle; anything that impedes his mobility is a blessing. Weave around the pillars to avoid his assaults until you are ready to renew your aggression. Another tactic that works well is to wait for him to perform his "rushing" attack (note the distinctive change in stance that foreshadows this), dodge, then attack as he passes. He will periodically heal throughout the confrontation, so be prepared for an extended encounter.

Consequences:

- The manner in which you defeat the Arishok has an effect on the closing cutscene of the Act.
- If Isabela does not return at the eleventh hour, or is taken away by the Qunari, she really *is* gone for good.

Companion Guidance:

- If you disagree with Aveline's comment ("That doesn't excuse murder") during the opening dialogue with the Arishok, you will experience a rivalry increase with her (and, if present, Sebastian as well).
- Allowing Isabela to be taken by the Arishok will lead to rivalry increases with Aveline, Merrill and Varric. Defending her will, naturally, lead to friendship boosts. Isabela's reaction to the latter depends on how your relationship has developed: anger for a rivalry, and gratitude in a friendship.
- There is a moderate rivalry increase with Fenris if he intervenes to arrange a duel and you refuse the offer; the opposite applies if you accept.

Night Terrors

Loot and Reward: 

Start Location:

Hawke Estate

Requirements:

Accept the letter from the Writing Desk.

Walkthrough:

- Speak to Arianni in Lowtown's elven alienage, then select your party for the journey.
- You can complete three "puzzles" to gain a total of four attribute points for Hawke before you continue with the quest. See the diagrams below for a step-by-step guide.
  - **Puzzle #1:** In the room that you arrive in, interact with the floating book to gain a single attribute point. In true Space Invaders tradition, focus on where the book *will* be – not where it actually is – to catch it.
  - **Puzzle #2 (Diagram 1):** In the corridor to the east you will find the first of two "barrel puzzles", where you must rearrange the containers into a specific order within a limited number of moves. If you fail, you lose the attribute point(s) on offer, and must fight a group of enemies. In this first instance you must rearrange the barrels so that the large ones are at the bottom, small ones at the top – and all within 18 moves.
  - **Puzzle #3 (Diagram 2):** There is another puzzle in a room to the east. The objective here is hinted at by the drums on either side of the room. You must rearrange the containers to have a block of four red barrels in the center. You have 18 moves to achieve this, with two attribute points given if you succeed – and a fight if you fail.
- Having claimed the available rewards, proceed into the central room. You will be greeted by the Sloth Demon (Torpor), who has a proposal: if Hawke can help him to possess Feynriel, he will offer a large reward.
  - If Anders is in your party, he will object to any prospective deal with this demon. If you choose the "Back off, Anders!" option (in order to take the demon's offer), you must fight him; his death expels him from the Fade, reducing your party by one (and with future repercussions – see Consequences).
  - If you choose to negotiate, the demon can fulfill one of three potential desires: **power** (four Attribute Points), **knowledge** (one Talent Point) or **magic** (the unique Torpor's Barrier Rune, which offers notable magic resistance when applied to armor). However, these rewards will only be delivered should Torpor actually take control of the elf. Your choice of payment is irreversible; the decision to sacrifice Feynriel is not. If you intend to go through with this betrayal, note that the Rune is a fine addition to companion armor.
  - If you refuse the Sloth Demon's advance, you must fight him and his cohorts immediately.
- Your actions within this shadowy realm influence Feynriel's mental state: too much disharmony will destabilize his mind. The goal is to ensure that he suffers as little anguish as possible. Note that Feynriel's mental state must be healthy to complete any deal with Torpor: again, see Consequences.
- Save your progress, then head into the east room first, via the door marked Feynriel's Desires. In the scene that follows, there are three resolutions:
  - If you attempt to persuade Feynriel to go with his father (in reality, the Desire Demon, Caress), his instability will increase dramatically.
  - If you try to convince Feynriel that the scene isn't real, his instability will increase marginally.
  - To avoid an instability increase entirely, convince Feynriel to reject his father.
- In the aftermath of this dialogue, the furious Caress will remonstrate with Hawke.
  - If Isabela is in your party, she will succumb to the Desire Demon's promise and turn on Hawke. Killing her will expel her from the Fade.
  - If Isabela is not in your party but Aveline is, she will turn on Hawke instead.

Diagram 1: **Puzzle #2 can be solved in 14 moves.**

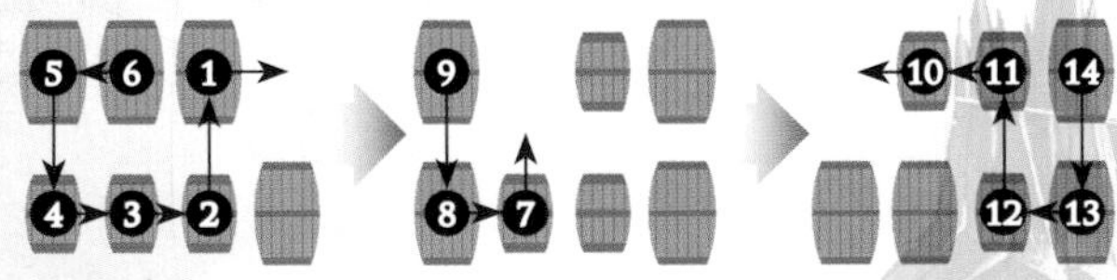

Diagram 2: **Puzzle #3 can be solved in 16 moves.**

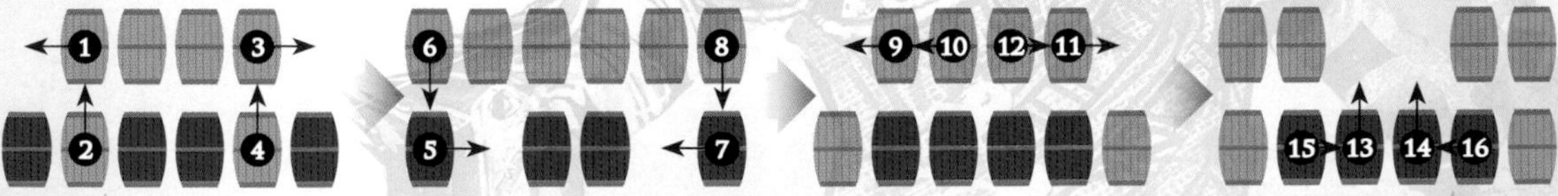

Night Terrors (Continued)

- You must defeat Pride (and Isabela or Aveline, if either are present) to continue. Take the initiative quickly, especially if you have been reduced to a single companion: strike with your most effective attacks and aim to at least incapacitate your opponents from the moment combat begins. Once the battle ends, travel through the main room to reach the Feynriel's Pride door. Save, then enter.
- As with the earlier scene, the lines you choose in this second charade will affect Feynriel's state of mind.
  - If you play along with the Pride Demon's attempt to make Feynriel accept his destiny as a Dreamer, and as prospective savior of the elves, his instability will greatly increase.
  - Attempting to reveal the true nature of the situation will lead to a small instability hike.
  - Encourage Feynriel to reject his "destiny" and raise concerns over what being a Dreamer could represent for no instability increase at all.
- The demon will not take kindly to Hawke's interference, and will seek a very personal form of retribution before conventional combat ensues. This plays out in the same way as the equivalent situation with the Pride Demon (Wryme).
  - If Merrill is in the party, she will accept the demon's offer.
  - If Fenris is in the party but Merrill is not, he will succumb to Wryme's promises instead.
  - If Varric is in the party but Merrill and Fenris are not, the storyteller will turn on Hawke.
- As with the battle with Caress, strike hard and fast to bring down Wryme before he can inflict any damage of note.
- On your return to the central room, the scene that greets you is dependant on your choices throughout the quest. If you made a deal with Torpor, there are three possibilities:
  - If Feynriel's mind has been twisted and wrought by Hawke's malevolent or clumsy interference, Torpor will be incapable of possessing the elf. It will attack Hawke, furious at his inability to complete his part of the deal.
  - If Feynriel's mental state is good, select the "You're safe" option to allow Torpor to take control of the Dreamer and deliver your desired boon.
  - You can renege on the deal to save Feynriel, but that means fighting the demon and forgoing the reward it promised you earlier.
- If Feynriel is not possessed by Torpor, he will leave the Fade immediately. If his instability is high, he will beg Hawke to kill him. Agreeing will make him Tranquil.

Consequences:

- If Feynriel emerges unscathed by his journey through the Fade, a small reactive quest may be unlocked at the start of Act 3.
- If Torpor possesses Feynriel, you get a very different concluding cutscene and will have access to a reactive event in Act 3.
- A third narrative wrap-up is available if Feynriel is made Tranquil. This leads to no follow-up events of note and is the least profitable outcome.

Companion Guidance:

- Striking a deal with Torpor will cause a large rivalry increase with Anders. Picking the "Quiet, Anders!" option during the conversation with Keeper Marethari at the end of the quest will also annoy him severely. Accepting the blame, by contrast, meets with surprised (albeit slight) approval.
- Any companion beguiled by a demon (or, in Anders' case, enraged by proxy) in the Fade will wish to speak to Hawke at their home or hangout when the quest ends. The possible results of these short companion quests are detailed below.

Night Terrors Reactivity

Depending on your selection of companions during the Night Terrors quest and your choices during your time in the Fade, certain companions may wish to talk to you once you return to Kirkwall.

- With Anders, there is a big friendship increase if you select "It was a ruse" having saved Feynriel at the end; you will meet with unavoidably massive disapproval if you did not. The latter eventuality will also end any ongoing romance.
- For Isabela, forgive her and flirt (or pick the diplomacy option) for +10 friendship. Lambast her as a backstabber for the same in rivalry points.
- With all other companions, friendship and rivalry increases are very minor – and the result of each conversational choice is fairly obvious. Interestingly, Sebastian is incorruptible in the Fade, which is very useful on the Nightmare difficulty.

Herbalist's Tasks

Loot and Reward: 

Start Location:

Gallows Courtyard

Requirements:

- You must have completed the equivalent quest during Act 1.
- Speak to Solivitus and offer your assistance once again.

Walkthrough:

- The Harlot's Blush Flower is located in the northwest of the Wounded Coast. It's just in front of the cave that you enter for the Search and Rescue side quest.
- Dalish Tattoo Ink can be acquired from a chest inside the Dalish Camp at the base of Sundermount. You can talk about this ingredient with Master Ilen, but his response is not favorable: you have to steal it.
- The Varterral Heart is obtained from the creature fought at the end of Merrill's companion quest, Mirror Image.
- Return the ingredients to Solivitus in the Gallows to pick up your payment.

Fool's Gold

Loot and Reward: 

Start Location:

Hightown

Requirements:

- Only available if Nathaniel died or wasn't recruited in Dragon Age: Origins – Awakening, or if you chose the Hero of Ferelden character background during the Prologue.
- Speak to Yevhen and agree to help.

Walkthrough:

- After accepting the quest, set out for the Deep Roads via the World Map. Ideally, try to equip your mages with weapons that inflict spirit or nature damage: the darkspawn await...
- When you reach Emrys you are given a choice between saving Merin or going to Iwan's aid in order to obtain an apparently powerful weapon. There is only time to complete one objective: rescue one brother, and the other will die. (Note that the area south of Emrys features two waves of assorted spider enemies: a potentially tricky battle, but certainly worth the XP and loot.)
  - If you choose **Merin**, he can be found a short walk to the north. There are two Darkspawn Emissaries here, powerful mages who can tear through a well-prepared party with disturbing ease. Deal with these immediately. After the battle ends, speak to Merin, then travel south to find Iwan's body and retrieve the Golem Control Rod.
  - If you choose **Iwan**, head straight to his position to the northeast. On arrival, you'll find him fighting a much smaller collection of darkspawn. In the conversation that follows you can either pay him for the Golem Control Rod, attempt to threaten him or have Varric step in to negotiate if present. The latter solution is the neatest of the three. You can optionally return to fight the collection of enemies that attacked Merin (see above) for additional XP before you continue.
- At this point, both paths converge. Interact with the Golem when you reach it to acquire a new ally, then fight your way past its less governable peers: cold and electricity attacks work best. There's a nasty battle with darkspawn just beyond this point that features an Emissary and an Ogre. You may find it prudent to pull back up the steps behind your position when they appear. The contents of the Treasure Cache depend on which brother you save. For noble Merin, you get a sizable sum of sovereigns; if you saved the conniving, heartless Iwan, there's substantially less currency but two unique weapons and a selection of loot.
- Whichever brother you save, collect the Lyrium-Laced Bilge Hoop from the treasure room at the end of the map to begin the side quest of the same name. Return to Hightown and speak with Yevhen.

Consequences:

- Those who save Iwan have the option of revealing his betrayal to his father.
- If you accept **Fool's Gold**, you cannot undertake the **Finding Nathaniel** quest in Act 3. It is only possible to play one of these two quests in a given playthrough.

Raiders on the Cliffs

Loot and Reward: 

Start Location:

The Wounded Coast

Requirements:

This quest is triggered by walking along the path that leads to the southernmost section of the Wounded Coast area.

Walkthrough:

- Approach Lieutenant Harley to hear an appraisal of the situation. Both Aveline and Isabela have interesting reactions to this quest, so it might be worth bringing them along. You have three choices:
  - You can offer to fight alongside the guardsmen. Players who favor diplomatic or aggressive speech responses can use a unique dialogue option to inspire these allies before the battle begins. This is definitely the easier option.
  - Walk away. You can return to complete the quest later, but Aveline will express mild disapproval if present.
  - Mount an attack on the gang without any support from the guardsmen. This is tough, but by no means insurmountable. Once again, Aveline will be a little irked by this: why can't her guards contribute to the fight?
- The area is littered with traps, with some being the complex variety (requiring 30 Cunning to disarm). Having your rogue lead the way can keep your party safe and act as a good source of XP. If you carefully micromanage this battle and head straight to the center of the roughly pretzel-shaped area (where most enemies are concentrated), you can actually disarm most of these afterwards.
- The most deadly opponent in this battle is Fell Orden, a blood mage. As is traditional in these instances, concentrate your party's fire on him to remove his baneful presence as soon as you can. Orden drops the Swatch of the Jackyard (which begins the related side quest), and the Flex-Chain – Guardsman Pattern armor upgrade for Aveline.
- Visit the Viscount's Keep and speak with Jelden to be reimbursed for your labors.

Consequences:

If you complete this quest, the leader of Evets Marauders may attempt to exact revenge during a visit to the Wounded Coast in Act 3.

Inside Job

Loot and Reward: 

Start Location:

Hawke Estate

Requirements:

- You must have completed The Bone Pit in Act 1.
- Complete Prime Suspect.
- Read the letter at the Writing Desk.

Walkthrough:

- Speak to Hubert in Hightown. Accepting the quest will automatically transport you to a location where Hubert has a man accused of theft tied to a chair. Pick diplomatic options (and promise to look after the miner's family) to learn the location of his stolen goods. After you decide the prisoner's fate, there is another automatic area transition.
- On arrival at the Outside Kirkwall map there is a short ambush by mercenaries. Scour the small area for collectibles, then travel to Darktown. Head to Lilley's waypoint marker. In the dialogue that follows, you can either persuade the Coterie representatives of your innocence, or fight them (via aggressive options) for additional XP.
- A small group of thugs await just inside Brekker's Hideaway, but these can be dismissed with ease. The second group features a Coterie Alchemist. Disable him immediately; if you don't, he will likely teleport to the upper level and rain destruction upon your party. The battle against Brekker at the waypoint starts slowly, but soon picks up momentum as three Coterie Rogues enter the fray. If you're quick, you can kill your principle target before they arrive.
- Leave the area via the nearby exit and return to Hubert.

Companion Guidance:

- Accepting the letter from the Writing Desk also causes Hubert's Fine Goods to reopen in Hightown.
- Unlocks a linear sequence of quests based around the Bone Pit Mines. This begins with Cave Crawling. If you took pity on Sabin and treated him with nothing but kindness, you will find Sabin's Stash in a crate when you next visit the Bone Pit.

Cave Crawling

Loot and Reward: 

Start Location:

The Bone Pit

Requirements:

- Complete Inside Job.
- Visit the Bone Pit and approach Jansen.

Walkthrough:

- After speaking with Jansen, collect the Petrified Human Finger from a sack south of the mine entrance to begin the Wentworth's Sixth Finger side quest.
- Enter the Bone Pit Mines. The Queen Spider is just inside the entrance and is supported by a few waves of her smaller kin. Anything that causes electricity damage will shorten this battle considerably. Scavenge the area for loot, then leave and return to Jansen.

Consequences:

Unlocks Cavern of Dead.

Cavern of Dead

Loot and Reward: 

Start Location:

The Bone Pit

Requirements:

- Complete Cave Crawling.
- Speak to Jansen.

Walkthrough:

- If you have only just completed Cave Crawling, note that you must leave the Bone Pit for another area and return to activate this quest.
- Access the Bone Pit Mines through a new entrance further east. As you face undead opponents throughout this short quest, weapons or attacks that cause spirit or electricity damage will be something of a boon.
- You can reach the central area where the Arcane Horror awaits by taking the north or east corridors. Both have traps placed across the first doorway that you reach, with a small but solid group of undead foes poised to take advantage of those caught unawares.
- The Arcane Horror is supported by a Revenant and other undead troops, with the Skeleton Archers being a particular headache for weaker mages. Retreating to the small chamber to the west will enable you to draw your opponents out gradually, and turn the access corridor into an avenue of easy slaughter.
- Pillage to your heart's desire, then report back to Jansen.

Consequences:

Unlocks Pick Up Pickaxes.

Pick Up Pickaxes

Loot and Reward: 

Start Location:

The Bone Pit

Requirements:

- Complete Cavern of Dead.
- Speak to Jansen.

Walkthrough:

- If you have only just completed Cavern of Dead, you must leave the Bone Pit and return to activate this quest.
- After agreeing to help, travel to Lowtown and visit the Smith standing next to the Armor Stand. The pickaxes cost a hefty 15 sovereigns, but this expense is the only way to complete the quest.

Consequences:

Hubert has short reactions to Cave Crawling, Cavern of Dead and Pick Up Pickaxes. The latter will confirm the sinking feeling that you may be experiencing after paying such an exorbitant sum for a relatively minor 1,000 XP...

COMPANION QUESTS

Social Calls

There are six small companion quests to complete at the start of Act 2. These provide an opportunity to further friendships and rivalries through dialogue choices and advance potentially intimate relationships.

Quest	Location
Plans for the Future	The Hanged Man
Visit Anders	Darktown Clinic
Calling on the Captain	Viscount's Keep Barracks
Speak to Fenris	Fenris's Mansion
Isabela's Ongoing Search	The Hanged Man
Consoling Words	Merrill's Hut

Repentance

Loot and Reward: 

Start Location:

Chantry

Requirements:

- You must have access to the Exiled Prince downloadable content (see dragonage.com/da2/addons).
- Complete **Duty**: see page 62 for details.

Walkthrough:

- Speak to Sebastian in the Chantry and agree to help, then travel to Hightown and enter the Harimann Estate. Sebastian will be locked into the party from this point forward. There are three chests with complex locks in this quest. Sebastian's automatically assigned Cunning attribute will not be sufficiently high to open these so bring your customary locksmith along as well.
- Your journey through the mansion will pass without incident until you reach a cutscene. Collect the Mail Undertunic from the nearby chest: this is an armor upgrade for Sebastian. You can find the Starkhaven Longbow, a gift for Sebastian that can be equipped, in the bedroom slightly north of the waypoint marker. Before you continue, take an (optional) detour to the east section of the mansion to forage for collectibles and view an amusing cutscene.
- On arrival at the waypoint, you will encounter Shades and two Desire Demons. Dispatch these, then enter the Underground Passage. As you will soon realize, the further you progress through this map, the more fraught the encounters will become. The first battle features a Rage Demon and numerous Shades. It's easy to get surrounded here: consider pulling back to the long staircase at the start of the fight. The next encounter is with a Revenant (a dangerous undead Commander weak against electricity and spirit damage) and a selection of Corpses. Beyond that, a confrontation with two Rage Demons awaits: anything that inflicts cold-based harm will make a big difference here. The final confrontation before the waypoint features a Revenant and an Arcane Horror (highly vulnerable to nature and cold) in quick succession with Corpses further complicating matters.
- Allure is a Desire Demon, while Lady Harimann is a powerful blood mage: a challenging combination. We would suggest that unleashing a fourfold storm of abilities in the direction of the mage would make sense here. Disable and destroy her before she can employ her more potent attacks.
- Return to the Chantry and speak with Sebastian to end the quest.

Consequences:

Sebastian joins as a permanent companion; you also unlock the **Faith** quest in Act 3.

Companion Guidance:

- In the opening quest dialogue, select the "You're not subtle..." option to score a high rivalry increase. A diplomatic approach will lead to a slight friendship increase.
- Attempting to secure a deal with the demon at the conclusion of the quest will not please Aveline, Anders or (especially) Sebastian. Diving straight into the battle with the "Die, fiend!" option when it appears will lead to friendship increases with most companions.

Sebastian

Devoted to the Chantry yet tormented by the demands of his lineage, this rogue archer pledges his support to Hawke after the completion of Repentance.

- Sebastian is morally upright in the most conventional sense. Ruthless killing will engender his ire, and mercy will solidify a friendship. While his vow of chastity precludes any romantic involvement, he'll enjoy the attention if a female Hawke flatters him with light flirting.
- Advising Sebastian to take back his lands at all costs, or insisting that he will be a good and just ruler, will only move your relationship along the rivalry path.
- This companion can only be recruited if you have the Exiled Prince downloadable content. For more details, see dragonage.com/da2/addons.

The Long Road

Loot and Reward: 

Requirements:

Complete Blackpowder Courtesy.

Walkthrough:

- Speak to Aveline in the Viscount's Keep barracks and agree to assist her. Make the delivery to Guardsman Donnic, interact with the Duty Roster, then speak to Donnic to arrange a meeting at The Hanged Man.
- Travel to The Hanged Man at night and speak with Donnic. If you restored Aveline to your party before travelling here, she will make an excuse and depart.
- Your next destination is the Wounded Coast. Follow the path marked by waypoints, clearing all hostiles you encounter before interacting with each Signal Fire. After the third, Aveline and Donnic will approach. When the dialogue ends, return to the Viscount's Keep and speak with the captain to bring this quest to a close.

Consequences:

May unlock the **Questioning Beliefs** companion quest: see the "Mid-Stage Relationship Quests" section on page 86 for further details.

Companion Guidance:

For friendship increases, go easy on Aveline: take the most sensitive and least confrontational approach during those awkward conversations.

Dissent

Loot and Reward: 

Requirements:

Complete Blackpowder Courtesy.

Walkthrough:

- Speak to Anders in his Darktown clinic and agree to help. With the mage in your party, head to the south of the district and enter the Gallows Dungeon.
- With the exception of a reasonably tough battle in the north of the map, the journey through this area is rather uneventful. Collect the Fine Dwarven Trousers collectible from a loot pile after this one notable encounter to begin **The One True Pantaloons** side quest. Lyrium Smuggler Foremen take time to kill, so temporarily disable them while you deal with their less resilient allies.
- The final battle with Ser Alrik and his assembled templars can be demanding. Fighting in such close confines makes AoE attacks extremely effective (except on Nightmare difficulty of course), but definitely leaves your ranged fighters vulnerable to the attentions of the Templar Hunters. If you can keep your opponents in front of you, the tight corridors work in your favor as you brutalize adversaries during their approach.
- Your dialogue choices in the aftermath of this battle can have serious repercussions – see Consequences.
- Collect Ser Alrik's papers from his corpse, then collect the Spirit Essence item (an armor upgrade for Anders) from the cave west of the exit. Return to speak with Anders in Darktown to end the quest.

Consequences:

- If you refuse to help Anders, the quest ends immediately (and with a large rivalry increase to express his bitter disappointment).
- There are two ways to deal with the flashpoint after the templar battle:
  - Calm Anders down with the special diplomacy option (green hue) that appears. He will flee the scene and return to his Darktown clinic.
  - Any other dialogue choice will lead to Ella's death.
- If Anders asks if you wish for him to leave, agreement really will remove him as a companion for the rest of the story.
- This may unlock the **Questioning Beliefs** companion quest for Anders: see the "Mid-Stage Relationship Quests" section on page 86 for further details.

Companion Guidance:

- There's a large friendship boost from Anders for simply accepting this quest, and another for preventing Ella's death by his hand (albeit at the behest of Justice).
- In the closing dialogue, pick "Anders, calm down" followed by green diplomatic responses only for a huge (+30) approval increase. If you'd prefer tough love and a shift towards rivalry, start with "What happened in there?", then select red aggressive responses at each stage of the conversation with the exception of those where he suggests that he leave. For these, insist that he stays. The consequence? A trifling +55 tilt in the direction of rivalry...
- If you are attempting to develop a friendship with Sebastian, it's better to leave him out of the party for this quest: many conversational choices that make Anders happy will displease the prince. It's perhaps telling that, if you dismiss the mage from your party at this crisis point, Sebastian will express moderate approval.

Mirror Image

Loot and Reward: 

Requirements:

Complete Blackpowder Courtesy.

Walkthrough:

- Speak with Merrill at her home and agree to help. She must be in your active party for this quest, so bring her into the fold before you leave for Sundermount. Note that Anders, Aveline and, to a lesser extent, Fenris and Sebastian all object if you support Merrill wholeheartedly throughout this quest.
- There is a small reactive event for those who sent Feynriel to live among the Dalish on arrival at Sundermount – see page 107 for details. You can also loot a chest just inside the camp to find the Dalish Tattoo Ink ingredient for the Herbalist's Tasks.
- Talk to Keeper Marethari to begin the Honoring the Fallen side quest. This is essentially the core of the Mirror Image quest so, rather than sending you elsewhere in the chapter, we'll continue the walkthrough here. Don't head up the mountainside – the waypoint marker you seek is actually accessed via the path to the left of the Keeper.
- Inside the Varterral Hunting Ground, a large group of spiders attacks when you head down the stone steps. These include the Wasp Spider: an especially hardy and vicious variant of the Poison Spider. Try to concentrate your party's fire (or, better still, lightning – their specific weakness) on one of these at a time, ideally incapacitating the others as you dispatch them in turn. After the battle, interact with Hunter Radha's corpse to collect the first amulet for Keeper Marethari.
- Further north, take the adjacent path leading south to find the body of Hunter Harshal. Continue deeper into the cavern to fight another group of spiders then, in the open area just beyond, look to the northeast to find the remains of Hunter Chandan.
- After the cutscene with Pol, a massive Varterral will attack. The speed and ferocity of this unique enemy is quite staggering, so it's vital that you curb such tendencies with spells and abilities that impede its chances to attack (and, indeed, move). When it employs a distinctive AoE assault, you may wish to manually reposition your companions away from the (rapidly deadly) effect radius.
- When the beast falls, scour the area for rewards: you should find a wealth of coin and assorted loot. Don't forget to rifle through the remains of the Varterral itself: this relinquishes the Varterral Heart, an ingredient required for Herbalist's Tasks. There is no shortcut back to the surface, so you'll need to fight your way through two groups of undead en route to the area exit. When you reach the second of these, locate and target the Frost Horror first.

Companion Guidance:

- Taking on this quest leads to a high friendship increase with Merrill. Refusing it will still enable you to change your mind at a later date, but there's an attendant rivalry increase that might be of interest to those seeking a more adversarial relationship with the Dalish mage.
- After the Varterral falls, the "Why did you run?" and "Don't waste your tears" lines lead to high and medium rivalry increases respectively. "Do you want some time?" and "Don't blame yourself" evoke equivalent boosts to friendship.
- Giving the Arulin'holm to Merrill leads to a large friendship increase with her, but rivalry increments with Anders, Aveline, Sebastian and Fenris; withholding it has the opposite effect.

Back from Sundermount

Loot and Reward: 

Requirements:

- Complete Mirror Image.
- Speak to Merrill at her home.

Companion Guidance:

This short conversation follows on from Mirror Image, and shows Merrill reflecting on the outcome of the quest. For those seeking to woo the Dalish mage, it offers another opportunity to flirt with her.

An Update

Loot and Reward: 

Start Location:

The Hanged Man

Requirements:

- Unlocked after you complete your first main plot quest in Act 2.
- Visit The Hanged Man and speak with Varric.

Consequences:

This conversation unlocks Varric's companion quest for Act 2: Family Matter.

Companion Guidance:

Select the "Let's go get some drinks" option and then agree to help find Bartrand to score a massive boost to friendship.

Family Matter

Loot and Reward: 

Start Location:

The Hanged Man

Requirements:

- Complete An Update.
- Varric must be in your party.

Walkthrough:

- Head to Hightown (Night) and enter Bartrand's Estate. This triggers a very interesting battle where Varric must fight alone against large waves of opponents. Employ AoE attacks to disable the larger groups, and you will find that default attacks will suffice to keep all other opponents under control.
- After the intermission, the Crazed Guards offer a more demanding test of your tactical prowess, especially when you face them in more threatening numbers as you progress through the mansion. The large central room pits you against two Crazed Commanders and an army of their subordinates; on higher difficulty levels, it could pay to station your party in a room outside, then draw successive waves to this position rather than engaging in a mass brawl.
- The small room just south of the waypoint marker has a chest that contains the Silverite-Reinforced Buckles – an armor upgrade for Varric.
- As you enter the final room, Bartrand fights alongside a final wave of Crazed Guards. Being of the Assassin archetype, it makes sense to keep him incapacitated as you chip away at his health gauge.
- In the post-fight dialogue with Bartrand, calling on Anders to intervene can provide a different narrative conclusion. Either way, you must help Varric make the decision on whether to let Bartrand live or die. See Companion Guidance for further information.

Consequences:

- Failing to complete this quest during Act 2 will cause Varric to reveal how he dealt with the situation himself in an Act 3 conversation. If you spare Bartrand, Varric will also have a few words to say on the subject during Act 3.
- May unlock the A Story Being Told companion quest: see the "Mid-Stage Relationship Quests" section on page 86 for further details.

Companion Guidance:

- Without the optional contribution from Anders, allowing Varric to kill Bartrand leads to a high friendship increase (and a nod of validation from Aveline). Insisting that he spare his brother leads to high rivalry (and a shake of the head from the guard captain, if present).
- If Anders steps in, you'll gain a friendship boost for sparing Bartrand, and a rivalry increase for his death.
- If Bartrand dies, dialogue choices that help to absolve Varric of guilt in the conversation outside will lead to high approval. Allowing him to kill his brother, then, is a great way to max out the friendship gauge.

A Bitter Pill

Loot and Reward: ★★★★★

Requirements:

- Complete the **Speak to Fenris** companion quest (see page 81).
- Travel to a destination in the Free Marches with the elf in your active party.

Walkthrough:

- Your party will be waylaid on the Outside Kirkwall map by a Tevinter Magister, Tevinter Mercenary and a number of slavers. Direct your aggression at the Magister: this mage is far more dangerous than his allies. The next stage of the quest unlocks irrespective of your response in the conversation with Fenris – but naturally, don't expect refusal or a lack of understanding to please him.
- **Optional:** When you leave the area, you will notice that the Holding Caves location appears on the Free Marches map. Rather than heading directly for this location, you can travel between destinations in Kirkwall to experience a second ambush on the Wrong Way map. Fenris must, of course, be in your active party for this to take place. After an opening cutscene, the battle that unfolds initially pits you against a Tevinter Mage and assorted henchmen. However, this confrontation matures into a fairly epic melee comprising undead, slavers, further mages and an Arcane Horror. Add traps into the mix, and you have a challenging aside. Fenris will react angrily in the battle's aftermath: see Consequences for details.
- At the Holding Caves, there are two battles with assorted slavers and Mercenary Archers in which your party will be assailed from both front and back. In the second fight, watch for the arrival of the Slaver Mage: it's easy to miss him until the harm he causes compels you to seek him out, so an early intervention is best here. Reconnoiter the area for loot, then enter the cave.
- The Abandoned Slaver Den is populated by a combination of slavers and undead that should be familiar by now. Watch out for pressure pads on the floor (these activate traps every time they are depressed, and cannot be disarmed) as you fight your way to the map marker.
- After speaking to the terrified elf, collect the Tevinter Chantry Amulet from the chest in the corner of the central room. This is a gift for Anders: see page 86. In the room that follows to the west, collect the Reinforced Straps – a timely armor upgrade for Fenris.
- In the final battle, defeat Magister Hadriana first: she's too powerful to leave unchecked while you contend with her bodyguards (or the Fade denizens and Corpses who arrive shortly afterwards). Fenris will leave after the closing dialogue, and remain unavailable for party selection until you next return to Hawke Estate. Take the nearby exit to return to the World Map.

Consequences:

- Failing to complete **A Bitter Pill** during Act 2 will mean that you cannot undertake Fenris's companion quest in Act 3, or advance his relationship with Hawke to its final stage.
- If you trigger the second Tevinter ambush, Fenris will rage at the player for not dealing with the situation earlier. He presents a choice: "We go *now*, or I do". Agree, and you will be automatically transported to the Holding Caves map when you exit the ambush area. Refusal will cause Fenris to leave the party permanently.
- It's possible to start this quest, then substitute Fenris from the party to prevent the second ambush from occurring. After a certain time, the furious elf may confront Hawke and leave the party for good.
- The scene on your return to Hawke Estate is an opportunity to begin a romance with Fenris if you have been fanning the flames up until now. If you prefer a platonic resolution, the responses that will engender his admiration and ire should be pretty self-evident.
- If you offered to employ Orana, she will become a permanent resident at Hawke Estate. There are a number of dialogue options to choose from while speaking to her: we'll leave your choices purely to your conscience...

Companion Guidance:

- In the first encounter, "He's not a slave!" leads to a small friendship boost with Fenris, while "Let's work out a deal!" leads to a small rivalry increase.
- You can offer to employ the elf you encounter in the Abandoned Slaver Den at the Hawke Estate. The "Come work for me" and "Slaves are useful" dialogue choices lead to significant rivalry increases; you can mitigate the effect of the first choice and gain a slight friendship boost with "I will pay her" as your second response. "Take this coin and go" leads to medium friendship, while sending her away empty-handed has no effect.
- When the time comes to question the Magister, let Fenris take charge with the green companion dialogue option and then insist that you can still find his sister for a friendship increase. Other paths (including a diplomacy option in which you ask him to calm down) generally lead to antagonism – though the romance option may be of interest to some.

The Captain's Condolences

Loot and Reward: ★★★★★

Requirements:

Complete the All That Remains main plot quest.

Companion Guidance:

In this short conversation, Aveline will express her sorrow at Hawke's loss. Blaming the captain or refusing to listen to her tale of her father both lead to rivalry increases.

Mid-Stage Relationship Quests

Completing major companion quests and reaching 50% friendship or rivalry with a companion will unlock a special conversation that marks the next stage in that individual's relationship with Hawke. The accompanying table details these minor quests, with tips on how you might react. See page 182 for further details.

Companion	Quest Name	Guidance
Anders	**Questioning Beliefs**	Flirting with Anders can lead to a romance (unless you've already rebuffed an advance from him). Questioning his sanity, casting doubt on Hawke's dedication to the friendship or dismissing his amorous advances will lead to rivalry increases and may end any prospect of future love.
Aveline	**Questioning Beliefs**	Select "You complain while helping me" followed by "You'd be bored" for a large friendship increase. Select from "Like they stabilize mages?", "A stupid provocation", "I need what I need" and "You're whining about yourself" for a shift towards rivalry.
Fenris	**Questioning Beliefs**	To flirt, select "Tell me anything you like". To start a romance, pick "I'm willing" or "This is a little sudden". To freeze any imminent ardor, pick "Stop right there".
Isabela	**Questioning Beliefs**	If you are on the friendship path with Isabela, pick "It all worked out", "Don't dwell on the past" or "I wouldn't bet on it" to please her. On the rivalry path, pick "You're not free" or "Helping others is rewarding/benefits me" to annoy her.
Merrill	**Questioning Beliefs**	If you have developed a friendship with Merrill, most options give a low boost in that direction. On the rivalry path, "Just making sure you're all right", "I'm here for you" and "She pays by the lecture" will all anger the mage.
Sebastian	**Questioning Beliefs**	Pick "You belong in the Chantry" for a high friendship increase, or "You must take Starkhaven!" for rivalry.
Varric	**A Story Being Told**	The easygoing Varric has no objections to anything Hawke might say in this conversation.

Companion Gifts

There is a unique "gift" to find for each companion during Act 2, with each one unlocking a short companion quest where you visit the individual in question at home. You can learn more about how these items can be used to develop relationships on page 182.

Companion	Quest Name	Item Required
Anders	**Tevinter Chantry Amulet**	Collect this gift from the Abandoned Slaver Den during Fenris's companion quest (**A Bitter Pill**).
Aveline	**The Shield of the Knight Herself**	Found in a container near the exit to Ser Varnell's Refuge during the **Offered and Lost** main plot quest.
Fenris	**The Book of Shartan**	During a visit to Hightown at night, collect the A Slave's Life item from a sack in the elven alienage.
Isabela	**A Ship for Isabela**	Collect the Ship in a Bottle from a chest in Smuggler's Cut during the Blackpowder Courtesy quest.
Merrill	**Wooden Halla**	Purchase the Wooden Halla Carving from Master Ilen's Shop at Sundermount's Dalish Camp.
Sebastian	**The Starkhaven Longbow**	Collected during the **Repentance** quest.
Varric	**The Tethras Signet Ring**	Purchase the Signet Ring from the Trinkets Emporium in Lowtown.

SIDE QUESTS

"Find and Deliver" Side Quests

Name	Start Location	Requirements
Lyrium-Laced Bilge Hoop	Deep Roads	• Find the Lyrium-Laced Bilge Hoop next to the Treasure Cache during the **Fool's Gold** quest. • Hand it to the Whiskey Master in Darktown.
Swatch of the Jackyard	The Wounded Coast	• Retrieve the item of the same name from the remains of Fell Orden during the **Raiders on the Cliffs** secondary quest. • Deliver it to the Ship Spotter in the Docks.
The One True Pantaloons	Gallows Dungeon	• After a battle with Lyrium Smugglers and Dwarf Mercenaries in the **Dissent** companion quest, collect the Fine Dwarven Trousers from a loot pile. • Present the garment to the Impeccable Bulf in Hightown.
Wentworth's Sixth Finger	The Bone Pit	• Collect the Petrified Human Finger from a sack south of the mine entrance. • Deliver it to Sister Phylias in front of the Chantry in Hightown.
Waxler's Hat	Disused Passage	• Collect Waxler's Hat from a sack beside a door on the east side of the Disused Passage – accessed via the Docks (Night). • Return it to Waxler in The Hanged Man at night.
Seal of the Old God Dumat	Disused Passage	• Retrieve the Seal of Dumat from a crate in a tiny room in the south of the Disused Passage – accessed via the Docks (Night). • Present it to Bolund the Amateur Annalist in Hightown.
The Eyes of Azure Jamos	Sundermount	• Defeat the Crazed Loner on the upper section of Sundermount – the mountain graveyard visited with Merrill during Act 1 – and collect this item from his corpse. • Deliver the item to Azure Jamos in the Gallows.
"South-Song" Gerralt's Corpse	Abandoned Thaig	• Collect "South-Song" Gerralt's Corpse from the Abandoned Thaig dungeon at Sundermount: see page 88 for details. • Return it to "East-Wise" Gerralt in Lowtown.
Ream-Rot Knife	Sundermount Caverns	• Pick up the Ream-Rot Knife from a sack close to the east exit. • Deliver it to Faj in Lowtown.
Goosegirl Cameo	Wounded Coast	• Only available if you have unlocked the **Bounty Hunter** quest – see page 90. • Collect the item from the corpse of Heborah de Soliere after you kill him at the Wounded Coast during the events of the **Bounty Hunter** side quest. • Return it to Vorse de Soliere in Lowtown.

Note: These quests generally lead to a reward of one sovereign and 750 XP in Act 2.

Sundermount

Two tiny find-and-deliver tasks aside, there are no quests that lead you to explore the full Sundermount area in Act 2. However, those who travel the winding path to its upper reaches will find it a fair source of XP and loot. There are also crafting resources to find.

- There is a Monstrous Spider just inside the Caverns, supported by smaller spiders. After a second arachnid attack, the final area by the exit to upper Sundermount features two unusually hardy Corpses and a Skeleton Archer. Collect the Ream-Rot Knife from the nearby sack to begin the side quest of the same name.
- Back outside, and closer to the peak, collect the Mighty Offense Potion recipe from a pile of bones a short walk west from the cave. On arrival at the graveyard you will encounter the Crazed Loner and a variety of undead. This is complicated by the later arrival of two Shadow Assassins and an Arcane Horror. The Crazed Loner drops an item called The Eyes of Azure Jamos; collect this to begin the side quest of the same name.
- Higher up the mountain, a pack of Dragonlings attacks. The reason for this sudden switch in local denizens becomes apparent when you reach the top to encounter a Mature Dragon. If you've been following advice set out by our Strategy & Analysis chapter, a mage armed with a cold-infused staff and the Elemental Weapons spell activated will shorten this battle considerably.
- Collect the Silver-Threaded Dalish Embroidery item (an armor upgrade for Merrill) before you head back down the slope. There is a final ambush by a Revenant and an Arcane Horror as you approach the Sundermount Caverns.

Forbidden Knowledge

Loot and Reward: 

Start Location:

Hawke Estate

Requirements:

- If you spared Idunna's life during **Enemies Among Us**, this quest is formally introduced by a letter at the Writing Desk.
- If Idunna died, you can start it by interacting with an Evil Tome in the Chantry or Viscount's Keep.

Walkthrough:

- It may be placed in the side quest category, but completing **Forbidden Knowledge** is an undertaking that eclipses many main plot quests in terms of size and reward. Tarohne's letter informs Hawke of books (known as Evil Tomes) that can be found in and around Kirkwall. When you find these, you are presented with three options:
  - **Destroy the book:** Choose this option for every book you find, with no exceptions. This is the only way to see the quest through to its conclusion.
  - **Read the book:** If you accept the book's deal, you will gain two free attribute points. This option is only available with a single Tome: for those that remain, only the "destroy" or "take" options are offered – thus preventing you from completing the quest. (You can claim these attribute points later, so don't feel at all tempted to accept them now.)
  - **Take the book:** Ignore this option – it offers no rewards.
- Regardless of your choice, interacting with each Tome leads to a fight with a group of enemies.
- There are two Evil Tomes in Kirkwall, and three in the Free Marches. The latter Tomes are potentially much harder to obtain.
- Collecting the Tome in the **Chantry** spawns a Desire Demon and Abominations.
- An Arcane Horror and Abominations will spawn when you interact with the Tome in the **Viscount's Keep**.
- The first of the "hidden" Evil Tomes is found on a map named, simply, **Cave**. The entrance is on the far east side of the Bone Pit. There are no enemies to fight beforehand: you can just stroll over to the book and do with it what you will. A Desire Demon and a handful of undead will appear to remonstrate afterwards.
- The second Evil Tome is located in the **Dank Cave**, an unmarked dungeon in the Wounded Coast. This can be found by heading west from the main area entrance, then taking the first path that leads south (excluding dead-ends). You'll see the entrance on your left. You may scoff at the small group of spiders just inside, but the opponent that follows should curb your mirth: a full-grown Dragon. Naturally, cold and constant incapacitation are called for here. You can collect a quite phenomenal cache of treasure once its fires have been quenched, and, of course, pick up the Tome. This spawns a Revenant, Abominations and Corpses.
- The fifth and final Evil Tome is situated in the **Abandoned Thaig**. This is accessed via the Recently Opened Passage entrance situated next to the western Sundermount exit.
  - This dungeon is packed with Stone Golems, undead, and Fade creatures of all varieties. The room to the west of the entrance is a dead-end, but features the oppressive combination of a Stone Golem and a Revenant – the target of priority – in addition to other troops. The important thing here is to avoid a situation where your party is divided between battles in the corridor and room itself.
  - The room to the north features a similar battle, but adds a Rage Demon. Direct your aggression at the deadly Revenant first, ideally while keeping the flaming Assassin quiet with Cone of Cold and Winter's Grasp. Through the east door, interact with "South-Song" Gerralt's Corpse to start a side quest.
  - The confrontation in the central room is epic, with waves of ever more powerful Fade creatures joining the engagement as it develops. The Desire Demon, Revenant and Arcane Horror are all opponents that you should eliminate with great haste. Even on the normal difficulty setting, some players may find this battle maddeningly difficult. The solution is to order your party to hold position in the room to the west, then lure your opponents back through in discrete groups.
  - The Nexus Golem is a special merchant who sells a few very interesting items.
  - Interacting with the Evil Tome will spawn a Revenant supported by Corpses.
- If you selected any option other than "Destroy the book", this is the end of the line. If all five books have been pulped, however, the quest will be updated. Ensure that you have a rogue in your party, then travel to Darktown and take the Evil Pit entrance.
- Inside the Forgotten Lair, pull the Disarming Switch then fight the Stone Golem. The door to the east is locked, which is where your rogue steps in. Have them lead the way in the corridor beyond to disarm the numerous traps; order the rest of your party to hold their position to avoid them being drawn forward by the handful of enemies you fight here.
- At the waypoint, prepare your party then collect the Fell Grimoire. This presents the same options as the other Tomes.
  - **Destroy the book** offers no additional reward.
  - **Read the book** gives you two attribute points.
  - **Take the book** allows you to obtain the Book of Forbidden Lore junk item. As this is sold for a little less than a single sovereign, it's safe to surmise that it's better to opt for the stat boost.
- At this point, Xebenkeck and three Rage Demons will attack. Xebenkeck is a Desire Demon, weak against nature and electricity elements (but immune to spirit damage on Nightmare difficulty). She imbues her allies with magic resistance, so do everything within your power to slay her quickly. Later in the battle, a Revenant, more Rage Demons and assorted Abominations join the melee. This is the time to refresh your party with Stamina Draughts and Lyrium Potions, then pummel your amassed opponents with a barrage of every AoE attack you can muster. Focus on the Revenant until it falls, and the final hurdle of any significance is over.
- Collect the (quite remarkable) selection of loot from the room, then leave via the nearby exit to bring this astonishingly rewarding side quest to a close.

Sketchy on the Details

Loot and Reward: 

Start Location:

Hightown

Requirements:

Accept the quest from the Chanter's Board.

Walkthrough:

- There are five groups of assailants that must be killed to complete this quest.
  - **Hightown (Night):** The Denerim Avengers can be found on the steps leading to the Viscount's Keep.
  - **Lowtown:** The Antivan Assassins are located close to the elven alienage entrance during daylight hours.
  - **The Gallows:** A Qunari Death Squad awaits in the far south of the area, just east of Solivitus.
  - **The Hanged Man (Night):** The Rivaini Legendary Beard group is found south of Varric's quarters.
  - **Darktown:** A band of Carta assailants awaits in the south of the district.
- With all factions dead and buried, head to the Docks at night to meet with Sketch and receive your reward.

The Lost Patrol

Loot and Reward: 

Start Location:

The Docks

Requirements:

- You must have gained a modicum of respect through your dealings with the Arishok during Act 1 (see Blackpowder Courtesy, page 72).
- Speak to the Qunari just inside the main Docks entrance.

Walkthrough:

- Head to the Wounded Coast and take the path that leads southwest from the area entrance. When you reach the waypoint marker, an Abomination and a handful of Shades will attack. Kill them.
- Report to the Qunari in the Docks to end this quest. However, you may first wish to continue to the southernmost area of the Wounded Coast to complete the Raiders on the Cliffs quest – see page 79.

Honoring the Fallen

Loot and Reward: 

Start Location:

Sundermount

Requirements:

Accept Merrill's companion quest, **Mirror Image**, then speak to Keeper Marethari with the elf in your party.

The Underground Railroad

Loot and Reward: 

Start Location:

- Hawke Estate

Requirements:

- You must have satisfied certain story requirements during Act 1 (see **Search and Rescue** and **How to Frame a Templar**).
- Accept the letter from the Writing Desk.
- Visit Mistress Selby at the Docks during the day.

Consequences:

Unlocks Mistress Selby's Board – a source of quests. If you fulfilled the requirements in Act 1, **Search and Rescue** and **How to Frame a Templar** will be available immediately.

Search and Rescue

Loot and Reward: 

Start Location:

The Docks

Requirements:

- Only available if you chose to let Grace and her fellow apostates go free at the conclusion of **Act of Mercy** in Act 1.
- Accept the quest from Mistress Selby's Board – see **The Underground Railroad** for details.

Walkthrough:

- Visit the Wounded Coast and head to the Bounty Hunter Getaway entrance.
- Collect the Harlot's Blush Flower just in front of the cave entrance. This is required for the **Herbalist's Tasks** secondary quest.
- Inside the Bounty Hunter Getaway, dispatch the first two groups of enemies. The battle that follows features a handful of Bounty Hunter Assassins and a Bounty Hunter Commander. There is a particularly nasty trap just inside the room, so have a rogue take point and disarm it before combat begins. You may find it efficient to have your party make a stand on the raised area on the east side of the cavern.
- Speak to the Captured Apostate. Don't neglect to explore the room east of her position – there's a reasonable cache of treasures inside. Return to Mistress Selby to claim your reward.

The Midnight Meeting

Loot and Reward: 

Start Location:
Hawke Estate

Requirements:

- You must have killed Ser Karras during the Act of Mercy quest in Act 1.
- After completing Blackpowder Courtesy, accept the letter that arrives at the Writing Desk.

Walkthrough:

- Travel to Hightown at night and approach the templars in the Merchant's Guild area. Your dialogue choice doesn't matter; they will attack regardless.
- Focus your party's aggression on the Templar Lieutenant: if you can kill her quickly, the rest of the battle will be much easier. Templar Archers and Hunters join the altercation after a short time, so it's better to deprive all hostiles of her beneficial presence.

Bounty Hunter

Loot and Reward: 

Start Location:
Hightown

Requirements:

- Only available if Grace and her fellow apostates were returned to the Circle of Magi at the conclusion of Act of Mercy.
- Accept the quest from the Chanter's Board.

Walkthrough:

- Jake the Black is located in Darktown. After speaking to him, he summons Shades and a Rage Demon before transforming into a resilient Pride Abomination – a trick duplicated by all primary targets in this quest.
- Innley of Starkhaven can be found at the top of Sundermount. He will summon assorted Fade creatures. A second wave includes a Desire Demon. If you activate this quest before defeating the Mature Dragon on top of Sundermount (see page 87), Innley replaces this optional adversary (and the Dragonlings on the path) on your first visit. If you wish to fight these, head back to the Sundermount Caverns, then revisit the upper area.
- Heborah de Soliere can be found at the Wounded Coast. After summoning a company of undead to defend himself (including a Revenant), he will make his transformation into a Pride Abomination.

A Debt in the Family

Loot and Reward: 

Start Location:
The Gallows

Requirements:

- Keran must have been expelled from the Order of the Templars after the events of Enemies Among Us.
- Speak to Templar Recruit Margitte.

Walkthrough:

Travel to the Docks at night and approach Senestra. She and her henchmen will attack with no provocation. This small quest ends after the last hostile has been killed.

The Fixer

Loot and Reward: 

Start Location:
Hawke Estate

Requirements:

- In Offered and Lost, you must have advised Viscount Dumar to burn the tortured Qunari.
- Accept the letter at the Writing Desk.

Walkthrough:

- This quest challenges you to locate and dispose of corpses. On arrival at the first two locations, you have a choice of either helping without comment, or attacking the murderers at the scene of the crime. If you opt for a fight, there is no way to complete the quest, though the enemies you slay in the Docks and Lowtown do drop a couple of fine items. If you decide to help, the next step is to dispose of the evidence at the waypoint marker.
- The first body is located in the Docks (Night). Enter the Habormaster's Office and speak to one of the Street Thugs. The next body is in Lowtown (Night). Speak to the Street Thug in the Residential District. The third corpse is found in the southwest end of Darktown. Simply collect and dispose of the body.
- Finally, travel to the Wounded Coast: this stage is only available if you have offloaded all three corpses so far. The final body is in the far southwest of the map. The Street Thugs there will attack immediately.
- Collect the final body and convey it to the Disposal Point, then return to Hawke Estate to claim your reward.

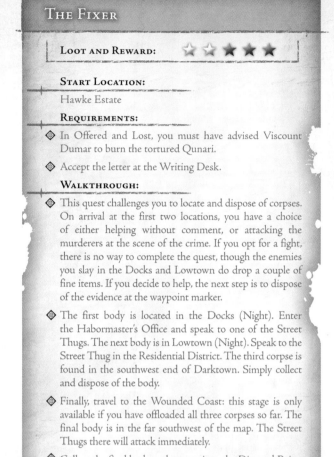

How to Frame a Templar

Loot and Reward: 

Start Location:
The Docks

Requirements:

- You must have persuaded Cullen to retain Keran's services at the end of the Enemies Among Us quest.
- Accept the quest from Mistress Selby's Board – see The Underground Railroad for details.

Walkthrough:

- Travel to The Hanged Man during daylight hours and speak with Ser Roderick. Pick any one of the available lies to cast aspersions on your victim, then head to the Gallows. Listen to the Harbormaster's Assistant, then interact with the Delivery Order. Choose to write in Conrad's name, then deliver the letter to the nearby Dockworker.
- Return to Mistress Selby. The letter that arrives at her board will explain the consequences of your actions.

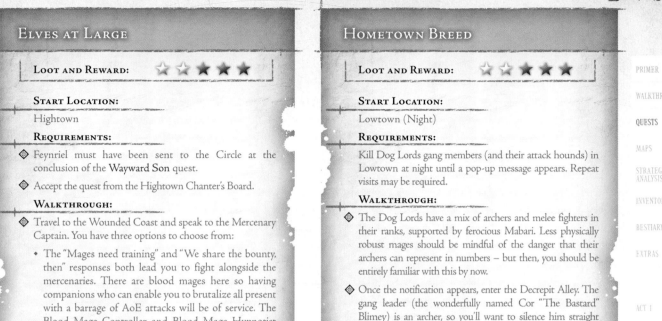

Elves at Large

Loot and Reward: 

Start Location:

Hightown

Requirements:

- Feynriel must have been sent to the Circle at the conclusion of the Wayward Son quest.
- Accept the quest from the Hightown Chanter's Board.

Walkthrough:

- Travel to the Wounded Coast and speak to the Mercenary Captain. You have three options to choose from:
  - The "Mages need training" and "We share the bounty, then" responses both lead you to fight alongside the mercenaries. There are blood mages here so having companions who can enable you to brutalize all present with a barrage of AoE attacks will be of service. The Blood Mage Controller and Blood Mage Hypnotist are the most dangerous of the opponents you face, and should bear the full brunt of your aggression.
  - Choose the "Let the elves go" option to fight the mercenaries instead. This leads to a slightly lower final reward, but potentially better loot drops.

Hometown Breed

Loot and Reward: 

Start Location:

Lowtown (Night)

Requirements:

Kill Dog Lords gang members (and their attack hounds) in Lowtown at night until a pop-up message appears. Repeat visits may be required.

Walkthrough:

- The Dog Lords have a mix of archers and melee fighters in their ranks, supported by ferocious Mabari. Less physically robust mages should be mindful of the danger that their archers can represent in numbers – but then, you should be entirely familiar with this by now.
- Once the notification appears, enter the Decrepit Alley. The gang leader (the wonderfully named Cor "The Bastard" Blimey) is an archer, so you'll want to silence him straight away. Hold position on the stairs to clear only the Dog Lords that detect you immediately, then push forward into the area to face the rest. Once the last hounds and handlers fall, leave via the marked exit.

Ladies' Lights Out

Loot and Reward: 

Start Location:

Hightown (Night)

Requirements:

Fight the Invisible Sisters in Hightown until a pop-up message appears. Repeat visits may be required.

Walkthrough:

- Though usually very weak, Invisible Sisters armed with dual daggers will exhibit Assassin-type behaviors. This gang has no ranged fighters when encountered on the streets; it's very melee-focused, which makes them vulnerable to AoE attacks.
- Once the quest formally begins, enter the Suspicious House. Ensure that all party members enter the main room, then set about killing the initial group of Invisible Sisters. Their leader, "Gracious" Gillian Winger, is actually an archer. She's not astonishingly tough, so try to dispose of her at an early stage in the fight. Ensure that you kill every last gang member to receive the quest completion notification, then return to Hightown.

Consequences:

As a reminder: if all nine gangs are eliminated across the three Acts, you can claim a special reward.

The Lowdown

Loot and Reward: 

Start Location:

Docks (Night)

Requirements:

Enter the Docks at night and kill Undercut Thrifters until a pop-up message appears. Repeat visits may be required.

Walkthrough:

- As with the Invisible Sisters, certain Undercut Thrifters have very low health but exhibit Assassin behaviors. They also have no ranged fighters.
- Once your labors on the streets unlock the hideout, enter the Run Down Alley to fight the gang leader: "Kanky" Hammertoe. Dispatch him quickly to avoid the nuisance value of his backstabs (and propensity for disappearing) while you devastate his cohorts. Explore the area to locate any stragglers, then depart once the quest is marked as complete.

ACT 3

COMPLETION ROADMAP

This diagram will help you plan your route through Act 3 by revealing the unlock progression for all main plot, secondary and companion quests. You will find fact sheets for these in the pages that follow, plus guidance for smaller side quests and their unlock conditions.

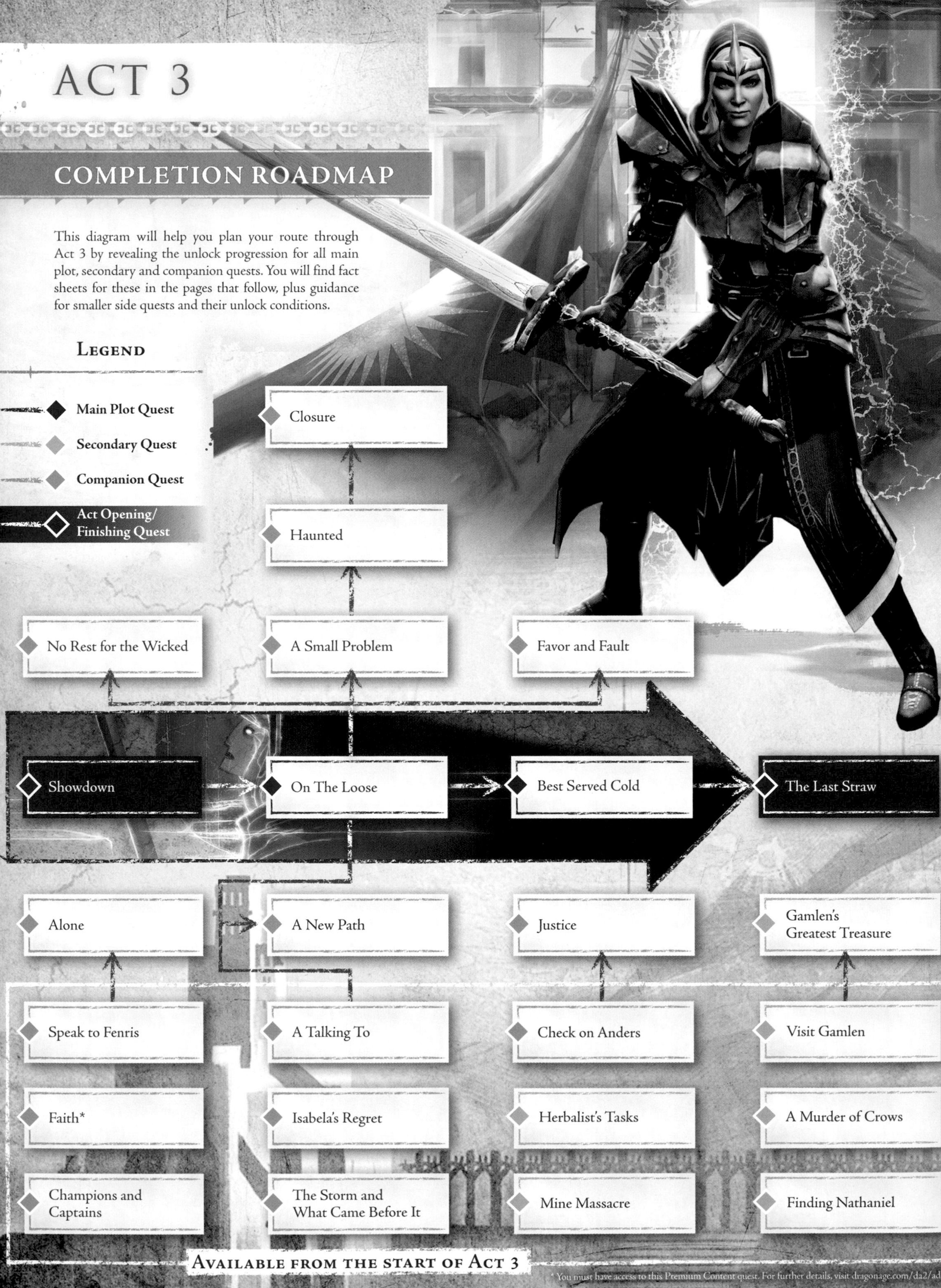

* You must have access to this Premium Content quest. For further details, visit dragonage.com/da2/add

MAIN PLOT QUESTS

Showdown

Loot and Reward: ★★★★★

Consequences:

- Though it does not appear as a Journal entry, your choices in the opening dialogue of Act 3 have an influence on who will contact Hawke for the Best Served Cold quest (Orsino if you favor the mages, or Meredith if you sympathize with the templars).
- If you pick a strictly neutral path through this conversation, the letter will most likely be sent by Orsino.

On The Loose

Loot and Reward: 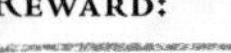

Start Location:

Hawke Estate

Requirements:

Accept the letter from the Writing Desk.

Walkthrough Addendum:

- If you have started The Lost Swords (see page 106), you will find one of the ten Qunari blades in the northeast room of the De Launcet Mansion. Even if he's not a regular travelling partner, it's worth taking Varric along just to see his brief reaction to the Comtesse.
- When you meet Emile, you can actually let him go free. This counts towards the "Arcane Defender" Achievement and Trophy. The other options are to insist that he returns immediately or to first permit him the night of passion he craves.
- If you chose the option to give money to Walter, it will cost five sovereigns. You can find the Rune of Devastation design in the chest next to the Sewer Passage exit.
- Those who opted to let Emile go free can brazenly admit this to Meredith at the end of the quest for a furious reaction or claim that they killed the misguided mage.

Consequences:

If you encouraged Emile to return to the Circle, the Comte de Launcet will send gold tokens of his appreciation via a letter at the Writing Desk. Emile will then make a cameo in a later quest.

Companion Guidance:

If Anders is in your party, he will take umbrage at the knight-commander during the closing conversation. Supporting his argument leads to a moderate friendship increase; telling him to be quiet evokes an equivalent increment in rivalry.

Best Served Cold

Loot and Reward: 

Start Location:

Hawke Estate

Requirements:

- Complete On The Loose.
- Accept the letter from the Writing Desk.

Walkthrough Addendum:

- The quest giver depends on your choices in the Act's opening set-piece squabble. See Showdown for further information. In all other respects, the actions you perform are identical.
- The Templar Lieutenant you fight in Hightown relinquishes Protection of the Faith, the final armor upgrade for Sebastian.
- After discovering which hostage the conspirators have taken, you can free Keran, threaten to report him, or kill him on the spot. Collect the Blade of Mercy from the nearby chest (a gift for Fenris – see page 104) and the Sigil of the Mage Underground armor upgrade for Anders from the northwest room before you leave.
- The party member who is kidnapped is chosen in the following order of priority:
  - If Bethany or Carver survived, they are the conspirators' primary target.
  - If Bethany or Carver died in the Deep Roads, the conspirators will kidnap Anders or Merrill if you are in an active romance with either – but only if they are not in the current party.
  - If you are in a romance with Isabela or Fenris, they will be taken if left at home for this quest.
  - If none of the above conditions are met, the kidnappers will simply snatch the companion with the highest friendship rating who is not accompanying Hawke when you speak to Keran.
- If you completed the Raiders on the Cliffs quest during Act 2 and the trip to the Wounded Coast is your first of Act 3, an individual named Evets will attack when you arrive.
- All conversations with Thrask lead to the same narrative destination. How you get there is purely a matter of playing the role of Hawke as you see fit.
- Cullen will ask if Hawke has a recommendation for Meredith. "Be merciful" will lead to no further deaths, while "Kill them all" will see the conspirators executed. "Give Samson another chance" will lead to the Fereldan being restored to his position as a templar. If you choose this option, he will appear in a later quest.

The Last Straw

Loot and Reward: 

Start Location:

Hawke Estate

Requirements:

- Complete **Best Served Cold**.
- Accept the letter from the Writing Desk.

Walkthrough Addendum:

- Be sure to wrap up any outstanding quests before you read the letter as there's no going back once you arrive at the Gallows. You should also note that any items stashed in the Storage chest at the Hawke Estate can be retrieved at a key stage in this quest. If you are playing on higher difficulty levels, placing extra potions inside may be useful.
- There is a lot of notable loot (including some valuable weapons, armor and accessories) in this quest, so don't assume that there's no need to forage for treasures. You may find them useful in future downloadable content, for instance.
- The heated confrontation between Meredith and Orsino in Lowtown places you at a crossroads: no matter which dialogue options you choose, you must commit Hawke to one side or the other. Your decision determines how the next section of the quest will play out and may cause one or more companions to leave Hawke's side.
  - If you side with the mages, Fenris will leave immediately unless you have completed all companion quests and his final-stage relationship conversation, **Questioning Beliefs**. If Fenris leaves, Aveline will stay no matter what happens. If Fenris stays, Aveline will only depart if her friendship level is below 50%.
  - If you side with the templars, Anders will leave the party.
- After choosing a side, you must either ask Anders to come with the party, set him free or execute him on the spot.
  - Unless you execute Anders, Sebastian will leave permanently. There is no further negotiation on this issue.
  - If you set Anders free, those siding with the mages will have an opportunity to ask him to rejoin later in the quest. Players who favor the templar path will have a very different encounter.
  - If you kill Anders, he plays no further part in the story.
- If Bethany or Carver joined the Grey Wardens and you completed the **Finding Nathaniel** quest during this Act, they will arrive as you make your way east through Lowtown. You can either let the surviving sibling join up or send them away; in the latter instance, they're gone for good.
- If you side with the templars, you take the same path through Lowtown and the Docks as you would if you sided with the mages, but templars will be your allies, not your foes. This makes the first fight in Lowtown rather easier.
- When you reach the Gallows, there is one last opportunity to persuade companions to stand by you in the final battles.
  - Aveline will rejoin if you are on the friendship path, but only if she didn't resign as captain after the events of **Favor and Fault**.
  - Fenris or Merrill can be swayed to come back if you are on the friendship path.
- After you've regrouped with whichever side you are supporting, you have one last chance to speak with Hawke's friends and rivals before the last part of the quest. If you are in a romance, this is the opportunity to "complete" it by speaking to them (and, if all conditions have been met, unlock the "Romantic" Achievement or Trophy). If Anders was set free earlier, he appears in the Gallows Prison and can be invited to rejoin the party. If Bethany survived the Prologue and joined the Circle, she will also be in attendance (in a pro-templar playthrough, you can then have her killed by Meredith in a special scene after the battle against Orsino).
- There is a special dialogue option available if you side with the templars and Aveline remains captain of the guard after **Favor and Fault**. Speak to her in the Gallows Courtyard after Meredith has addressed those assembled and select "The guards must fight with us". This will lead to additional help from allies in battles ahead.
- Mage sympathizers must battle from the Gallows Dungeon to reach the Gallows Courtyard, as detailed in the Walkthrough chapter. If you side with the templars, you must instead fight through the Templar Hall to reach the Gallows Dungeon, where Orsino awaits.
  - The first area of the Gallows Dungeon is lined with Circle Mages who snipe at your party from raised vantage points as you fight numerous Fade creatures. Unless you reduce the number of mages quickly, this becomes one of the most difficult battles in the game – far harder than the equivalent confrontation if you sided with Orsino.
  - After the confrontation ends, you can choose to kill or spare certain mages. Even on a pro-Meredith playthrough, it's worth allowing these to live just to see the look in her eyes...
  - There are more Circle Mages, Blood mages and Fade denizens in the east room, though the confined area makes this an easier fight.

The Last Straw (Continued)

- No matter which side you pick, the Templar Hall has a selection of optional battles. The two small rooms on the east side of the map both contain enemies to fight; the one to the north is a trap. To escape, have a rogue pick the lock on the door or defeat the Rage Demon. The area on the west of the map has two discretionary battles, including one where you face two Pride Demons simultaneously. You can collect some very fine rewards in these areas.
- You can also be confronted by Fenris, Aveline, Merrill or Anders at the Templar Hall if they left the party earlier. Though Aveline will leave, unwilling to draw her blade in anger, the others will attack.
- On a templar playthrough, Orsino is a more demanding foe. Unlike a mage playthrough, you have fewer allies to keep him occupied, so you'll need to micromanage your party and keep them in good working order. Also pay more attention to the Corpses that appear: they're more than a mere nuisance here, and dispatching them swiftly is essential. Perhaps acknowledging the greater challenge that this fight poses, you can shop with Sandal before you return to the Gallows.
- You can have up to eight allies active in the final battle against Meredith:
  - Hawke and the three members of the active party, plus Cullen: a mandatory fixture.
  - Dog counts towards the total, so you might wish to send him away in order to see other cameos.
  - As Meredith's health falls throughout the battle, additional companions can join the fray. In order of priority, these are Bethany, Carver, Varric, Anders, Aveline, Fenris, Isabela and Sebastian.

Finally, there are three additional cameos that can occur if you have completed specific quests: Donnic (if you completed **The Long Road** and have Aveline in the party), Zevran (**A Murder of Crows**) and Nathaniel (**Finding Nathaniel**).

Consequences:

After the final credits, Dragon Age II creates a "Post-Campaign" autosave. If you have just completed an optimal playthrough, it may be a good idea to load this and save a manual backup in anticipation of future downloadable content adventures.

SECONDARY QUESTS

Visit Gamlen

Loot and Reward: 

Requirements:

Available from the start of Act 3. This exists purely to draw you to Gamlen's House, accessed via Lowtown. After speaking with Hawke's uncle, read the Crumpled Note on the nearby table to begin the **Gamlen's Greatest Treasure** quest.

Gamlen's Greatest Treasure

Loot and Reward: 

Start Location:

Gamlen's House

Requirements:

Read the Crumpled Note in Gamlen's House.

Walkthrough:

- Speak to Gamlen, then head for Darktown and approach Mekel. This unsavory fellow and his henchmen will attack no matter which dialogue choices you favor. Rifle through Mekel's remains to find a note entitled The Wallop Mallet.
- Return to Gamlen's House. Speak to Hawke's uncle, then examine the Wallop Mallet on the north wall. Leave the house and head to the elven alienage, then interact with the tree.
- Travel to the Docks at night and enter Smetty's Fish Guttery. The container you seek, a red crate marked Shipment 1023, is on the raised area directly opposite the entrance. After the trap has been sprung, move your party out of the affected area, then slay the Mercenary Commander and his cohorts. Collect the Note for Gamlen item from the leader's corpse, then leave the area and journey to The Sink a new location in the Free Marches.
- On arrival at The Sink (see map on page 139), you are ambushed by Corpses, Skeleton Archers and – after a brief delay – a wave of Giant Spiders. Save your major AoE attacks for the arrival of the latter. When the path branches further south, the route to the west could be described as an "undead end": you can fight a few Corpses and Skeleton Archers, then pick up a few pieces of loot, but the door further south is sealed. Backtrack and take the east path to meet with the mysterious Charade.
- When Veld attacks, deal with him first: removing him from the conflict swiftly will deprive his allies of his buff effect. The benefits of doing so will become apparent as the battle progresses, with successive waves of enemies (including Mabari and a Mercenary Assassin) arriving in an attempt to grind your party down.
- In the post-battle dialogue, your decision in the final set of conversation options determines the conclusion of the quest:
  - "You should meet your father" is the diplomatic answer and the choice to make if you'd like to wrap this quest up with a heartwarming finale.
  - Selecting the "Give me the gem" or "I don't care" options will anger Charade, who will leave in disgust after relinquishing the Gem of Keroshek.
- Return to Gamlen to end the quest.

Consequences:

- If you told Charade to speak to Gamlen, she will be present on your arrival at his house. In this conclusion, the happy ending should be its own reward. You will also find a letter from Charade when you next return to the Hawke Estate.
- For those who prefer a more *tangible* payment for their labors, engineering immediate estrangement with the long-lost cousin will allow you to keep the mildly interesting Gem of Keroshek (see page 207) when Gamlen later decides that he does not want it. Choosing whether to tell him how you obtained the amulet or not is at your discretion: the end result is the same.

Mine Massacre

Loot and Reward: 

Start Location:

Hightown/The Bone Pit

Requirements:

If you completed The Bone Pit and Inside Job in previous Acts, speak to Hubert in the market area. Alternatively, the quest begins automatically if you arrive at the Bone Pit area.

Walkthrough:

- First things first: preparation is key for this battle, especially for those playing on the Hard or (heaven forefend) Nightmare difficulty levels. Stock up on Potions, draft in Anders to act as a healer (unless you adopt that role yourself), and consider applying poisons to all weapons. It also makes sense to take a tank along. If you have a mage with the Elemental Weapons spell, equipping a staff that inflicts cold damage will make a real difference (see page 199 to find out how to obtain Cold-Blooded or Mutiny for example).
- Jump headlong into the battle and see how it develops. If your first foray is humiliatingly truncated, that's probably the time to think about backtracking to invest in specialist equipment (such as armor, accessories or Runes that offer fire resistance).
- The High Dragon (see page 227) attacks the moment you reach the open space in the lower portion of the map. This is a multi-stage confrontation against an opponent with extremely high endurance and some truly vicious attacks:
  - The battle begins with the High Dragon facing your party on the ground. Keep ranged fighters well clear of the beast and spread out. If you brought a tank along, this character (most probably Aveline) can maintain its attention throughout this stage. Having to heal one character at a time is much less difficult than addressing an assortment of wounds.
  - The High Dragon will change position suddenly throughout this fight. When it lands on a perch overlooking the basin, successive waves of Dragonlings will enter the battle. These are not particularly challenging: the danger lies in the High Dragon's tendency to snipe at party members with homing fireball attacks. These inflict splash damage, so be sure to keep everyone spread out. This is the point where vigilance is everything and where having high fire resistance (for example thanks to a Rune of Fire Warding) makes a huge difference. Be ready to use Potions and healing spells at a moment's notice, especially when weaker mages are targeted. An efficient strategy in these instances is to have two party members (especially melee fighters) focus on the smaller enemies while the other pair continue to bombard the main target.
  - Once the Dragonlings have been defeated, the High Dragon returns to the lower level, and the cycle returns to the beginning. However, future Dragonling waves can also feature at least one Dragon. When these appear, it makes sense to direct all your aggression at them immediately.
- When the High Dragon eventually falls, its valediction is an incredible haul of loot – more than adequate recompense for the grind you have just (probably barely) survived. Of particular interest are the Dragon's Blood (a unique ingredient for crafting Runes – see page 214), the Enchanted Resin armor upgrade for Fenris, the Champion chestpiece, and the High Dragon Fire Gland.
- If you accepted this commission from Hubert, return to him now; otherwise, the quest ends here. No matter your choices in the final dialogue, if applicable, there is no further reward other than a final XP increase.

Consequences:

Collecting the High Dragon Fire Gland unlocks the final short stage of the Herbalist's Tasks quest.

A Murder of Crows

Loot and Reward: 

Start Location:

Hightown

Requirements:

- If you have imported a Dragon Age: Origins save game, Zevran must still be alive.
- We strongly advise that you complete **A Murder of Crows** before you embark on Merrill's Act 3 companion quest, **A New Path**. If you choose to kill the Dalish before they tell you where to find Zevran, the **A Murder of Crows** quest cannot be completed.
- Speak to Nuncio outside The Blooming Rose.

Walkthrough:

- If you can still count on Isabela's support, bring her along for this quest: her presence makes a big difference.
- Travel to Sundermount. If this is your first visit to the area in Act 3, you are ambushed by thieves shortly after you arrive. Plunder the Thief Leader's remains to obtain the Sylvanwood Ring, a gift for Merrill. You can also collect the Awiergan Scroll from the path that leads to the Dalish Camp to start **The Awiergan Scrolls: Third Aspect**.
- Speak to Variel and select the "I'm here for the Antivan" option, then head for the Mountain Cave via the path that leads northwest from the Dalish Camp. There is an Ogre supported by Hurlock Bolters near the Recently Opened Passage entrance, and a ferocious collection of Wasp Spiders outside your destination. Collect the Rune of Valiance Design from the pile of bones as you journey between the two battles.
- Inside the Mountain Cave, there is a multiple-wave attack by assorted spiders; pull back to the top of the wooden staircase to force them to approach in single file. Once the last arachnid has expired, loot the pile of bones to obtain the Boiled Leather Plates armor upgrade for Isabela.
- At the far north of the cave (up on the map), a Varterral will attack. You should be familiar with this opponent from your visit during Merrill's Act 2 companion quest but, if not, consult pages 83 and 228 for further details.
- In the conversation with Zevran, you can choose to take him back as a prisoner to Nuncio or let him go free (see Consequences). If Isabela is in your party, she and Zevran will engage in coquettish banter; Zevran may also playfully engage with Hawke. However, if you are using an imported world state from Dragon Age: Origins in which the Hero of Ferelden ended the game in a relationship with Zevran, his approach will be rather less flirtatious.
- After making your decision, loot the nearby treasure piles and leave. Travel to the Antivan Camp. After the cutscene, the Antivan Crows will attack. Deal with Nuncio first, or at least disable him while you reduce the number of blades and bows ranged against you. This battle is rather tough at the outset (and more so if you chose to take Zevran captive), but settles down after an initial difficulty spike. When the dust settles, speak with Zevran to conclude the quest.

Consequences:

- If you allow Zevran to leave the Mountain Cave, he will return to fight alongside Hawke when you reach the Antivan Camp. He also offers the player a rather fine dagger as an additional reward. Bind and deliver him to Nuncio, though, and he cannot participate in the combat that ensues. He is not particularly offended by this outcome but offers no additional expression of his gratitude.
- On the strict proviso that Zevran was not in a relationship with the Warden (living or dead) in an imported Dragon Age: Origins world state, there's additional fun to be had. If Isabela is in your party, she will proposition Zevran. Select the "All right, I'm game" option if you are currently romancing the Rivaini to initiate a threesome.

Herbalist's Tasks

Loot and Reward: 

Start Location:

Bone Pit Mines

Requirements:

- Slay the High Dragon to complete the Mine Massacre quest and claim the High Dragon Fire Gland.
- Visit Solivitus at the Gallows to claim a unique prize: Urzara's Tooth, a very powerful amulet.

Finding Nathaniel

Loot and Reward: 

Start Location:

Hightown

Requirements:

To play this quest, you must be using an imported Dragon Age: Origins world state in which you played the Awakening expansion, recruited Nathaniel, and he was *not* killed in the siege on Vigil's Keep. This is also available if you selected the Martyr preset world state during the initial character creation process.

Walkthrough:

- Agree to help Delilah Howe near the Chantry in Hightown, then set off for the Deep Roads. Ensure that you have an adequate supply of useful potions before you depart as this quest has a demanding finale. You will encounter Nathaniel Howe besieged by darkspawn. Nathaniel will accompany you as a guest party member for the duration of this quest. If he and Anders were acquainted from your Awakening playthrough, there are additional scenes and snatches of banter to enjoy as you progress through the area – so it's definitely worth bringing the brooding mage along.
- After speaking with Temmerin Glavonak, continue forward to trigger a battle with assorted darkspawn and an Ogre. The piles of rubble in this area make it easier to avoid the latter's charges, so be sure to take advantage of them. Pull the lever to open the way forward, then continue to the lower level.
  - If Bethany or Carver joined the Grey Wardens during the **Deep Roads Expedition**, they will be waiting here and will join in the ensuing battle.
  - If not, Nathaniel laments that his companions were killed; after this, it's straight into conflict.
- The climactic confrontation begins with waves of darkspawn attacking from multiple directions. Don't be too quick to congratulate yourself as they fall with little effort. After this easy start, two Ogres arrive and a third follows when these two have been dispatched. Direct most of your party's fire at one Ogre while using your tank and AoE attacks to suppress the surrounding darkspawn. If all else fails (including causing explosions with the levers), retreating to Temmerin's position at the start of the battle will enable you to face the waves of enemies in a more controlled manner.
- The battle over, Nathaniel (and Hawke's surviving sibling, if present) will bid the party farewell. Search the area for treasures (in particular the Drakeskin Leg Straps – the final armor upgrade for Varric), then depart via the door to the west.

Consequences:

If Carver or Bethany joined the Grey Wardens, completing this quest means that they can make a further (and more substantial) appearance later in the Act.

COMPANION QUESTS

Social Calls

As with the start of Act 2, this new chapter in Hawke's rise to prominence begins with a selection of short companion quests that enable you to catch up with Hawke's allies.

Quest	Location
The Storm and What Came Before It	The Hanged Man (Varric)
Check on Anders	Darktown Clinic
Champions and Captains	Viscount's Keep Barracks (Aveline)
Speak to Fenris	Fenris's Mansion
A Talking To	Merrill's Hut
Isabela's Regret	The Hanged Man

Notes

- If you have satisfied the conditions, speaking to Fenris will begin his Act 3 companion quest immediately.
- If you completed Aveline's Act 2 companion quest, she and Guardsman Donnic will be married.
- Any ongoing romantic relationship with Anders or Merrill may have led to them moving in with Hawke between Acts 2 and 3. If this is the case, there will be an opportunity to interact with the appropriate squeeze at the start of this Act.
- If you have Dog (see dragonage.com/da2/addons), a quest notification (Beware of Dog) will pop up when you first visit the Hawke Estate. To complete this, interact with Hawke's hound in the bedroom.

Faith

Loot and Reward: 

Requirements:

You must have the Exiled Prince downloadable content (see dragonage.com/da2/addons).

Walkthrough:

- Speak to Sebastian in the Chantry and agree to help him. Those seeking the "Chantry Historian" Achievement or Trophy can find the final required volume in the south of the map.
- Travel to Hightown at night and enter the Viscount's Keep. Approach the Throne Room and go through the door. A Blood Mage and a collection of Apostates will attack; deal with the former first. Note that Sebastian has the key to the locked door. After speaking with Leliana, return to the grand cleric in the Chantry.

Companion Guidance:

- There is a big friendship increase from Sebastian purely for accepting this quest.
- Return to Elthina and say "You won't leave?" followed by "Please reconsider" for a high friendship increase with the Starkhaven exile. Pick "You must be safe" followed by "Fine. But don't think you're my priority" for a large rivalry boost.

Alone

Loot and Reward: 

Start Location:

Fenris's Mansion

Requirements:

- Fenris must be an active companion, and you must have completed A Bitter Pill in Act 2.
- Complete Speak to Fenris.

Walkthrough Addendum:

- During the conversation with Danarius, there are a handful of options to choose from. If you select "Take him", a horrified Fenris will question Hawke's response. Confirm the choice, and he will be led away by Danarius. You will receive a payment in coin immediately and a further reward in a letter at the Writing Desk. All other options lead to combat.
- If you choose to fight, the first wave of Slavers are soon replaced by Shades and a Rage Demon. When the Corpses crawl in, Danarius will enter the fray. Ignore all other targets and direct your party to attack him immediately.
- In the closing dialogue, you can intervene and prevent Fenris from killing his sister. This determines how the quest ends and is very much a matter of personal preference.

Companion Guidance:

- Betraying Fenris leads to large rivalry increases with Aveline and Sebastian, with moderate ire from Merrill and Varric. Anders, if present, will express mild friendship feelings. If you intend to keep Fenris but wish to max out rivalry, initially refusing to support him, then changing your mind, will leave him utterly furious.
- The "He's no one's slave" option will please Aveline and Fenris. Expect a large rivalry boost from the elf if you attempt to negotiate with Danarius.
- Selecting "You deserve to die" when Fenris is poised to execute Varania leads to a large friendship boost. If you persuade him to spare her, note that the "She's not responsible" argument will lead to a rivalry increase – as will the "You're blaming magic?" dialogue choice in the aftermath.

Justice

Loot and Reward: 

Requirements:

- Anders must be an active companion.
- Complete Check on Anders.

Walkthrough:

- Speak to Anders at his clinic. Agree to help him if you wish to undertake this quest, as refusal will end it immediately – see Consequences. The next area you visit has several traps, so you may wish to bring a rogue along.
- Take a stroll to the south of Darktown and enter the Sewers. The objective here is to interact with all Sela Petrae deposits. The area just inside the entrance is populated by Lyrium Smugglers (with the Foreman variety being the most formidable) and Dwarven Mercenaries. To the south, a Raider Reaver and Apostate Mages offer a slightly sterner test. The biggest battle is in the north of the Sewers, where a larger group of the enemy types encountered at the start are joined by a Pit Boss – an Assassin. Collect the final two deposits, then depart through the nearby exit.
- Your next port of call is the Bone Pit. Head to the far east of the map and enter the Drakestone Mines. As with the Sewers, you must fight your way through an assortment of opponents while retrieving the Drakestone →

Justice (Continued)

deposits. The mines are infested with spiders of the Corrupted, Giant and Poisonous varieties, so electricity damage in any form will serve you well. The Monstrous Spider that awaits to the south is particularly vicious. Its movement and attack speed make it a relentless foe, so use everything in your power to grind it into submission rapidly and keep the spider's attention on your tank.

- After collecting the final deposit, return to Anders's Clinic in Darktown. If you pledge to help him in one last task, travel to the Chantry. Anders will leave as soon as you arrive; if present, Sebastian will also depart. Speak to the grand cleric on any topic that takes your fancy. After Anders intervenes, you are automatically returned to Darktown. Speak to the mage to end the quest.

Consequences:

Refusing to help Anders at two pivotal points in this quest (the start and the point when you return to the clinic after collecting the ingredients) will end it immediately.

Companion Guidance:

- In the opening dialogue, agreeing to help Anders leads to a moderate rivalry increase with Fenris; expect a friendship boost if you turn the mage down.
- If you aspire to friendship with both Anders and Sebastian, it's advisable to leave the Starkhaven noble behind for the final section of this quest. Agreeing to help Anders enter the Chantry by distracting the grand cleric will please the mage and perplex the pious prince. The reverse will lead to massive increases in rivalry with Anders and friendship with Sebastian.

Haunted

Loot and Reward: 

Start Location:

The Hanged Man

Requirements:

- Complete A Small Problem.

Walkthrough:

- You must have Varric in your active party to begin this quest. On arrival at Bartrand's Estate, visit the room in the northeast of the mansion to view a cutscene. This unlocks all nearby doors. Head into the central area and enter the bedroom to the east.
- Manually position your party in the lower area of the room when the Ethereal Golem attacks. This will allow your ranged fighters to maintain a discrete distance from your opponent. The Golem will disappear on the first two instances where its health gauge is depleted by one third, and a wave of Shades will attack in its stead. Use a couple of AoE attacks to banish these, then resume your assault. The Ethereal Golem is a heavy hitter, but is easily transfixed by a capable tank; this gives ranged fighters the luxury of bombarding it with near impunity.
- With the Golem dispatched, advising Varric to get rid of the shard leads to the best reward (see Consequences). All areas of the mansion are unlocked at this stage. Head into the bedroom in the southeast of the building to find a chest with a Master lock and a book marked Ledger, which triggers an optional cutscene. Once you are sure you have cleared the mansion of all valuables, return to Hightown.

Consequences:

If Varric keeps the Lyrium Shard, his weapon Bianca receives three additional Rune slots; the quest ends once you leave the mansion. If the shard falls into Hawke's possession, there is one final step to complete the quest: visit the Hawke Estate to consult Sandal. Rather than destroy it, Hawke's resident savant will create a Primeval Lyrium Rune. When applied to a weapon, this unique item will bless its user with a significant attack speed increase. Think long and hard before installing this irreplaceable Rune on an item that might be rendered obsolete in the not too distant future. If you have a soft spot for Varric as a key party member, Bianca might just be an appropriate place for it. Then again, just think about what Isabela might accomplish with it placed on a top-tier dagger...

Companion Guidance:

Varric's reaction to Hawke's counsel at the end of the quest depends on your relationship: a crystallized friendship will beget further friendship and so forth. Sebastian will approve if Hawke advises the dwarf to get rid of the Lyrium Shard.

A Small Problem

Loot and Reward: 

Requirements:

- Complete On The Loose.
- Speak to Varric at The Hanged Man. This conversation acts as a lead-in to his Act 3 companion quest, Haunted.

Closure

Loot and Reward: 

Requirements:

This quest is an epilogue to Haunted, in which Varric reflects on recent events.

Favor and Fault

Loot and Reward: 

Start Location:

Hawke Estate

Requirements:

- You must have completed Aveline's Act 1 companion quest, The Way it Should Be.
- Finish On The Loose.
- Accept the letter from the Writing Desk.

Walkthrough:

- Speak to Aveline at the Viscount's Keep barracks, then travel to the Docks at night with the guard-captain in your party. Your rendezvous with Guardsman Donnic sees him in the midst of a fracas with Coterie Thugs. After this first wave has been defeated, a second arrives just behind your position. These generic thugs are simple cannon fodder, though be careful not to miss the Coterie Alchemist and Coterie Rogue in their midst.
- Travel to the Gallows to speak with Cullen, then continue on to Lowtown at night. As with Donnic, Guardsman Brennan's contribution to the story is tailored to address whether Aveline married or not. (The impression, for those who cannot bear to miss a quest on a subsequent playthrough, is that Aveline is a harder individual who inspires less loyalty without the softening effect of her relationship with Donnic. Indeed, in this alternative plot strand, he is one of her most vocal critics.)
- On arrival at Darktown, Street Thugs and Mercenaries litter the streets before you reach the disgraced Jeven. Your first dialogue line with this embittered opportunist has a profound effect on how this quest ends:
    - If you completed Aveline's Act 2 storyline, no guardsmen will stand alongside Jeven: just a mob of insurrectionists. The best solution is to let Aveline take over with the companion dialogue option. This is the only way to keep the captain happy; it also has the effect of reducing the number of enemies you face by half. If you make a personal response to Jeven, expect increased rivalry: this isn't Hawke's battle to fight.
    - If you did not complete **The Long Road**, you can remove the assembled guardsmen from the fight ahead by suggesting that Aveline should bear partial responsibility for being so hard on her subordinates. This will piss her off mightily but make the resultant fight easier. The alternative is to comment that the guardsmen present have made their choice; Aveline will concur, which leads to combat with all in attendance. However, this last option will cause Aveline to resign as guard-captain: a development that will affect her loyalty to Hawke in a future crisis.
- Jeven is an Assassin with a colossal health gauge, so your best bet will be to keep him quiet while you deal with his angry mob. This will take a little micromanagement, but should be no great challenge at this stage in the game. Reinforcements arrive from behind your position on the staircase, so you may wish to greet them with AoE attacks and reposition any exposed ranged fighters. After the fight ends, collect the Deflecting Joints – Guardsman Pattern companion armor upgrade from Jeven's remains.
- Return to the Viscount's Keep to receive the captain's gratitude or admonishment.

A New Path

Loot and Reward: 

Start Location:

Merrill's Hut

Requirements:

- Complete A Talking To and On The Loose.
- Visit Merrill.

Walkthrough:

- After speaking to Merrill and travelling to Sundermount, you can have an optional conversation with Keeper Marethari before you begin your climb to the Pride's End cave entrance.
- To cut down on travel time, we suggest that you complete two of the Awiergan Scrolls side quests during this visit to the area: see page 103.
- There is a battle against spiders, Shades and a Shadow Warrior near the Sundermount Caverns exit. Destroy them in that exact order.
- At the graveyard, you can interact with graves. Three contain loot, two are empty and one spawns a wave of enemies when you interact with it. Expect Corpses, Skeleton Archers, a Shadow Warrior and, finally, a deadly Shadow Assassin. Clear the first three enemy types before the last arrives, then disable the Shadow Assassin with a concerted assault.
- After a profitable bout of graverobbing, interact with the shrine for an optional cutscene before you continue. There are Dragonlings and a Dragon as you approach the upper reaches, while Corpses and another Shadow Assassin await outside the cave entrance. Once again, try to keep the latter incapacitated at all times, as he may be capable of killing a slightly weakened mage with a single attack.
- Once inside Pride's End, collect the Felandaris (a rare crafting ingredient), then interact with the statue.
    - When the Pride Demon appears, brace yourself for a demanding confrontation. This opponent can alternate between two forms, each with distinct strengths and weaknesses: see page 231 to study these. In the first part of the battle, it favors melee attacks that have an AoE range. Keep your party spread out to minimize collateral damage.
    - This malevolent entity summons cruel facsimiles of Merrill's former Dalish clan that taunt her throughout the first stage of the fight. These are a distraction, nothing more: focus purely on the Pride Demon. (As an aside, killing the Dalish apparitions does marginally increase the XP that you gain from this fight.)
    - In the second stage, the Pride Demon favors its Crushing Prison attack. This is telegraphed by the appearance of an effect radius, so briefly pause your assault to move party members out of the danger zone before you resume hostilities.
- Once the Pride Demon falls, select the "You said you had to die" option to bring the battle to a close. Picking the "I'm glad that's over" dialogue choice leads to an additional third section of the fight, albeit with the creature damned to fairly swift destruction by a vastly diminished health gauge.
- When the confrontation ends, respectfully purloin items from the Keeper's corpse, including the Halla Horn Buckles – Merrill's final armor upgrade – before you leave the cavern.
- The remaining Dalish meet the party with escalating suspicion and hostility as you step out onto Sundermount. If Hawke takes responsibility for Merrill, they will grudgingly allow the party to leave. The other two dialogue options lead to a challenging battle with minimal rewards.

Consequences:

- If you do not complete this quest, you cannot reach the final stage in a romance with Merrill.
- Should you avoid conflict with the Dalish after defeating the Pride Demon, returning to Sundermount with Merrill in your party will cause the entire clan to attack without further provocation.

Companion Guidance:

- After Marethari's death, blame the Keeper to gain friendship with Merrill – but annoy Aveline, Anders and Fenris.
- For maximum rivalry, pick: "You weren't listening" then follow with "That's not up to you" or "Merrill, you were being crazy". If you chose to withhold the Arulin'holm at the end of her Act 2 quest, this will lead Merrill to give up the mirror. For the same outcome but with reduced rivalry, choose "She loved you".

No Rest for the Wicked

Loot and Reward: 

Start Location:

Hawke Estate

Requirements:

- Only available if Isabela was recruited in Act 1, returned to the fold at the climax of Act 2, and was not surrendered to the Arishok.
- Speak to Isabela in The Hanged Man.
- Complete On the Loose, then visit the Hawke Estate to find Isabela standing at the Writing Desk. Speak to her to begin the quest. If she is not there, return at a later date.

Walkthrough:

- After speaking with Isabela at the Hawke Estate, travel to The Blooming Rose via Hightown with the Rivaini in your party. Approach the waypoint to trigger a brief conversation, then enter the room and feign a betrayal. Any dialogue options will suffice, though the two aggressive options lead to the most interesting conclusion...
- Use the Gather Your Party point to recruit a replacement companion, then leave the brothel. Walk over each Isabela's Trail marker to activate those that follow until you reach the northwest area exit. Set off for Lowtown (Night). Once again, follow the trail markers in turn to reach the east area exit. From here, depart for the Docks (Night) where a final trail leads to the Castillon's Landing entrance.
- After entering the area, head through the north door and use the Disarming Switch. Wait for the trap sequence to end, then forage for some (rather nice) rewards. Enter the main room to trigger a battle with Velasco and his men. Loot Velasco's remains to collect the Office Key. Enter the northeast room to collect Ambrosia (the rarest of all potion ingredients), then loot the chest in the storeroom to the south to find the Incriminating Documents.
- Return to the main room to meet Castillon. At this point, you have two paths to pick from:
  - Agree with Isabela's plan ("If that's the way you want it"), and Castillon will walk free. The quest ends immediately.
  - Kill Castillon.
- If you opt to fight Isabela's nemesis against her wishes, kill the Raider Archer on the raised walkway to the south: he is standing on a pressure pad that activates the jets of flames that erupt on the lower level. Moving the entire party to the upper area (and, ideally, the room where the entrance is located) makes this fight much, much easier. Deal with Castillon first: he's a dangerous foe if left unchecked.

Companion Guidance:

- During the conversation with Isabela at the Hawke Estate, use humorous or witty dialogue options and suggest that Isabela be used as bait for a large friendship increase.
- If you make a deal with Castillon, the results of the final conversation with Isabela make you score more of the approval type that defines your relationship.
- If you kill Castillon, expect a large rivalry boost. Tell Isabela to stop whining for additional rivalry. Other options lead to friendship increases.

Companion Gifts

There are a trio of additional gifts to find in Act 3. These are necessary to take romances with Merrill, Fenris and Isabela to their optimum conclusion.

Companion	Quest Name	Gift Required
Merrill	Memento of the Dalish	Sylvanwood Ring found in the remains of the Thief Leader in Sundermount during A Murder of Crows.
Fenris	Blade of Mercy	Blade of Mercy found in a chest in the Secret Meeting Place map during Best Served Cold.
Isabela	A Rivaini Talisman	Rivaini Talisman found inside the Disused Passage, accessed via the Docks at night.

Final-Stage Relationship Quests

If you have completed all quests for a particular companion and have also reached a full 100% friendship or rivalry, the following quests will unlock to acknowledge the final stage in Hawke's relationship with that character. This guarantees the loyalty of *most* allies during Dragon Age II's epic denouement.

Companion	Quest Name
Fenris	Questioning Beliefs
Anders	Questioning Beliefs
Varric	An Anniversary
Aveline	Questioning Beliefs
Isabela	Questioning Beliefs
Merrill	Merrill, Friend or Foe
Sebastian	Questioning Beliefs

SIDE QUESTS

The Awiergan Scrolls: First, Second & Third Aspect

First Aspect

Loot and Reward: 

Start Location:

The Wounded Coast

Requirements:

Collect the Awiergan Scroll from the dead end just south of the main Wounded Coast entrance.

Walkthrough:

After collecting the scroll, continue along the path to reach the far western side of the area. When Corpses suddenly rise from the ground, you'll know that you've found the right spot. Proceed up the coast slowly and defeat each successive wave until Medan (an Arcane Horror) appears, then spread out and devote your energies to slaying this creature straight away.

Consequences:

If this is the last Aspect completed, you can embark on the main **Pride Unbound** quest.

Second Aspect

Loot and Reward: 

Start Location:

Sundermount

Requirements:

Collect the Awiergan Scroll hidden behind a wall just south of the Sundermount Caverns entrance.

Walkthrough:

- Travel through the caves to the upper section of the mountain area.
- The party is attacked by a Corpse named Bysmor and two Revenants: Gifre and Beacon. Dispatch Bysmor first – with a careful approach, you may be able to lure it down the slope before its allies notice you – then direct your aggression at a single Revenant at a time. Do everything you can to impede their movement and attack capabilities, favoring electricity and spirit damage whenever possible. On Nightmare difficulty, they are immune to nature and cold, though you can still ensnare or impede them temporarily with Winter's Grasp and Cone of Cold.

Consequences:

If this is the last Aspect completed, you can embark on the main **Pride Unbound** quest.

Third Aspect

Loot and Reward: 

Start Location:

Sundermount

Requirements:

Collect the Awiergan Scroll from the path leading from the main entrance to the Dalish Camp.

Walkthrough:

- After collecting this scroll, head for Sundermount Caverns. You will encounter an Arcane Horror on the path just before the cave entrance. Though initially alone, it will be joined by a huge number of Shades as the battle progresses. Keep these under control with a blanket of suppressing AoE attacks while you direct the majority of your firepower at the primary target. The battle will not last long once it falls.
- The Second Aspect scroll can be found just behind a low wall after the battle ends.

Consequences:

If this is the last Aspect completed, you can embark on the main **Pride Unbound** quest.

The Awiergan Scrolls: Pride Unbound

Loot and Reward: 

Requirements:

The Journal entry for this quest is unlocked by completing **The Awiergan Scrolls: First Aspect**, **Second Aspect** or **Third Aspect**. However, you cannot access the Hidden Dungeon in Darktown until you have completed all three.

Walkthrough:

- Enter the Hidden Dungeon via the door (marked on the map as "Hidden Lair") in the northeast of Darktown, just south of the clinic.
- Hybris is a resilient and highly dangerous Pride Demon (see page 231). Though it initially fights alone, it is joined by Shades and Rage Demons as the battle progresses. Crowd control, then, is a mandatory task until Hybris is reduced to his final slivers of health. At this point, it's better to pour everything into finishing him off, then deal with his minions afterwards.
- Beating Hybris unlocks the "Demon Slayer" Achievement and Trophy.

King Alistair

Loot and Reward: 

Start Location:

Hawke Estate

Requirements:

- Only available if you chose the Hero of Ferelden or The Martyr world state options during initial character creation or imported a Dragon Age: Origins save in which Alistair became king.
- Complete **On The Loose**, then accept the letter from the Writing Desk.

Walkthrough:

Travel to the Viscount's Keep to meet with King Alistair. The more devoted Dragon Age: Origins players will enjoy the references to Ferelden and events past. The quest ends once the interview with the king is complete. Both Aveline and Anders have short reactions to Alistair if they are present.

The Lost Swords

Loot and Reward: 

Start Location:

Hightown

Requirements:

- You must have gained the Arishok's respect during Act 2 (see **Blackpowder Courtesy** on page 72 for details).
- Speak to Taarbas outside the Hawke Estate.

Walkthrough:

- Taarbas asks Hawke to retrieve ten Qunari Swords from locations throughout Kirkwall and the Free Marches. Use the table below to find each one.
- You can turn in swords to Tarbaas at any time. He will ask if you require gold for your services. Unless you have no intention of collecting all ten, you should refuse this: the payments are nominal. However, handing over the entire collection without a reward in coin will lead him to give a unique gift, the Bassrath-Kata. This is an extraordinary weapon tailored to Hawke's class.
- The XP reward for collecting the Qunari Swords is bestowed on a per-sword basis, not as a final quest award – so those without a master lockpicker (or the dedication to find all ten) can still profit from this venture.

Qunari Sword Locations

Area	Location
Hightown	Purchase from Korval's Blades.
Lowtown	Purchase from Weaponsmithy.
Lowtown (Night)	Hidden in a pile of rubble in the Foundry District.
The Gallows	Purchase from the Weapon Shop.
Darktown	Inside a crate at Anders's Clinic.
Docks (Night)	Found in a pile of bones in the Harbormaster's Office area.
Docks (Night)	Inside a chest with a Master-grade lock in the Warehouse District.
De Launcet Mansion (Hightown)	Found in the northeast room of the building during your visit for the **On the Loose** main plot quest.
The Wounded Coast	Travel west from the main entrance until you can proceed no further, then head south (through a campsite) to a dead end. The sword is hidden in a pile of bones.
The Wounded Coast	Found among a pile of bones in the northwest of the region – you should remember this area as being the Tal-Vashoth camp from Act 1.

Reining It In

Loot and Reward: 

Start Location:

Docks (Night)

Requirements:

Fight the Slave Hunters in the Docks until a pop-up message appears. Repeat visits may be required.

Walkthrough:

- Slave Hunter groups consist of melee fighters and archers, though the latter tend to be less efficient than usual in the narrow streets and piers of the Docks – they're usually in range of the main pack if you lay down an AoE attack.
- After the pop-up notification, enter the Run Down Alley area. The gang leader (Jess "Leashmaster" Varvel) is a mage, so deal with her immediately after dispatching the initial group of Slave Hunters from the safety of the steps.

Kind of Want

Loot and Reward: 

Start Location:

Lowtown (Night)

Requirements:

Fight the gang members in Lowtown at night until a pop-up message appears. Repeat visits may be required.

Walkthrough:

- This gang boasts melee fighters and numerous archers, with an occasional Assassin popping up when you least expect it.
- After the quest notification appears, enter the Decrepit Alley. Fight from the top of the stairs until gang leader Hanker appears, then run down to kill her immediately.

Consequences:

Once you have dealt with the three gangs in Act 3, return to The Hanged Man to claim your final prize. There is a special bonus if you have eliminated all nine.

The Last Holdouts

Loot and Reward: 

Requirements:

- You must have sided with Meredith during the **Showdown** conversation at the start of Act 3.
- Talk to the Barmaid in The Hanged Man at night, then speak to Ser Mettin and agree to help.

Walkthrough:

- Travel to Darktown and enter the Hidden Sewer. Always deal with the Blood Mages first and the other enemies will put up very little resistance. Once you've defeated all hostiles, collect the four Blood Mage Dispatches, then journey to the Hawke Estate and accept the new letter from the Writing Desk.
- Take a locksmith to Sundermount as your destination features a locked chest with a worthwhile reward inside. Travel through Sundermount Caverns to reach the Blood Mage Base entrance. Ser Mettin and Ser Agatha fight alongside the party for the first two battles in this area. Head north to face Bancroft and a handful of Apostate Mages. Bancroft is a vicious Blood Mage, so incapacitate him instantly. You can ignore the other mages until he dies. When the combat ends, you have a choice:
    - If you attempt to persuade Ser Mettin to show mercy to the mages ("Mettin, stop") or express ambivalence ("Not my problem"), he will attack immediately; Ser Agatha will fight alongside the party.
    - If you support the templar ("Mettin is right"), you must fight Ser Agatha and her supporters. Mettin is grateful, though he offers no additional reward.

A Noble Agenda

Loot and Reward: 

Requirements:

- You must have sided with Orsino during the Showdown conversation at the start of Act 3.
- Speak to Ser Marlein Selbrech in Hightown and agree to help.

Walkthrough:

- Travel to Darktown, taking your favored locksmith with you as there are two secured chests with noteworthy loot, and enter the Hidden Supply Depot. Defeat the mercenaries that lie in wait when you arrive and the templars on the west side of the map.
- Visit Lowtown and approach Ser Mettin. Once he acknowledges the arrival of Hawke, he and his archer allies will attack. Try to kill Mettin quickly before a small wave of reinforcements (including a hunter) arrive.
- Return to the Hawke Estate to collect a letter detailing the next step, then head back to Lowtown at night. Approach Marlein, then fight off the templar ambush. This is a tough battle, so have a tank present and keep your weaker party members at a safe distance. Neutralize the dangerous Ser Edgert the Hound, the Templar Hunter and the Templar Lieutenant immediately. A subsequent wave of enemies features two more of the latter enemy type, so aim for survival over aggression if you experience difficulties (and don't skimp on Potion use).

Red Run Streets

Loot and Reward: 

Start Location:

Hightown (Night)

Requirements:

Fight the Bloodrager Thrall enemies in Hightown at night until a pop-up message appears. Repeat visits may be required.

Walkthrough:

- This gang is possibly the most challenging so far, as each group also features a mage (known simply as Bloodrager) in addition to archers and melee fighters. As their title suggests, these individuals employ blood magic – and should, therefore, be your exclusive target at the start of each fight.
- Once the final quest stage has unlocked, enter the Suspicious House. Jakeson "The Bleeder" Hall is the gang leader; launch the most vicious offensive you can muster to neutralize him before the blood magic begins. In addition to the rank and file, another Bloodrager mage arrives near the end of the battle, so keep a watchful eye on proceedings and act swiftly.

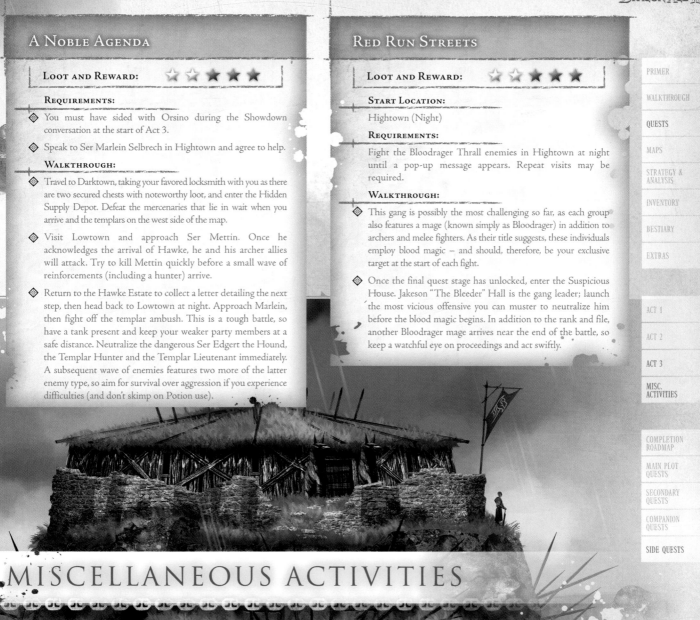

Miscellaneous Activities

The following section details a small assortment of optional cutscenes, conversations, events and activities that you can encounter during the three main Acts.

Act 1

- There is a special reactive event at the Wounded Coast that only occurs if you play with an imported Dragon Age: Origins save file in which you sided with the elves in the Nature of the Beast quest, or if you chose the Hero of Ferelden or The Martyr world states during the Prologue. On arrival in the area, take the south path to meet a Dalish Assassin remonstrating with a human.
- Corff the Bartender has news to share if you speak with him in The Hanged Man. Certain lines will reflect decisions you made in Dragon Age: Origins if you imported a save file.
- There is a Donation Box inside Lirene's Fereldan Imports. Placing money inside leads to a small XP reward: 50 XP for 50 silver, 100 XP for one sovereign and 200 XP for five sovereigns.

Act 2

- You can hire a prostitute in The Blooming Rose... with amusing results. If you are in an active romance and they are in the active party when you do this, there is a rivalry increase.
- If you sent Feynriel to live with the Dalish in the Wayward Son quest, there is a reactive event when you visit Sundermount for the first time in Act 2. You will encounter templars arguing with Dalish warriors. You can intervene and resolve the situation in many ways.

Act 3

- If you completed Magistrate's Orders and chose to kill Kelder, pay a visit to the elven alienage during the day to meet Lia, the young elf you saved. This brief cutscene is extended if Aveline is in your current party.
- Visit Sundermount at any time in Act 3 to explore the Hidden Dungeon. This "optional" map is not part of any quests and features a small selection of undead and high-rank Fade creatures to fight en route to the central area. On arrival you can shop with the Nexus Golem, who has a handful of remarkable items to sell. Use the nearby door to return to Sundermount.
- If Feynriel was possessed at the end of Night Terrors (the automatic conclusion if you did not undertake the quest), you will encounter an unusual scene in Lowtown's market area if you visit at night, where Feynriel appears to have become a Dream Stalker.

MAPS

While navigation is rarely an issue in Dragon Age II, plundering its countless locales of their finest treasures can be a demanding task. Help is at hand. This chapter reveals the locations of all noteworthy collectibles, including rare and unique items, locked chests and codex entries.

Introduction & Map Index

Before you continue, take a moment to familiarize yourself with the icons we will use throughout this chapter. As many points of interactivity (such as area exits and merchants) appear on the in-game maps, we instead focus exclusively on the countless collectibles that do not – which will make the process of tracking down treasures *much* easier.

Icon	Meaning	Notes
	Standard container	These can be opened by any character and include things like regular chests, but also piles of bones, corpses, furniture and so forth – in other words, any possible source of loot.
	Locked chest	Locked chests can only be opened by a rogue. There are 4 types of locks (basic, standard, complex and master), each requiring the rogue to have a minimum amount of points in the Cunning attribute (respectively 10, 20, 30 and 40).
	Rare item	Rare items include gifts, armor upgrades for companions, Codex collectibles, side quest items, and crafting ingredients or recipes. Note that some Codex collectibles are available in several areas: picking one up will deactivate the others that appear in different locations.

As a rule, all collectibles are removed from maps and replaced by new items at the beginning of each act. There are also certain collectibles that will only appear during a specific quest. Make sure you do not miss these items during the corresponding window of opportunity, as you will not be able to collect them later on. For maximum clarity, all collectibles are represented in color-coded sets on our maps, with their availability conditions (such as act or quest restrictions) clearly stated on each map's legend.

Most maps in the game are unique and used only for a given location. For example, the Hightown map is only ever used for the Hightown district. However there are a few "generic" maps that can appear on multiple occasions in different quests, each time with a new description. When this occurs, you will always find the name of each instance of a map clearly labeled. If in doubt, simply refer to the following map index. It lists all locales in Dragon Age II, with a page reference leading you to the corresponding map.

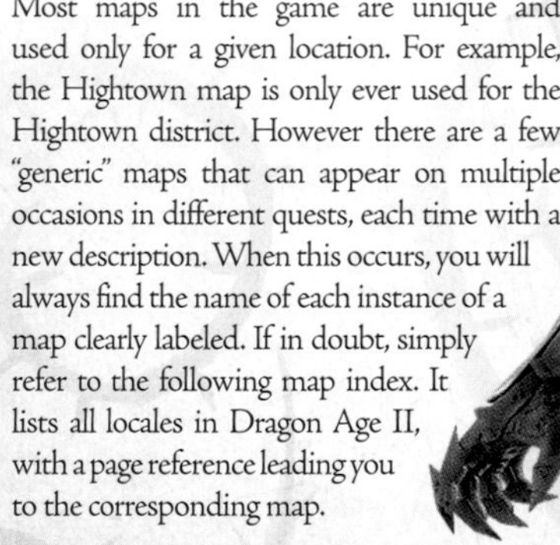

BLIGHTLANDS

LEGEND: ◆ Prologue

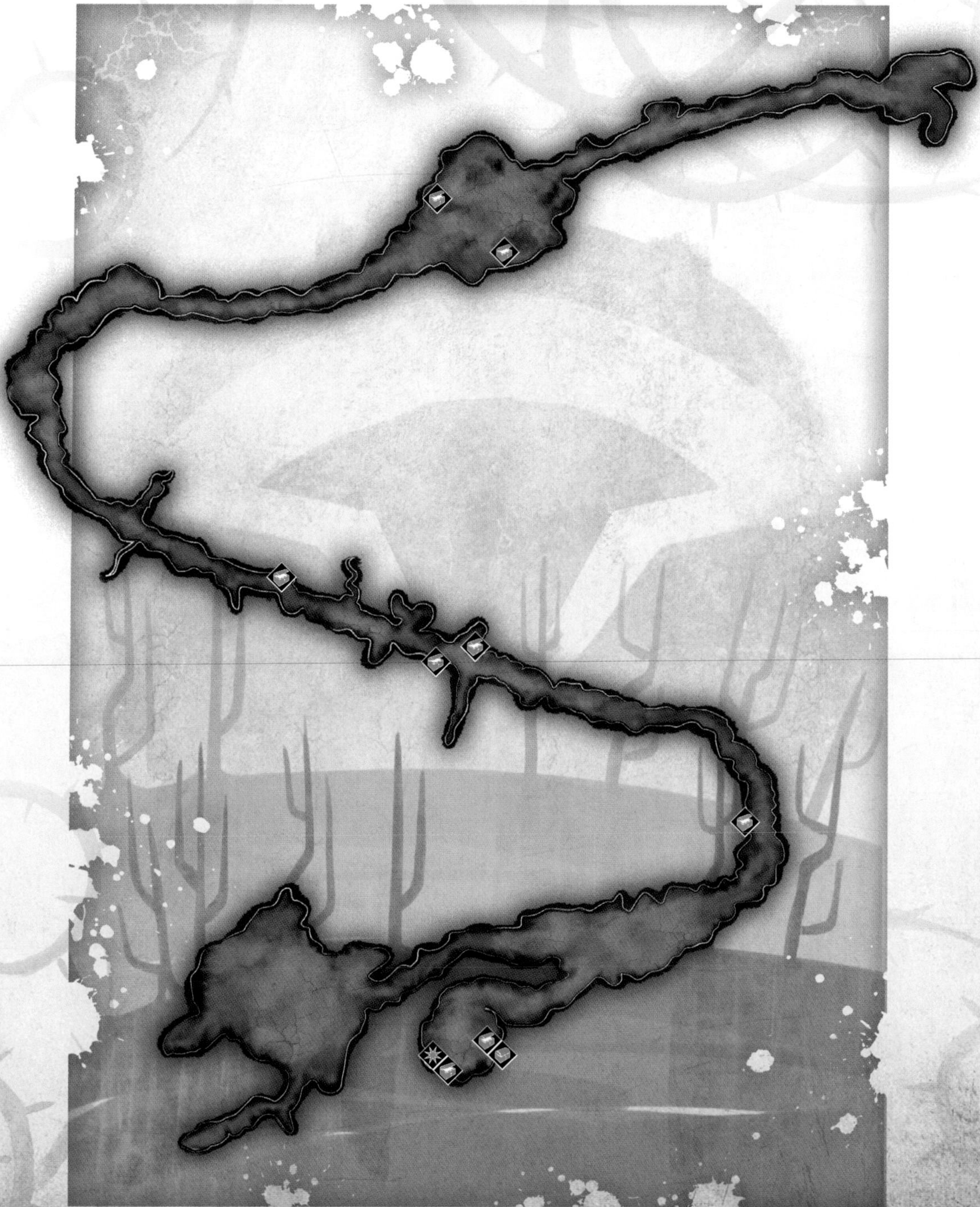

HIGHTOWN (DAY)

LEGEND: ◆ Act 1 ◆ Act 2 ◆ Act 3

HIGHTOWN (NIGHT)

LEGEND: ◆ Act 1 ◆ Act 2 ◆ Act 3 ◆ Demands of the Qun quest (Act 2)

LOWTOWN (DAY)

LEGEND: ◆ Act 1 ◆ Act 2 ◆ Act 3

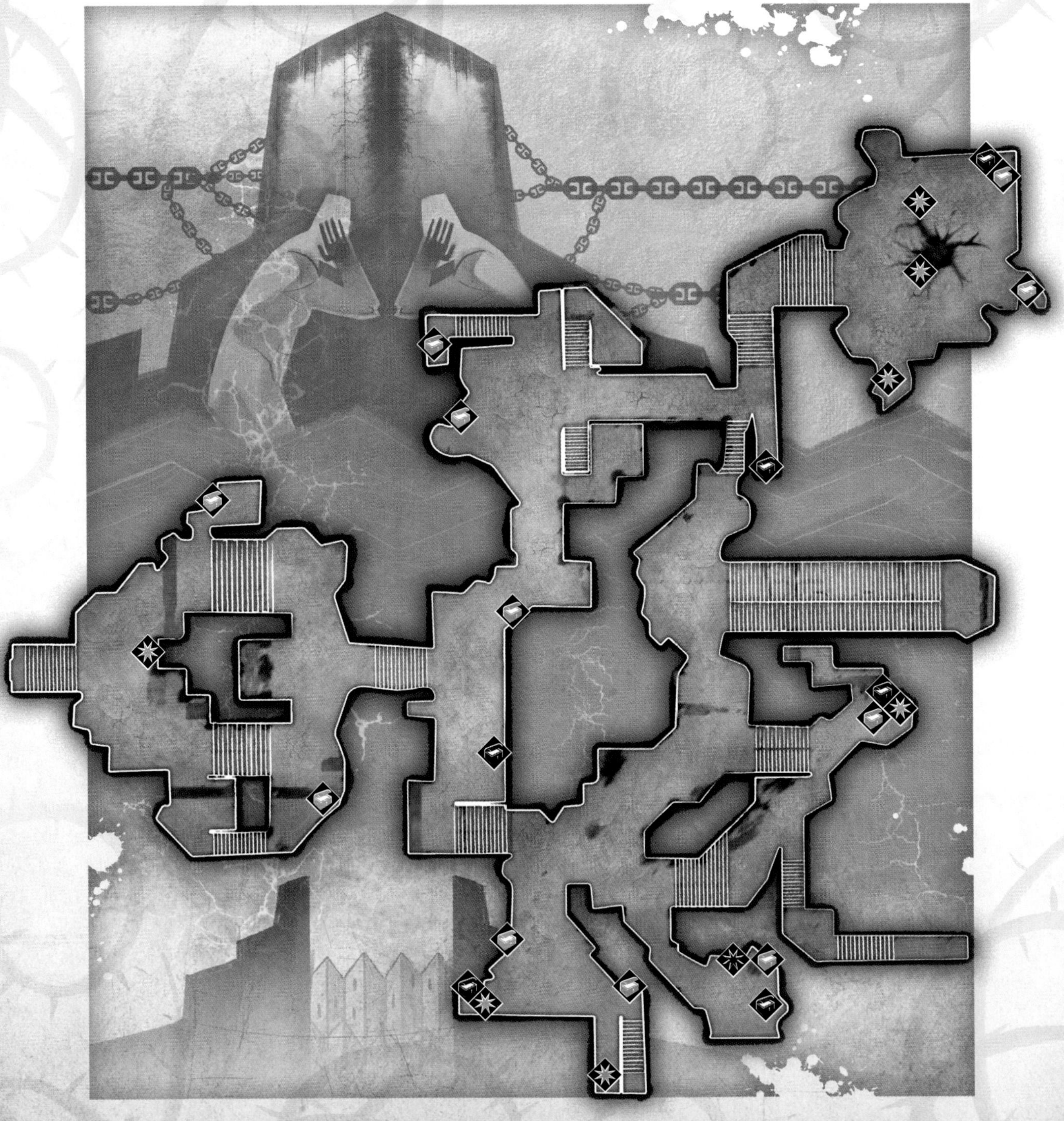

LOWTOWN (NIGHT)

LEGEND: Act 1 | Act 2 | Act 3 | Demands of the Qun quest (Act 2) | The Last Straw quest (Act 3)

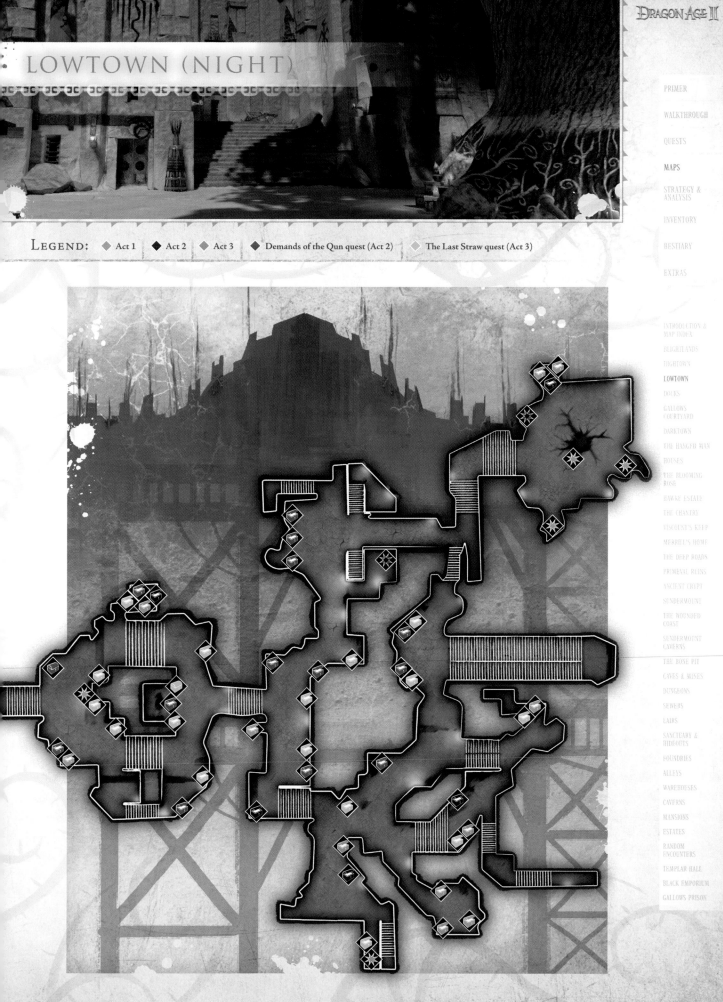

DOCKS (DAY)

LEGEND: ◆ Act 1 | ◆ Act 2 | ◆ Act 3

DOCKS (NIGHT)

LEGEND: Act 1 · Act 2 · Act 3 · The Last Straw quest (Act 3)

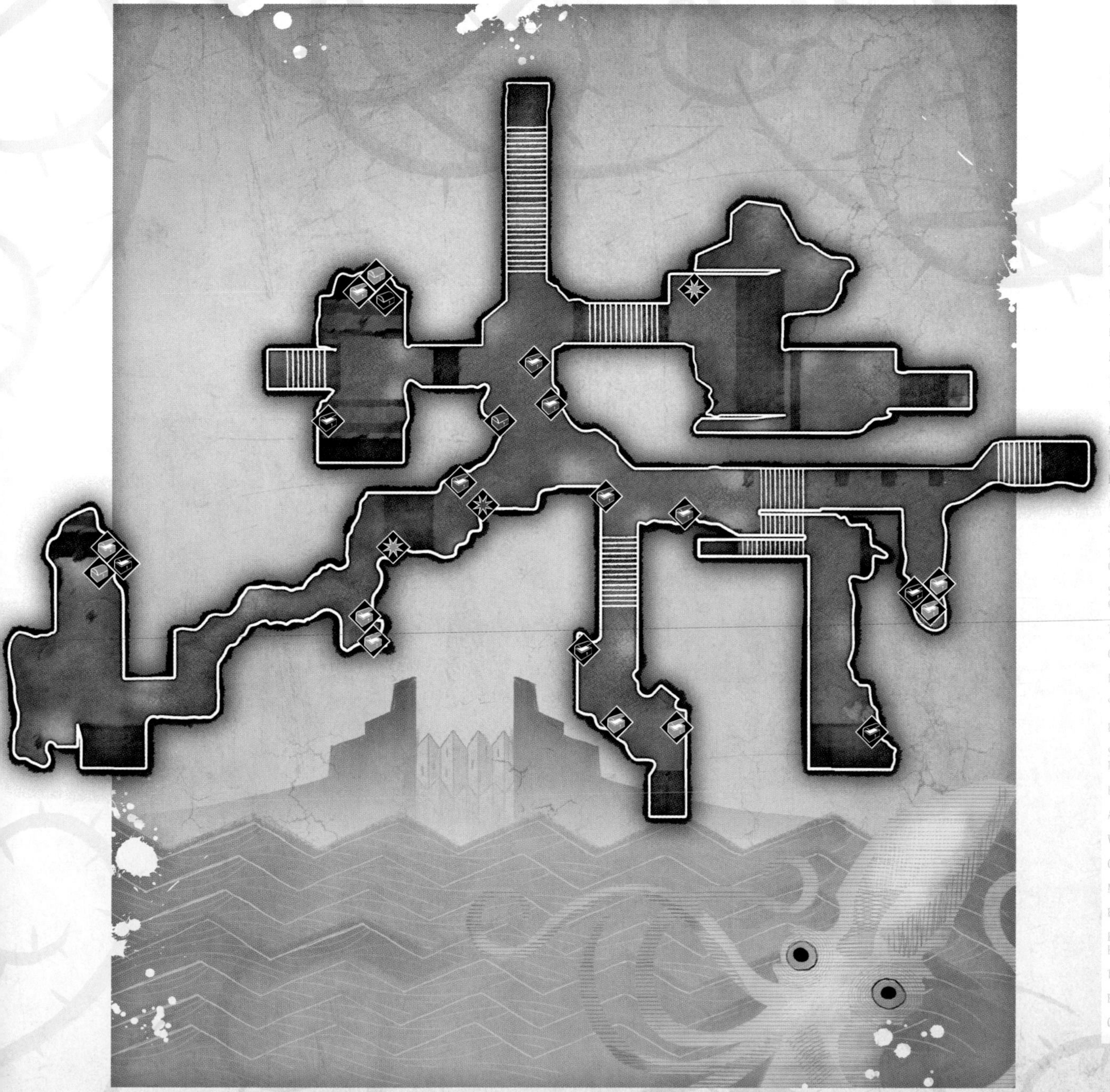

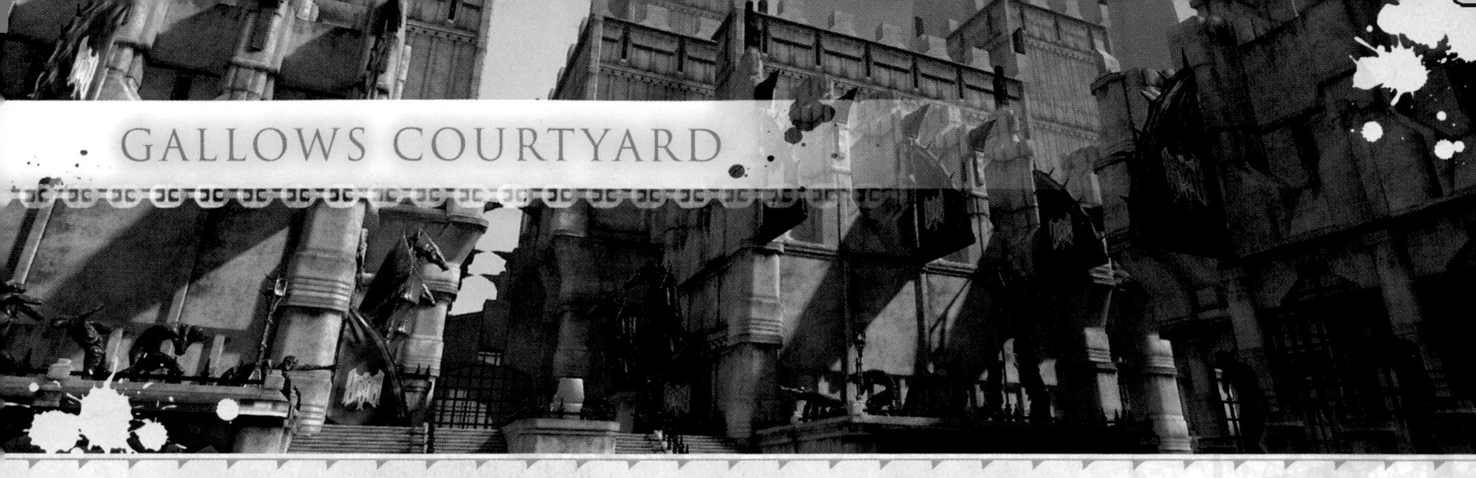

Gallows Courtyard

Legend: ◆ Act 1 ◆ Act 2 ◆ Act 3

DARKTOWN

LEGEND: Act 1 Act 2 Act 3

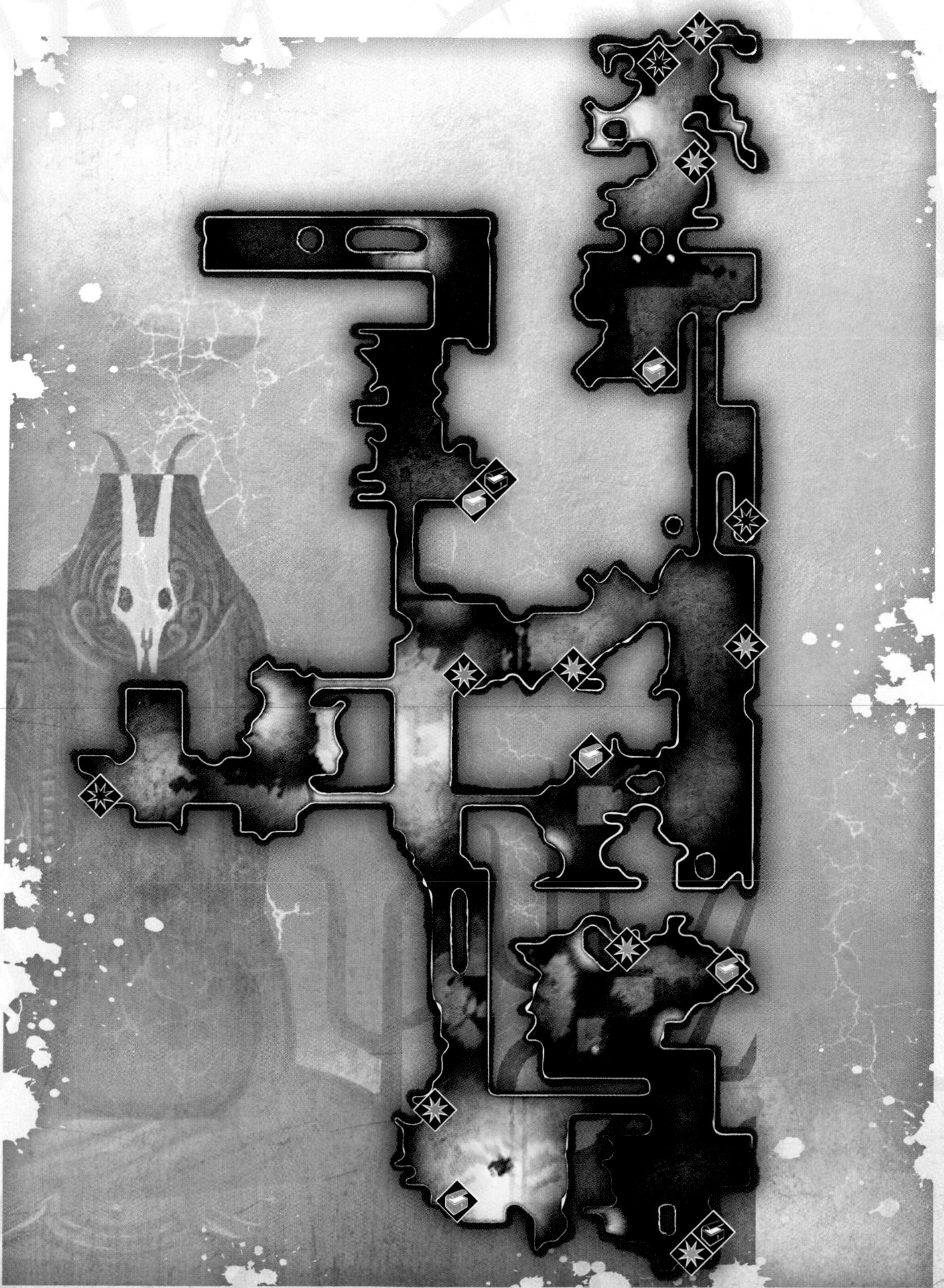

THE HANGED MAN (DAY)

Legend: ◆ Act 1 ◆ Act 2 ◆ Act 3

THE HANGED MAN (NIGHT)

Legend: ◆ Act 1 ◆ Act 2 ◆ Act 3

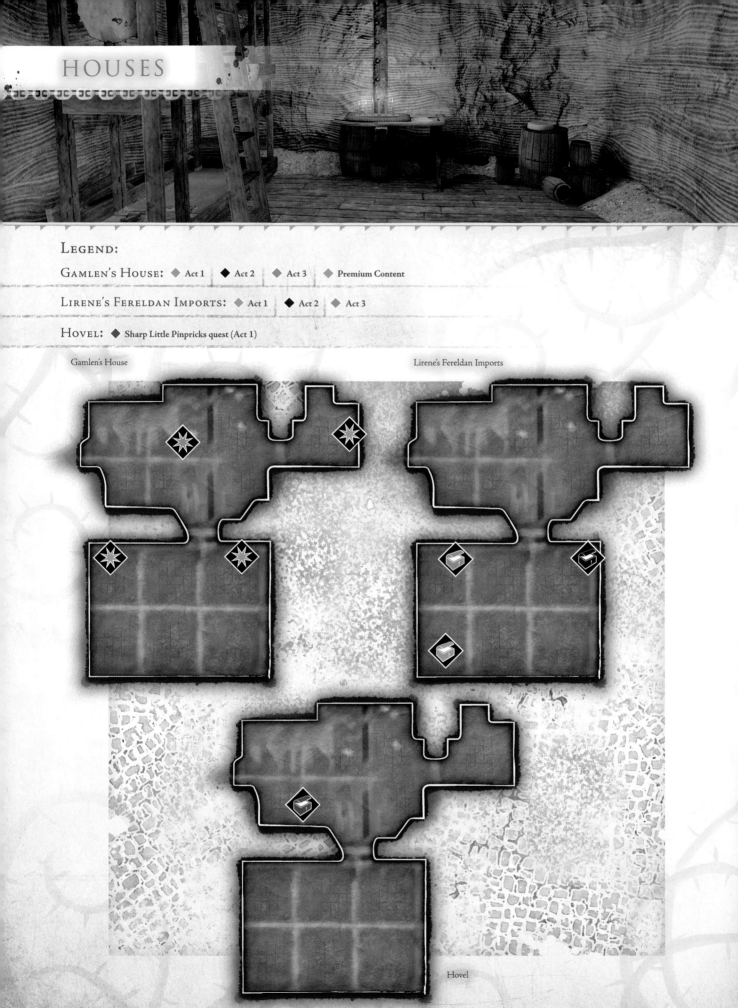

HOUSES

Legend:

Gamlen's House: ◆ Act 1 ◆ Act 2 ◆ Act 3 ◆ Premium Content

Lirene's Fereldan Imports: ◆ Act 1 ◆ Act 2 ◆ Act 3

Hovel: ◆ Sharp Little Pinpricks quest (Act 1)

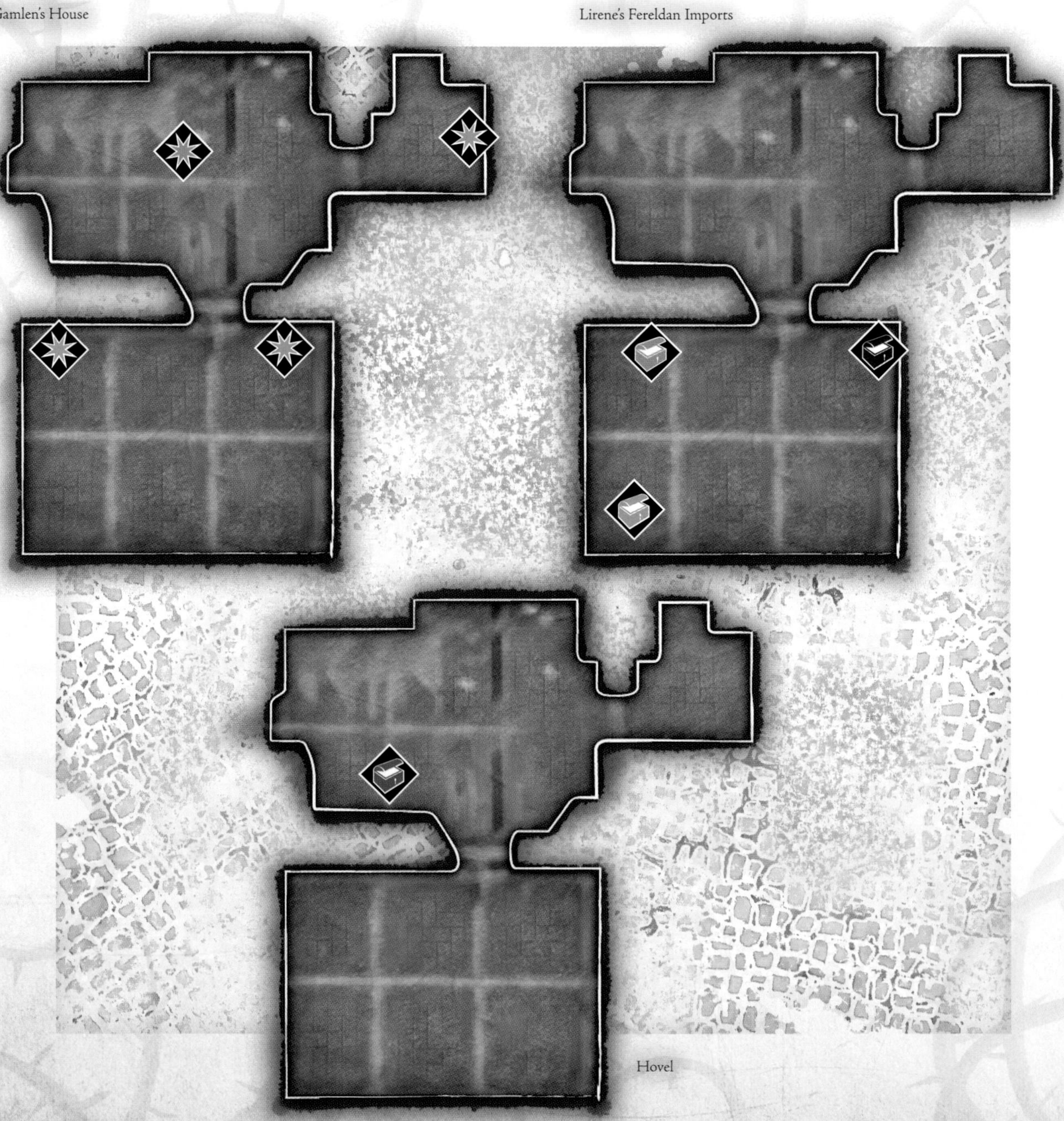

Gamlen's House

Lirene's Fereldan Imports

Hovel

THE BLOOMING ROSE

LEGEND: ◆ Act 1 ◆ Act 2 ◆ Act 3

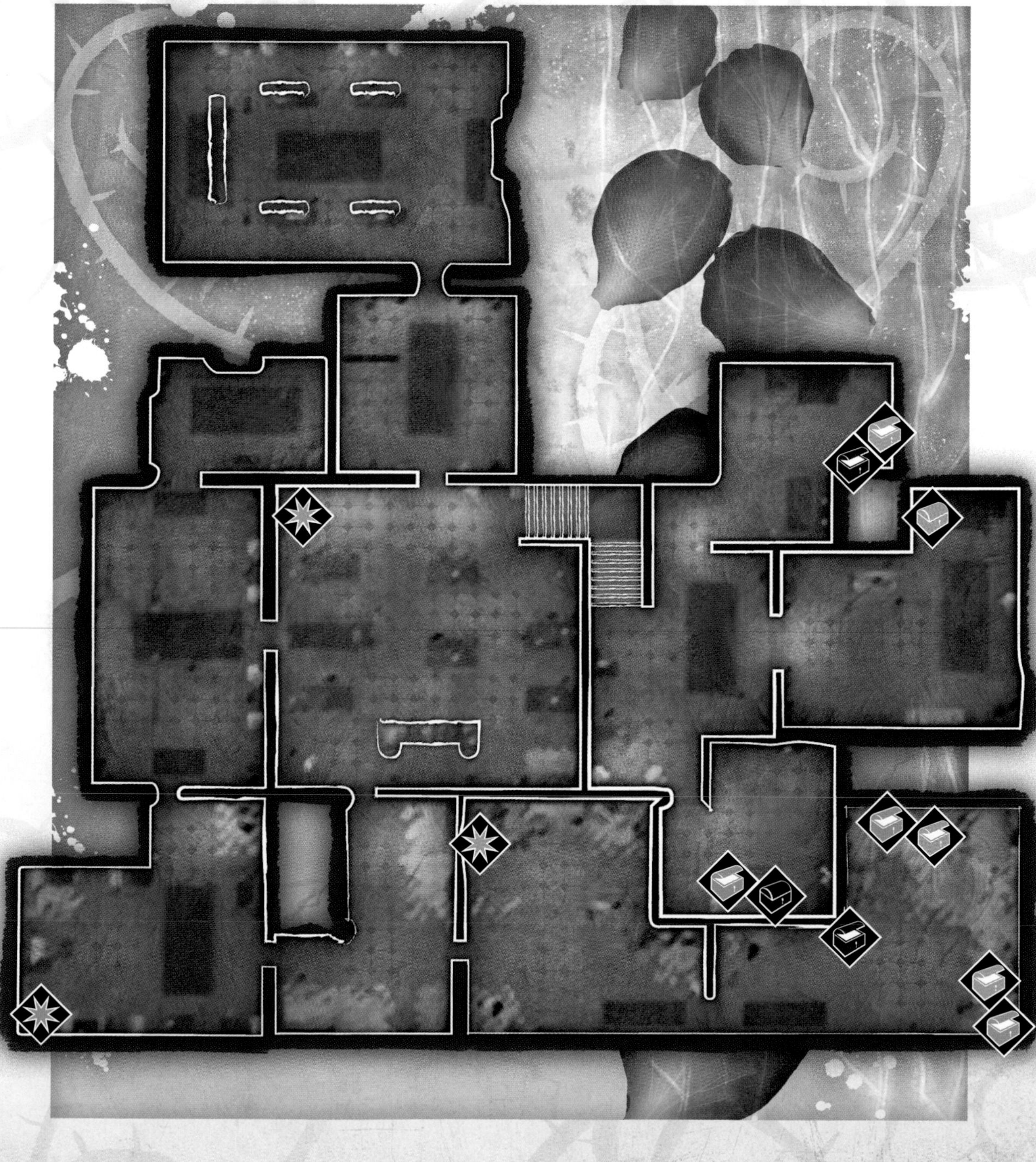

HAWKE ESTATE

Legend: ◆ Act 2 ◆ Act 3 ◆ Premium Content

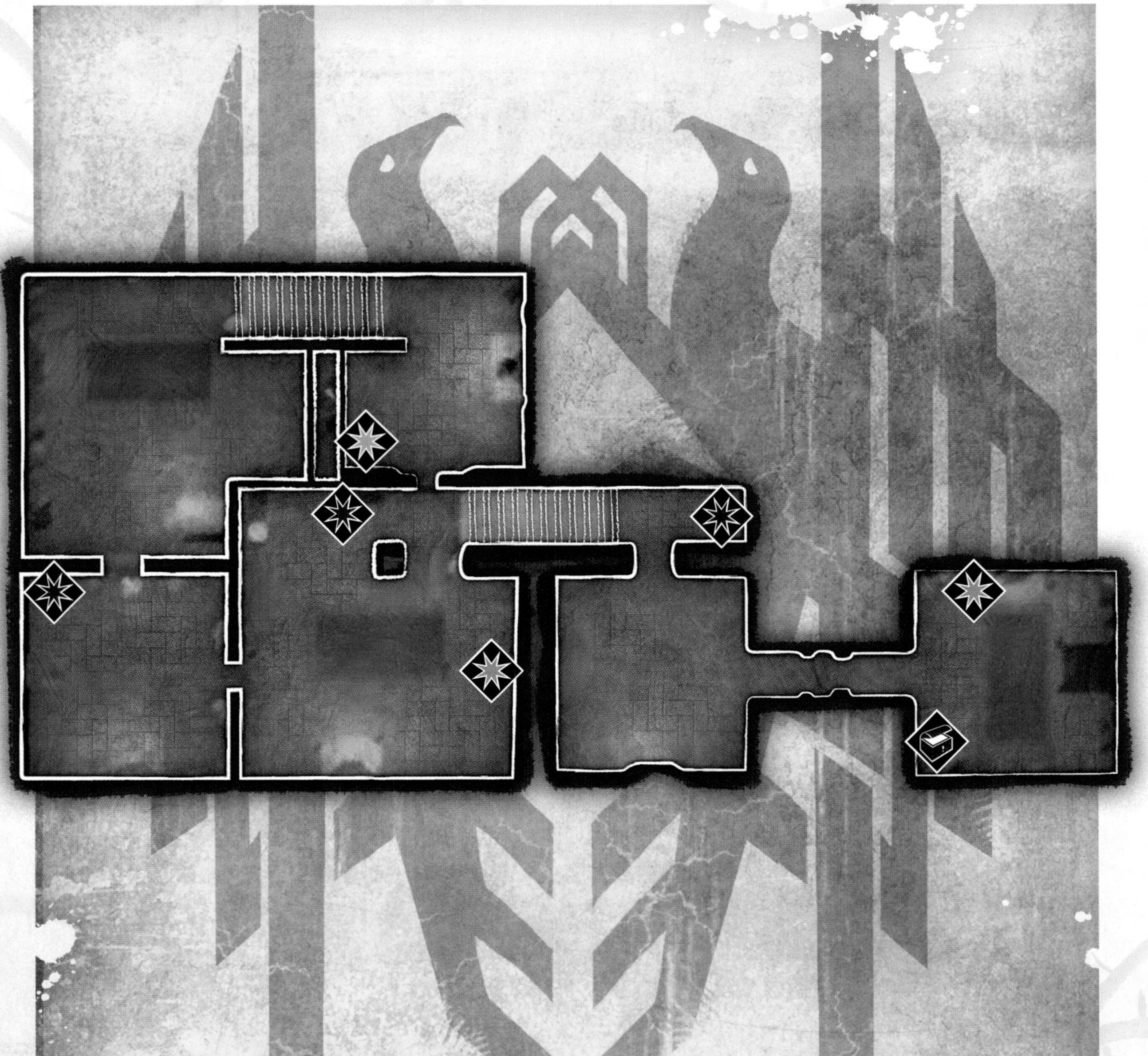

THE CHANTRY

Legend: Act 1 | Act 2 | Act 3 | Tranquility quest (Act 1)

VISCOUNT'S KEEP

LEGEND: ◆ Act 1 ◆ Act 2 ◆ Act 3 ◆ Demands of the Qun quest (Act 2)

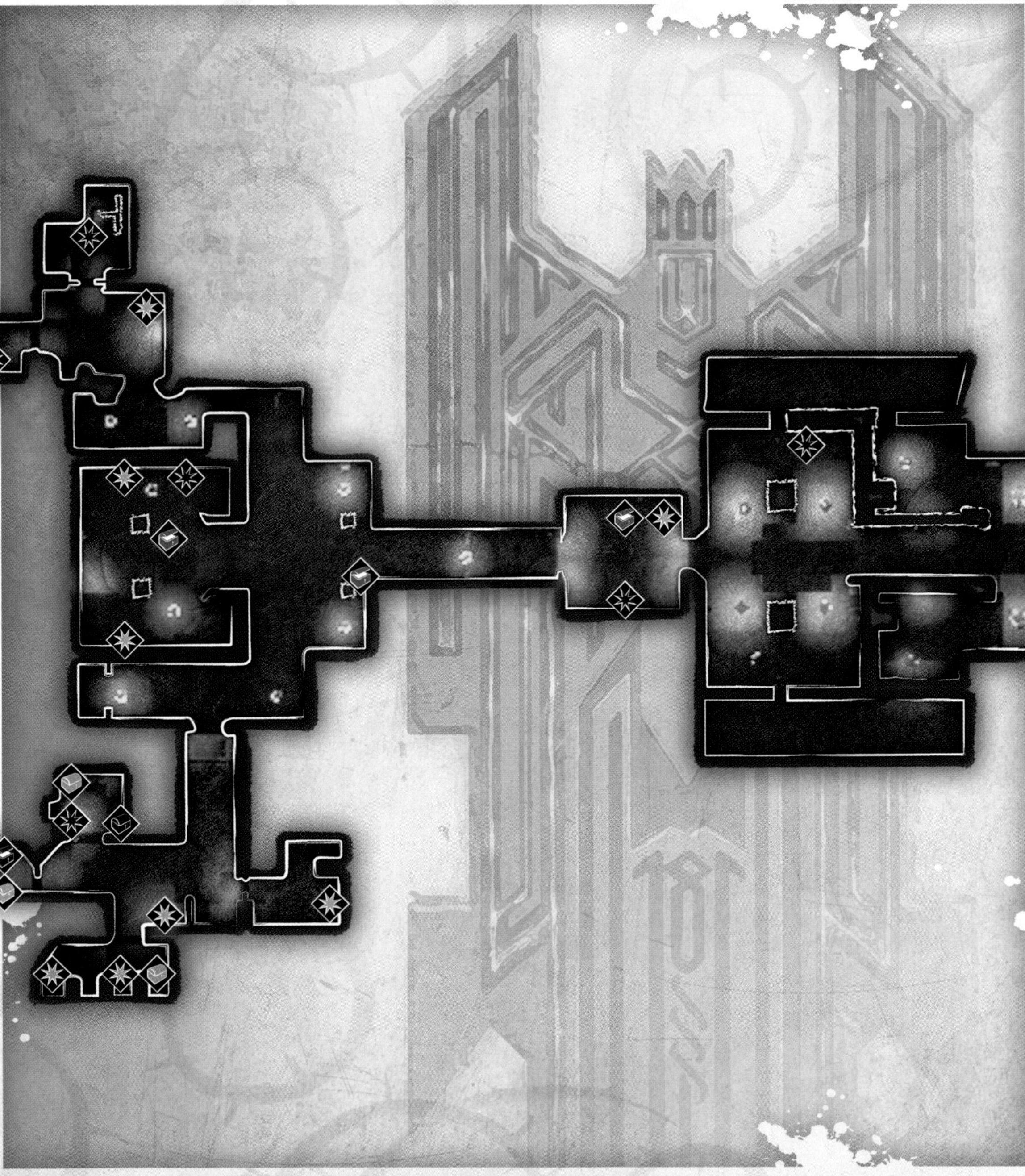

MERRILL'S HOME

LEGEND: ◆ Act 1 ◆ Act 2 ◆ Act 3

THE DEEP ROADS

PRIMEVAL RUINS

LEGEND: ◆ Act 1

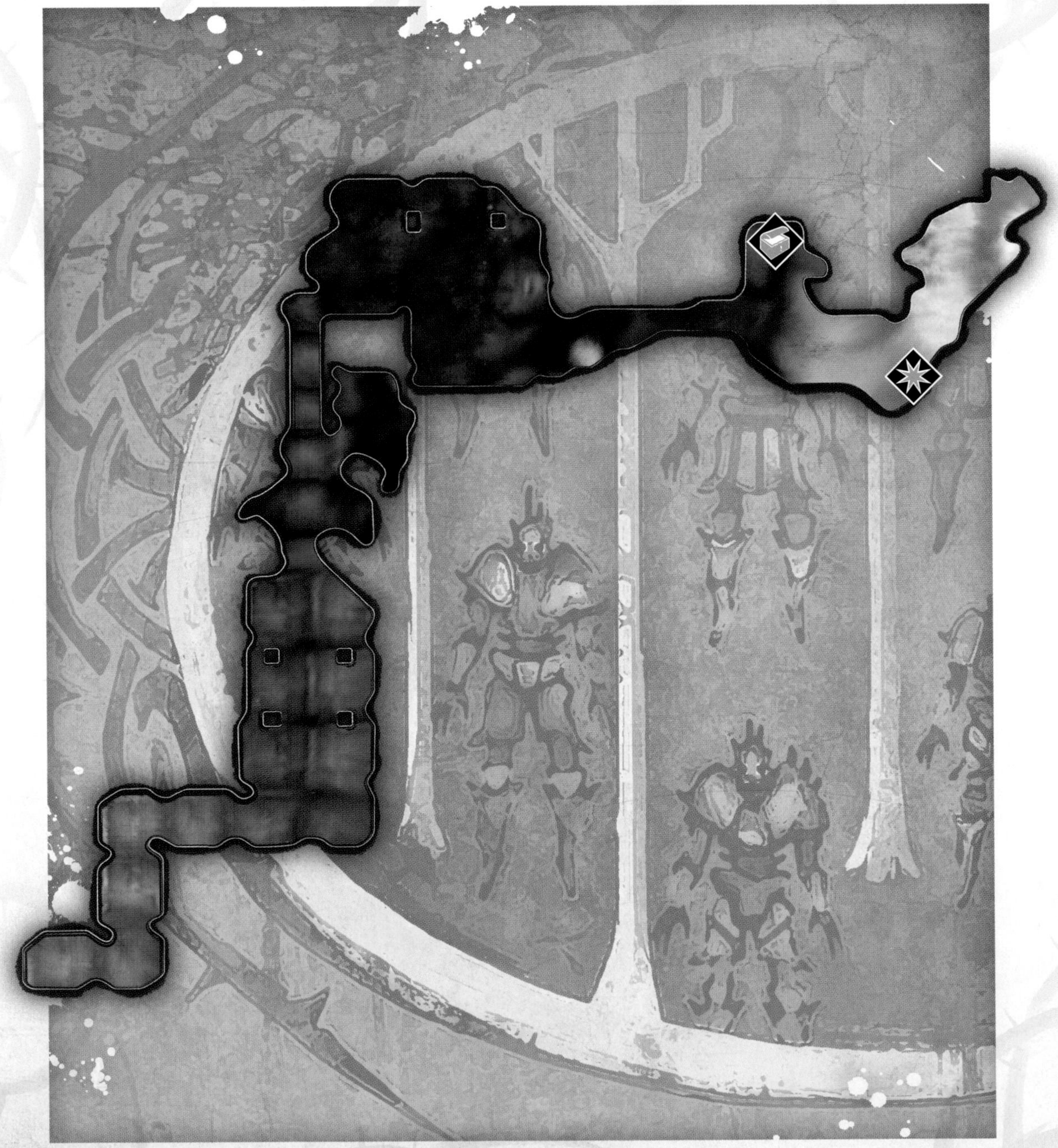

ANCIENT CRYPT

Legend: Act 1 Act 2 Act 3

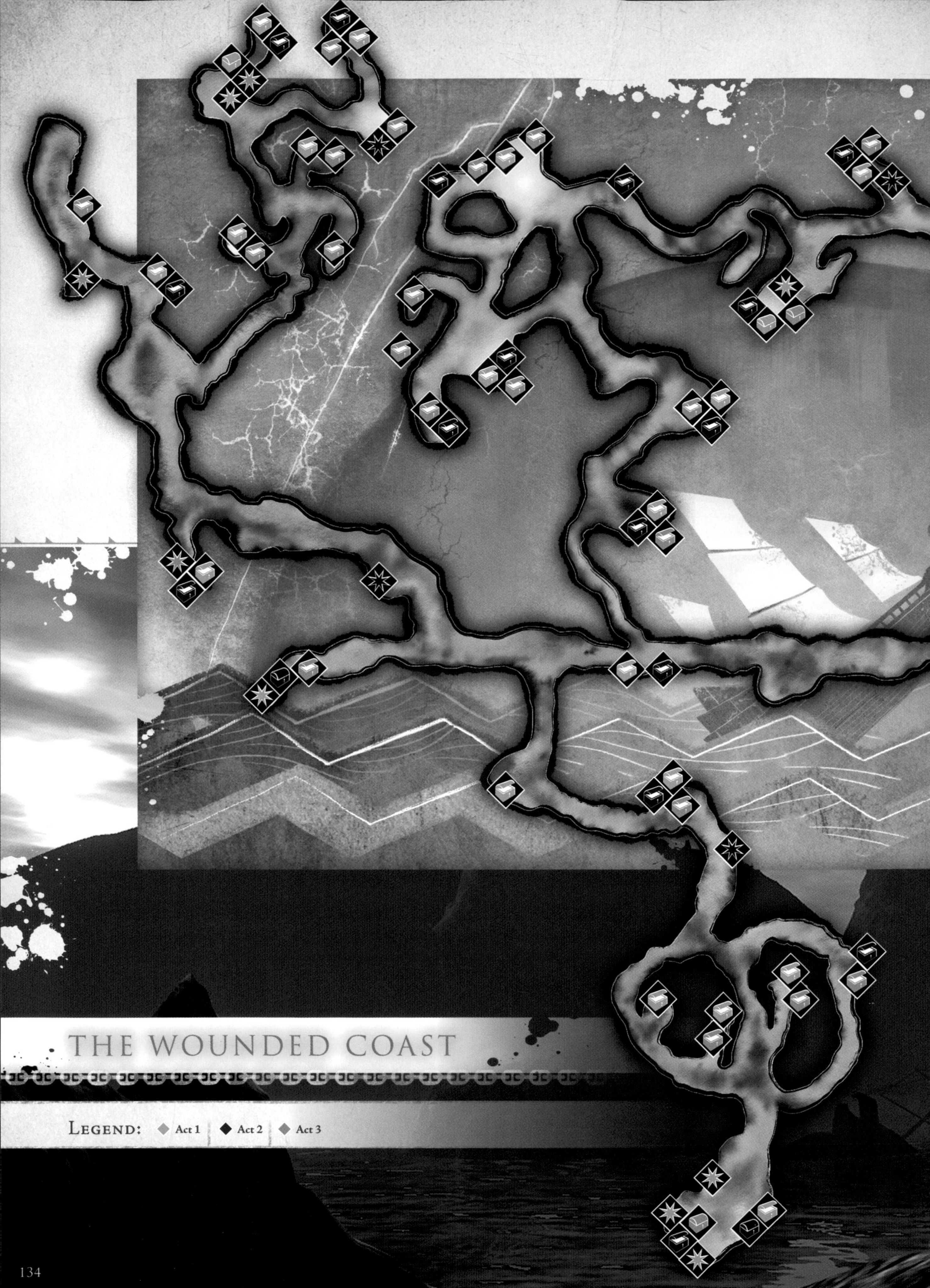
THE WOUNDED COAST
LEGEND: Act 1 Act 2 Act 3

SUNDERMOUNT CAVERNS

LEGEND: ◆ Act 1 ◆ Act 2 ◆ Act 3

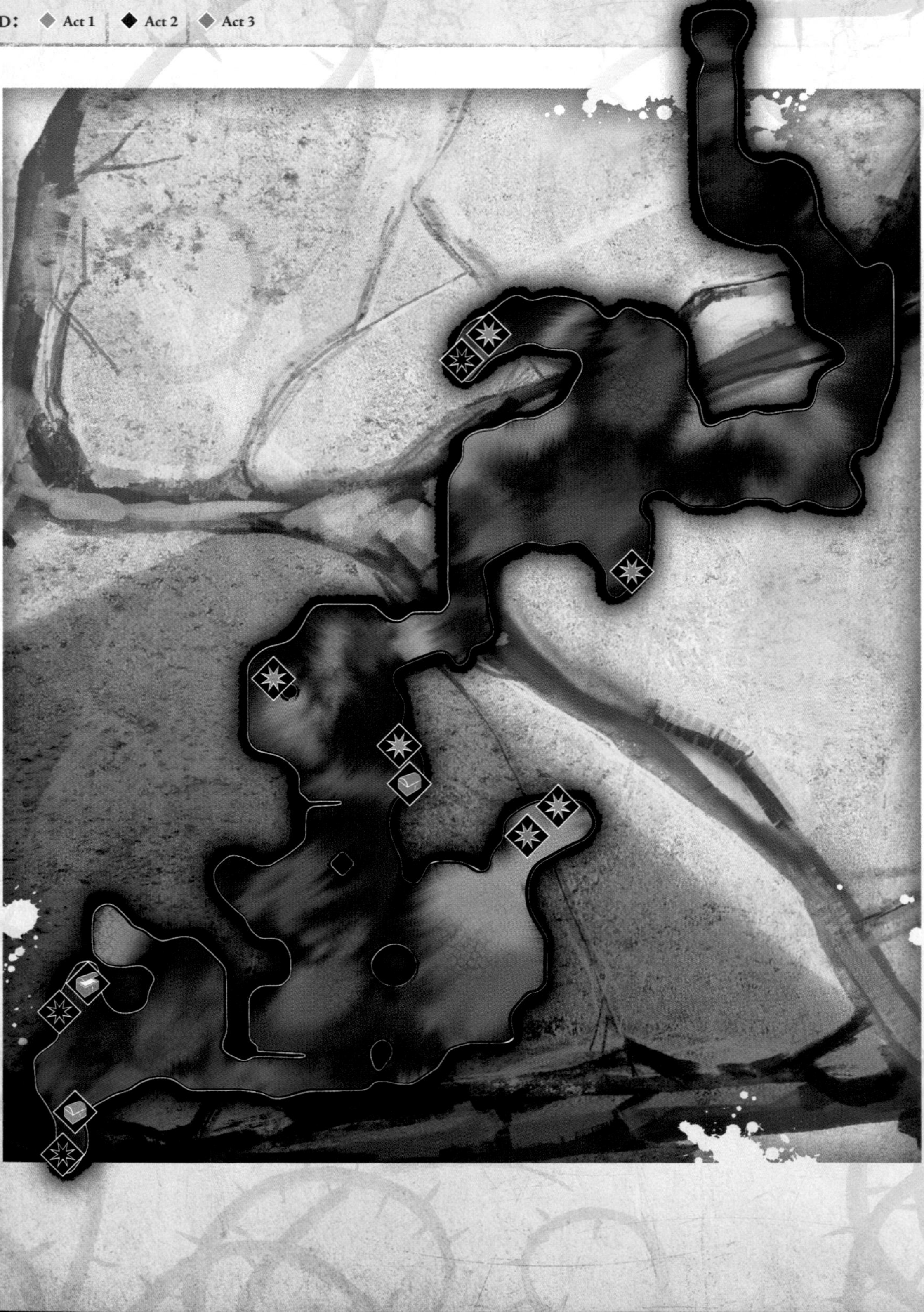

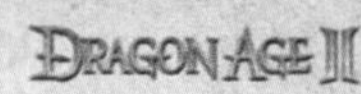

THE BONE PIT

Legend: ◆ The Bone Pit quest (Act 1) ◆ Cave Crawling quest (Act 2) ◆ Mine Massacre quest (Act 3)

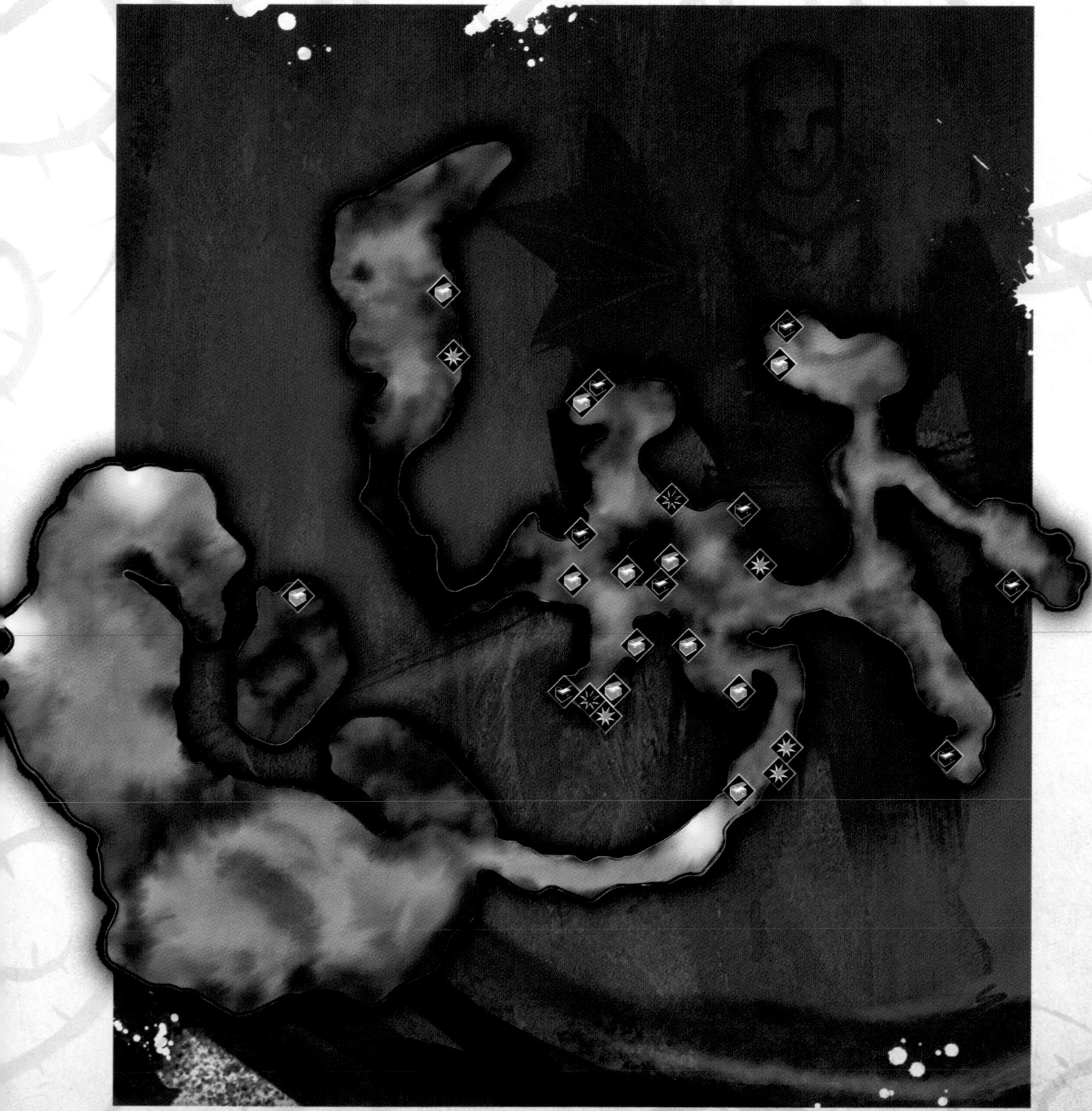

Legend:

Map	Quest
Bone Pit Mines	The Bone Pit (Act 1)
Smuggler's Cut	Blackpowder Courtesy (Act 2)
Gallows Dungeon	Dissent (Act 2)

CAVES & MINES (2)

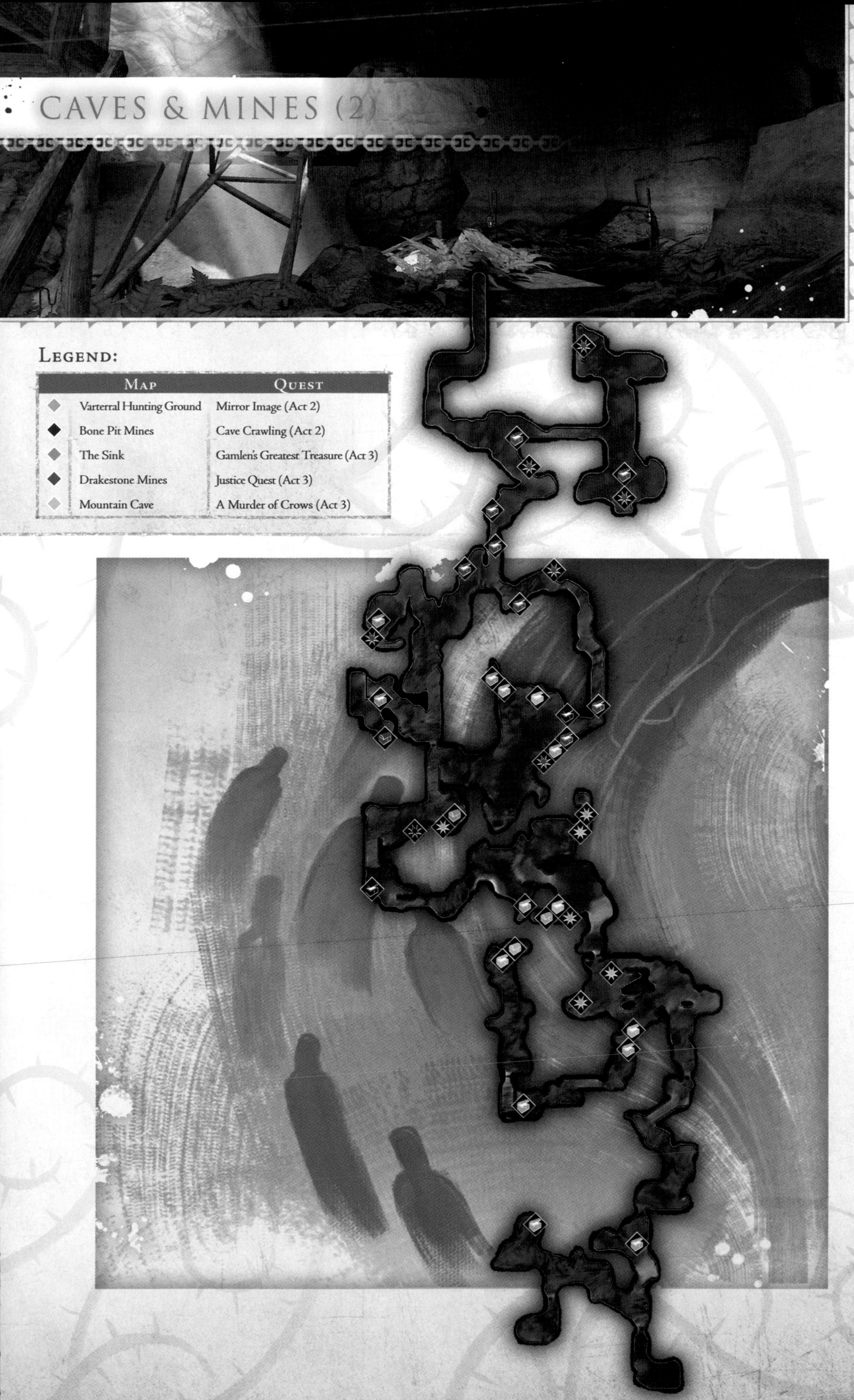

Legend:

Map	Quest
Varterral Hunting Ground	Mirror Image (Act 2)
Bone Pit Mines	Cave Crawling (Act 2)
The Sink	Gamlen's Greatest Treasure (Act 3)
Drakestone Mines	Justice Quest (Act 3)
Mountain Cave	A Murder of Crows (Act 3)

Legend:

	Map	Quest
◆	Ruined Passage	Magistrate's Orders (Act 1)
◆	Abandoned Thaig	Forbidden Knowledge (Act 2)
◆	Bone Pit Mines	Cavern of Dead (Act 2)
◆	Hidden Dungeon	Sundermount (Act 3)

SEWERS

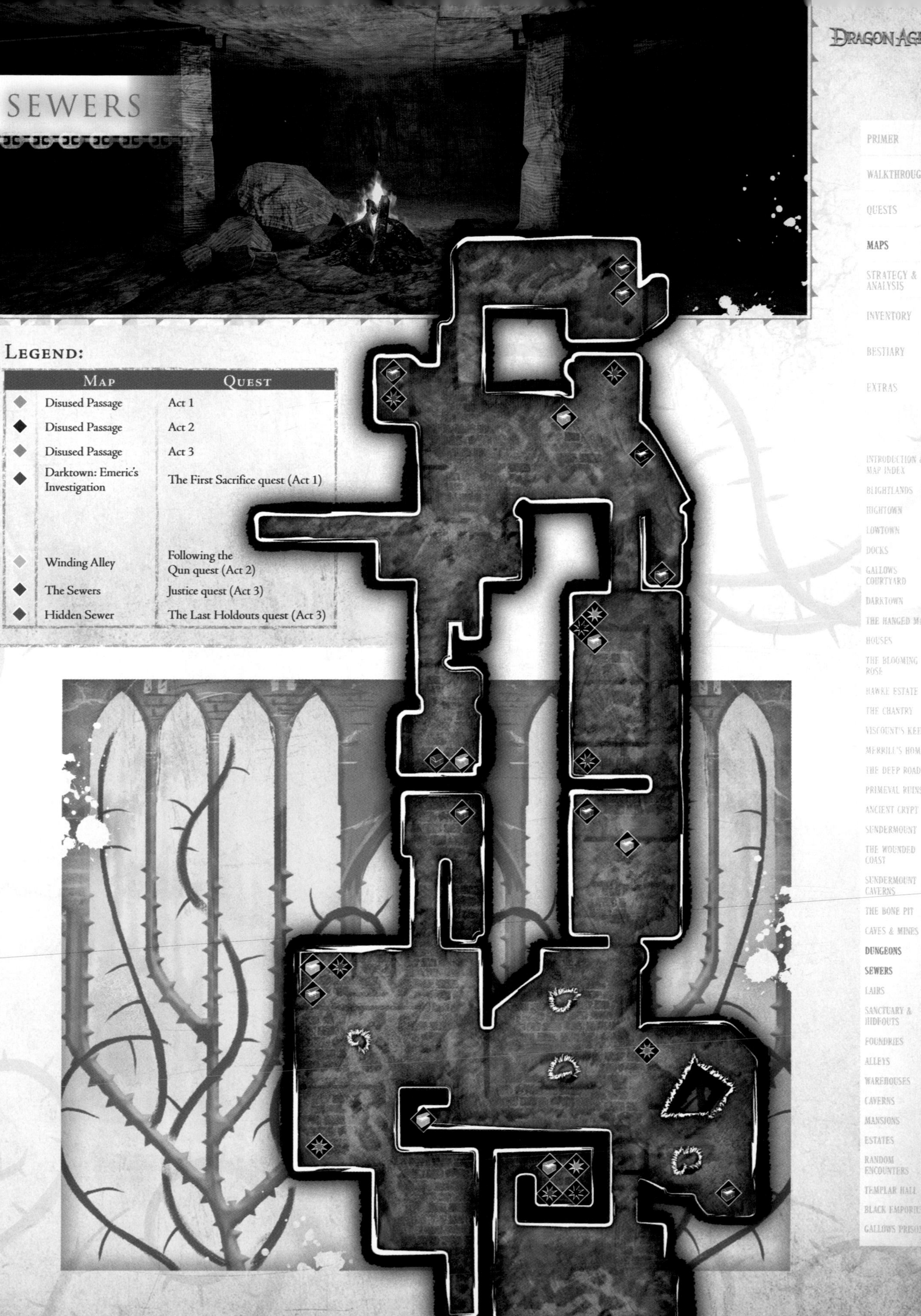

Legend:

Map	Quest
Disused Passage	Act 1
Disused Passage	Act 2
Disused Passage	Act 3
Darktown: Emeric's Investigation	The First Sacrifice quest (Act 1)
Winding Alley	Following the Qun quest (Act 2)
The Sewers	Justice quest (Act 3)
Hidden Sewer	The Last Holdouts quest (Act 3)

Legend:

	Map	Quest
◆ (grey)	Abandoned Slaver Den	A Bitter Pill (Act 2)
◆ (black)	The Forgotten Lair	Forbidden Knowledge (Act 2)

SANCTUARY & HIDEOUTS

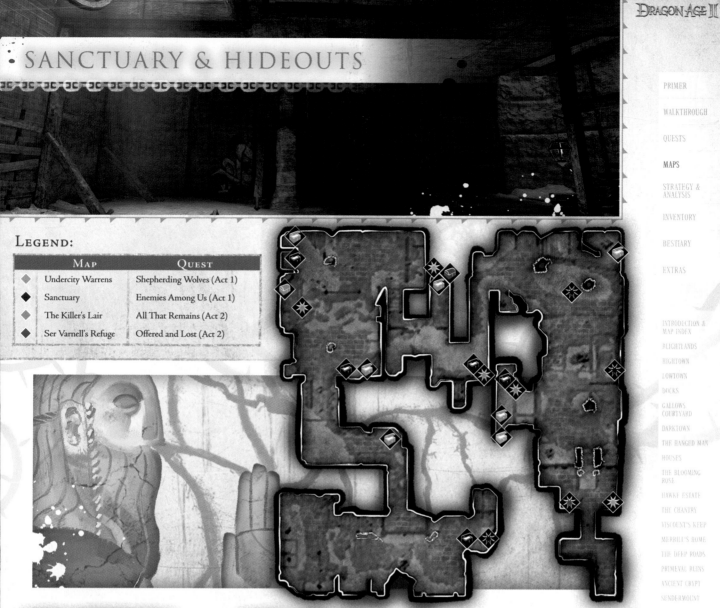

LEGEND:

Map	Quest
◆ Undercity Warrens	Shepherding Wolves (Act 1)
◆ Sanctuary	Enemies Among Us (Act 1)
◆ The Killer's Lair	All That Remains (Act 2)
◆ Ser Varnell's Refuge	Offered and Lost (Act 2)

LEGEND:

Map	Quest
◆ Brekker's Hideaway	Inside Job (Act 2)
◆ Sewer Passage	On the Loose (Act 3)
◆ Hidden Supply Depot	A Noble Agenda (Act 3)

FOUNDRIES

Legend:

	Map	Quest
◆ (grey)	Dark Foundry	The First Sacrifice (Act 1)
◆ (black)	Dark Foundry	All That Remains (Act 2)
◆ (grey)	Lost-End Foundry	To Catch a Thief (Act 2)

ALLEYS (1)

Legend:

	Map	Quest
◆ (grey)	Side Alley	Blackpowder Courtesy (Act 2)
◆ (black)	Blind Alley	Prime Suspect (Act 2)

ALLEYS (2)

Legend:

Map	Quest
◆ Run Down Alley	The Lowdown (Act 2)
◆ Decrepit Alley	Hometown Breed (Act 2)
◆ Run Down Alley	Reining It In (Act 3)
◆ Decrepit Alley	Kind of Want (Act 3)

WAREHOUSES

Legend:

Map	Quest
Arthuris's Private Dock	An Errant Letter (Act 1)
Woodrow's Warehouse	Finders Keepers (Act 1)
Warehouse	Pier Pressure (Act 1)
Smetty's Fish Guttery	Gamlen's Greatest Treasure (Act 3)
Secret Meeting Place	Best Served Cold (Act 3)
Castillon's Landing	No Rest for the Wicked (Act 3)

CAVERNS (1)

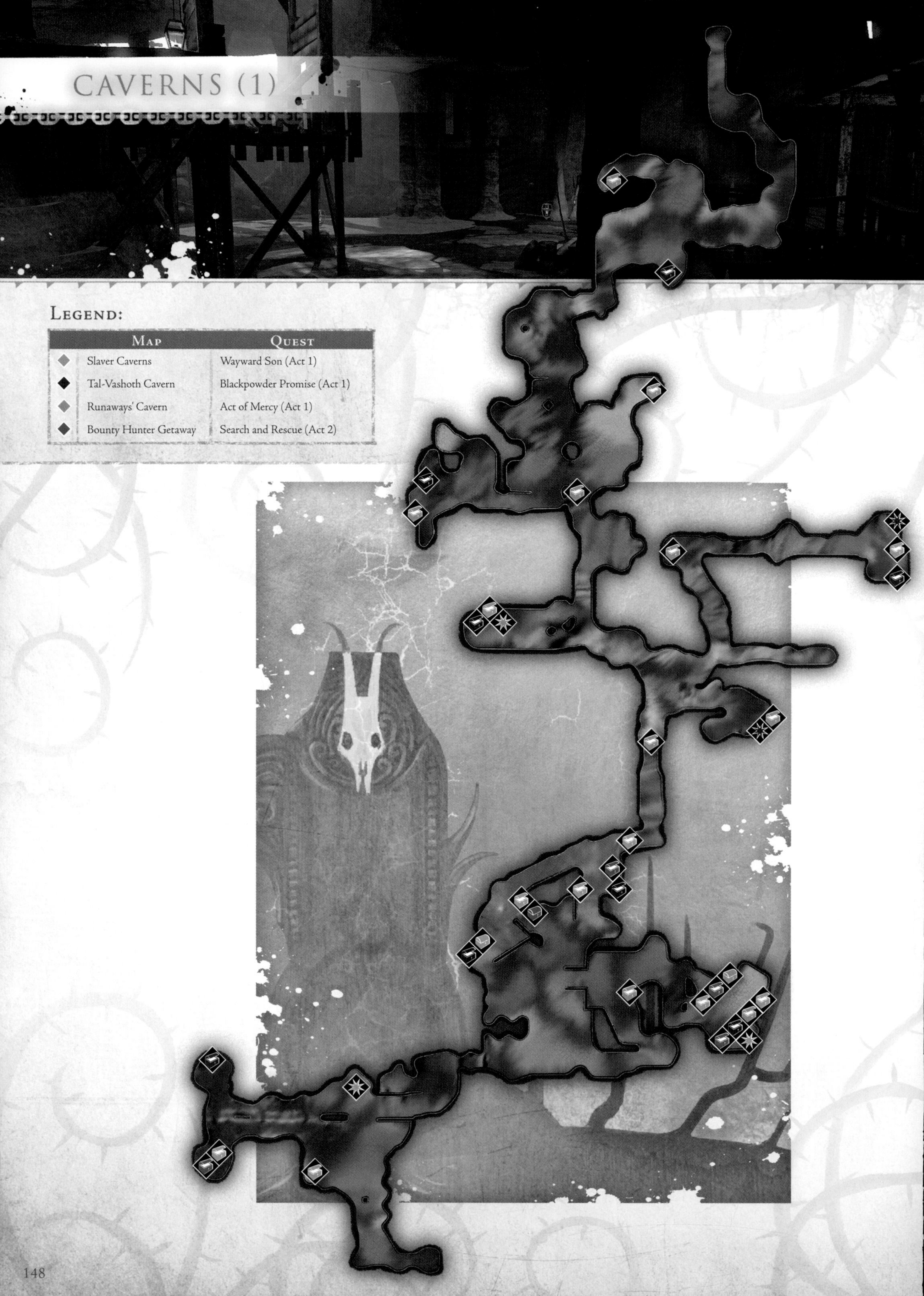

Legend:

	Map	Quest
◆	Slaver Caverns	Wayward Son (Act 1)
◆	Tal-Vashoth Cavern	Blackpowder Promise (Act 1)
◆	Runaways' Cavern	Act of Mercy (Act 1)
◆	Bounty Hunter Getaway	Search and Rescue (Act 2)

CAVERNS (2)

LEGEND:

	Map	Quest
◆	Dank Cave	Forbidden Knowledge (Act 2)
◆	Cave	Forbidden Knowledge (Act 2)
◆	Pride's End	A New Path (Act 3)
◆	Blood Mage Refuge	The Last Holdouts (Act 3)

Legend:

Map	Quest
Shallowguard Base	Night Lies (Act 1)
Bartrand's Estate	Family Matter (Act 2)
Suspicious House	Red Run Streets (Act 3)
De Launcet Mansion	On The Loose (Act 3)
Bartrand's Estate	Haunted (Act 3)

MANSIONS (2)

Legend:

	Map	Quest
◆ (grey)	Danarius's Manor	Bait and Switch (Act 1)
◆ (black)	Fenris's Mansion	Act 1
◆ (grey)	Fenris's Mansion	Act 2
◆ (black)	Fenris's Mansion	Act 3

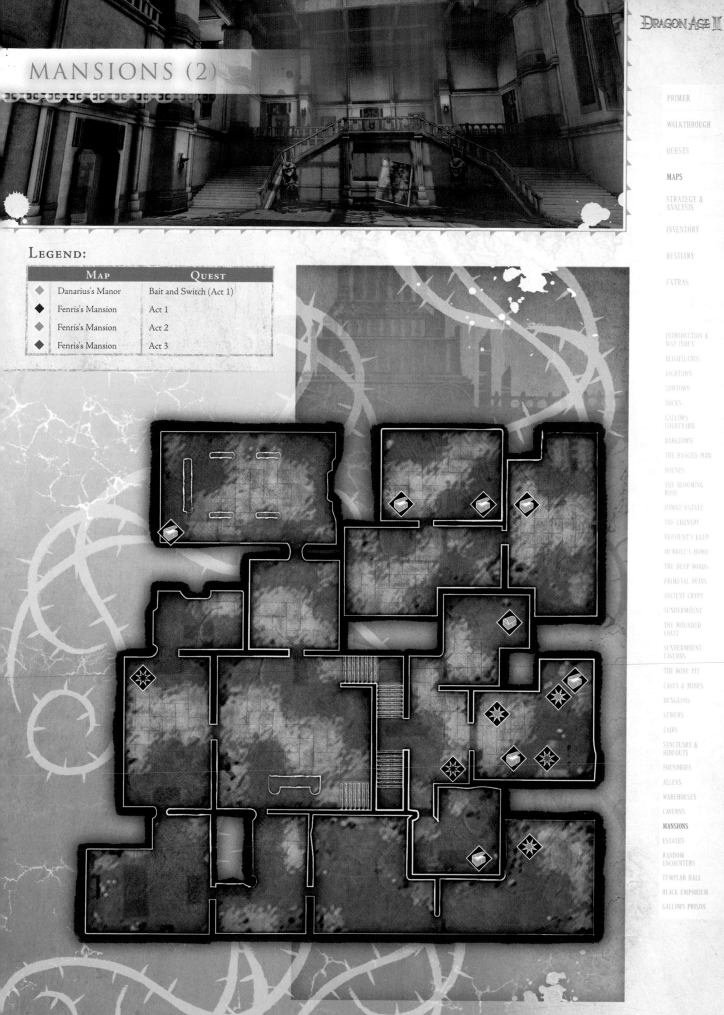

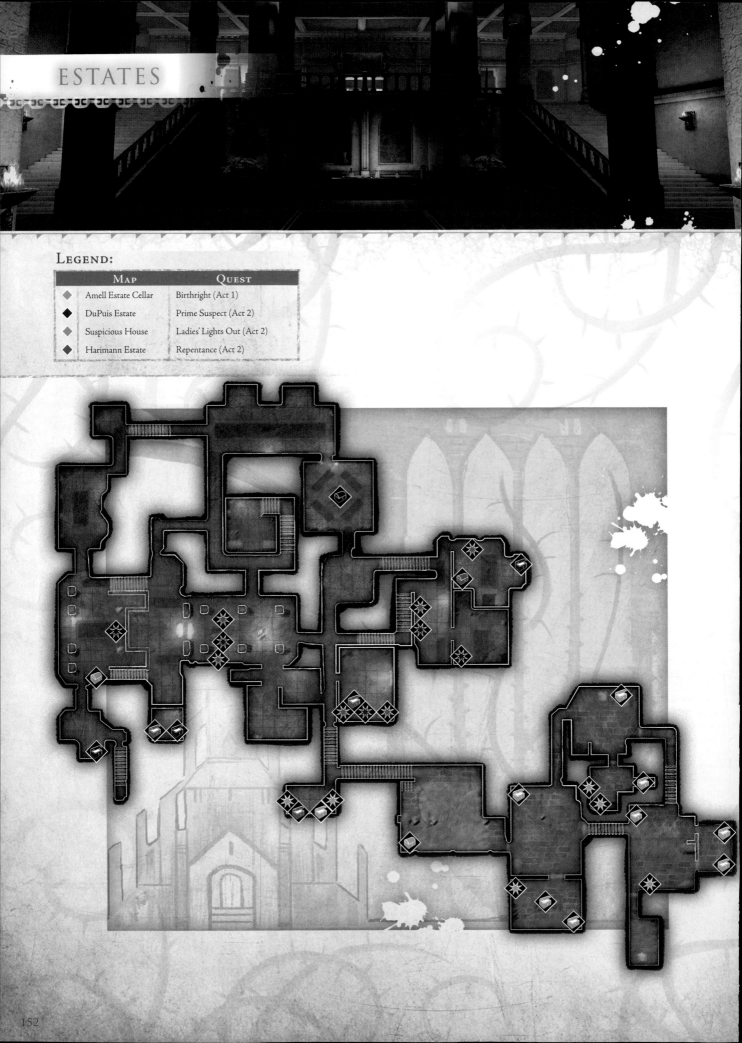

Legend:

	Map	Quest
◆	Amell Estate Cellar	Birthright (Act 1)
◆	DuPuis Estate	Prime Suspect (Act 2)
◆	Suspicious House	Ladies' Lights Out (Act 2)
◆	Harimann Estate	Repentance (Act 2)

Random Encounters (1)

Legend:

	Map	Quest
◆	Abandoned Ruins	Magistrate's Orders (Act 1)
◆	Vimmark Mountain Pass	Shepherding Wolves (Act 1)
◆	Ironwood Clearing	Herbalist's Tasks (Act 1)
◆	Outside Smuggler's Cut	Blackpowder Courtesy (Act 2)
◆	Outside Kirkwall	Inside Job (Act 2)

RANDOM ENCOUNTERS (2)

LEGEND:

	Map	Quest
◆	Sundermount Ambush Site	The Way It Should Be (Act 1)
◆	Wounded Coast Approach	Act of Mercy (Act 1)
◆	Antivan Camp	A Murder of Crows (Act 3)

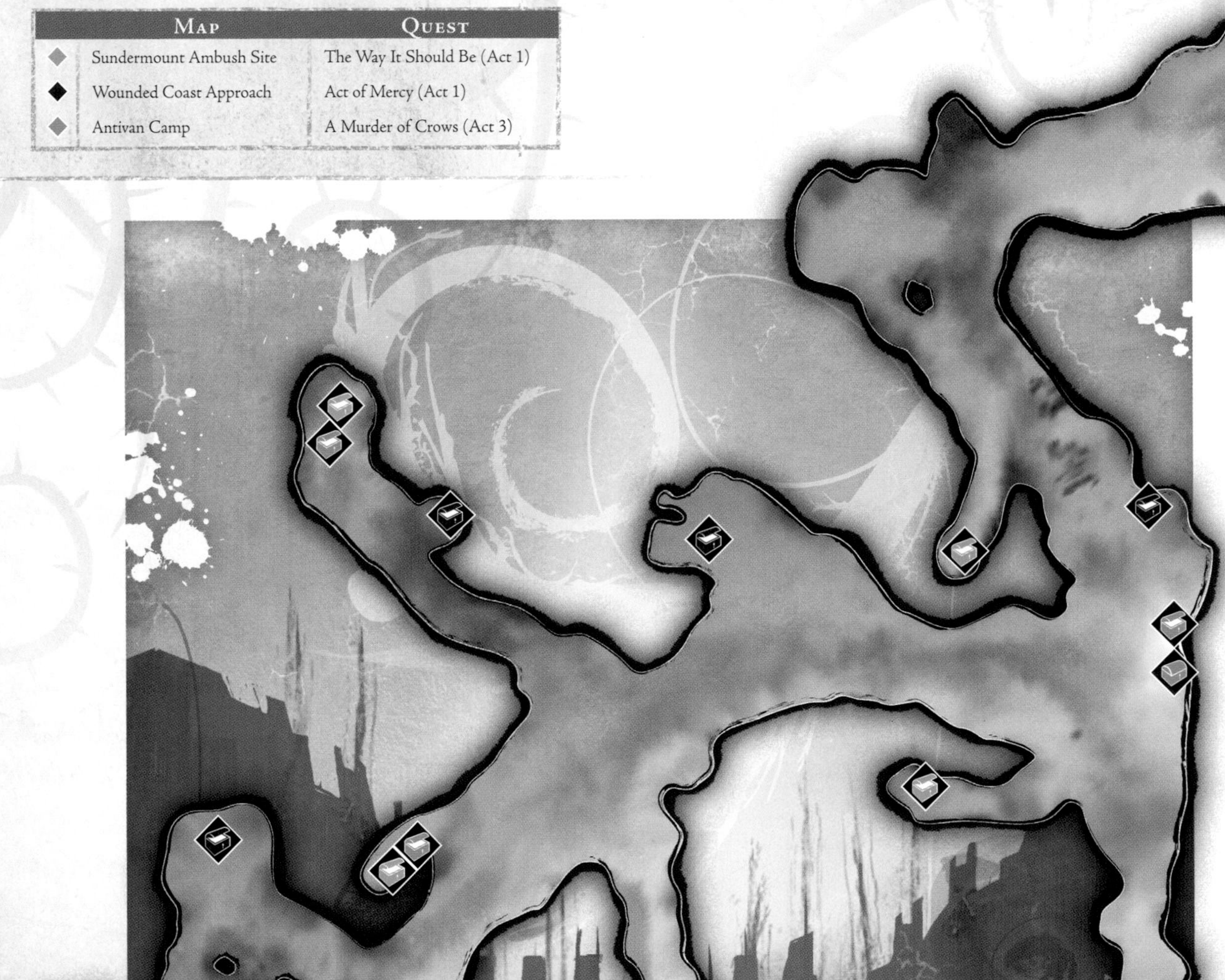

RANDOM ENCOUNTERS (3)

Legend:

	Map	Quest
◆	Wilmod's Camp	Enemies Among Us (Act 1)
◆	Dead Man's Pass	Blackpowder Promise (Act 1)
◆	Holding Caves	A Bitter Pill (Act 2)

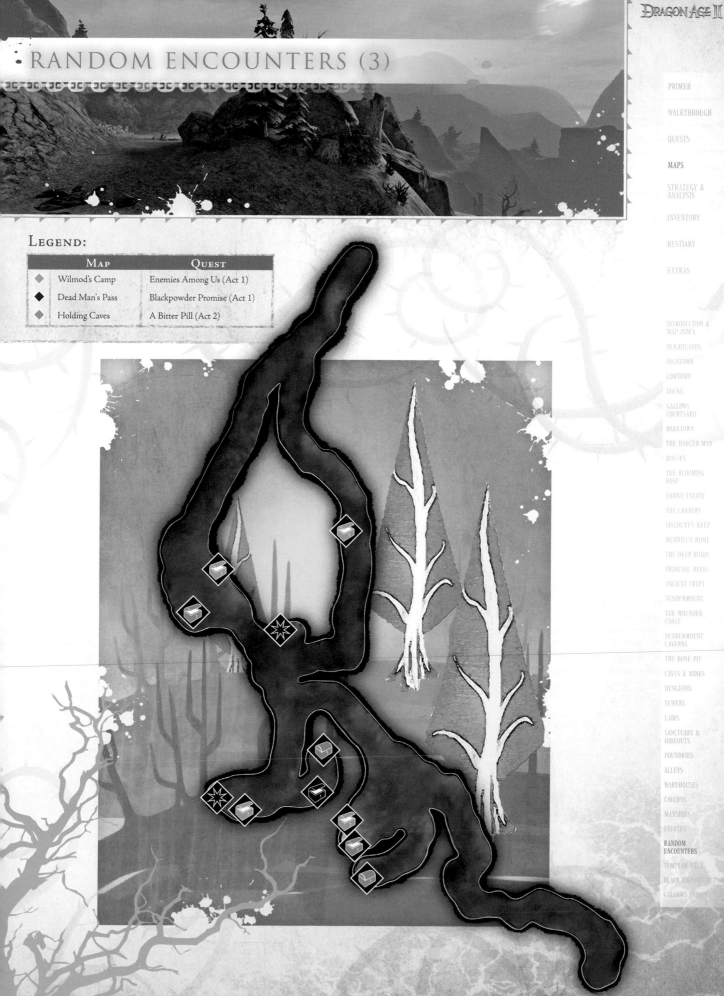

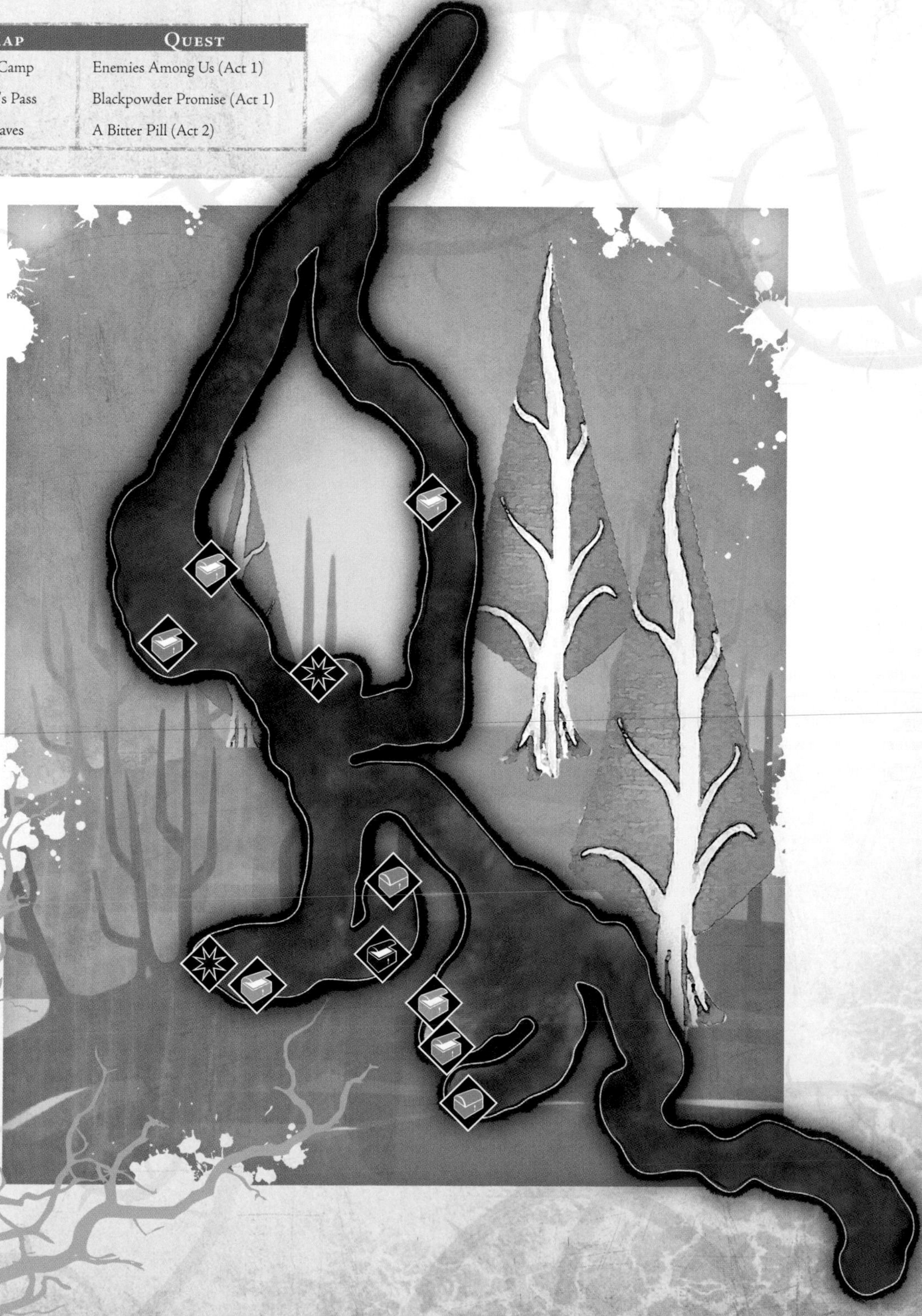

TEMPLAR HALL

Legend: ◆ Fade, Night Terrors quest (Act 2) | ◆ Act 3 | ◆ The Last Straw quest (Act 3)

THE BLACK EMPORIUM

GALLOWS PRISON

STRATEGY & ANALYSIS

Offering an advanced overview of Dragon Age II's most important gameplay systems, this chapter provides essential reading material for those who wish to build a commanding party, negotiate dialogue sequences in an optimal way and dismiss challenging adversaries with calculated ease.

IMPORTANT NOTE: While most of this chapter contains gameplay spoilers, the final Companion Analysis section features story spoilers of the most *abysmal* variety. We implore you to leave it well alone until you have completed your first playthrough.

THE DIALOGUE SYSTEM

Hawke's performance in conversations is almost as important as his or her prowess in battle. In this section, we look at what each conversational option entails and how you can shape Hawke's personality. You can find advice on key quest conversations (and the branching story paths that you can negotiate) throughout the mighty Quests chapter.

Dialogue Options

Icon	Description	Notes
	Diplomatic	Core dialogue choice for the Diplomatic personality type. Very rarely causes offense, likely to engender friendship increases.
	Helpful	Part of the Diplomatic personality type. Generally appears when Hawke is poised to volunteer his services to help someone or if sympathy or understanding is called for.
	Humorous	Core dialogue choice for the Humorous personality type. Rarely causes offense, tends to be a fairly "neutral" option where companions are concerned, though Isabela and Varric sometimes respond favorably.
	Charming	Secondary dialogue choice for the Humorous personality type.
	Aggressive	Core dialogue choice for the Aggressive personality type. Most likely to cause rivalry increases with companions.
	Direct	Secondary dialogue choice for the Aggressive personality type.
	Combat	Used to initiate combat immediately. The actual result (and effect on companion rivalry and friendship) depends on the context. Cutting short a conversation with a demon or brutal slavers to attack without compunction could be viewed favorably by those present; executing a misguided yet hapless pawn in a larger scheme might invite ire.
	Call on companion	Invites the specified companion to intervene in a conversation. These often lead to a unique (and, usually, non-violent or profitable) solution to a given situation. May also lead to a friendship increase.
	Flirt	Engage with a companion in an amorous or suggestive manner. Flirting is the only way to instigate a potential romance.
	End romance	Used to reject a romantic proposition from a companion or end an existing romance. Will often lead to a rivalry increase.
✓	Yes	Accept a proposal or offer as put forward by another character. Usually leads to new quests.
✗	No	Reject a proposal or offer as put forward by another character. Be very wary when rejecting potential quest opportunities: you may not get another chance.
	Choice	Appears when Hawke can choose from multiple responses that all address the situation in different ways. May lead to rivalry or friendship, your guide should be your knowledge of the person in question.
★	Special Choice	This rare dialogue option represents a "unique" choice that may lead to a special outcome. These appear in accordance with Hawke's personality, with Diplomatic, Humorous and Aggressive types all having their own opportunities appear at set points in the story.
	Pay/Extort	Used to pay or bribe people or to enquire about a possible quest's rewards. May also be used to press for further payment at the conclusion of a quest or even blackmail or extortion in certain instances.
	Lie	Attempt to lie in order to extricate Hawke from a difficult situation. A rare option, this may not always lead to the desired result.
?	Investigate	Choose this option to open a sub-menu where you can ask questions to learn more about a given topic. These may in turn offer further queries and even unlock otherwise unavailable dialogue options in other conversations.

HAWKE'S PERSONALITY

Though it may not be apparent at first, Hawke can exhibit one of three personalities based on the dialogue choices that you favor.

- **Diplomatic/Helpful:** Light blue or green highlight
- **Humorous/Charming:** Purple highlight
- **Aggressive/Direct:** Red highlight

The first dialogue choice you make sets Hawke's personality. If your first pick is a Diplomatic option, for example, Hawke's voice will adopt the Diplomatic tone in the next dialogue line that follows. As you keep choosing similar options at the dialogue wheel, they "stack". If you were to decide to change your personality later on, it would take more than twice the amount of (either Humorous or Aggressive) dialog lines to activate that version of Hawke's voice. The idea behind this system is to ensure a consistency in Hawke's delivery throughout each Act. After a certain number of specific dialogue choices, Hawke's personality is effectively crystallized.

At the start of each Act, Hawke retains his or her established personality, but the "stack" of previous personality choices is reduced. This gives you a window of opportunity to change your dominant tone.

FRIENDSHIP & RIVALRY

Hawke's relationship with his companions is measured on a 200-point scale that ranges from rivalry to friendship. You can study a visual representation of his current standing with his cohorts in the active party at the Character menu screen (Fig. 1).

01

- No matter if you are speaking to them directly or addressing a third party, companions will react to your conversational options in accordance with their own unique personality.
- We offer advice on major relationship shifts throughout the Quests chapter in the Companion Guidance sections that fall at the end of each quest fact sheet. Using these, you should find it easy to engineer a full friendship or rivalry.
- Completing companion quests and increasing the relationship gauge to the 50% and 100% thresholds in either direction will unlock special mid-stage and final-stage companion conversations that serve to advance and formalize Hawke's relationship with his associates.
- Another way to further a relationship is to find and deliver "gifts", a small selection of items that will usually increase friendship. We reveal the locations of these items in the Quests and Inventory chapters.
- Developing the relationship gauge to +100 in either direction will "freeze" it in perpetuity and (Bethany and Carver excepted) unlock a special ability on a talent tree unique to friendship or rivalry with the relevant companion. At this stage, further relationship adjustments are disabled: short of dismissal, betrayal or late-game plot developments, that companion will be completely dedicated to working with Hawke (as a friend or rival).
- Don't assume that developing a rivalry will lead a companion to desert Hawke. In fact, this side of the relationship spectrum can be just as powerful as an established friendship if you take it to its conclusion. In essence, a healthy rivalry means that an ally may not agree with your methods, but they respect your ability to shape the world around you – even though the way in which goals are achieved might not correspond with their individual ideologies.

ROMANCES

If you wish to initiate a romance with a companion, follow these simple guidelines:

- Flirt with the object of your affections whenever possible. However, note that the presence of a Flirt option isn't always a true indication that a romance is possible.
- In Act 2, try to ensure that your visits to Hawke's abode occur at night. If your desired squeeze is present on arrival, use the Flirt option to initiate the next stage. When the option arises in conversation, enquire about living together.
- After the romance begins, **do not** make come-hither eyes at other companions or NPCs: this will not end well. Nor, for that matter, will any degree of ambivalence or outright rejection.
- For the rest of the story, develop the relationship gauge to maximum friendship or rivalry, complete all companion quests (including any ambient situational conversations that may occur), deliver the necessary gifts, then share a moment with Hawke's loved one in the calm before the storm during Dragon Age II's epic conclusion (you'll know it when you get there).
- For Isabela and Sebastian, the above technique only partially applies. The Companion Analysis section at the conclusion of this chapter contains a complete guide to wooing both (though Sebastian only ever offers a chaste relationship) but is surrounded by heavy spoilers if you are still on your first playthrough.

ATTRIBUTES

MAIN ATTRIBUTES

Building an effective character requires a little extra insight into the game's workings, applying to both Hawke and the companion characters. The one thing to remember when leveling up is that your character can't do everything. Many abilities only come into their own at an advanced stage, earning their chance to cross-class combo when upgraded for example (see page 174), so specialization is the key to success. You will not be able to take every ability open to your characters – or even half the abilities – so having a specific goal in mind helps to create a much stronger party. Use the table below for a detailed appraisal of each main attribute.

Attribute Descriptions

Strength	The primary attribute for warriors, high Strength makes physical attacks more likely to connect and increases the damage inflicted. Every attribute point invested in Strength also gives a point in Fortitude, building resistance against the effects of knockdown from a powerful blow or elemental effects like being set aflame.
Dexterity	Rogues rely on Dexterity to attack successfully and cause damage with their standard blows. Higher Dexterity also benefits all classes by increasing the chance of scoring a critical hit.
Magic	This attribute determines the attack and damage of a mage when wielding a staff in combat, as well as the potency of their spells. Attribute points placed here also increase magic resistance, though the increase per point is so small that it is unwise for other classes to waste them here.
Cunning	Cunning increases defense for all classes, so it makes sense to spend attribute points in this attribute for ALL characters. This attribute also governs critical damage, raising the effectiveness of critical hits.
Willpower	This determines the size of a mage's mana pool and the stamina reserve of a warrior or rogue. Higher willpower grants more ability use or spellcasting before the character is exhausted and reduced to trading basic attacks. As a minimum requirement for equipping mage armor, even dedicated blood mages might benefit from some investment here.
Constitution	Constitution increases health (+5 per attribute point) and physical resistance. This attribute is also a minimum requirement for warriors wishing to equip certain pieces of armor. Every character can benefit from a little extra robustness, especially blood mages or those with little to start with, but there are equipment items that provide extra health so it's a decision you can delay until necessary.

There is a sweet spot for leveling up that makes most efficient use of the attribute points spent. To maintain an optimal value, you need to invest roughly 1.25 points per level (in other words, 5 points every 4 levels) in your primary attribute for attack, and 1 point of Cunning per level for optimal defense. The effect on derived attributes – such as attack, defense, damage and armor – is that a small investment sees little return, but ramps up quickly as you approach the optimal value for that level. Attribute points above that optimal value will still increase the character's power but will give diminishing returns in effectiveness.

Optimal Development Plan

Class	Primary Attribute	Secondary Attributes
Warrior	Strength	Constitution & Cunning
Rogue	Dexterity	Cunning (& Willpower in the later game)
Mage	Magic	Willpower & Cunning

DERIVED ATTRIBUTES

These attributes appear on the Character screen.

Attack

Your attack score is your chance of successfully hitting an enemy with a basic attack. This takes your attack percentage (derived from your primary attribute) and subtracts the enemy's defense and displacement percentages (if applicable). Attack scores are also modified against enemies of higher rank (-15% for a lieutenant and -30% against a boss). The final sum is the likelihood of success. If you fail to make your attack, you will strike a glancing blow that does 10% of your character's base damage.

Abilities such as Crushing Prison, Mighty Blow and Backstab never miss, although their effectiveness against the enemy isn't guaranteed.

Defense

Defense (derived from Cunning) is a character's ability to deflect, dodge or parry incoming attacks. With good defense, the enemy's blows miss or inflict only minimal damage. Defense is reduced against enemies of rank, by 20% for lieutenants and 40% against bosses. Every player has a base 5% defense, even if no points are invested in Cunning, and there is an 80% cap.

Damage

Damage determines the harm inflicted on an opponent, based on the equipped weapon and the character's primary attribute. The stated figure is a base rate for attacking an unarmored opponent, as armor absorbs some of the damage. Because the attack speed of a character can vary, the second figure gives DPS (damage per second) as a comparative calculation. A battle axe can inflict heavy damage but is slow to swing, while twin daggers can stab rapidly. It's important to note that your damage also determines the power of your abilities, so equipping a stronger sword or staff improves other talents beyond your standard attack.

Armor

Armor is resistance against physical assault, reducing the harm visited upon the character's health bar. The values of all equipped armor and armor bonuses are added together and converted into a percentage for the proportion of physical damage that is immediately disregarded from each attack. Armor's effectiveness is reduced by 10% against lieutenant ranks and by 20% against bosses.

Critical Chance

Every attack has a small possibility of generating a critical hit, as indicated by this Dexterity-based percentage. Items and abilities can influence critical chance, which is also increased by outflanking the enemy and attacking from behind or the side. A critical hit causes the enemy's health bar to flash white, indicating that they will take additional damage. The actual amount of critical damage is a percentage determined by Cunning, giving another reason for all classes to invest some points here.

Fortitude

The ability to withstand being knocked over or sent flying backwards is a combination of Fortitude and maximum health. Feeble spellcasters might consider specializing in Force Mage (with Fist of the Maker) at level 7 to obtain Unshakable at level 8, instantly gaining 100 points of Fortitude and an end to interrupted casting. On higher difficulties, many character builds can benefit from some points in constitution for greater maximum health.

RESISTANCES

Whether you think of armor as "physical resistance" or fire resistance as "armor against flames", the point to grasp is that they work identically. Each element is counteracted by a specific resistance in the same way that armor counteracts physical damage. For example, characters with 10% fire resistance suffer 10% less fire damage.

Checking your character's Resistance scores may reveal zero armor ratings against certain elements, meaning they suffer the full damage from such attacks. You can raise resistances through various means as revealed in the table below.

There are a few additional points worth noting:

- Damage resistance applies to damage of any kind and combines with all other resistances, making it the most useful resistance of all when weighing up items and abilities. Against a physical attack, it adds to armor; against a mage's Fireball, it adds to fire resistance and magical resistance for a cumulative damage reduction. Applying negative damage resistance to enemies (see the Entropy talent tree) increases the efficacy of subsequent attacks, a viable strategy against tough bosses.
- Dealing in the permeating energy of the Fade, spirit-based attacks are unique in rendering the victim's magic resistance and damage resistance only half as effective.
- Against magical attacks, magic resistance is added to the elemental or physical resistance. Mages develop magic resistance through their primary attribute, while other characters need protective accessories. Just like physical or elemental resistances, magic resistance counteracts a percentage of the damage that an attack would have inflicted. It also reduces the duration of hostile magical effects on a character in accordance with its percentage value.
- If enemies have significant resistance or immunity to a certain type of attack, a small shield appears next to their health bar whenever they're hit by that element.

Resistance	Protection from Abilities	Protection from Equipment (Examples)	Protection from Runes
Fire	Elemental Shield & Arcane Wall (Arcane tree); Elemental Aegis & Rally (Defender tree)	Dragon Hunter's Hauberk	Rune of Fire Warding
Cold		Regret	Rune of Frost Warding
Electricity		Illwan's Hood	Rune of Lightning Warding
Spirit		Chantry Amulet	Rune of Spirit Warding
Nature		Poisonwood Locket	Rune of Nature Warding
Physical	Rock Armor (Primal tree)	Any armor	Rune of Protection
Magical	Resolute (Defender tree)	Karasten's Belt	Torpor's Barrier Rune

ELEMENTS

There are actually six types of elemental damage – fire, cold, electricity, nature, spirit and physical – the last being associated with ordinary melee weapons. Most offensive spells produce one type of elemental damage and certain weapons (including most staves) inflict elemental instead of physical damage. Weapons that have been enchanted by Runes (see page 214) may inflict several different types of damage simultaneously.

Use the Bestiary chapter of this guide to discover the elemental weaknesses of enemies (which may include physical damage if they have weak armor) and select the appropriate weapons for the task. On Nightmare difficulty, enemies also have elemental resistances. A shield icon next to an enemy's health bar indicates an immunity to your current attack.

If you enable "Show Damage Numbers" in the Options screen, you can identify different types of damage by the color the text appears in.

Element	Text Color	Secondary Effect	Rune	Ability
Fire	Orange	Immolation	Rune of Fire	Fireball, Firestorm
Cold	Blue	Slows enemies	Rune of Frost	Winter's Grasp, Cone of Cold
Electricity	Yellow	Stunning jolt (holds enemies briefly)	Rune of Lightning	Chain Lightning, Tempest
Nature	Green	-	Rune of Nature	Wrath of the Elvhen, Ensnare
Spirit	Purple	Halves magic resistance and damage resistance	Rune of Spirit	Holy Smite, Spirit Bolt, Despair
Physical	White	-	Rune of Impact	Stonefist, Fist of the Maker, weapon attacks

STATUS EFFECTS

Certain spells and talents boast more interesting consequences than simply inflicting damage. They afflict the enemy with status effects, some of which serve as the opening conditions for cross-class combos, and all of which can be exploited by the informed player.

Status Effect	Description	Inflicted By (Ability)
Stun	This effect stops the enemy in their tracks for a couple of seconds, giving you the chance to retaliate or flee. Rogues can take advantage of stunned enemies for automatic critical hits. Victims forget their current target and may choose a new one when re-evaluating threat.	• Pommel Strike (warrior) • Mind Blast (mage) • Miasmic Flask (rogue) • Combustion Grenades (all)
Confused	Confusion disrupts enemy action and can occasionally cause opponents to attack each other.	• Confusion
Obscured	The rogue employs a smoke screen to hide the party and temporarily increase defense.	• Chameleon's Breath, Impenetrable Fog (rogue)
Brittle	When enemies are frozen in Brittle status, they are especially prone to damage multipliers from shattering blows.	• Winter's Grasp, Cone of Cold (mage) • Petrify, Desiccate (mage)
Disoriented	This extreme state of shock and bewilderment leaves the victim with heavily reduced defense.	• Chaos, Overpowering Fog (rogue)
Staggered	The enemy in Staggered status is dizzied and unsteady on their feet following a concussive force. They will try to fight on but suffer penalties to attack and defense.	• Pommel Blow, Aftershock, Pummel, Sunder (warrior)
Sleep	Targets only enemies and removes them briefly from combat. Sleepers awake on expiry of the spell's duration or earlier if attacked.	• Sleep, Entropic Cloud (mage)
Paralyzed	A creature in a state of paralysis cannot move, attack or cast spells.	• Glyph of Paralysis, Crushing Prison, Coma, Petrify (mage)
Dispel	Removes hostile magic and status effects on the player, including "debuffs" that negatively affect character attributes. Simultaneously, it cancels any sustained spells and magical "buffs" that boost enemy performance.	• Dispel Magic (mage)
Enslavement	Enemies subject to enslavement temporarily appear in the blue ground ring of an ally, fighting on the side of the player until their self-control is restored.	• Blood Slave (mage)
Silence	This templar sanction prevents enemies from casting spells or using abilities that demand mana/stamina.	• Silence (warrior)
Immobilized	A creature can be immobilized by a sticky substance, or an arrow that pins them to the spot, though they are still able to attack and defend.	• Tar Bomb (all) • Pinning Shot (rogue) • Traps (environment)
Knockback/ Knockdown	Every attack has its own degree of force, so you'll regularly see enemies stagger or swept from their feet by an impact. This applies to default weapon assaults and the vast majority of offensive abilities.	• Various

Brittle target

Disoriented target

Staggered target

ABILITIES

There are hundreds of different talents and spells to learn in Dragon Age II. To help you make the right decisions, this section offers analysis on all talent trees, offering targeted advice on which abilities might offer the best results for Hawke and his companions.

For those completely new to Dragon Age II, the following general guidelines will also be of assistance.

- **Activated abilities** last for a limited time and incur an immediate cost in stamina or mana. After you use them, there is generally a short Cooldown period before you can use them again. During the Prologue and early hours of Act 1, it can pay to prioritize activated abilities. The more you have, the better your party will perform in combat.
- **Sustained Abilities** remain constantly active until you disable them. These reserve a fixed percentage of the character's mana or stamina pool until you deactivate them.
- **Passive abilities** are permanent perks that do not consume stamina or mana.
- **Upgrades** are not abilities in themselves but instead improve an existing ability, usually in a very significant way. With precious few exceptions, all talents or spells that have upgrades are essentially restrained versions until you acquire the bolt-ons that augment their overall effect. Without Despair contributing huge spirit damage, Horror is just a temporary stun; on its own, Elemental Shield is just a moderately useful buff for a frail mage but, with Arcane Wall and Arcane Shield, it becomes a party-wide enhancement of great utility. For key abilities, we suggest that you acquire upgrades as soon as they become available. This is especially true with skills that set up cross-class combo opportunities (see page 174).
- Hawke can learn one **specialization** upon reaching level 7 and another at level 14. Three specializations are available for each class. Each grants a unique bonus and unlocks a new group of powerful talents or spells. Hawke's companions cannot learn specializations, but their personal ability trees include talents or spells that are related to the same specializations available to Hawke.

Don't focus too exclusively on abilities that offer heavy damage. While these are certainly worthwhile, passive perks and skills that contribute a strategic edge can be equally efficient. For example, many players might completely overlook the Sabotage tree common to all rogues. This would be a mistake: the talents it contains will enable a more tactically minded player to have entire groups of dangerous opponents reeling with the effects of its debuffs, incapable of striking back and ripe for cross-class combo finishes.

If you have access to the Black Emporium (see dragonage.com/da2/addons for details), you can buy a Maker's Sigh to reallocate every last ability point acquired during your adventure so far. This is great for those classic "buyer's remorse" moments where, on reflection, you may have approached the leveling process in a very different way.

Though it is of marginal importance until approximately midway through Act 1, especially on a first playthrough, we suggest that you experiment with the in-game Tactics system (see page 178) to fine-tune the way in which Hawke's companions make use of their abilities.

WARRIOR ABILITIES

Weapon and Shield

Used By: Hawke, Aveline, Carver

- This is essentially a dedicated "tank tree". **Shield Defense** cuts damage output by 25% but offers a commensurate boost to a warrior's capacity to withstand blows. **Perception** and **Safeguard** are passive abilities that offer immunity to flanking and critical hits respectively. Acquire them as soon as you can.
- Though the direct harm it inflicts is pitiful, **Shield Bash** is invaluable: with **Pummel**, it's an easy way to Stagger multiple enemies for mages and rogues to knock down in cross-class combos for massive damage.
- **Scatter** and **Assault** are the primary means by which a tank can inflict noteworthy damage. Upgraded, they're both highly effective against groups of Disoriented foes within range of the sword swing.

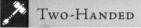

Two-Handed

Used By: Hawke, Fenris, Carver

- Every ability in this tree is of service to a two-handed warrior. Pick up **Giant's Reach**, **Mighty Blow** and **Scythe** early in the game: they're really that essential. The latter two work well against tightly packed groups of Brittle opponents.
- There is a special relationship between the **Sunder** passive ability and the upgraded **Whirlwind** talent: Sunder contributes a 50% chance of Staggering enemies with a critical hit, while Whirlwind plus **Tornado** has a critical chance of 100%.

Vanguard

Used By: Hawke, Aveline, Fenris, Carver

- **Might** and **Control** are mutually exclusive sustained abilities that enable a warrior to boost either attack or damage by 10%. For a standard warrior build, Might is probably the better choice. In both instances, think carefully before purchasing the upgrades for these: they're specific to very particular attack strategies and warrior roles.
- **Cleave** and **Massacre** are very useful for a warrior wielding a two-handed weapon.
- Having a mage cast the upgraded **Hex of Torment** on a target will enable a warrior armed with Might (plus the **Muscle** upgrade for improved critical hits), **Destroyer** and Cleave to cut them to pieces. This could be effective against the more sturdy mages you might encounter on higher difficulty levels.

Battlemaster

Used By: Hawke, Aveline, Fenris, Carver

- The bottom portion of this tree offers talents that can help you to maintain or replenish stamina and access abilities in Cooldown more rapidly. These are worth the investment if you are playing as a warrior: if not, **Bolster** alone may probably suffice for an AI-controlled companion.
- **Rally** is an interesting ability that enables a warrior to share temporarily the effects of sustained talents with other party members (in addition to a sudden surge in mana and stamina regeneration). The **Unite** upgrade extends the potential effects dramatically.
- **Battle Synergy** and its upgrades offer an alternative to Bravery as a means of drawing enemy attention towards a tank. Instead of increasing a warrior's threat within a set radius, the **Fearless Synergy** enhancement transfers 50% of *all* threat generated by companions to the user. While Bravery offers the better overall deal, the upgraded Battle Synergy could enable a tank to exert greater control of battles fought in wide-open spaces where Taunt's limited area of effect becomes problematic.

Defender

Used By: Hawke, Aveline, Fenris, Carver

- This tree offers warriors a variety of abilities that increase their capacity to withstand enemy aggression. The focal points (and gateways to two very interesting passive abilities) are **Turn the Blade**, which offers bonuses to Defense and Fortitude with upgrades, and **Elemental Aegis**, which offers elemental resistances. For a tank, a very strong case could be made for acquiring both, switching between the two sustained abilities as the situation demands. Note that Elemental Aegis is less important until at least late in Act 1.
- The 100% knockback resistance provided by **Resilience** is a fine skill for *any* warrior. The remaining talents are perhaps less essential, or a question of personal strategy.

Warmonger

Used By: Hawke, Aveline, Fenris, Carver

- **Pommel Strike** is a must for any warrior: it has a negligible stamina cost and, with **Pommel Blow**, has a high chance of leaving all but the most elite opponents Staggered. If you need to prevent an opponent from firing off an attack, this is one of the most convenient and reliable ways to interrupt them.
- For a tank, **Taunt**, **Bravery** and their respective upgrades are *mandatory* acquisitions. Acquire **Bellow** and **Bravado** as soon as you can.
- **Tremor** might be a good bet for a two-handed damage-dealer who regularly invites that little bit more threat than he or she can reasonably cope with.

Guardian

Specialization: Aveline only

- **Immovable** is actually rather counterproductive in many light, or only moderately challenging, battles. We would suggest that you remove this from Aveline's Tactics setup and activate it manually when a situation genuinely requires it. On higher difficulty levels, acquiring the **Retaliation** talent could enable you to address the overall damage deficit (and therefore threat decrease) that this sustained mode leads to.
- **Bodyguard** is of most use on Hard or Nightmare, when a frail mage critical to your party's strategy might fall to a single backstab from an Assassin.
- **Indomitable** and **Thick Skin** are essential, so invest in both once other core tanking abilities have been acquired. Indomitable stacks with Resilience in the Defender school to make Aveline peerlessly resolute.

Tevinter Fugitive

Specialization: Fenris only

- The top section of Fenris's unique tree features three passive abilities that you really need to acquire. Players seeking to maximize his DPS could consider creating specific healing conditions for all party members at the Tactics screen in order to get the most out of **Veneer of Calm**'s increase to damage whenever he is wounded.
- **Lyrium Ghost** is excellent, so have it active at all times. Another compulsory purchase is **Deflect**, offering a 25% increase in magic resistance.
- **Spirit Pulse** is an excellent alternative to Tremor in the Warmonger school: it's a get-out-of-jail card to play when Fenris gathers a little more threat than he can cope with. Though Tremor offers twice as much physical force and the possibility of Staggering opponents, Spirit Pulse causes a moderate amount of spirit damage.

Templar

Specialization: Hawke only

- This specialization is of specific interest if you are casting Hawke as a damage-dealer.
- **Cleanse**, **Silence** and, to a lesser extent, the **Righteous Strike** passive ability are designed to seriously impair the offensive capability of all enemies that use noteworthy abilities or spells. **Annulment** is a passive ability useful for a warrior of any type, though you'll need to go through the aforementioned talents to reach it.
- **Holy Smite** may not look like a particularly efficient talent, but its spirit damage can be devastating against Fade creatures (especially the undead) and mages.

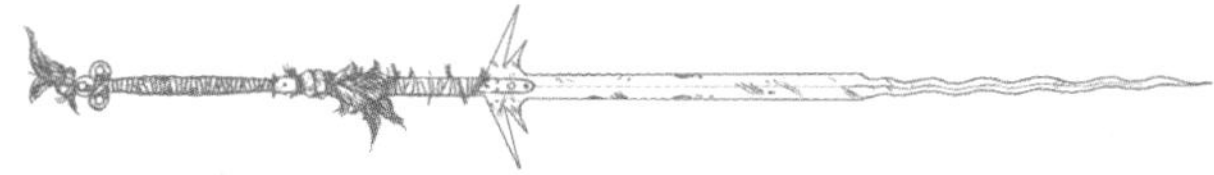

Reaver

Specialization: Hawke only

- **Blood Frenzy** and **Sacrificial Frenzy** are closely bonded: the passive ability provides a rising bonus to damage as Hawke's health meter depletes, while the activated ability temporarily doubles that increase for the relatively small price of -20 health.
- **Devour** is one of the most fascinating abilities. With its two upgrades, it enables Hawke to inflict damage and heal by an equivalent amount, with its effects increased by 300% against Disoriented targets. It also leaves enemies Staggered, essentially converting one cross-class combo opportunity into another. Use it in conjunction with **Sacrificial Frenzy** when Hawke is near death to maximize its effects.
- **Aura of Pain** inflicts spirit damage over a 6m radius every 4 seconds, but with an attendant 5% reduction in health with every "pulse". At the heart of a vicious melee, an artfully timed Aura of Pain → Sacrificial Frenzy → Devour sequence can greatly enhance Hawke's damage output.
- Fervor's bonus of +30% attack speed for 10 seconds after each kill is a hugely beneficial passive ability, but its position on the talent tree means that it requires 5 ability points to unlock.

Berserker

Specialization: Hawke only

- This talent tree is built around the core **Berserk** sustained ability, which offers a damage bonus in proportion to Hawke's remaining stamina (more = better), but drains the meter with each blow. Berserk must be active to employ the **Adrenaline** and **Barrage** activated abilities.
- Barrage offers a 50% boost to attack speed, but with a penalty to damage resistance (reduced from -20% to -10% with the **Resilient** upgrade).
- As is perhaps fitting for a school of combat that makes such perilously large demands on stamina, the **Death Blow** passive ability offers a minimum 5% increase to the meter with every enemy death.
- **Adrenaline** only lasts for 8 seconds, but it can be activated multiple times to "stack" a huge bonus to damage before the effect expires.
- While it takes a great deal of precision management, a combination of the Reaver and Berserker abilities can offer astonishingly high bursts of damage output.

ROGUE ABILITIES

Dual Weapon

Used By: Hawke, Isabela

- In most Isabela and dual-wielding Hawke builds, you will want to pick up pretty much everything in this talent tree.
- **Unforgiving Chain** and the upgraded **Explosive Strike** offer one of the best opportunities for heavy single-target damage. Ten consecutive standard attacks followed by an Explosive Strike finish against a Staggered opponent packs a malicious punch.
- **Backstab** and **Twin Fangs** are staple abilities for a rogue built for dual weapon fighting. Acquire them early in the story.
- The **Lacerate** sustained mode provides a 10% chance of inflicting bonus damage to any attack, which rises to 100% against Staggered targets with the Maim upgrade. This is not cumulative with Explosive Strike, which has priority when both are technically applicable.

Archery

Used By: Hawke, Varric (under the Bianca heading), Sebastian

- If Hawke or a companion focuses on archery, just assume that almost every ability and upgrade in this tree is pretty much essential. **Bursting Arrow** is an absolute killer for enemy groups rendered Brittle by Cone of Cold, while **Archer's Lance** causes cruciferous damage to anyone in its path. Set up Brittle with Winter's Grasp on a high-ranking opponent, and it's a commander killer.
- **Pinning Shot** can be employed to immobilize and (with an upgrade) Disorient a single high-priority target for a mage or warrior to knock down with a cross-class combo.
- **Hail of Arrows** isn't massively damaging, but its upgraded effect of slowing down opponents over a 15m radius for 4 seconds makes it useful for setting up cross-class combos or layered AoE barrages.

Sabotage

Used By: Hawke, Varric, Sebastian, Isabela

- With the exception of one upgrade, this entire talent tree offers no direct damage to opponents and is dedicated entirely to status effects. **Rush** is employed for knockdowns, **Miasmic Flask** for stuns, and **Fatiguing Fog** to slow groups of opponents down. **Confusion** has a 50% chance of causing enemies to fight among themselves for up to 20 seconds. In short, it's a school for those who favor advanced strategies, particularly cross-class combos.
- When upgraded, Fatiguing Fog and Confusion both have a chance of inflicting the Disoriented status effect over a small area, but you will need to invest at least 6 ability points to obtain these effects. Varric and Sebastian at least have Pinning Shot to Disorient single targets, but Isabela and a dual-wielding Hawke only have the Sabotage school to set up this effect.

Subterfuge

Used By: Hawke, Varric, Isabela, Sebastian

- The **Stealth** ability (and related **Ambush** passive ability) offers rogues the inexpensive option of disappearing from view, then striking a target for massive damage. The **Lingering Shroud** passive ability is a connected perk that is only of use if you regularly employ Stealth and use attacks that buff the party with the Obscure effect (such as Bursting Arrow and Fatiguing Fog). With Stealth and an obscure effect active on the rogue, they can make two (potentially critical) attacks before they become visible.
- Acquire **Evade** (and the **Tactical Withdrawal** upgrade) early in your rogue's development. **Subtlety** is another mainstay, offering a 25% threat reduction that benefits rogues of any variety.
- **Chameleon's Breath** has an AoE obscure effect and can be a good way to give brief respite to a beleaguered party, or augment the strike capacity of a rogue employing Lingering Shroud.

Specialist

Used By: Hawke, Varric, Isabela, Sebastian

- This tree offers three sustained abilities (and upgrades) that enhance a rogue's efficiency in distinct ways, plus a final passive ability that augments the effects of all three. However, you can only have one of these sustained modes active at a time.
- Complicating matters somewhat, the tree requires 4 to 6 ability points to gain the ability you desire and **Harmony**.
- The one individual who can definitely benefit from this tree is Varric. Spend the 6 points to pick up **Speed** (and upgrades) plus Harmony, then grab **Well-Oiled** and **Bianca's Song** (and its upgrade) in his personal talent tree to create your own walking, wise-cracking auto-cannon.

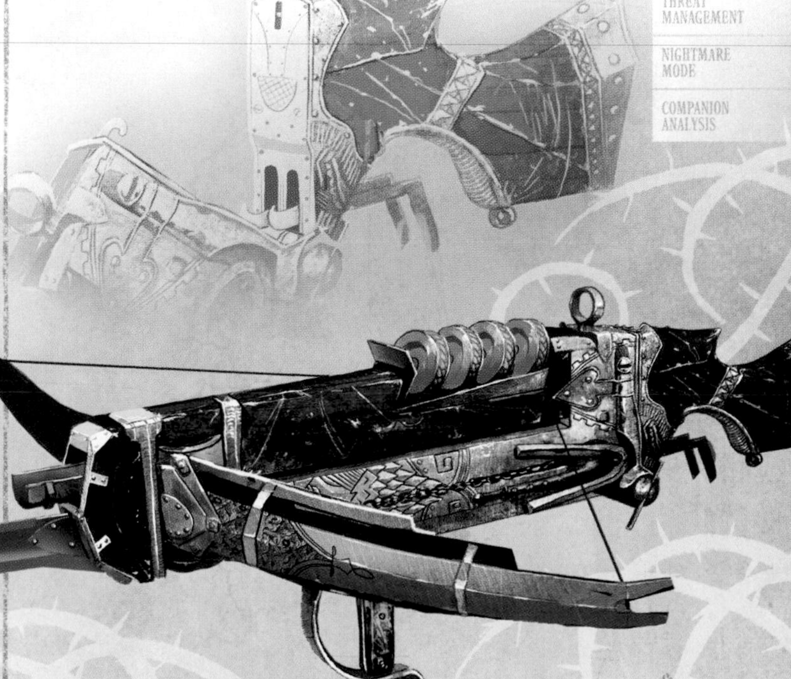

Scoundrel

Used By: Hawke, Varric, Isabela, Sebastian

- **Blindside** and **Twist the Knife** are passive abilities that offer damage upgrades in specific circumstances. The former boosts damage against enemies engaging other allies and is a great choice for any rogue; the latter offers assured critical hits against stunned opponents. With the upgraded Miasmic Flask or Evade, a rogue archer can stun groups of opponents and then immediately capitalize on this effect with an AoE finish.
- **Back to Back** is best used to teleport a dual-wield rogue to save a weaker party member from a strong and persistent enemy. It is also the gateway to **Brand** (an ability that only really pays for itself in protracted battles against strong single opponents) and **Follow-Through**, which offers a much-needed boost to stamina regeneration.
- **Armistice** and **Goad** are powerful threat management tools that come into their own on higher difficulty settings.

Swashbuckler

Specialization: Isabela only

- By route of **Across the Bow** and **Savvy**, the **Experienced Hand** and **Sea Legs** passive abilities are the only talents that might be of genuine interest in a Normal playthrough, though **All Hands on Deck** packs a punch against groups of enemies.
- Across the Bow and Savvy will be of most use to players who aim to micromanage threat and employ Isabela in an off-tank role. That said, the **Below the Waterline** upgrade offers an excellent 50% decrease to an enemy's defense stat for 20 seconds: a fine debuff when you face commander-grade enemies and higher.

Marksman

Specialization: Varric only

- Though you have to unlock **Rhyming Triplet** to get them, **Well-Oiled**, **Bianca's Song** and the **Embellishment** upgrade for the latter are the only essential upgrades in Varric's personal tree. Pick them up early in the game: the difference they make to his damage output is huge.
- **Overtime** is worth an ability point only if you already have Follow-Through and are still struggling with stamina issues. **Kickback** and its upgrade offer novelty value over palpable harm. The effect of landing a hit against a Staggered opponent is to launch them from a standing position with comedic velocity.

Royal Archer

Specialization: Sebastian only

- **Guardian Angel** is an intriguing ability: a decoy target (with all threat transferred from Sebastian as he disappears) will always be useful in sprawling melees, if just to keep certain enemies busy while you banish their peers. The main reason to acquire this talent, however, is to gain access to the **Holy Precision**, **Maferath's Advance** and (to a lesser extent) **Disciple's Discipline** passive abilities.
- The **Wounding Arrow** (and **Debilitating** upgrade) and **Righteous Chain** (with the **Arrow of Judgment** finish) both require that you link up to 10 uninterrupted default attacks before one augmented payoff. Unless you have the time or inclination to perform these manually, you may find that other talents and their upgrades in the Archery tree represent a better all-round choice.

Assassin

Specialization: Hawke only

- With its two upgrades, **Mark of Death** reduces its victim's damage resistance by 50% for 20 seconds. It's an excellent way to cut short battles against tough individual foes, especially if you can employ cross-class combos while the effect is active.
- **Pinpoint Strikes** increases critical chance to 100% for the duration of the effect. Augment this with the connected **Bloodlust** (stamina regeneration per each kill) and **Devious Harm** (+1% critical damage per point of Cunning), and Hawke becomes a near-tireless critical hit machine against groups of weaker opponents.
- **Assassinate** has colossal damage-dealing potential, especially on Brittle targets.

Shadow

Specialization: Hawke only

- Even if you only intend to invest ability points in one specialization, make this your second and pick up **Pinpoint Precision** for that superb 25% passive boost to critical damage.
- **Disorienting Criticals** increases critical damage by 25% and has a 100% chance of Disorienting a foe if Hawke lands a critical hit while obscured. With the **Shadow Veil** passive ability, the latter effect can be achieved simply by slipping into stealth. While obscured, land an Explosive Strike, Archer's Lance or Assassinate cross-class combo finish, and the automatic 100% critical chance of each ability will always inflict Disorient to set up another cross-class opportunity.
- In addition to the obvious merits of 100% critical chance for flanking attacks, the **Predator** passive ability will increase the frequency at which Hawke Disorients opponents through the **Disorienting Criticals** talent.
- **Decoy** is similar to Sebastian's Guardian Angel ability (see Royal Archer), but with two exclusive upgrades that increase the doppelganger's value. **Inconspicuous**, meanwhile, offers great benefits for Hawke if critical hits and high-impact talents are drawing more threat than the rogue can comfortably deal with.

Duelist

Specialization: Hawke only

- Duelist offers abilities that enable Hawke to perform an off-tank role with individual high-rank opponents.
- **Throw the Gauntlet** (plus upgrades) causes a single enemy to abandon their current target and pursue Hawke with a relentless fervor, with penalties to their damage and defense scores while the effect is active. The related **Parry** sustained mode offers notable perks to Hawke's defense, attack and critical chance (with **Riposte** and **En Garde**), but these are doubled while Throw the Gauntlet is in effect.
- The **Sure Strikes** and **Evasive Maneuvers** passive abilities offer +20% to attack and defense respectively. It is the **Vendetta** ability, however, that will most catch the eye. This is one of the best single-target assaults available, especially if the opponent is Staggered.

MAGE ABILITIES

Elemental

Used By: Hawke, Merrill, Anders, Bethany

- This talent tree is a staple for mages dedicated to dealing damage and contains two of the best AoE attacks for crowd control.
- **Cone of Cold** and **Winter's Grasp** are absolutely essential: both can inflict the Brittle status effect, and their capacity for impeding enemy movement (either through freezing or slowdown) is remarkably useful. Winter's Grasp has a very slight AoE effect: try to capitalize on this whenever possible.
- **Firestorm** is enormously efficient. Despite the protracted casting process and the fact that damage is not distributed evenly throughout the effect area, this is always a great leveler against large groups.
- For mages who favor this school, **Elemental Mastery** is a must: the perks (particularly the increased Brittle results for Cone of Cold and Winter's Grasp) are just too good to ignore.

Primal

Used By: Hawke, Merrill, Bethany

- The upgraded **Stonefist** and **Chain Lightning** spells are viciously efficient if you regularly employ cross-class combos; the latter is particularly devastating against opponents with a weakness to electricity.
- Compared to Firestorm, **Tempest** has the advantage of hitting all targets in the effect radius. It also causes no friendly fire damage on the Nightmare difficulty setting: a perk of inestimable merit.
- **Rock Armor** is an easy and inexpensive armor buff for any mage; useful if you are focusing on a build with attribute points dedicated to Magic and Willpower only.
- **Petrify** works against any target without a specific immunity to it. On its own, it's essentially a "stay there!" spell to temporarily remove powerful enemies from the fight while you deal with their allies. Upgraded, it's a boss-killer.

Spirit

Used By: Hawke, Anders, Merrill, Bethany

- **Spirit Bolt** is cheap, easy to use and twice as effective against opponents Disoriented by your resident rogue.
- The fully upgraded **Walking Bomb** is awesomely powerful against condensed packs of enemies but tends to be less efficient unless you deliver the payload manually: your companions just won't get the best out of it.
- **Death Syphon** can help cut the expense of Lyrium Potion usage; disable it during battles against single opponents. **Dispel Magic** really comes into its own on higher difficulty levels, where it's harder to keep enemy mages and commanders consistently debilitated through other means.

Arcane

Used By: Hawke, Anders, Merrill, Bethany

- **Elemental Weapons** and **Arcane Shield** (especially when applied to the entire party with upgrades) are a must for a support healer. The former is the cornerstone of a major tactic for maximizing party damage.
- Don't underestimate **Mind Blast**: though it causes no health loss, it's vital for redirecting attention away from a vulnerable mage.
- On higher difficulty levels, **Barrier** is a lifesaver in those instances where you anticipate a deadly attack before it lands, such as when an Assassin striding purposefully towards a mage disappears in a puff of smoke.
- **Crushing Prison** is one of the most powerful single-target spells, which should make it a key part of a nuke's repertoire.

Entropy

Used By: Hawke, Merrill, Bethany

- This school is all about debilitating individual foes and, as such, lends itself to playthroughs on Hard or Nightmare where commanders, assassins and bosses of any type pose a far graver threat. On Normal, only **Horror** and **Hex of Torment** are worthwhile investments.
- The upgraded Horror (inflicting spirit damage) can be employed to annihilate individual targets, especially if you weaken them with Hex of Torment beforehand.
- **Entropic Cloud** and **Sleep** are debuffs that make a world of difference when you cannot rely on Firestorm, Tempest or Cone of Cold to exert sufficient control over crowds.
- **Misdirection Hex** is a key tool for reducing the efficiency of more powerful opponents – useful against Assassins of all varieties.

Creation

Used By: Hawke, Anders, Bethany

- If Hawke is a mage, acquire **Heal**: even if you're playing as a nuke, a separate source of restorative magic is always useful.
- All spells in this school are suitable for a dedicated support healer. **Glyph of Paralysis** is useful for taking stronger foes out of the equation. **Glyph of Repulsion** has countless tactical applications: prevent enemy reinforcements from using a particular entrance, use it to fortify a choke point, or cast it on a weaker party member to give them a temporary force field.
- **Heroic Aura** is a worthwhile (though expensive) sustained buff. **Haste** can facilitate withering micromanaged onslaughts.

Vengeance

Specialization: Anders only

- Anders can only employ one set of abilities in this tree at a time, each linked to the **Panacea** and **Vengeance** sustained modes.
- With Panacea active, Anders boosts party health regeneration by 50 and can use **Aid Allies** to heal all party members as well as **Regroup** to revive the fallen. The cost, however, is 40% of Anders's total mana and the disabling of his offensive spells.
- The Vengeance mode, by contrast, renders him immune to conventional healing (both spells and potions) but offers a boost to damage output. To make the most of this mode, you must also acquire **Blood of my Enemy** to regenerate health, **Martyr** and **Swift Justice** to access spells in Cooldown more quickly, and the **Wrath** upgrade to enhance the damage increase. This mode is only truly efficient against large enemy groups. Against individual targets, it leaves Anders extremely vulnerable.

Dalish Pariah

Specialization: Merrill only

- Merrill's personal talent tree lends itself to some unique strategies for a mage, so only invest ability points in this area if you're certain of the benefits it will entail. Staves and poison aside, its spells are the only way that you can inflict nature damage.
- **Blood of the First** enables Merrill to call on blood magic, using health rather than mana to cast spells (which is why it will make sense to max out friendship with Merrill to gain the benefit of the **Solidarity** bonus). The only way that she can regain health in that mode is through the **Wrath of the Elvhen** spell.
- Wrath of the Elvhen inflicts constant nature damage within a set radius surrounding Merrill, also healing her in accordance with the number of foes affected. **Stone's Throw** and **Ensnare** are used to either send her into the heart of a melee or draw opponents to her position.
- In essence, the Dalish Pariah tree is geared towards a very unique approach to leveling Merrill: rather than investing in Willpower, you might assign all attribute points not placed in Magic into Constitution. This would both give her a huge pool of health (and, therefore, mana with Blood of the First active) and make her more capable of surviving at the centre of an enemy pack, causing constant damage.

Force Mage

Specialization: Hawke only

- Even if you don't intend to fully exploit this Specialization, the boost to physical and elemental force is a worthwhile perk. The principle reason to choose this tree, however, is the **Unshakable** passive ability: that +100 boost to Fortitude makes a world of difference.
- Without upgrades, **Fist of the Maker** is expensive and rather weak. With **Maker's Hammer** and **Maker's Fury**, however, it's a brutal punch that can be delivered to great effect (900% damage!) whenever a warrior Staggers a target.
- **Gravitic Ring**, **Telekinetic Burst** and **Pull of the Abyss** are all crowd-control spells with many defensive and offensive applications. The latter is especially important on the Nightmare difficulty setting as it enables you to draw opponents to a fixed point before you rain down an AoE barrage.

Spirit Healer

Specialization: Hawke only

- The Spirit Healer tree enables Hawke to keep the party healthy – but at the expense of vastly reducing his or her offensive capability while the **Healing Aura** ability is active.
- This tree offers two superb passive abilities. **Vitality**'s +10 boost to Constitution and +100 health regeneration are boons of obvious merit, while **Second Chance** completely disables the need to manage injuries – a welcome perk for a first-time Nightmare playthrough.

Blood Mage

Specialization: Hawke only

- This Specialization requires that you invest several ability points to really get the most out of it and necessitates a more planned approach to combat. With equipment that offers additional mana for each health point consumed and careful use of **Sacrifice** and **Grave Robber**, it offers virtually unlimited casting capabilities.
- As the **Blood Magic** sustained mode precludes the use of healing potions or spells, you must rely on Sacrifice and Grave Robber to make it viable. Sacrifice is obviously best employed as a direct transfusion of health from your party's tank (or a similarly hardy warrior). Grave Robber's boost to health is of most service in battles against large groups, with the spirit damage contributed by the **One Foot In** upgrade a fine perk against all affected enemies.
- Those who partake in this most malign of arcane arts can employ one of the most deadly spells available: **Hemorrhage**. Acquire the **Paralyzing** upgrade to unlock its true capacity and cause 900% damage against Staggered foes in the targeted area.

CROSS-CLASS COMBOS

Though you can *technically* survive without them, employing cross-class combos unlocks your party's full damage-dealing potential. If you are troubled by high-rank enemies, these two-part attacks are unrivalled in their capacity to neutralize resilient foes rapidly.

- Each class can set up a cross-class combo opportunity by hindering an enemy with a specific status effect (see tables). The combo occurs when a character of another class follows up with an ability that exploits this to deliver a very powerful attack. A cross-class combo can only be completed once per status effect.
- You must acquire all stated upgrades in order to use cross-class combos. For ease of use, we highlight in our tables the actual spell or talent employed to cause or exploit an effect in **bold**.
- Unless we specify otherwise, the likelihood of an effect being inflicted with an applicable status effect or exploited by a cross-class combo finish is 100% – enemy resistances and immunities notwithstanding.
- With Winter's Blast and Cone of Cold, you really need to invest points in the Elemental tree to obtain Elemental Mastery. This increases the probability of a frozen enemy becoming Brittle to 100%.
- Softening up a tough individual opponent with a debuff or two before you implement a cross-class combo is a great way to maximize damage. For example, dropping a Hex of Torment or Mark of Death on a target can make a real difference.
- If Hawke has access to the Reaver specialization, Devour and its two upgrades can be employed to take a big bite of an enemy's health, healing the warrior, but then automatically set up a Stagger for a rogue or mage to capitalize on.
- There's a similarly interesting effect with the Disorienting Criticals passive ability in the Shadow specialization tree: with a little management, it's possible to hit a Staggered or Brittle target for huge injury, then inflict the Disoriented condition in the aftermath.
- You can automate the process of exploiting the Brittle, Stagger and Disorient status effects with the Tactics system. See page 176 for details.

STAGGERED COMBOS (INITIATED BY A WARRIOR)

Caused By	Exploited By	Talents/Spells & Effects
• **Shield Bash** + Pummel (Weapon and Shield) • **Cleave** + Claymore (Vanguard; 40% chance) • **Pommel Strike** + Pommel Blow (Warmonger) • **Tremor** + Aftershock (Warmonger; 40% chance) • **Sunder** (Two-Handed; 50% chance after any critical hit) • **Devour** + Voracious (Reaver)	Mages	• **Chain Lightning** + Chain Reaction (Primal): 600% damage and 200% elemental force against all Staggered targets that are struck by each arc. • **Crushing Prison** + Paralyzing Prison (Arcane): 200% damage to single target, plus 100% chance to paralyze. • **Fist of the Maker** + Maker's Hammer (Force Mage): 900% damage to Staggered targets in AoE range. • **Hemorrhage** + Paralyzing Hemorrhage (Blood Mage): 900% damage to all Staggered foes in the AoE radius.
	Rogues	• **Explosive Strike** + Merciless Strike (Dual Weapon): 400% damage to a single target. • **Lacerate** + Maim (Dual Weapon): 100% chance of Lacerate success on Staggered targets. • **Kickback** + Backlash (Marksman): 800% physical force to single target. • **Vendetta** + Blood Feud (Duelist): 300% damage versus single target.

DISORIENTED COMBOS (INITIATED BY A ROGUE)

Caused By	Exploited By	Talents/Spells & Effects
• **Pinning Shot** + Disorienting Shot (Archery/Bianca) • **Fatiguing Fog** + Overpowering Fog (Sabotage) • **Confusion** + Chaos (Sabotage) • **Disorienting Criticals** (Shadow; caused by critical hits while obscured)	Mages	• **Stonefist** + Golem's Fist (Primal): 200% damage to a single target. • **Spirit Bolt** + Spirit Strike (Spirit): 200% damage and elemental force to a single target. • **Walking Bomb** + Corrosive Walking Bomb + Virulent Walking Bomb (Spirit): 200% damage to target, 200% damage to enemies affected by blast, and 200% physical force.
	Warriors	• **Assault** + Battery (Weapon and Shield): 400% damage to Disoriented targets in range on final hit. • **Scatter** + Disperse (Weapon and Shield): 300% damage to Disoriented targets in range. • **Devour** + Insatiable (Reaver): 300% damage to single target, 300% health gain to user.

BRITTLE COMBOS (INITIATED BY A MAGE)

Caused By	Exploited By	Talents/Spells & Effects
• **Winter's Grasp** + Winter's Blast (Elemental; 40% chance) • **Cone of Cold** + Deep Freeze (Elemental; 20% chance) • **Petrify** + Desiccate (Primal)	Rogues	• **Bursting Arrow** + Shattering Arrow (Archery/Bianca): 600% damage to all Brittle targets in AoE radius, and 400% elemental force. • **Archer's Lance** + Punishing Lance (Archery/Bianca): 600% damage to all affected Brittle targets, plus 400% physical force. • **Assassinate** + Annihilate (Assassin): 400% damage to single opponent.
	Warriors	• **Mighty Blow** + Shattering Blow (Two-Handed): 300% damage to all affected Brittle targets and 200% physical force. • **Scythe** + Reaper (Two-Handed): 200% damage to all affected Brittle targets and 200% physical force.

CHARACTER ROLES

Each of your companions will have a specific role to play if your party is to fight as an efficient unit. The following role descriptions include a few recommended sample character builds to show the extent to which your companions can be empowered by pursuing a very specific direction.

Tank

The role of the tank is to generate the most threat, drawing in all enemies or occupying the efforts of a boss so that your foes focus all attention on the tank and leave other characters alone. To this end, the tank is a sponge for damage and needs to be heavily armored, preferably possessing a high Constitution and enough Strength to equip the best. Assigning one character as a tank effectively protects weaker characters from facing too many assailants.

Holding the interest of so many enemies at once requires an understanding of the Threat system (see page 180). Although you can create a warrior Hawke in the tank mold, Aveline has been clearly crafted for this role – right down to her Guardian specialization and her unique Gift shield.

Favored Character Builds	Warrior Hawke, Aveline
Primary Attributes	Strength, Constitution
Essential Abilities	**Weapon and Shield:** All **Warmonger:** Taunt, Bellow, Bravery, Bravado, Bravura **Battlemaster:** Bolster, Second Wind **Guardian (Aveline):** Indomitable **Defender:** Elemental Aegis, Elemental Shroud
Aspirational Items	Etched Ring of the Twins, Bardin's Folly, Wardwall, Lord Bearing's Wall, Shield of the Knight Herself (Aveline), Champion armor set (Hawke), Perrin's Nail, Hack, Runes of Protection
Tactics	• Sustain Shield Defense (15%) and Bravery (30%), upgrading as you advance. Switch on Elemental Aegis (20%) only to match anticipated elemental attacks, turning off to enable more ability use. • Advance to draw enemies and Taunt early to ensure none slip past, repeating as Cooldown allows. • Reserve Shield Bash and Scatter for coordinated cross-class combos when a Chain Lightning or Fist of the Maker is ready and waiting. • Assault and Scatter enemies after a rogue has Disoriented them.
Desirable Equipment Properties	+ X damage resistance; + X% threat generation; + X fortitude; + X health; + X healing to this character; + X stamina; immunity to stun; immunity to knockback

Healer

In prolonged battles on higher difficulty settings, you will find your party suffering low health, unconsciousness and injury. The role of the healer is to monitor their companions and restore health when necessary. All spells having a set Cooldown, the healer benefits from possessing additional healing spells to share out simultaneously.

A healer will still spend their other time in either support or offense. Of the many options available, we suggest you pursue the Primal tree as a complement to Aveline. This opens up several cross-class combo opportunities and is especially effective at following up on her Staggered opponents.

Thanks to his Vengeance personal tree, Anders is the best choice for healing and support, though only a mage Hawke can opt for the Spirit Healer tree.

Favored Character Builds	Mage Hawke, Anders
Primary Attributes	Magic, Willpower
Essential Abilities	**Creation:** Heal, Greater Heal **Spirit Healer (Hawke):** All **Vengeance (Anders):** Panacea branch **Primal:** Chain Lightning, Chain Reaction, Petrify, Desiccate, Tempest, Strikes Twice, Galvanism **Entropy (Hawke):** Horror
Aspirational Items	Ring of the Ferryman, Bassrath-Kata, The Sylvan's Heart, Enchanter's Staff, Champion armor set, Vestments of Sacrifice, Cumberland Circle Robes, Elfroot Potions, Restoration Potions, Life Ward Potion, Mythal's Favor
Tactics	• Use Heal for individuals on low health, especially your tank. • Repeat the cheaper Aid Allies or Group Heal when all companions have taken damage and one is on low health. • Reserve Desiccate for coordinated combos, preparing the way for attacks that harm Brittle foes. • Cast Chain Lightning on enemies Staggered by the tank.
Desirable Equipment Properties	+ X% healing by this character; + X mana/mana regeneration; - X% threat generation; + X electricity damage

Damage-Dealer

A damage-dealer speeds up the process of dispatching the opposition by inflicting massive amounts of damage in very little time. As revealed in the table below, this can be achieved by virtually any character provided you specialize them accordingly.

Damage-Dealer Profiles

Class	Combat Style	Party Member
Mage	Spells	Hawke, Merril, Bethany, Anders (if not used as main healer)
Rogue	Archery	Hawke, Varric, Sebastian
Rogue	Dual Weapon	Hawke, Isabela
Warrior	Two-Handed Weapon	Hawke, Carver, Fenris

When facing massed opponents, the damage-dealing role – also known as "nuke" – is best fulfilled by a mage with an array of offensive AoE spells. To get the best bonuses for damage, it is important that the mage chooses the Elemental *or* Primal discipline and first fills out the entire tree (with upgrades), rather than spreading themselves thinly over both. Furthering their career, the mage can consider debuffer spells or specialization trees.

When it comes to inflicting large amounts of pain on single opponents, you have various options. A warrior in the Two-Handed Reaver/Berserker tradition can work wonders, with Fenris as your companion exemplar, but there is also plenty of provision for the role to fall to a rogue:

- Isabela's capacity as a damage-dealer is of such ferocity that she is likely to draw threat to her (and thus away from the tank). This is not necessarily a bad thing, though, as you could employ Isabela in an off-tank role (with the Across the Bow and Savvy talents being especially useful).
- Archer rogues can also deal large amounts of damage while enjoying the (relative) safety of range – a most welcome feature when Nightmare's friendly fire comes in. Varric is geared to be a very effective archer. This is especially true as the game uses base weapon damage in calculating the power of special moves, which greatly advantages Bianca. Taking Subterfuge for escape and Sabotage for combo potential, the archer sets up Stunned, Confused and Disoriented enemies for others while reserving Punishing Lance and Shattering Arrow for Brittle victims.

Additional Roles

Debuffer/Saboteur

This mage support role takes the entire Entropy tree, packing superbly useful Hexes for reducing enemy capabilities. Every sensible mage can cheaply cast Horror for a quick holding fix on many enemies otherwise immune to Stun. But it's the further upgrades and progression to Entropic Cloud that really make a difference when you need to incapacitate devastators, assassins and bosses – either to take them down quickly or to get rid of all other foes before the effect wears off.

Lockpicker

It's frustrating to pass up locked treasure chests or suffer traps, because you will lose out on thousands of XP over the game and on valuable loot. If you happen to find any items with a related property (bonus to lockpick or bonus to disarm traps) then hold on to them. Even if they're weaker than other pieces in your inventory, you can equip them purely for the duration of the task of opening a locked chest or disarming a trap.

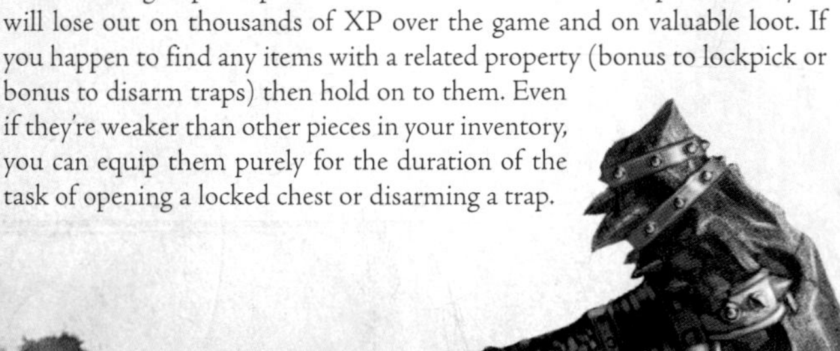

Party Builds

For sheer capacity to survive, the ideal party centers on a **tank.** Though in no way mandatory, this is the surest way to exploit the game's assumptions and advantages.

Players opting for the Hard and Nightmare difficulty settings will still find plenty of challenge in optimizing their party for the later extended battles. So the second step is to consider the inclusion of a **healer.** A good player may survive on Hard with only a Heal spell or a stack of potions, for the most part, hitting strong and fast to reduce battle ▶▶

Tactics

While you always manually control the currently selected character, the other party members behave according to the Tactics you define for them.

Tactics are built around a simple idea: you set a condition on the left side of the screen and if this condition is true in a battle, the corresponding action on the right side of the screen is executed; if not, the next condition is checked.

Of course, Tactics must be regularly adjusted as, for instance, the requirements of a party in Act 1 might be completely different for the same individuals at the start of Act 2. We can still offer a selection of useful tips that will enable you to fine-tune the default Tactics sets to get the most out of your party. ▶▶

times, but tougher moments will prompt a rethink. Again, this plays to the system, so at least one mage is recommended for the breadth and number of abilities they can bring to bear.

If the tank is good at their job then a second mage can be a candidate. There are enough magical disciplines and specializations for further mages to cover entirely different areas – especially damage-dealing and debuffing.

With an archer rogue as the fourth role, you can cover all adventuring needs with a one-melee, three-ranged party build in which your tank keeps the opposition firmly away from their companions. When threat is drawn away from the tank, the distance grants time to spot the break and call a Taunt or focus three-way fire.

Fenris and Isabela provide the companion choice of melee damage dealers. A two-melee party needs to manage threat more carefully but can exploit deathblows and crowd control (Whirlwind, Vendetta) to eliminate injured, hateful enemies as a priority.

General Tips

- Don't be intimidated! You can't "break" your party by dabbling with Tactics, as you can easily return to the default set.
- If you modify a character's Tactics, this custom set of parameters will be used until you specify otherwise. You will need to manually add new talents and spells to the list after each level-up.
- Don't forget that Tactics sets are read from top to bottom. Every time a Tactic is implemented, the system begins again from the top of the list. For this reason, high-priority Tactics (such as healing or "staple" abilities for crowd control and cross-class combos) should always be placed at the top.
- If you experience issues with companions using abilities while you are carefully executing a manual strategy in a tough fight, note that you can easily disable or enable entire sets at the Tactics screen with a simple key or button press.

Automating certain processes cuts out a lot of needless micromanagement, so we'll now look at two ways in which simple additions to the default Tactics sets can be of service (continued overleaf).

Healing & Supporting Tips

- The classic setup for Anders's Aid Allies ability is "Self: At least 3 party members below 50% health", though you may find that picking the version that only specifies two party members makes him more inclined to use the spell in a timely manner.
- If you find the required crafting ingredients and don't mind the expense, setting up your healer to automatically use Restoration Potions at low health instead of Heal will leave the spell available for other emergencies; as a secondary benefit, the tincture will also replenish your healer's mana.
- A healer can also play a role in enemy management. If you have Glyph of Paralysis, you can use this to temporarily disable stronger enemies throughout the battle. "Enemy: Highest health" is a useful condition that will generally impede a high-rank opponent such as a commander; if you are having problems with enemy Assassins, the "Enemy: Nearest visible rogue" condition can be of service.
- If you create a "nuke" mage, high on Magic and Willpower, but prone to shattering quickly under enemy blows, you could set up a "[Mage Name]: Being attacked by a melee attack", with "Glyph of Repulsion" as the following action.

Cross-Class Combo Tips

- To set up a Tactic that exploits the Brittle, Staggered or Disoriented status effects, select "Target: Condition", then select "Enemy" → "Status", then pick the appropriate condition from the list.
- Let's use the fully upgraded Winter's Grasp as an example. This generally freezes a single target, so set up "Enemy: Highest health" → "Winter's Grasp". Reposition this at the top of your mage's Tactics list. You can now set up the finishing move: we'll use the ever-useful Varric in this instance. With its upgrade, his Archer's Lance ability can inflict massive damage against a Brittle target (which is why we specify "Highest health" earlier). Create the "Enemy: BRITTLE" → "Archer's Lance" Tactic and move it to the top of the list, then go try it out in a live fire situation.
- For those who have the time and inclination, you can use the "Jump to tactic" action to create crude "subroutines" at the end of a Tactics list. This might help to encourage an AI-controlled character to differentiate between a single target ripe for a cross-class combo and groups more suited to an AoE finish. Here's a very rough-'n'-ready example, using Varric:

#	Tactic
1:	"Enemy: BRITTLE" → "Jump to: 18"
17:	"Self: Any" → "Jump to: 20"
18:	"Enemy: Clustered with at least 3 enemies" → "Bursting Arrow"
19:	"Enemy: BRITTLE" → "Archer's Lance"
20:	-

Combat Strategy

Combat Priorities

Open the battle by killing your most dangerous enemies (devastators and assassins) and incapacitating commanders. With the biggest hitters and annoyances removed, look to reduce enemy numbers by focusing on the weaker ones. Keep using basic stuns on the commander to keep his aura deactivated so that weak creatures can be eliminated. The commander's significant health bar can then be tackled with focused fire.

Pin-Down

Having identified a priority target such as an assassin or devastator, it is urgent that you prevent them from employing their powerful strikes and subsequent escape procedures. They must be pinned down while you undertake a potentially lengthy attempt to wipe out their entire health bar in one uninterrupted assault. There are many useful abilities that can be queued in succession to maintain a hold on the enemy for an extended duration: Horror, Pinning Shot, Glyph of Paralysis, Winter's Blast, Stonefist, Crushing Prison, and so forth.

Focused Fire

Focusing the damage of all party members on one enemy naturally speeds up their elimination, and ordering attacks into cross-class combos can earn enormous damage multipliers. However, there are other tactics that can be put in place to secure greater, faster damage. These work best the sooner they are placed:

- Damage resistance reduction on enemy (Death Hex, Entropic Cloud).
- Critical chance increases on enemy (Brand and Mark of Death).
- Attack or critical chance increases on party (Valiant Aura and Rally).
- Accelerated attacks by party (Haste, Speed).

Kiting

When an enemy decides to close on a target, there is no need for the target to stand and wait. Indeed, if the companion in question can outrun the opponents, then he or she can lead them around the battlefield, while other party members pile on ranged damage and closing attacks. This works best against bosses and large, slow enemies whose main attack is melee. Further slowing rounds of cold and electricity damage can keep a powerful foe tied up and unable to deliver its attack for a prolonged period. Additionally, the party can profit from healing and time to burn through Cooldowns while the enemy is being kited.

Peeling

Exploring a new area, your first sight of an enemy squad will be limited to the nearest targets. You can exploit this to peel off enemies from the main squad in small, manageable numbers:

- Order your party to Hold Position.
- Approach only as closely as you need to catch the attention of the nearest enemies.
- Use a ranged attack to attract them if required.
- Guide your scout in retreat back to your party, leading a few enemies in tow.

The Archer Trap Principle

This works for any team with ranged attacks, and can be initiated with peeling. The idea is to lead enemies into a hail of spells and projectiles in order to soften them up before they can initiate melee combat:

- Place your tank out front as the bait for enemies and Hold Position.
- Lay down a Glyph, Hail of Arrows, Miasmic Flask, Gravitic Ring or any other effects ahead of them to slow and halt approaching enemies.
- Unleash the fury of your bolts, arrows and spells upon easy targets.
- Use any other repellent force to drive enemies back into the firing zone. Even an upgraded Mind Blast, when confined to a corridor, can propel enemies like a walk-in cannon.
- Finally, enter melee combat against weakened opponents.

Bottlenecks

Using the environment is a valid tactic in dealing with large numbers of aggressors. Enemies can be channeled into a corridor or held at a doorway by a blocking tank, while other characters use ranged support from behind.

Solid obstacles provide cover, completely blocking ranged attacks and also any spell targeting. If you can't see your victim in line of sight, you can't cast a spell on them – although you could catch them with Area of Effect splash damage.

THREAT MANAGEMENT

Threat is the system by which enemies pick their targets. Much as you look out for Arcane Horrors or Blood Mages among the enemy ranks, so your enemies will first try to eliminate the biggest danger to themselves, and each enemy assesses threat individually. Managing threat enables you to control the fight, guiding the enemy to attack a strong character (your tank) instead of a frail one.

The initial threat rating when your party encounters trouble is based on class potential, so warriors will be the priority target. After that, the class threat generation applies to all subsequent actions and your characters' threat level is determined in real time by various factors:

- Proximity accounts for up to 100 points of threat when up close, falling to 1 point at 60m distance on a linear scale (the maximum amount of threat being 1,000). This factor naturally distinguishes melee fighters over ranged attackers. If you want to give your tank an early advantage, make sure he or she piles straight into the enemy to draw them in.
- Damage is the major factor and can alter threat priorities during a fight. Warriors can maintain their high threat by inflicting plentiful damage, although tanks will always do less than damage dealers in the long run. This is why your tank needs to Taunt opponents or to use other abilities to maintain their attention.
- The amount of threat generated by damage is directly proportional to the harm inflicted on the enemy. If a companion's attack cuts an enemy's health bar in half, the threat that your companion poses to the enemy will rise by 50% of maximum threat (so, +500). Damage dealers can thus generate threat spikes, especially when concluding a cross-class combo. This is when they need to use whatever abilities they have to lower or transfer threat, as revealed in the table to the right.
- Items that affect threat generation (such as Ghillie Brogues) impact directly on these amounts, so keep them for your most powerful damage dealers.
- Secondary damage also builds threat, albeit slowly, so mages and warriors with support skills will accrue threat from the damage buffs they apply to the whole party.
- Against a larger enemy or boss, a change in threat priorities can be a viable tactic to keep them occupied so that the previous target can recover. "Kiting" an enemy (see Combat Strategy on the previous page) can postpone their attacks and is especially effective if the boss can be slowed by magic or other talents.

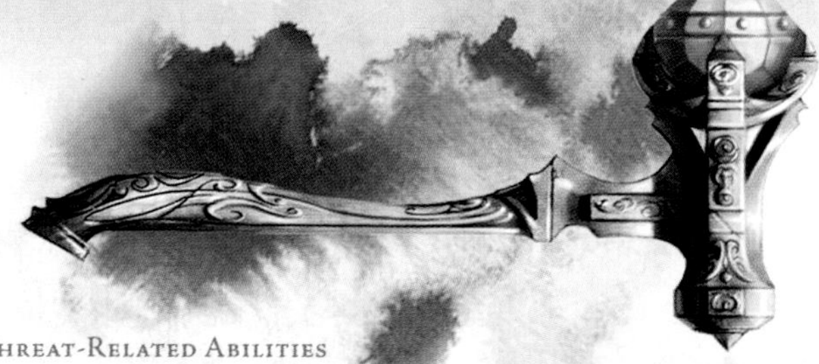

Threat-Related Abilities

Class	Threat Generation	Abilities	Effect
Mage	50%	Mind Blast	Clear threat on self
Rogue	75%	Evade, Inconspicuous	Lower threat on self
		Throw the Gauntlet, Across The Bow	Raise threat on self
		Goad, Armistice	Raise/lower threat on companion
		Decoy, Guardian Angel	Transfer threat from self to decoy
Warrior	100%	Taunt, Bellow	Raise threat on self
		Bravado	Raise threat on self
		Fearless Synergy	Transfer threat from companions to self

NIGHTMARE DIFFICULTY

The Nightmare difficulty setting introduces three major differences to combat:

1. Attacks cause friendly fire. This cuts both ways, as not only can you hurt your own companions but enemies can also hurt each other.

2. Enemies now boast elemental immunities. Refer to the Bestiary for details.

3. Enemy toughness is scaled up. They inflict even more damage on you and take more to kill. Assassins have a chance to steal potions from the party and their stealth attacks bypass the victim's armor completely. Commanders are able to direct their troops at party members for a concerted attack.

Playing on Nightmare therefore requires a more careful style of play. The following tips will help you get the right habits:

- You are your own worst enemy in Nightmare. The friendly fire of your best attacks will wipe out companions who get in the way. AoE spells that only target enemies include Sleep and the electricity attacks of the Primal tree.

- Micromanagement squeezes the most from your party members, ensuring they work in a coordinated fashion. Pause the game frequently to monitor their status and issue new orders.

- Cross-class combos are essential for grinding down enemies, which is why it is important that you choose when your companions unleash their talents. The damage multipliers possible against enemies you have deliberately set up with specific status effects make it possible to grind down the toughest enemies.

- If you have a Spirit Healer with Second Chance, you no longer need to worry about injuries. Otherwise, away from home, use any injury kits to cure as soon as possible: you'll force the game's generosity in providing up to the inventory limit of four from loot piles and containers. Such drops come as additional treasures and do not replace money or item loot.

- Battles remain ongoing while there are still enemies in the vicinity (red dots visible on the minimap). If you can retreat a sufficient distance, you can force the conclusion of the battle and some recovery time, not to mention a save game opportunity.

- Crafted poisons, potions and bombs are extremely effective combat aids. Imbuing a rogue's twin blades with slowing effects can turn the tide of a tough battle, and you don't have to be a mage to swig a Rock Armor Potion for impressive damage resistance.

- To perform any kind of Area of Effect ability safely, you will need to keep enemies grouped and isolated. The Force Mage specialization sacrifices damage for effects that repel, slow and pull enemies to where they can be hammered and blasted. Warriors can use Scatter to drive back a few enemies at once. Use Hold Position to stop your characters running off into the fray.

- One-hit kills from enemies can ruin your day. If your mage cannot survive long enough to raise a Barrier or Glyph when an assassin pops into stealth, buy more health with equipment properties and spend some attribute points in Constitution. Note that a character with less than 10% health remaining will bleed out to death unless healed.

- Crowd control is essential when critters and archers can pose a serious knockdown threat. Enemy damage and force scales with difficulty, and a mage can no longer afford to Mind Blast with allies in the vicinity because of the AoE effect.

COMPANION ANALYSIS

SPOILER WARNING! This section acts as an unexpurgated overview of companion relationships and romances. It is designed to assist players who intend to try different party builds and quests during repeat playthroughs. Unless you have completed the main storyline at least once, we strongly suggest that you do not read this section yet.

BETHANY & CARVER

Quick Facts

Recruitment	Mandatory: available from the start of the story.
Can Leave Party?	Yes – there's an unavoidable death for one in the Prologue, and the surviving sibling cannot continue in the party beyond the end of Act 1.
Personality Conflicts	Bethany will clash with Fenris in mage-related quests. Carver can clash with Anders and Merrill in mage storylines.
Companion Quest	**Birthright**
Armor Upgrades	• Act 1 – Carver: Fereldan Girded Plating (**Birthright**) • Act 1 – Bethany: Heirloom Amell Protective Sigils (**Birthright**)
Gifts	Tobrius's Documents (Carver), Portrait of Your Mother (Bethany) – both found during **Birthright**

General Notes

- Bethany is a fairly straightforward character. Building a friendship with her is easy if you favor helpful or diplomatic dialogue options; you should also side with mages whenever possible. To foment rivalry, the reverse applies.
- Carver begins the story with a preexisting tilt towards rivalry, so attempting to achieve full friendship is a challenge only for the dedicated repeat player. Supporting the templar position of controls for mages will please him, though don't assume that he's somehow the antithesis of Bethany: he's by no means brutal or ungallant.
- Unless you pick Carver or Bethany as permanent party members throughout Act 1 and make efforts to pander to their specific personalities, it's unlikely that you will reach full friendship or rivalry. If you do manage to max out the relationship gauge in either direction, this will give you access to extra reactive lines in the later game.

Crisis Points

- It is purely your choice of class that governs which sibling survives to reach Kirkwall: Carver if Hawke is a mage, or Bethany for rogues and warriors.
- If you refuse to take them on the **Deep Roads Expedition**, Bethany will be forcefully recruited to the Circle, while Carver will voluntarily join the templars on your return.
- Take Bethany or Carver to the Deep Roads with Anders in the party, and you have the choice of sending them to join the Grey Wardens or allowing them to die. If Anders is not present, death is unavoidable.

Later Appearances

If Carver/Bethany joins the Grey Wardens, they will appear in the following quests:

- The first encounter is in Lowtown during **Demands of the Qun** in Act 2 (see page 75).
- The second is during the **Finding Nathaniel** secondary quest in Act 3 (see page 99). This optional storyline has very specific unlock requirements.
- They will make a cameo appearance as the kidnap victim in **Best Served Cold** in Act 3.
- If **Finding Nathaniel** is completed, they will appear in Lowtown during **The Last Straw**. You have the option to take them with you (and even have them rejoin as active party members in later battles) or send them away. The latter option will prevent them from playing any further part in the conclusion of the story.

If Bethany or Carver joins the mage or templar factions:

- You will cross paths with one briefly during **Demands of the Qun** in Act 2 (see page 75).
- The surviving sibling will make a cameo appearance as the kidnap victim in **Best Served Cold** in Act 3.
- Bethany or Carver make more telling contributions during **The Last Straw**. They appear in the opening confrontation between Orsino and Meredith and can later be recruited back into the party for the final confrontations under very specific circumstances (see page 94).

There is one small consequence to having both Bethany and Carver die: this is the only condition under which another companion can be kidnapped during **Best Served Cold** (see page 93). This will be of interest to completionists who feel compelled to see every last potential outcome.

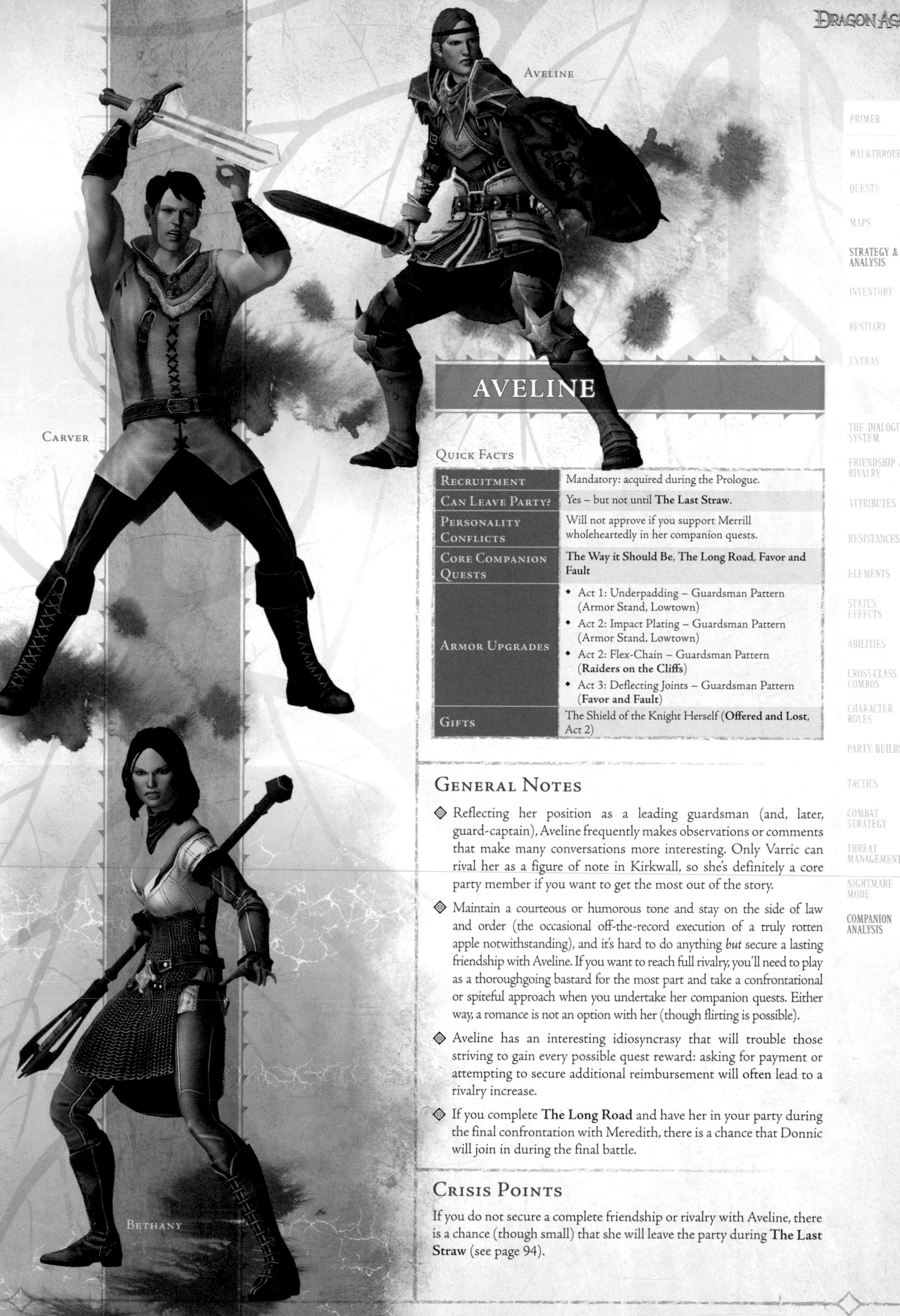

AVELINE

Quick Facts

Recruitment	Mandatory: acquired during the Prologue.
Can Leave Party?	Yes – but not until **The Last Straw**.
Personality Conflicts	Will not approve if you support Merrill wholeheartedly in her companion quests.
Core Companion Quests	**The Way it Should Be, The Long Road, Favor and Fault**
Armor Upgrades	• Act 1: Underpadding – Guardsman Pattern (Armor Stand, Lowtown) • Act 2: Impact Plating – Guardsman Pattern (Armor Stand, Lowtown) • Act 2: Flex-Chain – Guardsman Pattern (**Raiders on the Cliffs**) • Act 3: Deflecting Joints – Guardsman Pattern (**Favor and Fault**)
Gifts	The Shield of the Knight Herself (**Offered and Lost**, Act 2)

General Notes

- Reflecting her position as a leading guardsman (and, later, guard-captain), Aveline frequently makes observations or comments that make many conversations more interesting. Only Varric can rival her as a figure of note in Kirkwall, so she's definitely a core party member if you want to get the most out of the story.
- Maintain a courteous or humorous tone and stay on the side of law and order (the occasional off-the-record execution of a truly rotten apple notwithstanding), and it's hard to do anything *but* secure a lasting friendship with Aveline. If you want to reach full rivalry, you'll need to play as a thoroughgoing bastard for the most part and take a confrontational or spiteful approach when you undertake her companion quests. Either way, a romance is not an option with her (though flirting is possible).
- Aveline has an interesting idiosyncrasy that will trouble those striving to gain every possible quest reward: asking for payment or attempting to secure additional reimbursement will often lead to a rivalry increase.
- If you complete **The Long Road** and have her in your party during the final confrontation with Meredith, there is a chance that Donnic will join in during the final battle.

Crisis Points

If you do not secure a complete friendship or rivalry with Aveline, there is a chance (though small) that she will leave the party during **The Last Straw** (see page 94).

VARRIC

QUICK FACTS

RECRUITMENT	Mandatory: joins the party at the start of Act 1.
CAN LEAVE PARTY?	No – he's present until the bitter end, no matter what.
PERSONALITY CONFLICTS	None – this affable storyteller works well with everyone.
CORE COMPANION QUESTS	**Family Matter**, **Haunted**
ARMOR UPGRADES	• Act 1: Inscribed Leather Harness (Apparel Shop, Lowtown) • Act 2: Coat Lining with Concealed Pockets (Shady Merchandise, Docks) • Act 2: Silverite-Reinforced Buckles (**Family Matter**) • Act 3: Drakeskin Leg Straps (**Finding Nathaniel**)
GIFTS	The Tethras Signet Ring (Trinkets Emporium in Lowtown, Act 2)

GENERAL NOTES

- Unless you are obnoxious, petty or cruel, a gradual drift towards a full friendship with Varric is almost inevitable over the course of the adventure. Say the right things in his companion quests (he responds very well to humor), and you can accelerate this process dramatically. You cannot complete a romance with him, though.
- Varric's lack of a personal crusade means that he's easy to have around. Unless your Hawke is a truly nasty piece of work, you'll rarely need to worry about how the dwarf will react.
- Like Aveline, Varric has many interesting and unique reactions during dialogue sequences. He contributes a number of genuine laugh out loud moments to certain quests.
- Varric's final armor upgrade is only available in the **Finding Nathaniel** quest, which few players will have access to on a first playthrough. It could be considered a reward for those who chose to preserve **Nathaniel**'s life in Awakening.

VARRIC

ANDERS

QUICK FACTS

RECRUITMENT	Mandatory: early Act 1, after **Tranquility** is complete.
CAN LEAVE PARTY?	Yes – and on more than one occasion.
PERSONALITY CONFLICTS	Fenris and Sebastian do not combine well with Anders if you are aspiring to harmonious relationships; Carver will also clash with him, albeit to a lesser extent.
CORE COMPANION QUESTS	**Tranquility**, **Dissent**, **Justice**
ARMOR UPGRADES	• Act 2: Armor Struts (Lirene's Ferelden Imports, Lowtown) • Act 2: Lyrium Weave (Mage Goods, Gallows Courtyard) • Act 2: Spirit Essence (**Dissent**) • Act 3: Sigil of the Mage Underground (**Best Served Cold**)
GIFTS	Tevinter Chantry Amulet (**A Bitter Pill**, Act 2)

GENERAL NOTES

- On a mage-friendly playthrough, Anders is easy to please. Favor the templars, however, and complete rivalry is assured unless you make an effort to appease him in other ways, and leave him at home during storylines that might elicit the full extent of his fundamentalist fury.
- The **Dissent** quest offers massive boosts to friendship and rivalry (see page 82). With the correct decisions and a little forward planning, you could reach the maximum level in either direction early in Act 2 and therefore remove the need to consider his feelings as you spend the rest of the story appeasing templars.
- If you have not chosen the mage class for Hawke, Anders is the only candidate for the support healer role. Think very carefully before saying anything that might cause him to leave the party at key junctures in his personal storylines. Act 3 features many challenging battles, so you may sorely miss him later.

CRISIS POINTS

- If Hawke is less than understanding in the closing dialogue of **Dissent**, Anders will offer to leave the party. Accepting this will remove him from the game until the events of **The Last Straw**.
- In the aftermath of the Chantry's destruction, you can exact immediate retribution by killing Anders on the spot. If you send him away and side with Orsino, you can re-recruit him later – or fight him if you opt to serve the knight-commander's cause.

ROMANCE

To complete a full romance with Anders, you must satisfy the following requirements:

- Achieve 50% rivalry or friendship, then complete his **Questioning Beliefs** mid-stage relationship conversation during Act 2.
- Flirt with Anders at any point before or during **Questioning Beliefs**. If you don't, the romance cannot start.
- During **Questioning Beliefs**, Anders will intimate that a nocturnal visit is forthcoming. Returning to Hawke Estate in the evening at any point before the end of Act 2 will then trigger his arrival at the house. Flirt with him to begin the romance. In the conversation that follows, invite Anders to live with Hawke.
- Finish his remaining companion quests (including the delivery of his gift, the Tevinter Chantry Amulet) and any ambient dialogues that crop up. You must also reach a full 100% friendship or rivalry.
- You must side with the mages in **The Last Straw** (and, naturally, spare his life) and speak to him in the Gallows Prison to complete the romance.

MERRILL

ANDERS

MERRILL

QUICK FACTS

RECRUITMENT	Mandatory: enlisted by completing **Long Way Home** at the very start of Act 1.
CAN LEAVE PARTY?	Yes – but not until **The Last Straw.**
PERSONALITY CONFLICTS	Will clash with Fenris and Carver in mage-oriented storylines. You will please no one if you support her in her Act 2 and Act 3 companion quests.
CORE COMPANION QUESTS	**Long Way Home, Mirror Image, A New Path**
ARMOR UPGRADES	• Act 2: Samite Lining (Robes by Jean Luc, Hightown) • Act 2: Carved Ironwood Buttons (Ilen's Crafts, Sundermount) • Act 2: Silver-Threaded Dalish Embroidery (top of Sundermount) • Act 3: Halla Horn Buckles (**A New Path**)
GIFTS	• Wooden Halla Carving (Ilen's Crafts, Act 2) • Sylvanwood Ring (found in the remains of the Thief Leader during A Murder of Crows, Act 3)

GENERAL NOTES

- Another mage, another set of awkward sympathies to address for those on a templar-specific playthrough – though it's fair to say that Merrill is less touchy about the subject than Anders or Bethany.
- For a happy relationship with Merrill, treat her with kindness and complete her Act 2 and 3 companion quests to her satisfaction. For rivalry, disparage or discourage her throughout, withhold the Arulin'holm at the end of **Mirror Image**, then castigate her savagely for the death of Keeper Marethari at the conclusion of **A New Path**.

CRISIS POINTS

If you do not achieve 100% friendship or rivalry before **The Last Straw** and side with the templars, Merrill will leave the party. If she is a rival, but not at 100% on that side of the scale, you must fight her.

ROMANCE

To see a romance with Merrill through to its conclusion, you must satisfy the following requirements:

- Reach 50% friendship or rivalry, and flirt with Merrill at least once before or during the **Questioning Beliefs** mid-point relationship conversation in Act 2.
- After **Questioning Beliefs** has finished, Merrill will visit the Hawke Estate in the evening if her friendship or rivalry level remains at least 50% in either direction. Flirt with her to initiate the romance and invite her to move in.
- You must then reach 100% rivalry or friendship, complete her companion quests, give both gifts, speak to her in any ambient conversations that arise, then – finally – complete the **Friend or Foe** dialogue.
- If you are on the rival path, you will need to ally Hawke with the mages to guarantee that the romance reaches its optimum conclusion. On the friendship path, you can still side with the templars and complete the romance by convincing Merrill that the choice is not Hawke's to make: pick the "Anders tied our hands" option. Finally, speak with her in the Gallows Prison or Gallows Courtyard (during the **Last Straw**) to complete the romance.

ISABELA

Quick Facts

Recruitment	Optional: complete **Fools Rush In** to acquire her services.
Can Leave Party?	Yes – there are three instances where this could happen at the climax of Act 2.
Personality Conflicts	There's a *slight* variance of opinion regarding law and order with Aveline, but nothing major.
Core Companion Quests	**Fools Rush In**, **To Catch a Thief**, **No Rest for the Wicked**
Armor Upgrades	• Act 2: Rigid Boning (Apparel Shop, Lowtown) • Act 2: Supportive Corselet (Robes by Jean Luc, Hightown) • Act 2: Lambswool Insoles (**To Catch a Thief**) • Act 3: Boiled Leather Plates (**A Murder of Crows**)
Gifts	• Ship in a Bottle (**Blackpowder Courtesy**, Act 2) • Rivaini Talisman (Disused Passage, Act 3)

General Notes

- Isabela is one of the toughest companions to secure a full friendship or rivalry with. The only surefire way to develop the relationship to either extent is to pander to her shamelessly in her companion quests, deliver both gifts and sleep with her for good measure. As a rule, she tends to respond well to humor.
- An interesting facet of her character is that she really doesn't feel any fondness for Meredith. This isn't a case of her siding with the mages, but merely that she doesn't like working or bargaining with Meredith because she thinks the knight-commander is, well, *off her rocker*.

Crisis Points

- Isabela is unique in that you *must* secure 50% friendship or rivalry and complete her **Questioning Beliefs** mid-stage relationship conversation before the end of Act 2 if you wish to retain her as a companion. This should ideally be achieved before you begin **Following the Qun**.
- If you fail to help Isabela first when she and Aveline arrive at the Hawke Estate after **Following the Qun**, she leaves the party permanently – no matter what the current state of your relationship may be.
- Even if you complete **To Catch a Thief**, Isabela will only make her timely return during **Demands of the Qun** if you have satisfied the requirements detailed earlier. While handing her to the Arishok enables you to resolve the Qunari crisis without further bloodshed, this will lead to her permanent departure.

Romance

To sweep Isabela off her feet (despite her apparent disinterest in such an outcome beyond a purely physical interpretation of the phrase), you must complete the following objectives:

- You have to be on the friendship path to complete the romance with Isabela, though this isn't necessary for the first steps. She will sleep with Hawke no matter the state of their relationship.
- Flirt with the Rivaini during the **Isabela's Ongoing Search** companion quest, available from the start of Act 2. This will cause Isabela to make a random visit to Hawke Estate at night during the events of Act 2. Flirt again to sleep with her. In the following dialogue, you must ask why Isabela is hesitant to fall in love, then explore all "investigate" options (as denoted by the ? icon).
- Ensure that Isabela returns after **To Catch a Thief** (see Crisis Points).
- The final steps are to find and bestow both gifts, reach 100% friendship, then begin the **Questioning Beliefs** final-stage relationship conversation. When Isabela says the line that begins with "Now that I have my ship...", reply with "I'd like that". Last, but not least, converse with her in the Gallows Prison or Gallows Courtyard in **The Last Straw** to complete the romance.

FENRIS

Quick Facts

Recruitment	Optional: complete **A Bitter Pill** in Act 1.
Can Leave Party?	Yes – and on more than one occasion.
Personality Conflicts	With anyone wearing robes or wielding a staff – including Hawke.
Core Companion Quests	**Bait and Switch, A Bitter Pill, Alone**
Armor Upgrades	• Act 2: Tevinter Spirit Symbol (Robes by Jean Luc, Hightown) • Act 2: Lyrium Scales (Shady Merchandise, Docks) • Act 2: Reinforced Straps (**A Bitter Pill**) • Act 3: Enchanted Resin (**Mine Massacre**)
Gifts	• The Book of Shartan (Lowtown elven alienage, Act 2) • Blade of Mercy (**Best Served Cold**, Act 3)

General Notes

- To secure a friendship, leave Fenris out of the party for quests that involve the escalating mage/templar conflict if you intend to side with the practitioners of the arcane arts. Alternatively, just favor Meredith's worldview throughout the story.
- If you desire rivalry while siding with the templars, you'll need to be artfully unpleasant during his companion quests.

Crisis Points

You will permanently lose Fenris as a companion if you:

- Fail to complete **Bait and Switch**.
- Refuse to journey to the Slaver Camp after the second Tevinter ambush in **A Bitter Pill**.
- Substitute Fenris from the party after the first ambush that triggers **A Bitter Pill**, then fail to resume the quest. After a certain period of time, the outraged elf will confront Hawke and leave.
- Allow Danarius to take him during the **Alone** companion quest.

Unless you complete his companion quests, reach 100% friendship or rivalry and complete his final-stage relationship conversation, Fenris will abandon the party after the destruction of the Chantry if you support Orsino. He can be persuaded to rejoin during the negotiations at the Gallows if you have a solid friendship with him. If Fenris does not return to the fold, those siding with mages must fight him at the Templar Hall.

Romance

To see a romance with Fenris through to its conclusion, you must satisfy the following requirements:

- Reach 50% friendship or rivalry, then flirt with Fenris during the **Questioning Beliefs** mid-stage relationship conversation. If the friendship or rivalry level remains at least 50%, Fenris will subsequently visit the Hawke Estate if you return at night. Flirt with him to trigger the romance. The next step is to ask him to move in.
- Complete remaining companion quests and dialogues, give him both gifts, reach 100% rivalry or friendship, then complete the **Questioning Beliefs** final-stage relationship conversation before the start of **The Last Straw**.
- If you are on the rivalry path, you must ally yourself with the templars. If you are on the friendship path, you can convince Fenris to stay if you choose to support the mages. Speak with him at the Gallows Courtyard or Gallows Prison during **The Last Straw** to complete the romance.

SEBASTIAN

Quick Facts

Recruitment*	Optional: complete **Duty** and **Repentance**.
Can Leave Party?	Yes – but only during **The Last Straw**.
Personality Conflicts	Bears no love for Anders.
Core Companion Quests	**Duty, Repentance, Faith**
Armor Upgrades	• Act 2: Enhanced Articulation (Armor Shop, Gallows Courtyard) • Act 2: Reinforced Bracers (Olaf's Armory), Hightown) • Act 2: Mail Undertunic (**Repentance**) • Act 3: Protection of the Faith (**Best Served Cold**)
Gifts	Starkhaven Longbow (**Repentance**, Act 2)

* Sebastian is only available with the Exiled Prince downloadable content: See dragonage.com/da2/addons for details.

General Notes

Sebastian is a very "pure" character, which makes his responses fairly easy to anticipate. It's wise to leave him behind during the **Dissent** and **Justice** companion quests if you aspire to a friendship with both him and Anders.

Crisis Points

If you do not kill Anders following the destruction of the Chantry, Sebastian will leave the party permanently.

Romance

Though it may seem unlikely, it is possible to win Sebastian's heart. To achieve this feat, take the following steps:

- While all other potential love interests happily swing either way, Sebastian is resolutely heterosexual: only a female Hawke has any hope of success.
- The second requirement is equally pivotal: you must *never* flirt with another character at any point in the story.
- The remaining steps are to achieve 100% friendship and complete Sebastian's companion quests. Flirt with the Starkhaven exile both before and during the **Questioning Beliefs** final-stage relationship conversation to have him suggest an unconventional partnership.
- The execution of Anders in **The Last Straw** is the penultimate step required to complete the romance. A conversation with Sebastian at the Gallows Courtyard or Gallows Prison will lead to the conclusion you seek.

INTRODUCTION

After character builds and companion selection, inventory offers the most efficient method of enhancing and tuning a party to increase resilience or meet a specific threat. Individual abilities can be promoted by equipping items with supporting buffs and bonuses. Resistances can be increased to overcome a known foe. And for the player who relishes difficulty, party equipment can be coordinated to underpin a strong but precise battle tactic.

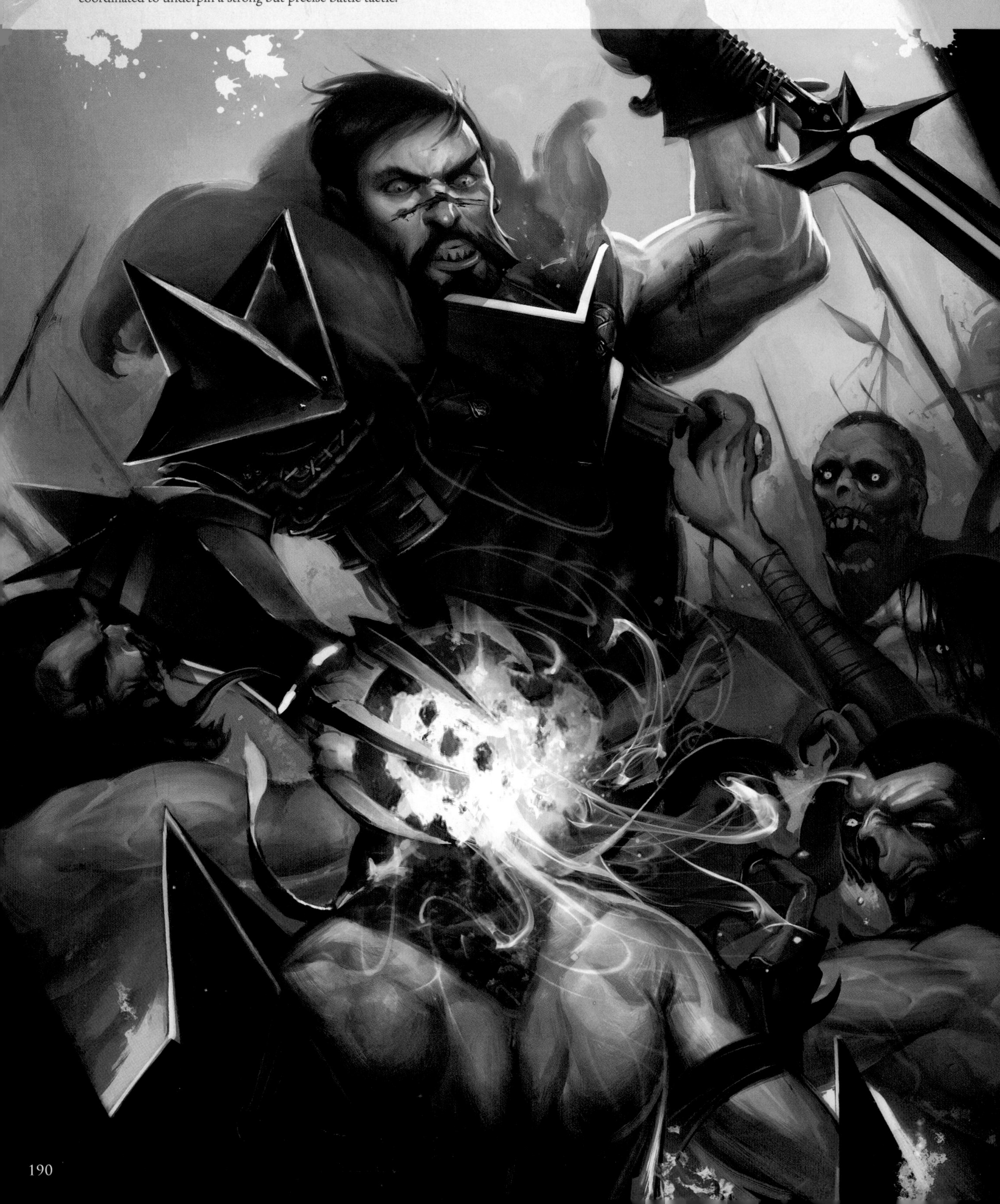

Unique Items & Generated Items

Unique items are those with set attributes and prices. These are usually better and far more valuable than their randomly generated counterparts. This chapter lists every single unique piece of equipment available in the game.

"Generated items" refers to a system in the game that takes a weapon, accessory or armor, assigns attributes, then scales the associated values to the level of your characters. As there are literally thousands of random items and possibilities therein, this guide focuses on unique items. If you would like to read a more detailed explanation of the generated items system, turn to page 209.

Ratings and Bonuses

The five-star rating system ( ) is the first guide to the relative power and usefulness of an item. When equipping a new sword, for instance, a two-star rating indicates a weapon that is average for your level. One star means the weapon is underpowered for the foes you can expect to face. Weapons of three to five stars will grant an excellent advantage if used correctly.

While the star rating provides a rough guide that is derived from the raw potential of the item, it does not reflect context. For example an amulet with no stars at all may actually serve an excellent purpose if it raises a rogue's 29 cunning to 30 cunning, thus enabling a complex grade of locks and traps to be tackled. Equally, a five-star item may be useless if it benefits talents that the character does not use, such as blood magic.

Weapon and Armor Attributes

Every weapon possesses a numerical base damage rating, which also indicates its elemental affinity. Swords, maces, bows, axes and daggers do physical damage – which is also an affinity, just like fire and cold – that can be countered by an enemy's physical resistance, otherwise known as armor. The higher the damage, the better the weapon. The character's total damage rating can be seen by the flash icon ( ) under Stats, and will be a higher number than the base rating if the character has bonuses to damage in effect. This is the theoretical amount of health that an attack would remove from an unarmored opponent.

Because characters can attack at different speeds, the figure in brackets provides a calculation of DPS (Damage Per Second) so that characters can be compared evenly on their basic weapon attacks.

Armor has a base protection rating that is added to all other items of armor being worn to create a cumulative armor value. This total is shown by the helmet icon ( ) under Stats and, again, may be higher if the character enjoys other bonuses. Armor is used to calculate the character's physical resistance, shown in brackets as a percentage, which functions just like other resistances in describing the amount of damage that is disregarded from a physical attack. Whatever damage penetrates is removed from the character's health.

Note that you will find a complete guide to attributes and resistances in the Strategy & Analysis chapter.

Requirements

Even if they possessed the muscles to pick it up, an untrained mage would have no idea how to swing a battle axe. A rogue would fare no better in guessing how to shake a spark from a staff of lightning. In other words many items simply cannot be used without the character meeting a set of minimum requirements that can relate to class, talent tree, level and attribute.

As a rule, the key requirements are down to two attributes that are essential for a corresponding class:

Armor Type	Class	Attributes Required
Heavy	Warrior	Strength & Constitution
Medium	Rogue	Dexterity & Cunning
Light	Mage	Magic & Willpower

It is sometimes possible for a high-level player to achieve attributes that would allow equipping armor of a different class, but of such a lower level that the items would almost certainly be useless.

There's a small trick that you may exploit which uses items that boost attributes. An accessory that boosts constitution, for instance, can be used to meet the minimum requirements of a piece of warrior armor, allowing the armor to be equipped. The accessory may then be removed and replaced with something else, but the armor will remain equipped (though grayed out) and its effects on stats will also stay active. In this way, you can equip items that the character couldn't otherwise use.

Rune Slots

Weapons and armor with slots for Runes are rare and highly prized for customization. This is reflected in their price and those with more than one Rune slot are precious indeed. Even if the item appears ordinary in other regards, the addition of an uncommon nature damage bonus, for instance, through the process of enchantment creates a rare form of weapon that can give you a significant advantage against specific enemies.

A few Runes may be found or purchased directly, but to source the best ones you will need to craft them for yourself. The details of enchantment are covered on page 213.

Default Items

In case you fancied a spot of wrestling, you should be aware that it's not possible to leave your characters undefended by removing their weapons. Every party member has a basic sidearm to call on if nothing else is equipped. For instance, the mage's default stick is a Basic Staff of fire, doing just 4 points of damage. Basic weapons are extremely weak and do not scale with the character's level.

01

If you decide to remove your character's armor as well, a fetching set of underwear protects their modesty – but little else, as there is no default armor. And yes, the effect persists for engine cut scenes (Fig. 1).

EQUIPMENT PROPERTIES

This section studies some of the most interesting properties offered by certain pieces of equipment in the game. These can often be used to further specialize characters fulfilling a specific role, such as tanks, lockpickers or damage-dealers. For more details on abilities, attributes and resistances, consult the Strategy & Analysis chapter.

Bonus to lockpicking | Bonus to disarm traps | Bonus to evade traps
The actual effect of these bonuses is to increase your character's cunning attribute by 50%, but purely in relation to the named task. So for instance a rogue with just 20 cunning but a bonus to lockpicking would be able to open complex chests, which normally require 30 cunning. With this property equipped, master chests become pilferable at 27 cunning.

25% chance to reduce movement speed | 25% chance to reduce attack speed
Every successful attack has a chance to reduce the enemy's movement speed or attack speed by 50% for a brief duration. Some enemies have specific immunities to these debuffs, but all others will become far less dangerous for the duration of the effect – a very useful way to hamper enemy damage-dealers.

+ X% threat generation
Intended for the tank in your party, this property raises their ability to draw the attention of enemies. These bonuses are small, especially when proximity plays a role, but can help to postpone that moment in battle when a daunting enemy decides that your mage or rogue is a greater threat. See page 180 for a better understanding of threat.

- X% threat generation
This makes the wearer more likely to be ignored during combat. Proximity can always offset a minor threat, so this bonus is most effective when trying to avoid enemy archers.

Blood magic: each point of health provides 1 additional mana
Blood magic ordinarily provides 3 points of mana for every 1 point of health, so with just two items possessing this property, the ratio would increase to 5:1, making the mana pool available huge. The ever-present risk of blood magic, though, is that the caster cannot be healed normally and sacrifices health to cast spells.

Immunity to stun
Though useful to all, this is one of the finer properties tanks can obtain as it prevents their defenses and generated threat from being reset.

+ X damage vs. humans
This is a powerful damage bonus useful against many enemy groups, such as thugs, mages and templars.

+ X% healing to this character
This property is intended primarily for your warriors with high constitution. It means that healing spells cast upon them will restore more health than they normally provide.

+ X% healing by this character
This property is useful for Spirit Healers and supporting mages. More effective healing spells will need to be cast less often, which counteracts lengthy Cooldown periods in long battles.

+ X damage resistance
One of the most useful resistances, as this applies to all types of damage taken. It's like having a few extra points of armor against any kind of attack.

+ X% attack speed
Individually, these bonuses tend to be small and often negligible. But if your character has abilities that enhance attack speed or companions who provide a speed buff, the cumulative effect can be worth pursuing. Increasing attack speed raises the probability of critical hits.

+ X% critical chance | + X% critical damage
The first of these bonuses raises the probability of landing critical hits; the second raises their power. Rogues will find that the latter becomes more important over time with the acquisition of automatic critical hits through ability or strategy. Stacking these bonuses can significantly increase a character's effectiveness.

+ X% chance to knock back
Knockback and Knockdown work best with a little micromanagement, so that the character leaves the victim out of the fight or open to others.

+ X physical damage across 2m
This increase in range suits both the tank encircled by aggressors and the two-handed damage-dealer who wades into a horde of foes.

+ X% magic resistance
This is armor against magic, absorbing the damage inflicted by spells, which becomes increasingly useful toward the end of the game. It also reduces the duration of enemy spells, so that you break free of hexes and paralyze magic much faster.

+ X mana/stamina | + X% mana/stamina
This increases your initial (and maximum) reserve of mana or stamina. Just 5 points of additional mana/stamina is equivalent to 1 attribute point spent on willpower, so a couple of +8 items would surpass a level up. You can forgo spending a warrior's or rogue's attribute points in willpower if you make use of items with these properties.

+ X mana/stamina regeneration
This increases the regeneration rate of mana or stamina, which becomes appreciable during long battles. All classes require plenty of mana or stamina for their many abilities. Some top-tier talents can be used for stamina recovery later in the game, but a substantial bonus here benefits characters early on.

+ X fire/cold/electricity/spirit/nature resistance
This really comes into its own when fighting against enemies with elemental attacks, such as Rage Demons. Even a modest resistance begins to downgrade them. If you can't find the elemental resistances you need, look for Rune slots and build your own. If you can find elemental armor *and* it has a Rune slot, apply a Rune of Warding of the same affinity for maximum protection.

+ X strength/dexterity/magic/willpower/cunning/constitution
These attribute bonuses are temporarily as effective as a Tome or level up in raising one attribute and can be transferred between characters in some instances. They can also help to meet the minimum requirements for other equipment.

+ X physical damage
Extra points of damage quickly add up when it's on a rogue's dagger, being applied at high speed on every strike.

+ X% fire/cold/electricity/spirit/nature damage
This is extremely useful for mages as it affects both their spells and their standard staff-based attacks. However this property can also be of benefit to other classes – for instance Bianca's Bursting Arrow deals fire damage, while Fenris can master spirit-based attacks.

+ X fortitude
As it takes 1 point of strength to raise a warrior's fortitude by 1 point, even small gains here can equate to increasing a level or two for a tank or for a class that doesn't wish to expend points on strength.

Immunity to flanking
Tanks usually have enough passive abilities to counter flanking after the first few levels, so its best application is with a damage-dealing warrior or rogue who likes to dive in.

X% chance to stealth when hit
Effectively, the rogue gains a small chance to enter stealth when hit. The rogue then has an opportunity to strike from stealth, with appropriate advantages.

100% of basic attack damage vs. enemies that attack in melee
When an enemy attacks the character equipped with this property, they suffer an instant counter with damage equal to the character's full basic attack damage. There is no animation for this retaliatory attack as it can occur instantly and simultaneously against multiple enemies. It does not apply to ranged attacks and magic.

Enemies drop more coin
With this property, coin drops are 5% larger than usual. So if you'd normally receive 20 silver from an enemy, you will now receive 21. The good news is that these properties stack, so having two items active would raise the haul by 10% – a significant sum over the course of a game.

Enemies drop better equipment
This increases the quality of enemy drops (a sword doing 24 instead of 22 damage, for instance, and having a better attack property). There is also a lower, secondary chance that the item gains an extra property or bonus. When you're trying to save money, keeping this equipped can turn up some better generic equipment that will fetch a more profitable sale price.

UNIQUE WEAPONS

WARRIOR WEAPONS

The minimum requirements for wielding a warrior weapon are based on strength (with shields also requiring constitution), in addition to specific talent trees.

Shields & One-handed Weapons

One-handed weapons and shields can only be used by a warrior with the Weapon and Shield talent tree. As you will mainly need such equipment for your tank, look for the following attributes:

- Improvements to armor, resistances and fortitude.
- Bonuses to health, regeneration and the healing applied to the character.
- Increased threat generation.
- Knockbacks, stuns and deathblows: these can reduce the number of opponents effectively dealing damage.

Furthermore, the high incidence of critical chance and attack speed modifiers can aid threat generation through damage.

As the game uses complex systems, note that all item attributes listed are average figures, so don't be surprised by a small degree of variation up or down. The format we use for many Acquisition notes is "item holder (location, quest)".

Shields

Name	Armor	Properties	Requirements	Acquisition	Act
Fereldan Soldier's Shield	37	-	12 Strength | 12 Constitution	Dead refugee (Blightlands, Prologue)	1
The Bann's Backhouse Door	72	1 Rune slot | +17 Health	18 Strength | 18 Constitution	Coterie Leader (Lowtown – Night)	1
Markham Head Stopper	66	+38 Attack | +7 Armor	18 Strength | 18 Constitution	Korval's Blades (Hightown)	1
Winter-Weight	86	+9 Armor | +8 Fortitude	20 Strength | 20 Constitution	Dragon (Deep Roads, The Deep Roads Expedition)	1
Oddsmaker	72	+41 Attack | +7% Physical damage	18 Strength | 18 Constitution	Revenant (Long Way Home)	1
Kirkwall Shield	72	+20 Defense | +7 Armor	18 Strength | 18 Constitution	Armor Merchant (Lowtown)	1
River's Wave	134	+33 Defense | +13 Armor	24 Strength | 24 Constitution	Qunari Delegate (Ser Varnell's Refuge, Offered and Lost)	2
Warstopper	94	+50 Attack | +4% Critical chance	21 Strength | 21 Constitution	Korval's Blades (Hightown)	2
Brink-Boaster	103	+10 Armor | +411 Nature resistance	22 Strength | 22 Constitution	Qunari Delegate (Ser Varnell's Refuge, Offered and Lost)	2
Spirit of 4:60 Black	146	1 Rune slot | +15 Armor | +7% Physical damage	25 Strength | 25 Constitution	Chest (Abandoned Slaver Den, A Bitter Pill)	2
Amell Family Shield	122	2 Rune slots | +12 Armor	23 Strength | 23 Constitution	Killer's Lair (All That Remains)	2
Defender of the Wall	122	2 Rune slots	23 Strength | 23 Constitution	Armor Shop (Gallows Courtyard)	2
Darkspawn Shield	122	+4 Mana/Stamina regeneration rate | +489 Fire resistance	23 Strength | 23 Constitution	Weaponsmithy (Lowtown)	2
Shield of the Knight Herself	190	1 Rune slot | +88 Attack | +5% Critical chance | 100% of basic attack damage vs. enemies that attack in melee	34 Strength | 28 Constitution | Aveline	Ser Varnell's Refuge (Offered and Lost)	2
Wardwall	190	+38 Armor | 100% of basic attack damage vs. enemies that attack in melee	27 Strength | 27 Constitution	Chest (Deep Roads, Finding Nathaniel)	3
Lord Bearing's Wall	208	1 Rune slot | +94 Attack | +47 Defense | +10 Fortitude	29 Strength | 29 Constitution	Hanker (Decrepit Alley, Kind of Want)	3
Cornerstone	208	+94 Attack | +21 Armor | Immunity to knock back	28 Strength | 28 Constitution	Jeven (Darktown, Favor and Fault)	3
Hearth Shield	174	1 Rune slot | +17 Armor | +4 Health regeneration rate | +19% Healing to this character	28 Strength | 28 Constitution	Quest reward from Meredith (Best Served Cold)	3
Volcanic Shield	227	1 Rune slot | +23 Armor | +12% Fire damage	29 Strength | 29 Constitution	Armor Shop (Gallows Courtyard)	3
Shield of the Resolute	248	2 Rune slots | +25 Armor | +8% Magic resistance	31 Strength | 31 Constitution	Pile of bones (Templar Hall, The Last Straw)	3
Mage's Friend*	271	3 Rune slots | +17% Magic resistance	32 Strength | 32 Constitution	Faith quest	3
Lady Rosamund's Bulwark*	86	3 Rune slots	20 Strength | 20 Constitution	Emporium's Relics and Antiques (Black Emporium)	1

* Downloadable content (see dragonage.com/da2/addons for details).

One-handed Weapons

Name	Damage	Properties	Requirements	Acquisition	Act
Overland Render	12 Physical	+38 Attack | +4% Critical chance	21 Strength	Ship Captain (The Docks – Night)	1
Edge of Song and Glory	16 Physical	+47 Attack | +7% Physical damage	24 Strength	Ser Karras (Gallows Courtyard, Act of Mercy)	1
Palvo's Cocksure Cleaver	12 Physical	+38 Attack | +14% Threat generation	21 Strength	"Captain" Qerth (Shallowguard Base, Night Lies)	1
Thudpucker's Fist	20 Physical	1 Rune slot | +57 Attack | 5% Chance to Stun	28 Strength	Bonny Lem's Wares (Disused Passage)	1
Trust and Cut Blade	12 Physical	+38 Attack | +14% Threat generation	21 Strength	Korval's Blades (Hightown)	1
Maelstrom	16 Physical	+4% Critical chance | +4% Attack speed	24 Strength	Weapon Shop (Gallows Courtyard)	1
Notched Sword	15 Physical	+18 Mana/Stamina | +7% Physical damage	23 Strength	Weaponsmithy (Lowtown)	1
Red Earth Long One	25 Physical	+76 Attack | +5 Fire damage	32 Strength	Bartrand (Bartrand's Mansion, Family Matter)	2
Sundarin Thunder	20 Physical	+438 Electricity resistance | +4 Electricity damage	28 Strength	Chest (Deep Roads, Fool's Gold)	2
Windsong Axe	27 Physical	+5% Critical chance | +12% Critical damage | +11 Electricity damage	35 Strength	Nexus Golem's Wares (Abandoned Thaig)	2
One-Cut	21 Physical	1 Rune slot | +61 Attack | +8% Physical damage | Messy Kills	30 Strength	Innley of Starkhaven (Sundermount, Bounty Hunter)	2
Markham Heart Stopper	27 Physical	+5% Critical chance | +12% Critical damage | Messy Kills	33 Strength	Weapon Shop (Gallows Courtyard)	2
Royeaux One and Two	13 Physical	1 Rune slot | +41 Attack | +4% Critical chance	22 Strength	Amaranthine Conspirator (Sundermount, The Conspirators)	2
Darktown Blade	23 Physical	1 Rune slot | +4% Critical chance	30 Strength	Weaponsmithy (Lowtown)	2
Sataareth	29 Fire	1 Rune slot | +94 Attack | +8% Physical damage | +8% Magic resistance	38 Strength	Quest reward for defeating the Arishok (Viscount's Keep, Demands of the Qun)	2
The Wailer	20 Physical	+4% Critical chance | +11% Critical damage | +8% Physical damage	28 Strength	Veld (The Sink, Gamlen's Greatest Treasure)	3
Bassrath-Kata	31 Physical	+100 Attack | +4% Attack speed | +20% Chance of Deathblows | +9 damage vs. humans	39 Strength	Quest reward (The Lost Swords)	3
Perrin's Nail	25 Physical	1 Rune slot | +76 Attack | +19% Healing to this character	32 Strength	Korval's Blades (Hightown)	3
The Weight	29 Physical	1 Rune slot | +94 Attack | +11 Fortitude | 5% Chance to knock back	38 Strength	High Dragon (The Bone Pit, Mine Massacre)	3
The Bringer of Silence	28 Physical	1 Rune slot | +5% Critical chance | +12% Critical damage | +5% Chance to dispel hostile magic	36 Strength	Quest reward (Finding Nathaniel)	3
Woodsman's Ire	27 Physical	1 Rune slot | +32 Health | +81 Attack | +16% Threat generation	35 Strength	Jess "Leashmaster" Varvel (Run Down Alley, Reining It In)	3
Raider Sword	29 Physical	1 Rune slot | +5% Critical chance | +12% Critical damage	36 Strength	Shady Merchandise (The Docks)	3
City Guard Sword	29 Physical	1 Rune slot | +94 Attack | +4% Attack speed	36 Strength	Weapon Shop (Gallows Courtyard)	3
Sword of the Antaam	32 Physical	1 Rune slot | +108 Attack | +10 damage vs. humans	38 Strength	Lirene's Fereldan Imports (Lowtown)	3
Aurvar's Prize	33 Physical	1 Rune slot | +116 Attack | +3 Armor | +17% Threat generation	41 Strength	Chest (Deep Roads, Finding Nathaniel)	3
The Vague Blade	33 Physical	3 Rune slots | Enemies cannot dodge attacks	41 Strength	Chest (Blood Mage Refuge, The Last Holdouts)	3
Glandivalis	33 Electricity	1 Rune slot | +116 Attack | +3 Armor | 2.5% Chance to enslave normal enemies	41 Strength	Hybris (Hidden Dungeon, The Awiergan Scrolls)	3
Fade's Fury*	25 Physical	2 Rune slots | +5% Critical chance | +3 Spirit damage across 2m	34 Strength	Desire Demon (Harimann Estate, Repentance)	2
Desdemona's Blade*	17 Nature	2 Rune slots | +50 Attack	25 Strength	Emporium's Relics and Antiques (Black Emporium)	1
Blade of a Thousand Battles*	35 Physical	2 Rune slots | +5% Critical chance | +8% Physical damage | 5% Chance to knock back	42 Strength	Emporium's Relics and Antiques (Black Emporium)	3

* Downloadable content (see dragonage.com/da2/addons for details).

Two-handed Weapons

Suited to the damage-dealer, two-handed weapons deliver significant physical damage. Minimum requirements in strength top out at 40-43 for the best weapons and may need some early dedicated investment before focus switches to other attributes. Increases in cunning will help to offset the lack of shield by raising the chance to dodge attacks while improving critical damage.

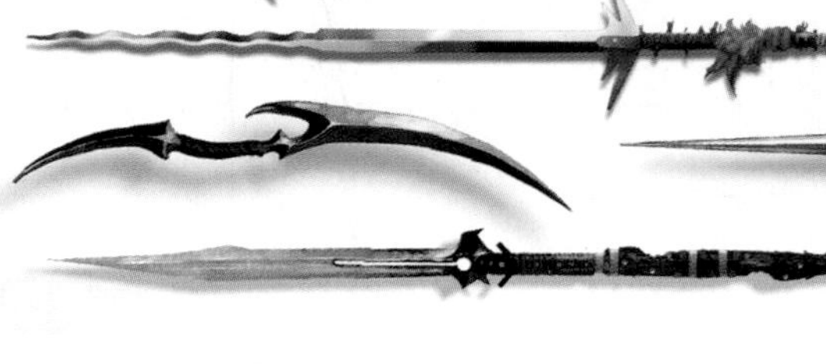

Supporting accessories and equipment can take several different paths but work best if they concertedly follow the lead of the weapon itself:

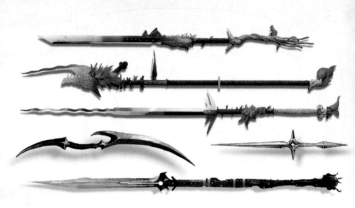

- Add multiple physical damage properties, increasing tough regular hits.
- Add critical chance and damage properties, complementing attribute points in cunning.
- Add attack speed bonuses, increasing the hit rate.
- Add stamina regeneration for more ability use.

Two-handed Weapons

Name	Damage	Properties	Requirements	Acquisition	Act
The Ream-Ward	17 Physical	+55 Attack | +9% Physical damage	23 Strength	Tevinter Hunter Captain (Lowtown – Night, Bait and Switch)	1
Red Grace	18 Physical	+59 Attack | +4 Fire damage	24 Strength	Chest (Tal-Vashoth Cavern, Blackpowder Promise)	1
Caskhead's Portable Anvil	20 Physical	+63 Attack | 5% chance to knock back	25 Strength	Chest (Deep Roads, The Deep Roads Expedition)	1
Templar Great Sword	14 Physical	+4% Attack speed | +3 Fire damage	21 Strength	Weapon Shop (Gallows Courtyard)	1
Oath-Breaker	26 Physical	1 Rune slot | +82 Attack | +23% Healing to this character	30 Strength	Chest (Deep Roads, The Deep Roads Expedition)	1
The Brothers' End	28 Physical	+88 Attack | +10% Physical damage	31 Strength	Elven Fanatic (Side Alley, Blackpowder Courtesy)	2
Persuasion	26 Physical	+82 Attack | +8 damage vs. Qunari	30 Strength	Chest (Bone Pit Mines, Cavern of Dead)	2
All-Fall	21 Physical	+5% Critical chance | +4 Fire damage	27 Strength	Korval's Blades (Hightown)	2
Potency	25 Physical	+6% Critical chance | +14% Critical damage	29 Strength	Treasure Cache (Deep Roads, Fool's Gold)	2
Binky's Comfort	23 Physical	+30 Health | +5 Health regeneration rate | +22% Healing to this character	28 Strength	Quest reward (The Lost Patrol)	2
The Subtle Brute	26 Physical	+10% Physical damage | 5% chance to knock back	30 Strength	Weapon Shop (Gallows Courtyard)	2
Void's Hammer	28 Physical	1 Rune slot | +6% Critical chance | +5% Attack speed | +3 Physical damage across 2m	33 Strength	Magnus's Wares (The Wounded Coast)	2
Blade of Mercy	34 Physical	2 Rune slots | +117 Attack | +5% Attack speed | Fenris	-	Chest (Secret Meeting Place, Best Served Cold)	3
Bassrath-Kata	35 Physical	+126 Attack | +6% Critical chance | +10% Physical damage | +11 damage vs. humans	39 Strength	Quest reward (The Lost Swords)	3
Limbtaker	35 Physical	1 Rune slot | +126 Attack | +10% Physical damage | +25% Chance of Deathblows	39 Strength	Korval's Blades (Hightown)	3
Roadhammer	32 Physical	1 Rune slot | +10% Physical damage | 25% Chance to reduce attack speed | 25% Chance to reduce movement speed	35 Strength	Pile of Bones (Hidden Dungeon, Sundermount)	3
Double-Bearded Axe	32 Physical	+42 Mana/Stamina | +15% Critical chance | +10% Physical damage	35 Strength	Sten (Hightown – Night)	3
Her Song	34 Physical	1 Rune slot | +117 Attack | +5 Health regeneration rate | +26% Healing to this character	38 Strength	Pile of Bones (Sundermount Caverns)	3
Top-Chop Brand	31 Physical	+102 Attack | +6% Critical chance | +10% Physical damage	33 Strength	Jakeson "The Bleeder" Hall (Suspicious House, Red Run Streets)	3
Widow's Fury	34 Physical	1 Rune slot | +15% Critical chance | 5% Chance to Stun	36 Strength	Weapon Shop (Gallows Courtyard)	3
Dwarven Great Axe	35 Physical	3 Rune slots	37 Strength	Korval's Blades (Hightown)	3
Sundering	38 Electricity	+6% Critical chance | +16% Critical damage | +10% Physical damage | +5 Mana/Stamina regeneration rate	41 Strength	Nexus Golem's Wares (Hidden Dungeon)	3
The Celebrant	38 Spirit	1 Rune slot | +3 Strength | +3 Willpower | +21% Threat generation	41 Strength	Beacon (Sundermount, The Awiergan Scrolls)	3
Bloom	38 Cold	2 Rune slots | +16% Cold damage | +5% Chance to regenerate 4% Health	41 Strength	Arcane Horror (Sundermount, The Awiergan Scrolls)	3
The Anderfel Cleaver*	20 Fire	2 Rune slots | +63 Attack | No Physical damage bonus	25 Strength	Emporium's Relics and Antiques (Black Emporium)	1
The Barbarian's Blade*	29 Physical	1 Rune slot | +10% Physical damage | +5% Attack speed | 5% Chance to Stun	34 Strength	Emporium's Relics and Antiques (Black Emporium)	2

* Downloadable content (see dragonage.com/da2/addons for details).

Rogue Weapons

The player rogue has the choice of mastering Archery or Dual Weapons. In playing terms, this translates into the lone ranged tactician or the dual-wielder in the thick of the action. Both roles will focus attacks on a single enemy at a time to remove it from the fight as quickly and cleanly as possible.

Dual Weapons

Requirements for the best weapons range from 38 to 42. At all stages of the game, dexterity is important for both attack and critical chance.

The first thing to realize about dual wielding is that you have two sets of weapon attributes. These work best if they can complement each other with similar stacking bonuses, but much of the time you'll be picking the best two by their relative level. Additional item properties can take this further:

- Add bonuses for critical hits.
- Increase attack speed.
- Add elemental damage to Rune slots to be more effective against specific enemy weaknesses.

Weapons and armor with rogue skill bonuses don't need to be used for combat. Just equip them before performing the skill check (such as opening a locked chest) and revert to better items for fighting.

Dual Weapons

Name	Damage	Properties	Requirements	Acquisition	Act
Bloodletter	20 Physical	+35 Attack | Messy Kills	24 Dexterity	Captain Reiner (Arthuris's Private Dock, Wayward Son)	1
The Bodice Ripper	17 Physical	+3% Critical chance | +7% Critical damage	22 Dexterity	Hayder (The Chantry, Fools Rush In)	1
Blade of Red Birth	22 Physical	1 Rune slot | +38 Attack | +4 Fire damage	25 Dexterity	Chest (Deep Roads, The Deep Roads Expedition)	1
Thrice-Bound	15 Physical	+29 Attack | Bonus to disarm traps | Bonus to lockpicking	21 Dexterity	Weaponsmithy (Lowtown)	1
Cruel Dagger	20 Physical	+8% Critical damage | +6 damage vs. humans	24 Dexterity	Shady Merchandise (The Docks)	1
Tarnished Dagger	20 Physical	+35 Attack | +4 Fire damage	24 Dexterity	Lirene's Fereldan Imports (Lowtown)	1
Arm of Adruil	20 Physical	1 Rune slot | +35 Attack | +3% Attack speed	24 Dexterity	Shadow Warrior (Sundermount)	1
Chum-Cutter	25 Physical	+43 Attack | +6% Physical damage	28 Dexterity	Senestra (The Docks – Night, A Debt in the Family)	2
Honeycut	28 Physical	+49 Attack | +20 Mana/Stamina	30 Dexterity	Pile of Treasure (Varterral Hunting Ground, Mirror Image)	2
Stitch-Maker	30 Physical	1 Rune slot | +3% Critical chance | +9% Critical damage	31 Dexterity	Chest (Ser Varnell's Refuge, Offered and Lost)	2
Shine	25 Physical	+3% Critical chance | +5 Spirit damage	28 Dexterity	Mercenary Captain (The Wounded Coast, Elves at Large)	2
The Tiny Cut (413 of 1000)	25 Physical	1 Rune slot | +43 Attack | +5 Physical damage	28 Dexterity	Templar Hunter (Hightown – Night, Midnight Meeting)	2
Seven Deaths	27 Physical	1 Rune slot | +3% Critical chance | +6% Physical damage	29 Dexterity	Weapon Shop (Gallows Courtyard)	2
Guild Dagger	28 Physical	1 Rune slot | +49 Attack	30 Dexterity	Korval's Blades (Hightown)	2
Coterie Shiv	30 Physical	+9% Critical damage | 25% Chance to reduce attack speed | 25% Chance to reduce movement speed	31 Dexterity	Weaponsmithy (Lowtown)	2
The Offhand Blade	35 Physical	+65 Attack | +4% Critical chance | +9% Critical damage	35 Dexterity	High Dragon (The Bone Pit, Mine Massacre)	3
Bassrath-Kata	39 Physical	+4% Critical chance | +9% Critical damage | +6% Physical damage | +12 damage vs. humans	39 Dexterity	Quest reward (The Lost Swords)	3
Blade of the Many	40 Physical	2 Rune slots | +81 Attack | +4 Physical damage across 2m	40 Dexterity	Bonny Lem's Wares (Disused Passage)	3
Red Jenny Backbiter	37 Physical	2 Rune slots | +15% Chance of Deathblows | Messy Kills	38 Dexterity	Weaponsmithy (Lowtown)	3
Tine	37 Physical	1 Rune slot | +70 Attack | +26 Mana/Stamina	36 Dexterity	Quentin (The Killer's Lair, All That Remains)	3
The Pairing Knife	35 Physical	1 Rune slot | +65 Attack | 5% Chance To Regenerate 2% Mana/Stamina	35 Dexterity	Velasco (The Blooming Rose or Castillon's Landing, No Rest for the Wicked)	3
Ragged Edge	35 Physical	+65 Attack | +6% Physical damage | +11 damage vs. humans	35 Dexterity	Velasco (The Blooming Rose or Castillon's Landing, No Rest for the Wicked)	3
Spider's Heart	37 Physical	1 Rune slot | +9% Critical damage | +7 Nature damage	36 Dexterity	Weapon Shop (Gallows Courtyard)	3
Shadow's Claw	35 Spirit	1 Rune slot | +4% Critical chance | +3% Attack speed	35 Dexterity	Weaponsmithy (Lowtown)	3
Carta's Right-Hand	42 Physical	+87 Attack | +4% Critical chance | +10% Critical damage | 5% Chance to Stun	41 Dexterity	Bonny Lem's Wares (Disused Passage)	3
Finesse	42 Physical	1 Rune slot | +4% Critical chance | +10% Critical damage | +8 Nature damage	41 Dexterity	Quest reward (A Murder of Crows)	3
Carta's Left-Hand	42 Physical	+87 Attack | +10% Critical chance | Immunity to knockback | 25% Chance to reduce movement speed | 25% Chance to reduce attack speed	41 Dexterity	Hanker (Decrepit Alley, Kind of Want)	3
The Low Blade*	44 Nature	2 Rune slots | +10% Critical damage | +3% Attack speed | 25% Chance to reduce movement speed | 25% Chance to reduce attack speed	42 Dexterity	Random Enemy (Viscount's Keep, Faith)	3
Song of Sorrows*	13 Physical	2 Rune slots | +27 Attack	20 Dexterity | Level 5	Discarded Weapons and Armor (Black Emporium)	1
Shard of the Fallen*	32 Physical	1 Rune slot | +3% Critical chance | 5% Chance to regenerate 5% Health	34 Dexterity	Emporium's Relics and Antiques (Black Emporium)	2
The Maker's Kiss*	26 Spirit	+4% Critical chance | +10 Spirit damage	42 Dexterity	Emporium's Relics and Antiques (Black Emporium)	3

* Downloadable content (see dragonage.com/da2/addons for details).

Bows

Bows are limited to archers. Once you pass 40 in dexterity, you can equip the best bows in the game.

Power summarizes the use of the bow in terms of damage and knockback, balanced by an initially painful rate of fire. As with the talent trees, an archer has the choice of bolstering power or speed:

- If playing for power, focus on damage properties.
- If enhancing critical hits, look to attack speed too. Two rolls of the dice are better than one.
- Abilities hit automatically, without fail. Equip to promote the devastation of their success.

Bows

Name	Damage	Properties	Requirements	Acquisition	Act
Nevarran Lancer	70 Physical	+5% Critical chance | +13% Critical damage	25 Dexterity	Dragon (Deep Roads, The Deep Roads Expedition)	1
The Runt's Spiker	53 Physical	+5% Critical chance | +11 Physical damage	22 Dexterity	Ignacio Strand (Hovel, Sharp Little Pinpricks)	1
Longtouch	53 Physical	1 Rune slot | +51 Attack | +9% Physical damage	22 Dexterity	Ilen's Crafts (Sundermount)	1
The Trepanner's Gift	53 Physical	+5% Critical chance | +12% Spirit damage	22 Dexterity	Quest reward (Changing One's Nature)	1
Cracked Bow	59 Physical	+5% Critical chance | +5% Attack speed	23 Dexterity	Weaponsmithy (Lowtown)	1
Mont de Glace Strand	59 Physical	1 Rune slot | +55 Attack | +5% Critical chance	23 Dexterity	Chest (Ruined Passage, Magistrate's Orders)	1
Swarm	70 Physical	+63 Attack | +7 Nature damage across 2m	25 Dexterity	Mature Dragon (Bone Pit Ledge, The Bone Pit)	1
Borderfall	75 Physical	+67 Attack | +5% Critical chance	27 Dexterity	Varterral (Varterral Hunting Ground, Mirror Image)	2
Felons' Punch-Gut	80 Physical	1 Rune slot | +5% Critical chance | 25% Chance to reduce attack speed | 25% Chance to reduce movement speed	28 Dexterity	Chest (Abandoned Slaver Den, A Bitter Pill)	2
Quills of the Heretic	75 Physical	+67 Attack | +15 Cold damage	27 Dexterity	Ilen's Crafts (Sundermount)	2
The Heavens' Answer	107 Physical	1 Rune slot | +6% Critical chance | +15% Critical damage | 5% Chance to Stun	35 Dexterity	Bonny Lem's Wares (Disused Passage)	2
Recurve Bow	91 Physical	1 Rune slot | +6% Critical chance	30 Dexterity	Lirene's Fereldan Imports (Lowtown)	2
The Runner's Retort	113 Physical	+109 Attack | +6% Critical chance | 25% Chance to reduce attack speed | 25% Chance to reduce movement speed	35 Dexterity	Street Thug (Lowtown – Night, The Fixer)	2
Starkhaven Longbow	86 Physical	2 Rune slots | +9 Nature damage across 2m	Sebastian	Harimann Estate (Repentance)	3
Bassrath-Kata	123 Physical	+126 Attack | +6% Critical chance | +10% Physical damage | +37 damage vs. humans	39 Dexterity	Quest reward (The Lost Swords)	3
Cynoeswr Sain	113 Physical	1 Rune slot | +15% Critical damage | +23 Nature damage	35 Dexterity	Chest (Hidden Supply Depot, A Noble Agenda)	3
Crosscut Composite	102 Physical	1 Rune slot | +15% Critical damage | +10% Physical damage | 5% Chance to Stun	34 Dexterity	Weaponsmithy (Lowtown)	3
Righteous Rain	118 Physical	+117 Attack | +6% Critical chance | +12 Cold damage across 2m	36 Dexterity	Treasure Pile (Mountain Cave, A Murder of Crows)	3
Truebow	102 Physical	1 Rune slot | +95 Attack | 5% Chance to knock back	32 Dexterity	Ilen's Crafts (Sundermount)	3
Jackal's Longbow	134 Fire	+145 Attack | +16% Fire damage | +27 Fire damage	39 Dexterity	High Dragon (The Bone Pit, Mine Massacre)	3
Absolution	134 Physical	1 Rune slot | +6% Critical chance | +16% Critical damage | +27 Nature damage	41 Dexterity	Nexus Golem's Wares (Hidden Dungeon)	3
Arlathan Replica Bow*	70 Physical	+5% Critical chance | +13% Critical damage | +5% Attack speed	25 Dexterity	Emporium's Relics and Antiques (Black Emporium)	1
Sliver*	102 Physical	1 Rune slot | +6% Critical chance | +5% Attack speed | +10 Nature damage across 2m	34 Dexterity	Emporium's Relics and Antiques (Black Emporium)	2

* Downloadable content (see dragonage.com/da2/addons for details).

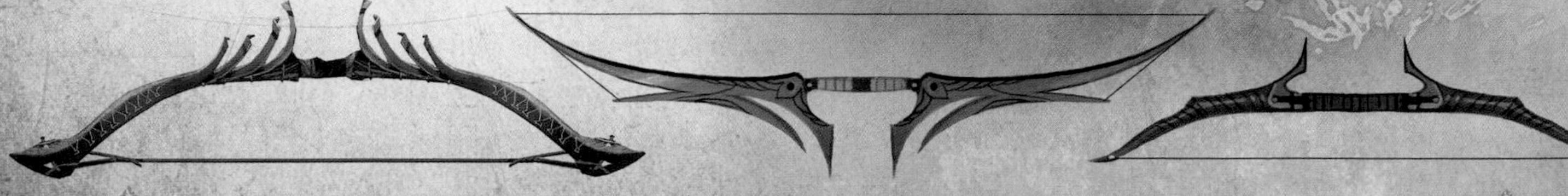

MAGE WEAPONS

Staves deal damage at range with bolts of energy and up close with physical blows (though that may not suit the disposition of most mages). They can score critical hits with their basic attacks like any other weapon and their shots can be blocked by obstacles between wielder and target. The magic attribute determines a staff's attack value.

Staves

High magic is the only requirement to equip the best staves, though you'll also need to place a certain amount of investment in willpower to equip fine mage armor.

The first rule for any party-minded mage is to acquire a wide collection of staves to cover all the elemental affinities for every enemy and occasion. The second rule is to acquire the Elemental Weapons talent so that others share the benefit. But after finding a strong damage rating in the correct element, it is the other properties that distinguish exceptional staves from ordinary fare. In its ideal form, the staff is a support tool that enhances the power of your chosen spell disciplines. Unlike other classes, the mage excels at Area of Effect magic and crowd control. Things to look for include:

- Raw elemental damage enhancement for your strongest spells.
- Mana pool assistance.
- Defensive properties to balance out the mage's weakness.

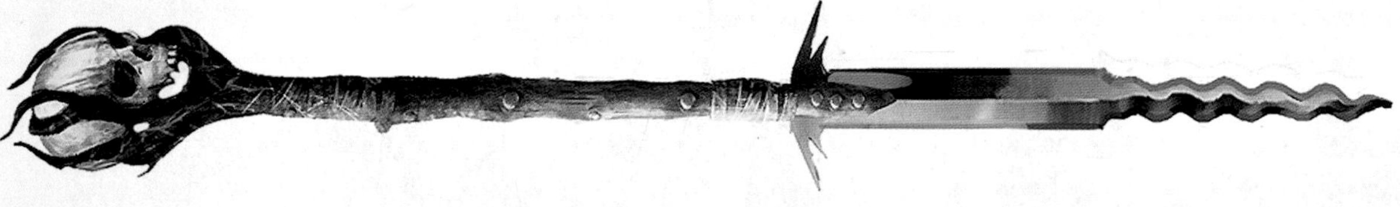

Staves

Name	Damage	Properties	Requirements	Acquisition	Act
Chanters' Staff	22 Spirit	+24 Mana/Stamina | +21% Healing by this character	-	Reward from Grace (Act of Mercy)	1
The Hypnotist's Staff	22 Electricity	+59 Attack | +8% Magic resistance	-	Decimus (Runaways' Cavern, Act of Mercy)	1
The Turncoat's Walking Stick	17 Fire	+48 Attack | +12% Fire damage	-	Mage Goods (Gallows Courtyard)	1
Staff of the Primal Order	28 Cold	1 Rune slot | +14% Fire damage | +14% Cold damage	28 Magic	Bonny Lem's Wares (Disused Passage)	1
Acolyte's Staff	33 Physical	+5 Mana/Stamina regeneration rate | +14% Fire damage | +178 Fire resistance	31 Magic	Apparel Shop (Lowtown)	1
Stone's Breath	26 Spirit	1 Rune slot | +13% Spirit damage | 5% Chance to knock back	-	Reward for saving Sandal (The Deep Roads Expedition)	1
Valdasine	28 Spirit	1 Rune slot | +2 Willpower | +5 Mana/Stamina regeneration rate	-	Crypt Treasure (Ancient Crypt, The Deep Roads Expedition)	1
Hubris	22 Physical	+24 Health | +5 Mana/Stamina regeneration rate	-	Frost Horror (Varterral Hunting Ground, Mirror Image)	2
Crooked Staff	29 Spirit	+6% Critical chance | +14% Spirit damage	-	Chest (Gallows Dungeon, Dissent)	2
Sketch's Resplit-Shaft	22 Fire	1 Rune slot | Blood Magic: Each point of health provides 1 additional mana | +4 Physical damage	-	Reward from Sketch (Sketchy on the Details)	2
Acolyte's Staff	22 Physical	+5 Mana/Stamina regeneration rate | +13% Fire damage	31 Magic	Robes by Jean Luc (Hightown)	2
Enchanter's Staff	31 Physical	1 Rune slot | +14% Cold damage | +14% Spirit damage	30 Magic	Apparel Shop (Lowtown)	2
Cold-Blooded	37 Cold	+6 Magic | +40 Mana/Stamina | +10 Mana/Stamina regeneration rate | +30% Cold damage | Blood Magic: Each point of health provides 1 additional mana	35 Magic	Magnus's Wares (The Wounded Coast)	2
Bassrath-Kata	42 Fire	+46 Mana/Stamina | +5 Mana/Stamina regeneration rate | +26% Healing by this character | +13 damage vs. humans	39 Magic	Quest reward (The Lost Swords)	3
Voracity	41 Fire	+117 Attack | Blood Magic: Each point of health provides 1 additional mana | +4 Fire damage across 2m	-	Xebenkeck (The Forgotten Lair, Forbidden Knowledge)	3
The Tiger's Tail	39 Fire	+109 Attack | +6% Critical chance | +15% Critical damage	-	Grace (The Wounded Coast, Best Served Cold)	3
Torch of Falon'Din	42 Fire	2 Rune slots | +16% Fire damage | +8 Fire damage	-	Marethari (Sundermount)	3
Eye of the Storm	37 Electricity	1 Rune slot | +15% Electricity damage | 5% Chance to Stun	-	Danarius (The Hanged Man, Alone)	3
Mutiny	37 Cold	1 Rune slot | +40 Mana/Stamina | +102 Attack	33 Magic	Mage Goods (Gallows Courtyard)	3
Corrupted Acolyte's Staff	42 Physical	+46 Mana/Stamina | +16% Electricity damage | Blood Magic: Each point of health provides 1 additional mana	37 Magic	Apparel Shop (Lowtown)	3
Staff of Violation	41 Spirit	+3 Willpower | +15% Spirit damage | 2.5% Chance to infect with Walking Bomb	-	Orsino (Gallows Prison)	3
Allure's Crook*	35 Spirit	2 Rune slots | +38 Mana/Stamina | +5 Mana/Stamina regeneration rate	34 Magic	Allure (Underground Passage, Repentance)	2
The Magister's Scythe*	24 Physical	+63 Attack | Attacks ignore Enemy Armor | 5% Chance to regenerate 3% Health	25 Magic	Emporium's Relics and Antiques (Black Emporium)	1
The Final Thought*	48 Physical	1 Rune slot | +4 Magic | 5% Chance to regenerate 9% Mana/Stamina | +104 Mana/Stamina | +33% Nature damage | +33% Spirit damage	42 Magic	Emporium's Relics and Antiques (Black Emporium)	3

* Downloadable content (see dragonage.com/da2/addons for details).

UNIQUE ARMOR

Hawke can equip up to four pieces of armor at the same time, each covering a specific body part. Companions do not have access to armor per se, but they can still receive armor upgrades (see page 211).

WARRIOR ARMOR

Minimum requirements must be met in strength and constitution to carry the heaviest plate or chain mail. Good armor is the savior of the tank, but a player warrior is likely to opt for a more hands-on damage-dealer role and will need to account for the absence of shield or Defender talents.

Warriors would do well to look for Rune slots. With weak magic resistance and likely very little elemental resistance, Runes of Warding can make the difference between an easy victory and a barbecued Hawke in fighting the likes of Dragons.

Gloves

Name	Armor	Properties	Requirements	Acquisition	Act
Wyvernscale Gauntlets	19	+11 Attack | +78 Fire resistance	17 Strength | 17 Constitution	Olaf's Armory (Hightown)	1
Hands of Stone	28	+3 Armor | +3 Fortitude	20 Strength | 20 Constitution	Chest (Ancient Crypt, The Deep Roads Expedition)	1
Handcrafted Dwarven Cuffs	33	1 Rune slot | +3 Armor | Immunity to Stun	22 Strength | 22 Constitution	Quest reward (Last of His Line)	1
Gauntlets of the Fallen	30	+7 Health | +1% Critical chance	21 Strength | 21 Constitution	Rubble (Sundermount Caverns, Long Way Home)	1
Alunduris	33	+1% Critical chance | +3% Critical damage	22 Strength | 22 Constitution	Ilen's Crafts (Sundermount)	2
Surfacer Stone Gauntlets	39	1 Rune slot | +10 Defense | +4 Armor	23 Strength | 23 Constitution	Olaf's Armory (Hightown)	2
Gauntlets of the Champion	79	1 Rune slot | +12 Health | +35 Attack | +1% Attack speed	31 Strength | 31 Constitution	Quest reward (Demands of the Qun)	2
Stonehammer Gauntlets	51	1 Rune slot | +10 Health | +24 Attack	25 Strength | 25 Constitution	Chest (The Killer's Lair, All That Remains)	2
Gauntlets of the Dark Breath	47	+23 Attack | 2% chance to Stealth when hit	25 Strength | 25 Constitution	Olaf's Armory (Hightown)	3
Ashen Gauntlets	51	1 Rune slot | +2% Physical damage | +204 Fire resistance	25 Strength | 25 Constitution	High Dragon (The Bone Pit, Mine Massacre)	3
Ser Maura's Gauntlets*	87	2 Rune slots | +1 Strength | +9 Armor | +3% Physical damage	32 Strength | 32 Constitution	Random enemy (Viscount's Keep, Faith)	3
Gauntlets of the Nug*	28	+3 Armor | +2% damage resistance | Enemies drop better equipment	20 Strength | 20 Constitution	Emporium's Relics and Antiques (Black Emporium)	1

* Downloadable content (see dragonage.com/da2/addons for details).

PRIMER
WALKTHROUGH
QUESTS
MAPS
STRATEGY & ANALYSIS
INVENTORY
BESTIARY
EXTRAS

INTRODUCTION
EQUIPMENT PROPERTIES
UNIQUE WEAPONS
UNIQUE ARMOR
UNIQUE ACCESSORIES
GENERATED EQUIPMENT
SPECIAL ITEMS
CRAFTING
SHOPS

Boots

Name	Armor	Properties	Requirements	Acquisition	Act
The March of Thunder	32	+18 Attack | +2% Critical chance	18 Strength | 18 Constitution	Mature Dragon (Bone Pit Ledge, The Bone Pit)	1
Surfacer Stone Boots	35	1 Rune slot | +8 Health	18 Strength | 18 Constitution	Olaf's Armory (Hightown)	1
Boots of the Fallen	45	+10 Health | +24 Attack	21 Strength | 21 Constitution	Chest (Undercity Warrens)	1
Blackened Greaves	45	+24 Attack | +3% Physical damage	21 Strength | 21 Constitution	Chest (Bartrand's Mansion)	2
Avvarian War Boots	49	1 Rune slot | +26 Attack | +2% Critical chance	22 Strength | 22 Constitution	Brekker (Brekker's Hideaway)	2
Golem's Leg	59	1 Rune slot | +30 Attack	23 Strength | 23 Constitution	Olaf's Armory (Hightown)	2
Stonehammer Boots	77	1 Rune slot | +14 Health | +37 Attack	25 Strength | 25 Constitution	Chest (Bartrand's Mansion, Family Matter)	2
Boots of the White Spire	109	+10% Healing to this character | +5 Fortitude	29 Strength | 29 Constitution	Armor Shop (Gallows Courtyard)	3
Dragonscale Boots	84	1 Rune slot | +39 Attack | +334 Fire resistance	26 Strength | 26 Constitution	Chest (The Sewers, Justice)	3
Boots of the Champion	119	1 Rune slot | +18 Health | +52 Attack | +4% Physical damage	31 Strength | 31 Constitution	Huon (On The Loose, Lowtown – Night)	3
Boots of Tremendous Weight*	41	1 Rune slot | +11 Defense | +4 Armor	20 Strength | 20 Constitution	Emporium's Relics and Antiques (Black Emporium)	1

* Downloadable content (see dragonage.com/da2/addons for details).

Chestpieces

Name	Armor	Properties	Requirements	Acquisition	Act
Dragon Hunter's Hauberk	115	+12 Armor | +460 Fire resistance	20 Strength | 20 Constitution	Ser Karras (Act of Mercy)	1
Marcher Battle Plate	81	1 Rune slot | +8 Armor | +19% Healing to this character	17 Strength | 17 Constitution	Olaf's Armory (Hightown)	1
Armor of the Wall	97	+10 Armor | +386 Spirit resistance	18 Strength | 18 Constitution	Armor Shop (Gallows Courtyard)	1
Surfacer Stone Armor	97	+22 Health | +27 Defense | +10 Armor	18 Strength | 18 Constitution	Pile of bones at the top of Sundermount	2
Warplate of the Fallen	126	+28 Health | +67 Attack	21 Strength | 21 Constitution	Dragon (Deep Roads, The Deep Roads Expedition)	1
Trevisian Breastplate	126	+67 Attack | +13 Armor	21 Strength | 21 Constitution	Olaf's Armory (Hightown)	2
Dissension	137	+36 Defense | +9% Physical damage	22 Strength | 22 Constitution	Ser Alrik (Dissent)	2
Monolith's Heart	163	+34 Health | +16 Armor | +5 Health regeneration rate	23 Strength | 23 Constitution	Armor Shop (Gallows Courtyard)	2
Red Breastplate	195	+95 Attack | +20 Armor | +778 Fire resistance	25 Strength | 25 Constitution	Olaf's Armory (Hightown)	3
Proving Battle Tunic	213	1 Rune slot | +102 Attack | +6% Critical chance	25 Strength | 25 Constitution	Chest (Antivan Camp, A Murder of Crows)	3
Chains of the Vaarad	254	1 Rune slot | +44 Health | +1014 Electricity resistance	27 Strength | 27 Constitution	Shady Merchandise (The Docks)	3
Warplate of the Champion	331	2 Rune slots | +50 Health | +145 Attack	31 Strength | 31 Constitution	High Dragon (The Bone Pit, Mine Massacre)	3
Cuirass of the Centurion	331	+33 Armor | +27% Healing to this character	29 Strength | 29 Constitution	Danarius (The Hanged Man, Alone)	3
Stonehammer Plate	213	1 Rune slot | +40 Health | +102 Attack	25 Strength | 25 Constitution	Olaf's Armory (Hightown)	3
King Something the Forgotten's Armor*	213	+3 Constitution | +152 Defense | +43 armor | +5% Attack speed | +20% damage resistance | Immunity to Stun	27 Strength | 27 Constitution	Emporium's Relics and Antiques (Black Emporium)	2

* Downloadable content (see dragonage.com/da2/addons for details).

Helms

Name	Armor	Properties	Requirements	Acquisition	Act
Imperial Bloodhelm	32	+7 Health | +8% Healing to this character	17 Strength | 17 Constitution	Master Slaver (Amell Estate Cellar, Birthright)	1
Helm of Victory	35	+8 Health | +20 Attack	18 Strength | 18 Constitution	Rubble (The Bone Pit, The Bone Pit)	1
Roar	35	+20 Attack | +2% Attack speed	18 Strength | 18 Constitution	Armor Shop (Gallows Courtyard)	1
Helmet of the Fallen	50	+11 Health | +27 Attack	21 Strength | 21 Constitution	Tarohne (Sanctuary, Enemies Among Us)	1
Chevalier Silverite Helm	50	+27 Attack | +5 Armor	21 Strength | 21 Constitution	Olaf's Armory (Hightown)	2
Helm of the Emerald Knights	60	+31 Attack | +239 Nature resistance | Immunity to flanking	22 Strength | 22 Constitution	Chest (Bone Pit Mines, Cavern of Dead)	2
Stonehammer Helm	85	+16 Health | +41 Attack | +2% Critical chance	25 Strength | 25 Constitution	Thug Leader (Winding Alley, Following the Qun)	2
Warden's Coif	121	+54 Attack | +4% damage resistance	29 Strength | 29 Constitution	Armor Merchant (Lowtown)	2
Dwarven Battle Helm	85	1 Rune slot | +41 Attack | +5 Fortitude	25 Strength | 25 Constitution	Ogre (Deep Roads, Finding Nathaniel)	3
King's Bounty	111	1 Rune slot | +10% Healing to this character | +443 Spirit resistance	28 Strength | 28 Constitution	Armor Shop (Gallows Courtyard)	3
Helm of the Champion	132	1 Rune slot | +20 Health | +58 Attack | +3% Critical chance	31 Strength | 31 Constitution	Grace (The Wounded Coast, Best Served Cold)	3
Garahel's Helm	132	1 Rune slot | +58 Attack | +4% Physical damage	29 Strength | 29 Constitution	Quest reward (A Noble Agenda)	3
Helm of Appreciation*	30	1 Rune slot | +9 Defense | +3 Armor	16 Strength | 16 Constitution | Level 5	Discarded Weapons and Armor (Black Emporium)	1
Helm of a Thousand Battles*	144	2 Rune slots | +2 Strength | +14% damage resistance | +16% Magic resistance | Immunity to critical hits	32 Strength | 32 Constitution	Emporium's Relics and Antiques (Black Emporium)	3

* Downloadable content (see dragonage.com/da2/addons for details).

ROGUE ARMOR

Minimum requirements peak at 31 dexterity and cunning, though it would take a high-level rogue to meet both. Runes can broaden protection, but the rogue's investment in cunning should help to avoid more physical attacks rather than hoping to absorb the damage.

Gloves

Name	Armor	Properties	Requirements	Acquisition	Act
Alchemist's Protective Handguards	23	1 Rune slot | +14 Attack | +2 Armor | +2% Magic resistance	20 Dexterity | 20 Cunning	Chest (Slaver Caverns, Wayward Son)	1
Bloody Butcher's Gloves	20	+1% Critical chance | +3% Critical damage	18 Dexterity | 18 Cunning	Ignacio Strand (Hovel, Sharp Little Pinpricks)	1
Raider Gloves	21	+7 Defense | +1% Attack speed	18 Dexterity | 18 Cunning	Shady Merchandise (The Docks)	1
Last Descent Gauntlets	28	+1% Critical chance	21 Dexterity | 21 Cunning	Rubble (Sundermount Caverns, Long Way Home)	1
Stoneclutcher's Gloves	26	+15 Attack | +3 Fortitude | Bonus to lockpicking	20 Dexterity | 20 Cunning	Crypt Treasure (Ancient Crypt, Deep Roads Expedition)	1
Gauntlets of the Ashaad	28	+1% Critical chance | +1 Mana/Stamina regeneration rate	21 Dexterity | 21 Cunning	Tevinter Enchanter (Lost-End Foundry, To Catch a Thief)	2
Rat-Nibbled Gloves	36	+20 Attack | +1% Attack speed	23 Dexterity | 23 Cunning	Armor Merchant (Lowtown)	2
Gloves of Enasalin	47	+1% Critical chance | +4% Critical damage	25 Dexterity | 25 Cunning	Chest (The Killer's Lair, All That Remains)	2
Gloves of the Wilder	47	+24 Attack | +2% Physical damage	25 Dexterity | 25 Cunning	Varterral (Mountain Cave, A Murder of Crows)	3
Hands of Glory	52	1 Rune slot | +26 Attack | +1% Critical chance | Enemies drop better equipment	28 Dexterity | 28 Cunning	Chest (Darktown, Favor and Fault)	3
Quick Hands	61	+30 Attack | +1% Attack speed | +266 Fire resistance	28 Dexterity | 28 Cunning	Armor Merchant (Lowtown)	3
Gloves of the Champion	73	1 Rune slot | +2% Critical chance | +4% Critical damage	31 Dexterity | 31 Cunning	Quest reward (Demands of the Qun)	2
Ser Isaac's Gauntlets*	23	+2 Armor	19 Dexterity | 19 Cunning	Downloadable content (Ser Isaac's Armor Set)	-
Gauntlets of the Nug*	28	+3 Armor | +2% damage resistance | Enemies drop better equipment	20 Dexterity | 20 Cunning	Emporium's Relics and Antiques (Black Emporium)	1
Invisible Gloves*	26	+8 Defense | -4% Threat generation | Enemies drop better equipment	20 Dexterity | 20 Cunning	Emporium's Relics and Antiques (Black Emporium)	1

* Downloadable content (see dragonage.com/da2/addons for details).

Boots

Name	Armor	Properties	Requirements	Acquisition	Act
Lowtown Stompers	29	+4% Critical damage | +3% Physical damage	18 Dexterity | 18 Cunning	Ignacio Strand (Hovel, Sharp Little Pinpricks)	1
Footpad's Secret	29	+18 Attack | +3% Physical damage	18 Dexterity | 18 Cunning	Leech (Warehouse, Pier Pressure)	1
Hunter's Boots	32	+2% Critical chance | Bonus to evade traps	18 Dexterity | 18 Cunning	Lirene's Fereldan Imports (Lowtown)	1
Last Descent Boots	42	+2% Critical chance | +5% Critical damage	21 Dexterity | 21 Cunning	Chest (Undercity Warrens, Shepherding Wolves)	1
Boots of Enasalin	71	+2% Critical chance | +5% Critical damage | Bonus to disarm traps	25 Dexterity | 25 Cunning	Chest (Bartrand's Mansion, Family Matter)	2
Zoey's Battered Horde-Kickers	46	1 Rune slot | +2% Critical chance | +5% Critical damage	22 Dexterity | 22 Cunning	Chest (Deep Roads, Fool's Gold)	2
Highwayman's Lambskin Boots	42	+2% Critical chance | +4 Armor | Enemies drop more coin	21 Dexterity | 21 Cunning	Pile of Bones (Varterral Hunting Ground)	2
Worn Leather Boots	54	+15 Defense | +5% Critical damage	23 Dexterity | 23 Cunning	Shady Merchandise (Docks)	2
Windstrider Boots	65	1 Rune slot | +34 Attack | +2% chance to Stealth when hit	26 Dexterity | 26 Cunning	Ilen's Crafts (Sundermount)	3
Boots of the Champion	110	1 Rune slot | +2% Critical chance | +6% Critical damage | Bonus to disarm traps	31 Dexterity | 31 Cunning	Huon (On The Loose, Lowtown – Night)	3
Ser Isaac's Boots*	35	+4 Armor	19 Dexterity | 19 Cunning	Downloadable content (Ser Isaac's Armor Set)	-
Stealth Boots*	71	+2 to all attributes | +37 Defense | +21% Critical damage | Bonus to evade traps	27 Dexterity | 27 Cunning	Emporium's Relics and Antiques (Black Emporium)	2

* Downloadable content (see dragonage.com/da2/addons for details).

Chestpieces

Name	Armor	Properties	Requirements	Acquisition	Act
Stalker's Boar Hides	75	+5% Critical chance | +12% Critical damage	17 Dexterity | 17 Cunning	Swindler (Lowtown, Miracle Makers)	1
Kirkwall Squire's Jerkin	75	+48 Attack | +9% Physical damage	17 Dexterity | 17 Cunning	Armor Merchant (Lowtown)	1
Longshadow Hauberk	180	1 Rune slot | +95 Attack | Bonus to lockpicking	25 Dexterity | 25 Cunning	Armor Merchant (Lowtown)	1
Last Descent Armor	116	+5% Critical chance | +13% Critical damage	21 Dexterity | 21 Cunning	Dragon (Deep Roads, The Deep Roads Expedition)	1
Quickstring's Tunic	116	+67 Attack | +5% Critical chance	21 Dexterity | 21 Cunning	Quest reward (A Matter of Pride)	2
Chestguard of the Scoundrel	116	+13% Critical damage | Bonus to lockpicking | Enemies drop more coin	21 Dexterity | 21 Cunning	Armor Merchant (Lowtown)	2
Vain	165	1 Rune slot | +88 Attack | +9% Magic resistance	24 Dexterity | 24 Cunning	Lirene's Fereldan Imports (Lowtown)	2
Guardian of Enasalin	197	1 Rune slot | +6% Critical chance | +15% Critical damage	25 Dexterity | 25 Cunning	Patron (The Hanged Man, Offered and Lost)	2
Dragonhide Mantle of the Predator	234	+6% Critical chance | +15% Critical damage | +1014 Fire resistance	27 Dexterity | 27 Cunning	Chest (Templar Hall)	3
Nightingale's Lamellar Armor	197	1 Rune slot | +6% Critical chance | Bonus to evade traps | Bonus to disarm traps	27 Dexterity | 27 Cunning	High Dragon (The Bone Pit, Mine Massacre)	3
Arms of the Champion	306	2 Rune slots | +6% Critical chance | +16% Critical damage	31 Dexterity | 31 Cunning	High Dragon (The Bone Pit, Mine Massacre)	3
Cuirass of the Winds	306	+3 Cunning | +145 Attack	29 Dexterity | 29 Cunning	Castillon (Castillon's Landing, No Rest for the Wicked)	3
Ser Isaac's Cuirass*	98	2 Rune slots | +20 Armor	20 Dexterity | 20 Cunning	Downloadable content (Ser Isaac's Armor Set)	-
Flint Company Cuirass*	106	+2 Dexterity | +31 Defense | +5% Critical chance	20 Dexterity | 20 Cunning	On a mercenary (Duty quest)	1
Ancient Leather Cuirass*	69	1 Rune slot | +5% Critical chance | +298 Electricity resistance	16 Dexterity | 16 Cunning | Level 5	Discarded Weapons and Armor (Black Emporium)	1

* Downloadable content (see dragonage.com/da2/addons for details).

Helms

Name	Armor	Properties	Requirements	Acquisition	Act
Mask of the Imperium	30	+19 Attack | +2% Critical chance	17 Dexterity | 17 Cunning	Chest (Amell Estate Cellar, Birthright)	1
Henchman Cowl	30	+7 Mana/Stamina | +2% Critical chance	17 Dexterity | 17 Cunning	Armor Merchant (Lowtown)	1
Last Descent Helmet	46	+2% Critical chance | +5% Critical damage	21 Dexterity | 21 Cunning	Tarohne (Sanctuary, Enemies Among Us)	1
DuPuis Family Chapeaux	60	1 Rune slot | +2% Critical chance | Enemies drop more coin	23 Dexterity | 23 Cunning	Robes by Jean Luc (Hightown)	2
Blackguard Shroud	55	+4% Physical damage | 2% chance to Stealth when hit	22 Dexterity | 22 Cunning	Jake the Black (Darktown, Bounty Hunter)	2
Mariner's Trust	66	1 Rune slot | +2% Critical chance	24 Dexterity | 24 Cunning	Shady Merchandise (The Docks)	2
Helm of Enasalin	79	+2% Critical chance | +6% Critical damage | Bonus to lockpicking	25 Dexterity | 25 Cunning	"Kanky" Hammertoe (Winding Alley, The Lowdown)	2
Cap of Kings	72	1 Rune slot | +2% Critical chance | Enemies drop better equipment	25 Dexterity | 25 Cunning	Armor Merchant (Lowtown)	3
Tenebral Cowl	86	+44 Attack | +2% Critical chance	26 Dexterity | 26 Cunning	Chest (Blood Mage Refuge, The Last Holdouts)	3
Helm of the Champion	122	1 Rune slot | +3% Critical chance | +6% Critical damage | Bonus to lockpicking	31 Dexterity | 31 Cunning	Grace (The Wounded Coast, Best Served Cold)	3
Ser Isaac's Helm*	39	1 Rune slot | +5% Critical damage | +8 Armor	20 Dexterity | 20 Cunning	Downloadable content (Ser Isaac's Armor Set)	-
Cap of the Antivan King*	43	+1 to all attributes | +4% Critical chance	20 Dexterity | 20 Cunning	Emporium's Relics and Antiques (Black Emporium)	1

* Downloadable content (see dragonage.com/da2/addons for details).

MAGE ARMOR

Much like the staff, mage robes are more useful in their supporting properties than when called on to act like armor in deflecting blows. While some outfits have protective qualities, especially in elemental resistances and magic resistance, mana enhancement and generation is a more common property. Fortunately, mage clothes feature some exceptional bonuses in areas that would well serve the party that defends its weaker members.

A magic resistance focus would be a well-rewarded tactic for dealing with some of the later enemies in the game, and with deft use of storage the mage could stock costumes like staves for every occasion. Minimum requirements in both willpower and magic may disadvantage the blood mage who chose to invest attribute points in constitution, but it's possible to get by with less than 30 in each.

Gloves

Name	Armor	Properties	Requirements	Acquisition	Act
Rune-Covered Gloves	17	+11 Attack | +3% Nature damage	17 Magic | 17 Willpower	Mage Goods (Gallows Courtyard)	1
Silverite-Threaded Gloves	18	+5 Mana/Stamina | +1 Mana/Stamina regeneration rate	18 Magic | 18 Willpower	Dead Messenger (The Wounded Coast, Dark Epiphany)	1
Gloves of the Spiral Eye	26	+7 Mana/Stamina	21 Magic | 21 Willpower	Rubble (Sundermount Caverns, Long Way Home)	1
Gloves of the Overseer	43	+10 Mana/Stamina | +24 Attack	25 Magic | 25 Willpower	Chest (The Killer's Lair, All That Remains)	2
Gloves of the Void	43	1 Rune slot | +12 Defense | +4% Spirit damage	25 Magic | 25 Willpower	Apparel Shop (Lowtown)	2
Gauntlets of the Magister	28	+7 Mana/Stamina | +3% Electricity damage	22 Magic | 22 Willpower	Magister Hadriana (Abandoned Slaver Den)	2
Gloves of the Champion	67	1 Rune slot | +1 Magic | +12 Mana/Stamina | +35 Attack	31 Magic | 31 Willpower	Quest reward (Demands of the Qun)	2
Lyrium Embroidered Gloves	40	+9 Mana/Stamina | +1 Mana/Stamina regeneration rate | +2% Magic resistance	25 Magic | 25 Willpower	Mage Goods (Gallows Courtyard)	3
Gauntlets	47	1 Rune slot | +26 Attack | +4% Fire damage | +4% Cold damage	28 Magic | 28 Willpower	High Dragon (The Bone Pit, Mine Massacre)	3
Gloves of June	52	1 Rune slot | +6% Healing by this character | +243 Nature resistance	27 Magic | 27 Willpower	Ilen's Crafts (Sundermount)	3
Vir Atish'an	67	+13% Healing by this character	29 Magic | 29 Willpower	Hidden Dungeon (Sundermount)	3
Gloves of the Unknowable Unknown*	15	1 Rune slot | +1 Health regeneration rate | +1 Mana/Stamina regeneration rate	16 Magic | 16 Willpower | Level 5	Discarded Weapons and Armor (Black Emporium)	1
The Hands of Fate*	40	+1 Willpower | +3% Spirit damage | Blood Magic: Each point of health provides 1 additional mana	26 Magic | 26 Willpower	Emporium's Relics and Antiques (Black Emporium)	2

* Downloadable content (see dragonage.com/da2/addons for details).

Boots

Name	Armor	Properties	Requirements	Acquisition	Act
Formari Work Boots	27	+7 Mana Stamina | +18 Attack	18 Magic | 18 Willpower	"Captain" Qerth (Shallowguard Base, Night Lies)	1
Boots of the Isolationist	27	1 Rune slot | +18 Attack | +2 Mana/Stamina regeneration rate	18 Magic | 18 Willpower	Ilen's Crafts (Sundermount)	1
Boots of the Elder	30	1 Rune slot | +5% Nature damage	18 Magic | 18 Willpower	Robes by Jean Luc (Hightown)	1
Boots of the Spiral Eye	38	+10 Mana/Stamina | +24 Attack	21 Magic | 21 Willpower	Chest (Undercity Warrens, Shepherding Wolves)	1
Enchanter's Spatterdashes	65	+1 Magic | +14 Mana/Stamina | +18 Defense | +9% Healing by this character	27 Magic | 27 Willpower	Magnus's Wares (The Wounded Coast)	2
Ghillie Brogues	35	+11 Defense | -6% Threat generation	20 Magic | 20 Willpower	Chest (Ancient Crypt, The Deep Roads Expedition)	2
Boots of the Redd	54	+2 Mana/Stamina regeneration rate | +256 Fire resistance	24 Magic | 24 Willpower	Apparel Shop (Lowtown)	2
Boots of the Overseer	65	+14 Mana/Stamina | +37 Attack | +2 Mana/Stamina regeneration rate	25 Magic | 25 Willpower	Chest (Bartrand's Mansion, Family Matter)	2
Harlan's Jackboots	85	+2 Mana/Stamina regeneration rate | +4% damage resistance | +5 Fortitude	28 Magic | 28 Willpower	Robes by Jean Luc (Hightown)	3
Boots of the Champion	101	1 Rune slot | +18 Mana/Stamina | +52 Attack | +2 Mana/ Stamina regeneration rate	31 Magic | 31 Willpower	Huon (On The Loose, Lowtown – Night)	3
Sandals of the Mystic*	35	+1 Willpower | +11 Defense | -6% Threat generation	20 Magic | 20 Willpower	Emporium's Relics and Antiques (Black Emporium)	1

* Downloadable content (see dragonage.com/da2/addons for details).

Chestpieces

Name	Armor	Properties	Requirements	Acquisition	Act
Robe of Hidden Pockets	98	+21% Healing by this character | Enemies drop better equipment	20 Magic | 20 Willpower	Sophia Dryden (Wounded Coast, Terror on the Coast)	1
Flocked Wool Robe	69	+24 Defense | +7 Armor	17 Magic | 17 Willpower	Mage Goods (Gallows Courtyard)	1
Apostate's Robes	82	+22 Mana/Stamina | +27 Defense	18 Magic | 18 Willpower	Apparel Shop (Lowtown)	1
Robes of the Spiral Eye	107	+28 Mana/Stamina | +67 Attack	21 Magic | 21 Willpower	Dragon (Deep Roads)	1
Heavy Velvet Robes	107	+67 Attack | +34 Defense | +11 Armor	21 Magic | 21 Willpower	Mage Goods (Gallows Courtyard)	2
Robe of the Notorious Pirate	107	1 Rune slot | +28 Mana/Stamina | +67 Attack | Enemies drop more coin	22 Magic | 22 Willpower	Fell Orden (Wounded Coast, Raiders on the Cliffs)	2
Robes of the Void	151	+36 Mana/Stamina | +88 Attack | +712 Electricity resistance	24 Magic | 24 Willpower	Robes by Jean Luc (Hightown)	2
Aequitarian Robes	151	+36 Mana/Stamina | +88 Attack | +5 Mana/Stamina regeneration rate	24 Magic | 24 Willpower	Dead body (Hightown, Demands of the Qun)	2
Cumberland Circle Robes	197	1 Rune slot | +42 Mana/Stamina | +5 Mana/Stamina regeneration rate | +25% Healing by this character	28 Magic | 28 Willpower	Reward from Orsino (Best Served Cold)	3
Battlemage Armaments	165	+47 Defense | +15% Fire damage | +10% Magic resistance	25 Magic | 25 Willpower	Mage Goods (Gallows Courtyard)	3
Circle Robes	257	1 Rune slot | +16% Electricity damage | +1210 Electricity resistance	29 Magic | 29 Willpower	Robes by Jean Luc (Hightown)	3
Robes of the Champion	281	2 Rune slots | +50 Mana/Stamina | +145 Attack	31 Magic | 31 Willpower	High Dragon (The Bone Pit, Mine Massacre)	3
Vestments of Sacrifice	98	1 Rune slot | +5 Mana/Stamina regeneration rate | +21% Healing by this character	20 Magic | 20 Willpower	Chest (The Deep Roads, Finding Nathaniel)	3
Robes of the Overseer	181	1 Rune slot | +40 Mana/Stamina | +102 Attack	25 Magic | 25 Willpower	Grave (Sundermount, A New Path)	3
Vestments of the Mystic*	98	2 Rune slots | +2 Willpower	20 Magic | 20 Willpower	Emporium's Relics and Antiques (Black Emporium)	1
Robes of Unblemished Cleanliness*	307	+2 to all attributes | +24% Fire damage | +24% Cold damage | +24% Electricity damage | +24% Nature damage | +28% Healing by this character	32 Magic | 32 Willpower	Emporium's Relics and Antiques (Black Emporium)	3

* Downloadable content (see dragonage.com/da2/addons for details).

Helms

Name	Armor	Properties	Requirements	Acquisition	Act
Slaver Lord's Cowl	25	1 Rune slot | +6 Mana/Stamina | +2% Critical chance	16 Magic | 16 Willpower	Chest (Danarius's Manor, Bait and Switch)	1
Thinking Cap	30	+8 Mana/Stamina | +20 Attack	18 Magic | 18 Willpower	Corpse (Sanctuary, Enemies Among Us)	1
Illwan's Hood	33	+2 Mana/Stamina regeneration rate | +154 Cold resistance | +154 Electricity resistance	18 Magic | 18 Willpower	Robes by Jean Luc (Hightown)	1
Hood of the Spiral Eye	43	+11 Mana/Stamina | +27 Attack	21 Magic | 21 Willpower	Tarohne (Sanctuary, Enemies Among Us)	1
Gascard DuPuis's Favorite Hat	43	+13 Defense | +2% Critical chance	21 Magic | 21 Willpower	Gascard DuPuis (Killer's Lair, All That Remains)	2
Tevinter Enchanter's Cap	51	+31 Attack | +6% Fire damage	22 Magic | 22 Willpower	Chest (Holding Caves, A Bitter Pill)	2
Cowl of the Overseer	72	+16 Mana/Stamina | +41 Attack | +2 Mana/Stamina regeneration rate	25 Magic | 25 Willpower	Thug Leader (Winding Alley, Following the Qun)	2
Circlet of the Dreamer	103	+3 Magic | +2 Mana/Stamina regeneration rate | +6% Spirit damage	30 Magic | 30 Willpower	Bonny Lem's Wares (Disused Passage)	3
Hood of the Formari	72	1 Rune slot | +41 Attack | +2% Critical chance	25 Magic | 25 Willpower	Mage Goods (Gallows Courtyard)	3
Regret	86	+6% Cold damage | +10% Healing by this character | +406 Cold resistance	27 Magic | 27 Willpower	Robes by Jean Luc (Hightown)	3
Hood of the Champion	112	1 Rune slot | +20 Mana/Stamina | +58 Attack | +2 Mana/Stamina regeneration rate	31 Magic | 31 Willpower	Grace (The Wounded Coast, Best Served Cold)	3
The Resolutionist's Cap*	123	2 Rune slots | +1 Magic | +4 Mana/Stamina regeneration rate	32 Magic | 32 Willpower	Faith quest	3
The Ponderer*	66	2 Rune slots | +1 Magic | +1 Willpower	26 Magic | 26 Willpower	Emporium's Relics and Antiques (Black Emporium)	2

* Downloadable content (see dragonage.com/da2/addons for details).

ARMOR SETS

There are three unique, complete armor sets to collect in each Act, one for each class that Hawke may play. Equipping the entire suit of armor on the main character confers an additional bonus for completing the uniform. Note that these items are class-specific: you can only acquire those corresponding to your class in a single playthrough.

Armor Sets

Set Name	Act	Class	Piece #1	Piece #2	Piece #3	Bonus
Fallen	1	Warrior	Gauntlets of the Fallen	Boots of the Fallen	Warplate of the Fallen	1 strength, 20 health
Last Descent	1	Rogue	Last Descent Gauntlets	Last Descent Boots	Last Descent Armor	1 dexterity, 20 stamina
Spiral Eye	1	Mage	Gloves of the Spiral Eye	Boots of the Spiral Eye	Robes of the Spiral Eye	1 magic, 20 mana
Stonehammer	2	Warrior	Stonehammer Gauntlets	Stonehammer Boots	Stonehammer Plate	2 strength, 3% armor
Enasalin	2	Rogue	Gloves of Enasalin	Boots of Enasalin	Guardian of Enasalin	2 dexterity, 3% displacement
Overseer	2	Mage	Gloves of the Overseer	Boots of the Overseer	Robes of the Overseer	2 magic, 3% defense
Champion	3	Warrior	Gauntlets of the Champion	Boots of the Champion	Warplate of the Champion	3 strength, 5% armor
Champion	3	Rogue	Gloves of the Champion	Boots of the Champion	Arms of the Champion	3 dexterity, 5% displacement
Champion	3	Mage	Gloves of the Champion	Boots of the Champion	Robes of the Champion	3 magic, 5% defense

UNIQUE ACCESSORIES

Even if you steadfastly pick your weapon for its damage and your outfit for its armor rating, accessories are the opportunity to put an edge or tactical spin on your character. The only difference between the four slots is the restriction placed on different types. Up to one amulet, one belt and two rings can be equipped simultaneously by player characters and companions alike, and with no requirements.

The important thing to remember in equipping accessories with items is that effects can 'stack', or add together. Two cheap rings of +8 health will add 16 to your total health, surpassing a level-up spent on constitution. Four high-quality accessories can work together for exceptional bonuses. For this reason, accessories with more than one property are valuable in underpinning a stacked bonus while offering additional benefits.

Belts

Name	Properties	Acquisition	Act
Enchanted Silverite Chain Belt	+1 To All Atributes | +11 Defense | +3% Magic resistance	Bonny Lem's Wares (Disused Passage)	1
Sailors' Rope Belt	+3% Physical damage | +3 Fortitude	Hayder (The Chantry, Fools Rush In)	1
Handlers' Whip	+16 Attack | +2% Critical chance	Arvaarad (Vimmark Mountain Pass, Shepherding Wolves)	1
String of Pearls	+6 Health | Enemies drop more coin	Chest (Danarius's Manor, Bait and Switch)	1
Pirate Sash	+16 Attack | +2% Critical chance	Shady Merchandise (The Docks)	1
Belt of Unknowing	+8 Mana/Stamina | +2 Mana/Stamina regeneration rate	Crypt Treasure (Ancient Crypt, Deep Roads Expedition)	1
Belt of the Brigand	+16 Attack | +8 Defense | +1% Attack speed	Pile of Bones (Top of Sundermount)	2

Belts (Continued)

Name	Properties	Acquisition	Act
Belt of the Primevals	+4% Fire damage | +4% Cold damage | +4% Electricity damage | +4% Nature damage	Chest (Bartrand's Mansion, Family Matter)	2
Seneschals' Leather Strap	+23 Attack | +2% Critical chance | +3% Physical damage	Patron (The Hanged Man, Offered and Lost)	2
Dalish Embossed Belt	+30 Attack | +1% Attack speed | +510 Nature resistance	Nexus Golem's Wares (Abandoned Thaig)	2
Cord of the Weyr-Beast	+30 Attack | +3% Physical damage	Trinkets Emporium (Lowtown)	2
Sash of the Tirashan	+21 Attack | +3% Physical damage	Chest (Deep Roads, Fool's Gold)	2
Belt of Vigor	+22 Health | +2 Health regeneration rate	Hubert's Fine Goods (Hightown)	2
Andruil's Braid	+12 Mana/Stamina | +2 Mana/Stamina regeneration rate | +7% Healing by this character	Grave (Sundermount, A New Path)	3
Seven Deadly Cinch	+2% Critical chance | +9% Critical damage | +3% Physical damage	Magnus's Wares (The Wounded Coast)	3
Griffon-Feather Belt	+13 Health | +33 Attack | +13 Mana/Stamina	Corpse (Drakestone Mines, Justice)	3
Belt of Woven Elf Hair	+1 Constitution | +43 Attack | +15 Mana/Stamina | +2% Critical chance	Nexus Golem's Wares (Hidden Dungeon)	3
Rock Band	+1 Armor | +8 Fortitude	Ethereal Golem (Bartrand's Estate, Haunted)	3
Fereldan Circle Sash	+1 Willpower | +38 Attack | +19 Defense	Evelina (Sewer Passage, On the Loose)	3
The Hanged Man's Girdle	+12 Health | +30 Attack | +15 Defense	Hubert's Fine Goods (Hightown)	3
Belt of the Silent Sisters	+15 Health | +43 Attack | +22 Defense	Trinkets Emporium (Lowtown)	3
Deepstalker's Belt	+11 Health | +28 Attack | +14 Defense	Reward for saving Sandal (The Deep Roads Expedition)	3
Sash of the Halla	+19 Defense | +2 Health regeneration rate | +3% damage resistance	Ilen's Crafts (Sundermount)	3
Concealer's Sash	+18 Defense | +5% Spirit damage | +3% Magic resistance	Apparel Shop (Lowtown)	3
Templar Ceremonial Cummerbund	+10% Magic resistance | +2 Health regeneration rate	Chest (Templar Hall, The Last Straw)	3
Karasten's Belt	+1 Armor | +3% damage resistance | +3% Magic resistance | +4 Fortitude	Magnus's Wares (The Wounded Coast)	3
Girdle of the Elders	+13 Health | +8% Healing to this character | +3% damage resistance	Medan (The Awiergan Scrolls, Wounded Coast)	3
Sturdy Belt*	+8 Health | +9 Defense | +2 Health regeneration rate	Emporium's Relics and Antiques (Black Emporium)	1
The Belt of Promise*	+3 Dexterity | +3 Cunning | +10% Magic resistance | +10% damage resistance | +1% XP gain	Emporium's Relics and Antiques (Black Emporium)	3

* Downloadable content (see dragonage.com/da2/addons for details).

Amulets

Name	Properties	Acquisition	Act
Lifestone	+10 Health | +8% Healing by this character	Crypt Treasure (Ancient Crypt, Deep Roads Expedition)	1
Pewter Pendant of Wolves Howling at the Moon	+22 Attack | +2% Critical chance	Chest (Ruined Passage, Magistrate's Orders)	1
The Liar's Charm	+10 Defense | +1 Armor	Hubert's Fine Goods (Hightown)	1
Meraas	+1 Armor | +4 Fortitude	Chest (Tal-Vashoth Cavern, Blackpowder Promise)	1
Amulet of Serenity	+8% Healing by this character | +8% Healing to this character	Solivitus (Gallows Courtyard)	1
Amulet of Influence	+7 Health | Enemies drop more coin	Trinkets Emporium (Lowtown)	1
Brass Nug Charm	+10 Health | +10 Mana/Stamina | +2 Health regeneration rate	Crypt Treasure (Ancient Crypt, Deep Roads Expedition)	1
Talisman of Saarebas	+2 Health regeneration rate | Blood Magic: Each point of health provides 1 additional mana	Quest reward (Shepherding Wolves)	1
Polished Whitewood Amulet	+2 Health regeneration rate | +9% Healing to this character	Pile of Bones (Varterral Hunting Ground, Mirror Image)	2
Moonstone Amulet	+5% Spirit damage | +3% Magic resistance	Hubert's Fine Goods (Hightown)	2
Poisonwood Locket	+ 41 Attack | + 12% Nature damage | + 340 Nature resistance	Bonny Lem's Wares (Disused Passage)	2
Gaudy Amethyst Pendant	+16 Defense | Enemies drop better equipment	Chest (The Killer's Lair, All That Remains)	2
Magister's Lifestone	+15 Defense | Enemies drop better equipment	Chest (Holding Caves, A Bitter Pill)	2
Split Bone Necklace	+2 Health regeneration rate | +9% Healing to this character | +239 Fire resistance	Trinkets Emporium (Lowtown)	2
Fen'Harel's Tooth	+15 Defense | +239 Nature resistance | Bonus to evade traps	Ilen's Crafts (Sundermount)	2
The Sacred Heart	+35 Attack | +2% Critical chance | +4% Physical damage	Reward from Alistair (Lowtown, Demands of the Qun)	2
White Scapular of the Defender	+17 Health | +22 Defense | +1 Armor	Reward from Gascard DuPuis via a letter if you let him live in All that Remains	3
Four-Fingered Eddie's Lucky Talisman	+ 2 Dexterity | + 2 Cunning | + 8 Critical chance | + 4% Attack speed | Enemies drop better equipment | Enemies drop more coin	Bonny Lem's Wares (Disused Passage)	3
Warden's Oath	+17 Health | +22 Defense | +1 Armor	Corpse (Drakestone Mines, Justice)	3
Rhinestone-Studded Symbol of Andraste	+15 Mana/Stamina | +38 Attack | +10% Healing by this character	Hubert's Fine Goods (Hightown)	3
Filigreed Orlesian Pendant	+41 Attack | +2% Critical chance | +4% Physical damage	Evelina (Sewer Passage, On the Loose)	3
Van Markham's Heirloom	+38 Attack | +2% Critical chance | +4% Physical damage	Hubert's Fine Goods (Hightown)	3
Chantry Amulet	+16 Health | +6% Cold damage | +340 Spirit resistance	Formari Herbalist (Gallows Courtyard)	3
Amulet of the Tempest	+44 Attack | +4% Physical damage | +2% Attack speed	Lirene's Fereldan Imports (Lowtown)	3
Urzara's Tooth	+2 to all attributes | +20 Health | +529 Fire resistance	Reward for completing all Herbalist's Tasks	3
Tranquility	+1 to all attributes	Trinkets Emporium (Lowtown)	3
Gem of Keroshek	+44 Attack | Enemies drop more coin	Quest reward (Gamlen's Greatest Treasure)	3
Meghan Vael's Locket*	+1 Willpower | +184 Fire resistance | +184 Cold resistance	On a mercenary (Duty)	1
Jewel of the Ether*	+1 Willpower | +42 Health | +9% Magic resistance	Faith quest	3
Dull Brass Amulet*	+1 to all attributes | +15 Health | +1 Armor | Immunity to flanking	Emporium's Relics and Antiques (Black Emporium)	2

* Downloadable content (see dragonage.com/da2/addons for details).

Rings

Name	Properties	Acquisition	Act
Ring of the Magister	+6 Mana/Stamina | +4% Fire damage	Arcane Horror (Sundermount, Long Way Home)	1
Runed Silverite Ring	+18 Attack | +3% Physical damage	Quest reward (Wayward Son)	1
Gentleman's Puzzle Ring	+17 Defense | +3 Fortitude	Hubert's Fine Goods (Hightown)	1
Gallows Slave Finger-Cuffs	+7 Health | +9 Defense	Rubble (Bone Pit Mines, The Bone Pit)	1
Guild Ring	+8 Defense | +106 Fire resistance	Trinkets Emporium (Lowtown)	1
Dirthamen's Secret	+4% Electricity damage | +116 Nature resistance	Ilen's Crafts (Sundermount)	1
Carved Ring of the Vhenadahl	+19 Attack | +2% Critical chance	Chest (Primeval Ruins, Deep Roads Expedition)	1
Rivaini Seer's Brand	+4% Fire damage | +4% Spirit damage	Chest (Varterral Hunting Ground, Mirror Image)	2
Ring of Incandescence	+10 Mana/Stamina | +4% Fire damage | +196 Fire resistance	Hubert's Fine Goods (Hightown)	2
The Seal of Kirkwall	+26 Defense | +1 Armor | +2 Health regeneration rate	Dead body (Viscount's Keep, Demands of the Qun)	2
Etched Ring of the Twins	+2 Strength | +4% Critical chance | +9% Critical damage | +15% Healing to this character | Immunity To Knockback	Nexus Golem's Wares (Abandoned Thaig)	2
Twice-Blessed Ring	+2% Critical chance | +4% Critical damage	Dead body (Viscount's Keep, Demands of the Qun)	2
Ring of the Seven Watchers	+2% Critical chance | +4% Critical damage	Corpse (Bounty Hunter Getaway, Search and Rescue)	2
Ring of the Faithful	+11 Defense | +7% Healing to this character | +179 Spirit resistance	Formari Herbalist (Gallows Courtyard)	2
Ring of Ruin	+4% Spirit damage | Blood Magic: Each point of health provides 1 additional mana	Trinkets Emporium (Lowtown)	2
Tear of Ferelden	+10 Health | +2% Critical chance | Enemies drop better equipment	Lirene's Fereldan Imports (Lowtown)	2
Puzzle Ring of the Black Fox	+2 Dexterity | +2 Cunning | +9% Critical chance | Bonus to lockpicking | Enemies drop better equipment	Bonny Lem's Wares (Disused Passage)	2
Warden's Promise	+4% Critical damage | +3% Physical damage | +3% Magic resistance	Reward from Stroud (Lowtown, Demands of the Qun)	2
The Jade Serpent	+33 Attack | +5% Nature damage | +278 Nature resistance	Dragon (Sundermount, A New Path)	3
Onyx Ring of the Dales	+11 Health | +28 Attack | +1 Armor	Mage Goods (Gallows Courtyard)	3
Orsino's Signet Ring	+14 Health | +14 Mana/Stamina | +5% Spirit damage	Orsino (Gallows Prison, The Last Straw)	3
Mark of the Fallen	+38 Attack | +2% Critical chance | Blood Magic: Each point of health provides 1 additional mana	Chest (Templar Hall, The Last Straw)	3
Three Wolf Boon	+2% Critical chance | +5% Critical damage | +3% Physical damage	Enchanter (Hightown – Night or Secret Meeting Place, Best Served Cold)	3
Ring of the Shadow Hunter	+4% Critical damage | +3% Physical damage | +3% Magic resistance	Treasure Pile (Mountain Cave, Murder of Crows)	3
Band of Silvery Gold	+4% Critical damage | +3% Physical damage | +3% Magic resistance	Hubert's Fine Goods (Hightown)	3
Ring of the Emerald Knights	+5% Critical damage | +3% Physical damage | +3% Magic resistance	High Dragon (The Bone Pit, Mine Massacre)	3
Demon's Eye	+3% Magic resistance | +4 Fortitude | Immunity to Stun	Shady Merchandise (The Docks)	3
Pretty Little Thing	+332 Fire resistance | +332 Cold resistance | Enemies drop more coin	Trinkets Emporium (Lowtown)	3
Awakened's Might	+30 Attack | +4% Fire damage | Blood Magic: Each point of health provides 1 additional mana	Lirene's Fereldan Imports (Lowtown)	3
Ring of the Wounded Coast	+13 Health | +278 Fire resistance | +278 Cold resistance	Apparel Shop (Lowtown)	3
Ring of the Ferryman	+2 Magic | +9 Mana/Stamina regeneration rate | +24% Fire damage | +24% Electricity damage | Immunity to Stun	Magnus's Wares (The Wounded Coast)	3
Bardin's Folly	+2 Strength | +116 Attack | +58 Defense | +6% Physical damage | +3% Attack speed	Nexus Golem's Wares (Hidden Dungeon)	3
Sylvanwood Ring	+2% Critical chance | +8% Critical damage | +4% Nature damage	Thief Leader (Sundermount, A New Path)	3
Ring of Unheeded Wisdom*	+1 Cunning | +5 Health | +2% damage resistance | Level 5	Discarded Weapons and Armor (Black Emporium)	1
The Fallen Star*	+1 to all attributes | +23 Health | +7% damage resistance | +1% XP gain	Emporium's Relics and Antiques (Black Emporium)	1
Ring of No Wishes*	+1 to all attributes | +8% Healing to this character | Immunity to critical hits | Immunity to Stun	Emporium's Relics and Antiques (Black Emporium)	3

* Downloadable content (see dragonage.com/da2/addons for details).

GENERATED EQUIPMENT

Besides the unique items, with their names and history, you'll also find plenty of ordinary equipment with useful but unexceptional attributes. Such items are randomly generated, from their names to their bonuses, by intelligent selection from predetermined loot categories. They can be found as enemy drops, in most containers throughout Kirkwall and the Free Marches, and even in shops where they represent the bulk of merchant inventories. These items are generated upon entering the map in which they are situated.

You'll quickly learn to spot such items by their use of adjectives rather than individually imagined names. While "The Bann's Backhouse Door" is a fairly memorable title that marks out an early unique shield, the "Superior Shield" and "Heavy Shield" are examples of many generic items that will come your way.

Perhaps the most relevant factor in the generation of items is Hawke's level. Weapons and armor will scale accordingly, keeping pace with the party's need for increasingly powerful gear. Older items can be confidently traded away for silvers and bits.

The most useful items endow the user with multiple bonuses, but costs rise exponentially with each additional bonus. Furthermore, generated items never feature Rune slots and their bonuses cannot match the power or specialization of unique items. But when you are trying to be frugal in your expenditure, such finds can usefully fill gaps in your party's inventory. Mages will want to collect staves of every element, while accessories with the same bonus can be equipped on one character for a dedicated, stacked advantage to a specific attribute.

Loot Drops

Enemies are sometimes scripted to drop specific items as the fixed rewards for quests. They may also leave coins or Potions as plunder to be claimed for defeating them in battle. Most of the time, though, the treasure dropped by enemies consists of generated items. These are randomly selected from within a range of objects that belong to the loot category associated with the creature group (as revealed in the Bestiary chapter of this guide). The following table of loot categories shows the useful types of reward for each group.

Loot Category	General Contents	Useful For
Generic	Weapons, armor, accessories	All classes
Apostates	Weapons, armor, rings, Heretic's Manual, Bedroll	Mages
Beasts	Claws, Liver, Kidney, Pelt, Dragon Eyes, Dragon Scales, Dragon Glands, Spider Fangs, Spider Glands, Spider Silk	All classes
Chantry	Shields, rings, belts	Warriors, Rogues
Circle of Magi	Staffs, armor, amulets	Mages
Coterie	Bows, daggers, armor, rings, belts	Rogues
Dalish	Weapons, armor, amulets, belts	Warriors, Rogues
Darkspawn	Weapons, amulets	Warriors
Demonic	Weapons, armor, amulets, rings, belts	Mages
Dwarven	Weapons, armor	Rogues
Kirkwall	Weapons, armor	Warriors, Rogues
Profane	Weapons, amulets, rings	Mages
Qunari	Weapons, armor, amulets, belts	Warriors, Mages
Raiders	Weapons, armor	Warriors, Rogues
Slavers	Weapons, armor	Warriors, Mages
Templars	Weapons, armor	Warriors, Rogues

Potions work slightly differently, as the game assists players who are short on supplies. The chance of a Potion drop is greatest when your inventory is empty, the probability decreasing until you hit the limit for the current difficulty level. If the number of Potions in your inventory matches or exceeds the limit, they will stop appearing as loot. This limit applies to each type of basic Potion individually. As soon as the number of Potions in your inventory falls below the limit, you will be getting some as loot drops again.

Difficulty level	Potion Drop Limit
Casual	16
Normal	12
Hard	8
Nightmare	4

Although they are cheap goods, you can always exploit the game's generosity in the early stages by forcing the drops. For example, try placing all of your Lyrium Potions in storage at Gamlen's House so that your inventory is empty of them before opening some of the containers around Kirkwall.

SPECIAL ITEMS

Backpacks

The total amount of treasure, accessories and equipment that you may carry at any one time is determined by the capacity of your inventory. You begin with a default capacity of 50 slots, which may be increased by purchasing Backpacks from specific merchants. Each additional Backpack permanently adds 10 slots to your inventory. The capacity meter on the lower right of the inventory screen also indicates how many Backpacks you have already obtained, extending to a potential 100 slots if you acquire all five.

Slots should not be confused with items, as a single slot in your inventory can sometimes hold many identical items. Every time you wish to add a new type of item to your inventory, such as a dagger or your first Stamina Potion, it needs an empty slot to be free. Should you add a second Stamina Potion, it will join the first and the slot will then indicate "x2", or "x3" for a third, and upwards as you stack more items in the same slot. However, Runes and equipment have unique identities – even if they appear interchangeable – so a second dagger will need a new slot, even if its attributes appear similar. Note that crafting paraphernalia, letters, keys and other quest items are all stored separately and do not require a space in your inventory.

Backpacks

Backpack	Shop	Act
#1	Robes by Jean Luc	1
#2	Apparel Shop	1
#3	Mage Goods	2
#4	Robes by Jean Luc	2
#5	Robes by Jean Luc	3

Tomes & Special Potions

The life-affirming value of reading a good book has never been so apparent – nor so immediate – as in the case of these edifying publications. Tomes are one-use items that grant a permanent increase to Hawke's abilities or attributes. Since the only other way to enjoy such an advance in character development is by gaining an experience level, these volumes are very rare and extremely expensive. They take effect as soon as they are purchased, the points becoming available to spend through the usual Level Up menu. Tomes of Technique teach a single ability, while Tomes of the Mortal Vessel improve attributes.

Tomes & Special Potions

Name	Effect	Shop	Act
Tome of Technique	Teaches a single ability	Hubert's Fine Goods	1
Avernus's Experimental Draught	Grants 2 attribute points	Dark Epiphany quest (see page 66)	1
Greater Tome of the Mortal Vessel	Grants 2 attribute points	Trinkets Emporium	2
Tome of Technique	Teaches a single ability	Ilen's Crafts	2
Arcane Tome of the Mortal Vessel	Grants 1 attribute point	Korval's Blades	3
Tome of Technique	Teaches a single ability	Black Emporium	*
Greater Tome of the Mortal Vessel	Grants 2 attribute points	Black Emporium	*
Greater Elixir of the Mortal Vessel	Grants 2 attribute points	Black Emporium	*
Elixir of Arcane Technique	Teaches a single ability. Restriction: mage	Black Emporium	*
Elixir of Physical Technique	Teaches a single ability. Restriction: warrior or rogue	Black Emporium	*
Maker's Sigh	Grants reallocation of all points previously spent on attributes, specializations and abilities	Black Emporium	*

* See dragonage.com/da2/addons for further details on this Premium Content.

Gifts

Beyond the consequences of your actions and conversations, your relationships with your companions can be further influenced by presenting them with Gifts. A single Gift will usually strengthen the relationship further in the direction of friendship.

Gifts are personalized for a specific character and only influence the individual relationship with a one-time bonus, which may be undone by later actions and events. Some Gifts can even be equipped as useable items. See the corresponding sections in this chapter for details on the Shield of the Knight Herself, the Blade of Mercy, the Sylvanwood Ring and the Starkhaven Longbow.

Gifts

Companion	Name	Location	Related Quest
Anders	**Tevinter Chantry Amulet**	Abandoned Slaver Den	A Bitter Pill (page 85)
Aveline	**Shield of the Knight Herself**	Ser Varnell's Refuge	Offered and Lost (page 72)
Bethany	**Portrait of Your Mother**	Amell Estate Cellar	Birthright (page 63)
Carver	**Tobrius's Documents**	Amell Estate Cellar	Birthright (page 63)
Fenris	**Blade of Mercy**	Secret Meeting Place	Best Served Cold (page 93)
	A Slave's Life	From a sack in the elven alienage, Lowtown (Night)	-
Isabela	**Ship in a Bottle**	Smuggler's Cut	Blackpowder Courtesy (page 72)
	Rivaini Talisman	Disused Passage, Act 3, Docks	-
Merrill	**Sylvanwood Ring**	Thief Leader remains, Act 3, Sundermount	A Murder of Crows (page 98)
	Wooden Halla Carving	Ilen's Crafts shop, Act 2, Sundermount	-
Varric	**Signet Ring**	Trinkets Emporium shop, Act 2, Lowtown	-
Sebastian	**Starkhaven Longbow**	Harimann Estate	Repentance (page 81)

Companion Armor Upgrades

Companion	Name	Acquisition	Act
Bethany	Heirloom Amell Protective Sigils	Final room in the Birthright quest (see page 63)	1
Carver	Fereldan Girded Plating	Final room in the Birthright quest (see page 63)	1
Anders	Lyrium Weave	Mage Goods shop (Gallows)	2
	Armor Struts	Lirene's Fereldan Imports shop (Lowtown)	2
	Spirit Essence	Dissent quest, Gallows Dungeon (see page 82)	2
	Sigil of the Mage Underground	Best Served Cold quest (see page 93)	3
Aveline	Underpadding – Guardsman Pattern	Armor Merchant shop (Lowtown)	1
	Flex-Chain – Guardsman Pattern	Raiders on the Cliffs quest, on Fell Orden (see page 79)	2
	Impact Plating – Guardsman Pattern	Armor Merchant shop (Lowtown)	2
	Deflecting Joints – Guardsman Pattern	Favor and Fault quest, on Jeven (see page 102)	3
Fenris	Lyrium Scales	Shady Merchandise shop (Docks)	2
	Tevinter Spirit Symbol	Robes by Jean Luc shop (Hightown)	2
	Reinforced Straps	A Bitter Pill quest, Abandoned Slaver Den (see page 85)	2
	Enchanted Resin	Mine Massacre quest, on Dragon (see page 97)	3
Isabela	Lambswool Insoles	To Catch A Thief quest, in a chest in the Lost-End Foundry (see page 74)	2
	Rigid Boning	Apparel Shop, (Lowtown)	2
	Supportive Corselet	Robes by Jean Luc shop (Hightown)	2
	Boiled Leather Plates	A Murder of Crows quest (see page 98)	3
Merrill	Silver-Threaded Dalish Embroidery	Sundermount, near the top of the path	2
	Carved Ironwood Buttons	Ilen's Crafts shop (Sundermount)	2
	Samite Lining	Robes by Jean Luc shop (Hightown)	2
	Halla Horn Buckles	A New Path quest, on the Pride Demon (see page 103)	3
Varric	Inscribed Leather Harness	Apparel Shop (Lowtown)	1
	Silverite-Reinforced Buckles	Family Matter quest, Bartrand's Estate (see page 84)	2
	Coat Lining with Concealed Pockets	Shady Merchandise shop (Docks)	2
	Drakeskin Leg Straps	Finding Nathaniel quest (see page 99)	3
Sebastian*	Enhanced Articulation	Armor Shop (Gallows)	2
	Mail Undertunic	Repentance quest, Harriman Estate (see page 81)	2
	Reinforced Bracers	Olaf's Armory shop (Hightown)	2
	Protection of the Faith	Best Served Cold quest, Hightown (Night), on a Templar Lieutenant (see page 93)	3

* See dragonage.com/da2/addons for further details on this Premium Content.

Companion Armor Upgrades

Companions cannot equip the armor made available to Hawke but they each have the option of upgrading their personal outfit with a series of bolt-on components. Every armor upgrade is permanently applied on acquisition and confers estimable protective bonuses. Diligently tracking down upgrades for all of your fellow travelers, even those who see less action, will maintain party balance and keep later options open.

There is one early armor upgrade for Hawke's sibling while all other companions can expect four upgrades over the course of the game. The effects vary greatly, and in addition to improving the base armor rating they can introduce Rune slots, add resistances and increase defense.

Consumables

Potions can be consumed in mid-battle, requiring the character to cease other actions and taking immediate effect. Potion use is limited by a Cooldown period, which is extended to similar replenishing items on activation, and may be automated through Tactics when a companion is in danger.

Icon	Name	Effect	Acquisition
	Health Potion	Health regeneration: 60% Cooldown: 30 seconds	Standard loot from enemies and containers
	Mana Potion	Mana regeneration: 40% Cooldown: 30 seconds	
	Stamina Potion	Stamina regeneration: 40% Cooldown: 30 seconds	
	Injury Kit	Heals an injury	

When it comes to availability, always try to ration your Potion consumption and establish a reserve for emergency use that you have accumulated from those you find. You will most likely need to raid your stock of Potions at some point, as you'll be facing many lengthy battles and challenging boss encounters where Potions will come in handy as your "fifth NPC medic" when forsaking healers and support for a more aggressive party roster.

When your character is knocked unconscious during battle, they will incur an injury (indicated by a red skull icon beside their portrait) on revival. Injured characters must endure a constant reduction in maximum health, proportional to the number of injuries received, that remains with them until cured. The Injury Kit will heal the condition, but take note that this sticking-plaster item is intended mainly for use mid-quest, when you are deep in a cave or dungeon and unable to leave the current path. Returning to Gamlen's House or the Hawke Estate cures all injuries just as effectively and at no cost, while the Spirit Healer's Second Chance passive ability prevents injury altogether.

Junk

Don't concern yourself with saving anything that automatically turns up in your trash can ( ). That's not to say it's worthless, as you'll generate a small amount of welcome revenue every time you trade in your haul at a merchant's. Some objects fetch more than others, with antiques and pouches of chipped gemstones demanding a higher price than bottles of rotgut or a moth-eaten scarf. But if an item is clearly labeled as junk on discovery then it is meant to be sold: there are no hidden treasures, crafting items or secret valuables in this category that will contribute to quests later on.

If you need to make inventory space for real equipment, the ragged objects in the junk category can be permanently removed with the Destroy option. In a pinch, you may even transfer unwanted weapons and gear to the trash can for destruction. As a rule, though, it's far wiser to manage your inventory, sell items and use the Storage in Gamlen's House to clear out your clutter before embarking on a new quest. Acquiring Backpack expansions for additional capacity slots also tends to make things much easier.

CRAFTING

Some of the more useful items in the game must be made by the process of crafting. There are three distinct fields of crafting, each generating different kinds of objects, but the requirements are broadly the same for all disciplines:

1. **Recipes, Designs and Formulas:** Knowledge, in the form of a set of instructions to follow.
2. **Reagents:** The discovery of sufficient raw ingredients, by type and quantity.
3. **Crafters:** The expertise of a professional who must be paid 1 silver for their services in creating each item.

The one thing to understand about crafting is that the ingredients you find will stay with you permanently. They are not spent when you make an item: instead, they add to a growing resource list that increases your capacity to make more complicated combinations.

As an example, an Elfroot Potion recipe asks for 1 Elfroot. When you have found at least one of the game's 9 Elfroots, you may begin ordering as many Elfroot Potions as you like. Expanding the operation to make a Restoration Potion then demands the acquisition of the new recipe, which will tell you that crafting takes 3 Elfroot and 2 Spindleweed. With only 1 Elfroot on your list, you will need to find another 2 Elfroot and at least 2 Spindleweed to meet the required combination.

Potions

To concoct a Potion or Elixir, you must first discover a Recipe. The herbal ingredients of Elfroot, Spindleweed, Embrium and Ambrosia must then be sourced and picked from the wild reaches of the Free Marches.

Lady Elegant is one of the first characters that Hawke may encounter on an initial visit to Lowtown. She immediately offers her services and provides a complimentary Elfroot Potion Recipe to unlock her Crafting Station.

Potion Recipes

Icon	Name	Effect	Acquisition	Ingredient 1	Ingredient 2	Ingredient 3	Ingredient 4
	Elfroot Potion	Restores 80% of health and removes one injury. Cooldown: 30 seconds	Lady Elegant (Lowtown, Act 1)	Elfroot (x1)	-	-	-
	Elixir of Purity	Increases damage done to darkspawn by 10%. Duration: 30 minutes. Cooldown: 5 minutes	The Black Emporium*	Elfroot (x2)	-	-	-
	Restoration Potion	Restores 80% of health and 40% of mana/stamina. Cooldown: 30 seconds	Formari Herbalist shop, Gallows	Elfroot (x3)	Spindleweed (x1)	-	-
	Life Ward Potion	Revives the user if taken prior to being knocked unconscious, though an injury is still sustained. Health restored: 40%. Duration: 20 minutes. Cooldown: 5 minutes	Formari Herbalist shop, Gallows	Elfroot (x2)	Spindleweed (x2)	-	-
	Rock Armor Potion	Improves resistance to all damage types. Damage resistance: +10%. Duration: 30 minutes. Cooldown: 5 minutes	Lowtown (Act 2)	Elfroot (x1)	Spindleweed (x1)	Embrium (x1)	-
	Mighty Offense Potion	Increases all forms of damage dealt by 10%. Duration: 30 minutes	Sundermount (Act 2)	Elfroot (x2)	Embrium (x2)	-	-
	Elixir of Heroism	Grants the party a bonus level (one-time use)	Hightown (Act 3)	Elfroot (x1)	Spindleweed (x1)	Embrium (x1)	Ambrosia (x1)

* See dragonage.com/da2/addons for further details on this Premium Content.

Potion Ingredients

Name	Aquisition (Act 1)	Aquisition (Act 2)	Aquisition (Act 3)
Elfroot	Sundermount (x2), Wounded Coast (x2), Sundermount Ambush Site (The Way It Should Be quest)	Sundermount, Wounded Coast	Wounded Coast
Spindleweed	Lowtown (x2), Slaver Caverns (Wayward Son quest), Wounded Coast	Lowtown	Lowtown
Embrium	Dead Man's Pass (Blackpowder Promise quest)	Sundermount, Wounded Coast (x2), Holding Caves (A Bitter Pill quest)	Wounded Coast
Ambrosia	-	-	Castillon's Landing

Runes

Runes are magical symbols that can be grafted onto other items to enhance their power with a specific enchantment. Weapon Runes can be used to enchant a bow, a staff, a sword or similar sidearm by adding damage and effects to the weapon's existing attack attributes. Armor Runes can be placed on chain mail, boots, gloves, a helm or even a shield, to add magical protection. Only some of the game's unique named items (as opposed to randomly generated items – see page 209) have the requisite slots to hold such enchantments. The most prized of all feature more than one Rune slot.

The creation of a Rune first requires a Design. The raw materials of Lyrium, Silverite, Orichalcum and Dragon's Blood must then be sourced in sufficient quantity and combination. Shortly after gaining entry to Kirkwall, Hawke will catch up with a vendor and artisan by the name of Worthy, who keeps a Crafting Station in Hightown Market. True to his name, the dwarf is eminently qualified to craft Runes to order.

To use the Runes so acquired, you must also apply them to the slot of an accommodating weapon, shield or piece of armor by hiring the services of an enchanter. Bodahn Feddic's son, Sandal, offers enchantment services in Hightown from Act 1. He relocates to the Deep Roads during the expedition and can be found at the Hawke Estate from Act 2 onwards.

Although the attribute of a Rune is determined by its Design, its potency derives from the power of the item to which it is attached. The Weapon Rune's bonus is 20% of the weapon's base damage rating. The resistance bonus Rune of Warding is derived from the armor value. So a Rune is always best used on powerful equipment. And in case you were wondering, the effects of the Rune of Fortune do not stack with similar items.

Rune Designs

Icon	Name	Type	Effect	Aquisition	Ingredient 1	Ingredient 2	Ingredient 3
	Rune of Protection	Armor	Improves physical damage resistance	Worthy shop (Hightown, Act 1)	Lyrium (x1)	-	-
	Rune of Fortune	Armor	Increases money dropped by creatures	The Black Emporium*	Lyrium (x2)	-	-
	Rune of Frost Warding	Armor	Improves cold damage resistance	Enemies Among Us quest, Sanctuary (see page 32)	Lyrium (x1)	Silverite (x1)	-
	Rune of Fire Warding	Armor	Improves fire damage resistance	Wounded Coast (Act 1)	Lyrium (x1)	Silverite (x1)	-
	Rune of Lightning Warding	Armor	Improves electricity damage resistance	Mage Goods shop (Gallows, Acts 1 & 3)	Lyrium (x2)	Silverite (x1)	-
	Rune of Nature Warding	Armor	Improves nature damage resistance	Blackpowder Courtesy quest, Smuggler's Cut (see page 36)	Lyrium (x2)	Silverite (x2)	-
	Rune of Spirit Warding	Armor	Improves spirit damage resistance	Mage Goods shop (Gallows, Acts 2 & 3)	Lyrium (x1)	Silverite (x1)	Orichalcum (x1)
	Rune of Defense	Armor	Improves defense	Wounded Coast (Act 2)	Lyrium (x1)	Silverite (x2)	Orichalcum (x1)
	Rune of Valiance	Armor	Applies Valiance, a non-stacking effect that improves all attributes	Sundermount (Act 3)	Lyrium (x1)	Dragon's Blood (x1)	-
	Rune of Impact	Weapon	Adds a physical damage bonus	Enemies Among Us quest, Wilmod's Camp (see page 32)	Lyrium (x1)	-	-
	Rune of Frost	Weapon	Adds a cold damage bonus	Lirene's Fereldan Imports shop (Lowtown)	Lyrium (x1)	Silverite (x1)	-
	Rune of Fire	Weapon	Adds a fire damage bonus	The First Sacrifice quest, Dark Foundry (see page 62)	Lyrium (x1)	Silverite (x1)	-
	Rune of Lightning	Weapon	Adds an electricity damage bonus	Sundermount (Act 1)	Lyrium (x2)	Silverite (x1)	-
	Rune of Nature	Weapon	Adds a nature damage bonus	Ilene's Crafts shop (Sundermount, Acts 2 & 3)	Lyrium (x2)	Silverite (x1)	Orichalcum (x1)
	Rune of Spirit	Weapon	Adds a spirit damage bonus	Inside Job quest, Brekker's Hideaway (see page 79)	Lyrium (x3)	Orichalcum (x1)	-
	Rune of Striking	Weapon	Increases critical strike chance	Prime Suspect quest, DuPuis Estate (see page 38)	Lyrium (x1)	Orichalcum (x2)	-
	Rune of Devastation	Weapon	Applies Devastation, a non-stacking effect that improves all forms of damage	On the Loose quest, Sewer Passage (see page 42)	Lyrium (x1)	Dragon's Blood (x1)	-
	Torpor's Barrier Rune	Armor	Increases magic resistance	Night Terrors quest (see page 76)	-	-	-
	Sandal's Special Rune	Weapon	Enchants a weapon with Knockback	Reward from Sandal at the beginning of Act 2	-	-	-
	Primeval Lyrium Rune	Weapon	Increases attack speed	Reward from Sandal in the Haunted quest (see page 101)	-	-	-

* See dragonage.com/da2/addons for further details on this Premium Content.

Rune Ingredients

Name	Aquisition (Act 1)	Aquisition (Act 2)	Aquisition (Act 3)
Lyrium	Bone Pit Mines (The Bone Pit quest), Runaways' Cavern (Act of Mercy quest), Deep Roads (x2), Tal-Vashoth Cavern (Blackpowder Promise quest)	Bone Pit Mines (Cavern of Dead quest), Dank Cave (x2) (Forbidden Knowledge quest)	Sundermount Caverns
Silverite	Vimmark Mountain Pass (Shepherding Wolves quest), Deep Roads, Tal-Vashoth Cavern (Blackpowder Promise quest), Sundermount Caverns (Long Way Home quest)	Sundermount Caverns, Smuggler's Cut (Blackpowder Courtesy quest)	-
Orichalcum	Primeval Ruins (Deep Roads Expedition quest)	Deep Roads, Varterral Hunting Ground (Mirror Image quest), Sundermount Caverns, The Killer's Lair (All That Remains quest)	Sundermount Caverns
Dragon's Blood	-	-	High Dragon (Mine Massacre quest)

Poisons & Bombs

Poisons and Bombs require a Formula to obtain the correct toxic or combustible reagents. Such substances are extracted from Deep Mushroom, Deathroot, Glitterdust and Felandaris, which tend to thrive when nature finds a foothold in some dark, insalubrious corner.

Poisons enjoy a lengthy duration, potentially lasting many battles, and are applied to the weapon of every party member when used. They can be considered as a purchased form of additional combat buff.

Bombs require no special skill to deliver and can be thought of as an additional attack or ability available to any and every party member. Though costly if used to excess, they can be kept in reserve for times of trouble. The revival grenade of Mythal's Favor is a perfect example, turning the last man or woman standing into an ad hoc Spirit Healer.

City elf Tomwise operates a stall near the western exit of Darktown. Another of the acquaintances met by Hawke in the year spent gaining entry to Kirkwall, the dabbler is happy to provide his services and offers the Formula of Debilitating Poison to unlock his Crafting Station.

Poison and Bomb Formulas

Icon	Name	Type	Effect	Aquisition	Ingredient 1	Ingredient 2	Ingredient 3
	Combustion Grenade	Bomb	Inflicts fire damage and stuns targets in range	Tal-Vashoth Leader, Blackpowder Courtesy quest, Tal-Vashoth Cavern (see page 72)	Deep Mushroom (x1)	-	-
	Tar Bomb	Bomb	Immobilizes targets in range	Shady Merchandise shop	Deep Mushroom (x1)	Deathroot (x1)	-
	Mythal's Favor	Bomb	Resuscitates friendly targets in range	Wounded Coast (Act 2)	Deep Mushroom (x1)	Deathroot (x1)	Glitterdust (x1)
	Fel Grenade	Bomb	Causes significant damage	Wounded Coast (Act 3)	Glitterdust (x2)	Felandaris (x1)	-
	Debilitating Poison	Poison	Decreases by 15% the damage a targeted enemy inflicts. Duration: 30 minutes	Tomwise (Darktown, Act 1)	Deep Mushroom (x1)	-	-
	Crow Venom	Poison	Slows a targeted enemy's movement speed and attack speed by 25%. Duration: 30 minutes	The Black Emporium*	Deep Mushroom (x2)	-	-
	Deathroot Toxin	Poison	Deals +4 nature damage per hit to targets	Shady Merchandise shop (Docks)	Deathroot (x2)	-	-
	Arcane Poison	Poison	Decreases a target's magic resistance by 15%. Duration: 30 minutes	Elven Fanatic, Blackpowder Courtesy quest (see page 36)	Deathroot (x1)	Glitterdust (x1)	-
	Fel Poison	Poison	Leeches health from its targets (+1% of the user's maximum health). Duration: 5 minutes	Huon (Lowtown at night, see page 42)	Deep Mushroom (x3)	Felandaris (x1)	

* See dragonage.com/da2/addons for further details on this Premium Content.

Poison & Bomb Ingredients

Name	Aquisition (Act 1)	Aquisition (Act 2)	Aquisition (Act 3)
Deep Mushroom	Slaver Caverns (Wayward Son quest), Deep Roads (x2), Sundermount, Bone Pit Mines (The Bone Pit quest)	Smuggler's Cut (Blackpowder Courtesy quest), Gallows Dungeon (Blackpowder Courtesy quest), Varterral Hunting Ground (Mirror Image quest)	Drakestone Mines (Mine Massacre quest)
Deathroot	Darktown, Sewers, Sanctuary	Darktown, Holding Caves (A Bitter Pill quest)	Darktown
Glitterdust	Wounded Coast	Sundermount, Bone Pit, Varterral Hunting Ground (Mirror Image quest), Holding Caves (A Bitter Pill quest)	Sundermount
Felandaris	-	-	Pride's End (A New Path quest)

SHOPS

Some of the game's finest items are not to be wrested from demon sentinels or filched from dragon hordes. The only way to obtain them is to engage with the sharp-eyed vendors and stallholders of the city plazas and beyond.

The unique items that are sold by the many traders of Kirkwall and the Free Marches are all listed in this section, but as the following directory of shopkeepers comprehensively reveals, the more obscure outlets are harder to locate. It's worth noting that shop stock changes from Act to Act, introducing even better items but also removing earlier items.

Excluding the unique items and regular supplies in store, all other traders' goods are generated randomly (see page 209) when you enter the local map. A quick place to test this is Lirene's Fereldan Imports, where you can see her wares and those of the bazaar vendors change by stepping in and out of her premises in Lowtown. Determined shoppers might "roll the dice" a few times to see if luck delivers them something special in their size.

The cost of items can vary within a set margin: **prices listed are average figures**, intended to give a comparative sense of value, but don't be surprised by a certain degree of variation up or down. Items sold to vendors fetch 10% of their cost price, though again certain shops will apply a mark-up to that base value (see the notes in the bottom-right corner of each double-page spread).

If you sell an item but immediately regret the decision, switch to the Buy menu and use the Buy Back option to reclaim your goods at sale price. This is only possible before you leave the store, though. The Sell Back option will similarly allow you to review your shopping basket.

Gallows

Formari Herbalist[1]

Act	Item for Sale	Price
1	Health Potion	32 34
1	Injury Kit	37 73
1	Lyrium Potion	43 12
1	Stamina Draught	43 12
1	Amulet of Serenity	2 6
1	Recipe: Restoration Potion	16 96
1	Elfroot Potion	36 52
1	Restoration Potion	91 30
2	Health Potion	32 34
2	Injury Kit	37 73
2	Lyrium Potion	43 12
2	Stamina Draught	43 12
2	Ring of the Faithful	6 30
2	Recipe: Restoration Potion	16 96
2	Recipe: Life Ward Potion	26 63
2	Elfroot Potion	36 52
2	Restoration Potion	91 30
2	Rock Armor Potion	1 9 56
3	Health Potion	32 34
3	Injury Kit	37 73
3	Lyrium Potion	43 12
3	Stamina Draught	43 12
3	Chantry Amulet	7 94 12
3	Recipe: Restoration Potion	16 96
3	Recipe: Life Ward Potion	26 63
3	Elfroot Potion	36 52
3	Restoration Potion	91 30
3	Life Ward Potion	91 30
3	Rock Armor Potion	1 36 95
3	Mighty Offense Potion	1 36 95

Armor Shop[1]

Act	Item for Sale	Price
1	Armor of the Wall	2 24 12
1	Roar	2 44 68
1	Rune of Protection	80
1	Monolith's Heart	9 60
2	Rune of Lightning Warding	1
2	Defender of the Wall	3 33 20
2	Boots of the White Spire	5 69 62
2	King's Bounty	11 86
3	Rune of Protection	80
3	Volcanic Shield	9 70 75

Mage Goods[1]

Act	Item for Sale	Price
1	Flocked Wool Robe	2 37 50
1	Rune-Covered Gloves	2 2 25
1	Design: Rune of Lightning Warding	26 63
1	Rune of Lightning Warding	1
1	The Turncoat's Walking Stick	2 46 12
2	Heavy Velvet Robes	7 86 50
2	Hood of the Formari	10 27 70
2	Design: Rune of Lightning Warding	26 63
2	Design: Rune of Spirit Warding	26 63
2	Rune of Spirit Warding	1
2	Lyrium Weave	2 28 25
2	Backpack	67 37
2	Free Man's Staff	15 50
3	Onyx Ring of the Dales	7 57 75
3	Battlemage Armaments	10 84 75
3	Lyrium Embroidered Gloves	9 16 37
3	Design: Rune of Lightning Warding	26 63
3	Design: Rune of Spirit Warding	26 63
3	Rune of Spirit Warding	1

Weapon Shop[1]

Act	Item for Sale	Price
1	Rune of Fire	40
1	Maelstrom	2 28 70
1	Templar Great Sword	2 40 25
2	Rune of Impact	10
2	Seven Deaths	6 17 17
2	Markham Heart Stopper	7 91 62
2	The Subtle Brute	5 1 60
3	Rune of Striking	1 80
3	Spider's Heart	8 64
3	City Guard Sword	8 39 62
3	Widow's Fury	13 31 37

Hightown

Olaf's Armory (Day)[1]

Act	Item for Sale	Price
1	Surfacer Stone Boots	2 59 43
1	Marcher Battle Plate	4 81 60
1	Wyvernscale Gauntlets	2 2 97
2	Golem's Leg	4 16 50
2	Trevisian Breastplate	3 90
2	Surfacer Stone Gauntlets	8 21 43
2	Chevalier Silverite Helm	3 20 50
3	Red Iron Breastplate	10 89
3	Stonehammer Plate	11 32 37
3	Gauntlets of the Dark Breath	4 26 75

Robes by Jean Luc (Day)[1]

Act	Item for Sale	Price
1	Boots of the Elder	2 60 31
1	Illwan's Hood	5 41 80
1	Backpack	67 37
2	Robes of the Void	10 18 30
2	DuPuis Family Chapeaux	8 71 20
2	Tevinter Spirit Symbol	2 28 25
2	Supportive Corselet	2 28 25
2	Samite Lining	2 28 25
2	Backpack	67 37
2	Acolyte's Staff	10 74 40
3	Harlan's Jackboots	11 58 75
3	Circle Robes	29 90
3	Regret	11 30 12
3	Backpack	67 37

Korval's Blades (Day)[1]

Act	Item for Sale	Price
1	Trust and Cut Blade	1 64 5
1	Markham Head Stopper	1 88 98
2	Guild Dagger	3 26 3
2	Warstopper	2 72 8
2	All-Fall	4 8 85
3	Arcane Tome of the Mortal Vessel	21 93 25
3	Perrin's Nail	7 18 75
3	Limbtaker	35 3 50
3	Dwarven Great Axe	13 86

Hubert's Fine Goods' (Day)*

Act	Item for Sale	Price
1	The Liar's Charm	1 68 75
1	Gentleman's Puzzle Ring	1 67 12
1	Rune of Frost Warding	1
1	Health Potion	40 42
1	Injury Kit	47 16
1	Lyrium Potion	53 90
1	Stamina Draught	53 90
1	Tome of Technique	21 93 25
2	Moonstone Amulet	2 98 87
2	Belt of Vigor	7 2
2	Ring of Incandescence	6 71
2	Rune of Fire	40
2	Health Potion	32 34
2	Injury Kit	47 16
2	Lyrium Potion	43 12
2	Stamina Draught	43 12
3	Rhinestone-Studded Symbol of Andraste	7 47
3	Van Markham's Heirloom	7 57 75
3	The Hanged Man's Girdle	7 92 25
3	Band of Silvery Gold	7 63 12
3	Rune of Fire	40
3	Health Potion	32 34
3	Injury Kit	47 16
3	Lyrium Potion	43 12
3	Stamina Draught	43 12

* Hubert's stall will vanish if you do not complete the Bone Pit quest (see page 58).

Docks

Shady Merchandise (Western Warehouse District, Day)[2]

Act	Item for Sale	Price
1	Pirate Sash	2 9
1	Raider Gloves	2 54 12
1	Formula: Tar Bomb	1 91
1	Formula: Deathroot Toxin	1 91
1	Cruel Dagger	2 25 50
2	Worn Leather Boots	4 20
2	Mariner's Trust	4 94 87
2	Formula: Tar Bomb	1 91
2	Formula: Deathroot Toxin	1 91
2	Lyrium Scales	2 28 25
2	Coat Lining with Concealed Pockets	1 82 60
3	Demon's Eye	9 37 12
3	Chains of the Vaarad	12 55 75
3	Formula: Deathroot Toxin	1 91
3	Tar Bomb	67 85
3	Raider Sword	8 40 62

Bonny Lem's Wares (Disused Passage)[1]

Act	Item for Sale	Price
1	Enchanted Silverite Chain Belt	5 93 50
1	Staff of the Primal Order	8 82
1	Thudpucker's Fist	5 26 12
2	Poisonwood Locket	20 9 25
2	Puzzle Ring of the Black Fox	88 14 75
2	The Heavens' Answer	30 40
3	Four-Fingered Eddie's Lucky Talisman	108 1 62
3	Circlet of the Dreamer	31 72 25
3	Blade of the Many	23 58 25
3	Carta's Right-Hand	24 96

[1] This shop applies a +25% mark-up to the normal price of items. [2] This shop applies a -10% mark-down to the normal price of items.

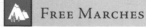

Lowtown

Vincento's Northern Merchandise (Day)*

Act	Item for Sale	Price
1	Fereldan Shortbow	18 ● 12 ●
1	Fereldan Dagger	5 ● 75 ●
1	Fereldan Long Sword	11 ● 62 ●
1	Fereldan Greatsword	18 ● 25 ●

* You can see Vincento arrested as a consequence of the Wayward Son quest (see page 28), after which his stall will vanish from the bazaar.

Lirene's Fereldan Imports (Day)

Act	Item for Sale	Price
1	Hunter's Boots	2 ● 34 ● 87 ●
1	Design: Rune of Frost	21 ● 30 ●
1	Backpack	67 ● 37 ●
1	Health Potion	32 ● 34 ●
1	Tarnished Dagger	2 ● 23 ● 75 ●
2	Tear of Ferelden	6 ● 76 ● 75 ●
2	Vain	10 ● 20 ●
2	Design: Rune of Frost	21 ● 30 ●
2	Armor Struts	1 ● 82 ● 60 ●
2	Recurve Bow	4 ● 76 ● 12 ●
3	Amulet of the Tempest	8 ● 40 ●
3	Awakened's Might	7 ● 96 ●
3	Design: Rune of Frost	21 ● 30 ●
3	Sword of the Antaam	9 ● 41 ● 75 ●

Armor Merchant (Day)

Act	Item for Sale	Price
1	Kirkwall Squire's Jerkin	2 ● 38 ●
1	Henchman Cowl	2 ● 16 ●
1	Underpadding – Guardsman Pattern	1 ● 82 ● 60 ●
1	Kirkwall Shield	2 ● 10 ● 25 ●
2	Chestguard of the Scoundrel	7 ● 93 ●
2	Rat-Nibbled Gloves	4 ● 5 ● 87 ●
2	Warden's Coif	6 ● 17 ● 87 ●
2	Impact Plating – Guardsman Pattern	1 ● 82 ● 60 ●
3	Longshadow Hauberk	10 ● 83 ● 50 ●
3	Quick Hands	11 ● 25 ● 62 ●
3	Cap of Kings	9 ● 80 ●

Apparel Shop (Day)

Act	Item for Sale	Price
1	Apostate's Robes	2 ● 97 ● 50 ●
1	Inscribed Leather Harness	1 ● 82 ● 60 ●
1	Backpack	67 ● 37 ●
1	Acolyte's Staff	10 ● 74 ● 37 ●
2	Boots of the Redd	4 ● 44 ●
2	Gloves of the Void	9 ● 67 ● 37 ●
2	Rigid Boning	1 ● 82 ● 60 ●
2	Enchanter's Staff	10 ● 8 ●
3	Concealer's Sash	8 ● 84 ●
3	Ring of the Wounded Coast	8 ● 40 ●
3	Corrupted Acolyte's Staff	13 ● 86 ●

Martin's Contraband (The Hanged Man, Night)*

Act	Item for Sale	Price
1	Formula: Debilitating Poison	13 ● 57 ●
1	Combustion Grenade	45 ● 65 ●
1	Debilitating Poison	45 ● 65 ●
1	Crow Venom	45 ● 65 ●
1	Deathroot Toxin	91 ● 30 ●
2	Formula: Debilitating Poison	13 ● 57 ●
2	Combustion Grenade	45 ● 65 ●
2	Tar Bomb	67 ● 85 ●
2	Debilitating Poison	45 ● 65 ●
2	Crow Venom	45 ● 65 ●
2	Deathroot Toxin	91 ● 30 ●
3	Formula: Debilitating Poison	13 ● 57 ●
3	Combustion Grenade	45 ● 65 ●
3	Tar Bomb	67 ● 85 ●
3	Mythal's Favor	1 ● 91 ● 30 ●
3	Debilitating Poison	45 ● 65 ●
3	Crow Venom	45 ● 65 ●
3	Deathroot Toxin	91 ● 30 ●
3	Fel Poison	1 ● 71 ● 18 ●

* Martin's Contraband must be unlocked by completing the Finders Keepers quest (see page 60).

Trinkets Emporium (Day)

Act	Item for Sale	Price
1	Amulet of Influence	1 ● 19 ● 75 ●
1	Guild Ring	1 ● 88 ●
1	Rune of Fire Warding	1 ●
1	Health Potion	32 ● 34 ●
1	Lyrium Potion	43 ● 12 ●
1	Stamina Draught	43 ● 12 ●
2	Split Bone Necklace	5 ● 1 ● 60 ●
2	Cord of the Weyr-Beast	3 ● 94 ● 25 ●
2	Ring of Ruin	2 ● 66 ● 24 ●
2	Rune of Spirit	40 ●
2	Health Potion	32 ● 34 ●
2	Lyrium Potion	43 ● 12 ●
2	Stamina Draught	43 ● 12 ●
2	Greater Tome of the Mortal Vessel	16 ● 44 ● 93 ●
2	Signet Ring	9 ● 13 ●
3	Tranquility	2 ● 49 ●
3	Belt of the Silent Sisters	10 ● 75 ●
3	Pretty Little Thing	9 ● 37 ● 12 ●
3	Rune of Frost	40 ●
3	Health Potion	32 ● 34 ●
3	Lyrium Potion	43 ● 12 ●
3	Stamina Draught	43 ● 12 ●

Weaponsmithy (Day)

Act	Item for Sale	Price
1	Cracked Bow	3 ● 22 ● 25 ●
1	Thrice-Bound	3 ● 31 ● 75 ●
1	Notched Sword	2 ● 4 ● 37 ●
2	Coterie Shiv	3 ● 51 ● 87 ●
2	Darktown Blade	3 ● 27 ● 50 ●
2	Darkspawn Shield	3 ● 34 ● 25 ●
3	Crosscut Composite	28 ● 66 ● 50 ●
3	Red Jenny Backbiter	21 ● 87 ● 37 ●
3	Shadow's Claw	8 ● 25 ● 50 ●

Free Marches

Ilen's Crafts (Dalish Camp, Sundermount)[1]

Act	Item for Sale	Price
1	Dirthamen's Secret	2 ● 24 ● 87 ●
1	Boots of the Isolationist	4 ● 39 ● 37 ●
1	Rune of Nature	40 ●
1	Health Potion	32 ● 34 ●
1	Injury Kit	47 ● 16 ●
1	Lyrium Potion	43 ● 12 ●
1	Stamina Draught	43 ● 12 ●
1	Longtouch	5 ● 3 ● 50 ●
2	Fen'Harel's Tooth	6 ● 37 ● 50 ●
2	Alunduris	3 ● 65 ● 87 ●
2	Design: Rune of Nature	26 ● 63 ●
2	Rune of Nature	40 ●
2	Carved Ironwood Buttons	2 ● 28 ● 25 ●
2	Health Potion	32 ● 34 ●
2	Injury Kit	47 ● 16 ●
2	Lyrium Potion	43 ● 12 ●
2	Stamina Draught	43 ● 12 ●
2	Tome of Technique	21 ● 93 ● 25 ●
2	Quills of the Heretic	4 ● 6 ● 87 ●
2	Wooden Halla Carving	5 ●
3	Sash of the Halla	9 ● 24 ●
3	Windstrider Boots	9 ● 48 ● 12 ●
3	Gloves of June	10 ● 21 ● 12 ●
3	Design: Rune of Nature	26 ● 63 ●
3	Rune of Nature Warding	1 ●
3	Health Potion	32 ● 34 ●
3	Injury Kit	47 ● 16 ●
3	Lyrium Potion	43 ● 12 ●
3	Stamina Draught	43 ● 12 ●
3	Truebow	11 ● 34 ●

Magnus's Wares (Wounded Coast, northwest paths)[1]

Act	Item for Sale	Price
2	Void's Hammer	27 3
2	Cold-Blooded	113 9 73
2	Enchanter's Spatterdashes	26 27
3	Seven Deadly Cinch	24 84
3	Karasten's Belt	25 92
3	Ring of the Ferryman	109 95 62

Bodahn's Provisions (Deep Roads Expedition)[1] & Sandal's Enchantments (The Last Straw)[1]

Act	Item for Sale	Price
1	Health Potion	32 34
1	Injury Kit	47 16
1	Lyrium Potion	43 12
1	Stamina Draught	43 12

Nexus Golem's Wares (Abandoned Thaig, via Sundermount)[1]

Act	Item for Sale	Price
2	Dalish Embossed Belt	20 28 25
2	Etched Ring of the Twins	84 68
2	Windsong Axe	19 69 75
3	Belt of Woven Elf Hair	31 36 50
3	Bardin's Folly	105 5 12
3	Absolution	38 34
3	Sundering	38 40

The Black Emporium*

Unlike normal stores, The Black Emporium retains unsold stock from previous Acts so that late purchasers don't miss out.

See dragonage.com/da2/addons for further details on this Premium Content.

Emporium's Crafting Materials[1]

Act	Item for Sale	Price
1	Recipe: Elixir of Purity	16 96
1	Formula: Crow Venom	16 96
1	Design: Rune of Fortune	16 96
1	Rune of Fortune	70
1	Elixir of Arcane Technique	27 6 87
1	Elixir of Physical Technique	27 6 87
1	Greater Elixir of the Mortal Vessel	10 82 75
1	Rock Armor Potion	1 36 95
1	Maker's Sigh	1 34 75
1	Health Potion	40 42
1	Lyrium Potion	53 90
1	Stamina Draught	53 90
1	Injury Kit	47 16
1	Fel Poison	1 71 18
1	Crow Venom	45 65
1	Combustion Grenade	45 65
2	Restoration Potion	91 30
2	Elfroot Potion	45 65
2	Debilitating Poison	45 65
2	Tar Bomb	67 85
2	Rune of Fire	40
2	Rune of Frost Warding	1
2	Rune of Protection	80
2	Crow Venom	45 65
2	Health Potion	40 42
2	Lyrium Potion	53 90
2	Injury Kit	47 16
2	Stamina Draught	53 90
3	Rune of Lightning Warding	1
3	Rune of Nature Warding	1
3	Mythal's Favor	1 91 30
3	Rune of Lightning	40
3	Rune of Nature	40
3	Elixir of Purity	45 65
3	Crow Venom	45 65
3	Deathroot Toxin	91 30
3	Elfroot Potion	45 65
3	Health Potion	40 42
3	Lyrium Potion	53 90
3	Injury Kit	47 16
3	Stamina Draught	53 90

Emporium's Relics and Antiques[1]

Act	Item for Sale	Price
1	The Anderfel Cleaver	7 56
1	Desdemona's Blade	4 91 37
1	Lady Rosamund's Bulwark	5 2 25
1	Arlathan Replica Bow	7 66 75
1	The Magister's Scythe	70 8
1	Vestments of the Mystic	7 21 12
1	Cap of the Antivan King	6 55 50
1	Gauntlets of the Nug	6 21 12
1	Invisible Gloves	6 19 12
1	Sandals of the Mystic	6 36 25
1	Boots of Tremendous Weight	6 34 12
1	The Fallen Star	48 18
1	Sturdy Belt	4 99 12
1	Maker's Sigh	1 34 75
2	The Barbarian's Blade	27 24 25
2	Shard of the Fallen	18 95 37
2	Sliver	27 7 25
2	King Something the Forgotten's Armor	111 82 62
2	The Ponderer	24 70 37
2	The Hands of Fate	23 14 12
2	Stealth Boots	84 42 67
2	Dull Brass Amulet	19 39 50
3	Blade of a Thousand Battles	94 75 12
3	Helm of a Thousand Battles	133 4 25
3	Robes of Unblemished Cleanliness	140 75 25
3	The Final Thought	126 47 25
3	The Maker's Kiss	94 45 50
3	Ring of No Wishes	26 93 75
3	The Belt of Promise	112 87

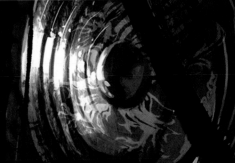

[1] Items that you sell at this shop will be bought at 125% of the base value.

BESTIARY

Death wears many faces in the Free Marches. Cautious explorers of the wilds expect to glimpse him in bared teeth and flexed talons, but the seasoned traveler knows he is as likely to be met in fine robes. This section reveals the hidden strengths and weaknesses of every enemy type – people, beasts, demons and the damned – and identifies the lethal resources that each can call on to vanquish the unprepared.

CHAPTER STRUCTURE

To help you understand exactly what you're up against, this chapter will categorize enemies by their group. All enemies within a group share the "group traits" listed up front, such as the weakness to nature that applies to all darkspawn.

Within each group, every monster and enemy in Dragon Age II also belongs to a specific archetype that determines its general behavior – much as the rogue, mage and warrior classes define a player's character. Archetypes are described in the following section and subsequently identified for each creature. While standard archetypes need no further explanation, the talents of the more powerful "elite" archetypes are examined using individual analysis sheets.

Finally, every enemy has a rank, that can vary, to describe its relative strength compared to others of the very same kind. If you're lucky, you might find yourself facing a weedy specimen of Hurlock that won't put up much of a fight. Or it could be a vicious Hurlock veteran, if you and luck aren't getting along.

As a complete example for using the guide, let's suppose you encounter a female Dalish Assassin. The Dalish have an innate weakness to electricity as a group, so this applies to all Dalish units. This specialized combatant belongs to the assassin archetype, which reveals more of her behavior and stealth abilities. Finally, she may be a lieutenant in rank – slightly more powerful than weak or normal Dalish units and with a larger health bar. As the Dalish Assassin is an "elite" unit, you will find all of the information about her advanced attributes gathered in a dedicated analysis sheet in the Dalish section (see page 230).

For each analysis sheet, the icon-based key immediately reveals the elemental immunities (**only used in Nightmare difficulty – replaced by neutral affinities in the other difficulty levels**) and weaknesses to exploit with your spells or magic weapons. Indeed, it is worth noting that all groups have a weakness, even if it is slight or not always obvious from play.

If you're unsure of the meaning of a special trait (such as "weak armor" or "high defense"), read the Secondary Attributes section on page 163 of the Strategy & Analysis chapter.

When a creature is defeated, there is often a chance that it will drop some kind of loot. This can take the form of coins or junk that can be sold. However, it's also possible for loot drops to contain useful equipment. Enemies are therefore assigned a "loot category" so that the randomly generated treasure they leave is appropriate to them and the context of the encounter. Hunted mages surrender Apostate robes and staves; Kirkwall Guards leave behind their Reacher armor. Refer to page 209 for more details on the various categories of randomly generated items.

ARCHETYPES

Though you will encounter many different enemies and factions, there are combat roles that are common to all groups. Categories called archetypes define those roles, from the humble frontline standard trooper to the inspiring commander, and establish the further advantages assigned to them. Weapons and abilities also determine the tactical behavior of such archetypes.

Trooper

Archetype Traits: None

Archetype Analysis:
The standard warrior archetype picks a target on the battlefield, influenced by the threat generation system (see page 180), and rushes to engage directly in melee assault. This broad category also covers creatures with natural weapons, such as spiders and the mabari. Crowd control measures can focus them around a companion or hold them in one spot for Area of Effect attacks. Alternatively, Glyphs of Paralysis and single-target stalling attacks like Pinning Shot, Stone Fist and Winter's Grasp can break up an advancing wave of troopers so that your fighters can deal with each foot-soldier in turn. Finally, your fighters can use Stun, Stagger and Knockback moves to temporarily reduce the number of opponents engaged. These can set up cross-class combo opportunities for other companions (see page 174).

Trooper – Weapon and Shield

Archetype Traits:

- Medium armor bonus
- Moderate defense bonus
- Weak magic resistance

Archetype Analysis:
Troopers with skills in "sword and board" benefit from increased resistance to physical attacks but they are correspondingly weaker against magic. They adopt the same melee rush tactics as basic Troopers.

Trooper – Two-Handed Weapons

Archetype Traits:

- Medium damage bonus
- Moderate attack bonus
- Weak defense

Archetype Analysis:
This soldier has been designated a damage-dealer, a shock troop who inflicts bigger hits but is less adept at dodging blows. Concentrating your attacks on these soldiers as a priority can eliminate their effectiveness altogether. Slow two-handed weapon strikes can also be avoided simply by moving your character clear.

Trooper – Dual Weapons

Archetype Traits:

- Moderate damage bonus
- Medium attack bonus
- Weak armor

Archetype Analysis:
Dual-wielding troopers increase their damage per second with a rapid flurry of attacks. Only lightly armored for speed, they take more damage from successful hits.

Trooper – Archery

Archetype Traits:

- Moderate damage bonus
- Medium attack bonus
- Weak armor

Archetype Analysis:
This archetype covers all physical ranged attackers and marks a change in tactics to match the weapon. Archers will advance into range and no further, keeping their distance and firing missiles in support of other troopers. They are weak against melee attackers, but heavier projectiles can still pack enough punch (testing against Fortitude) to cause Knockback. Archers will happily identify weak companions as a priority risk when staying beyond range of your tank's Taunts and threat generation.

Party members can foil ranged attacks by exploiting the environment and avoiding line of sight. Missiles will be blocked by intervening objects. You may also trick archers into moving closer by hiding in cover and forcing them to advance in search of a clear shot.

Otherwise, you may use Ensnare or rogue tactics such as Miasmic Flask to temporarily remove or distract artillery support until your own fighters have a chance to move in. Maintaining distance means that grouped enemy archers are susceptible to Area of Effect spells without the risk of friendly fire, and disoriented enemies are especially weak against Walking Bomb, Spirit Strike and Golem's Fist.

Trooper – Staff

Archetype Traits:

- Moderate damage bonus
- Moderate magic resistance bonus
- Weak armor

Archetype Analysis:
Mages follow similar rules to archers in their preference for ranged attacks, but not all spells demand clear line of sight and hiding in cover may not protect you from Area of Effect splash damage. Furthermore, their resistance to spells encourages physical retaliation. Employing direct assault to counter those resistances, rogue stealth attacks and battlefield teleportation skills can swiftly disrupt an enemy's magical rearguard. Mages typically lack Fortitude and can be interrupted or knocked back by a strong archery shot.

Assassin

Archetype Traits:

- Medium attack bonus
- Weak armor
- Weak health

Archetype Analysis:
This specialist can wreak havoc and confusion during even a modest skirmish. Every assassin is capable of invisible movement through stealth and a Disengage ability, which returns them to stealth after knocking their enemies back a short distance. Between those events, they have two special attacks they can deliver from hiding. The announcing Backstab briefly paralyzes the target and inflicts a heavy amount of damage. The second stealth attack inflicts additional damage over time, of a type determined by the group or faction.

To tackle an assassin effectively, they must first be pinned down and exposed to heavy assault. Tagging additional stuns and freezes can prolong the opportunity for damage, though you may need to repeat the process.

Even when unseen, assassins have physical presence and can trigger protective Glyphs or take untargeted damage from Area of Effect magic.

Bruiser

Archetype Traits:

- Very high damage
- Medium attack bonus
- Moderate armor bonus
- Very weak defense

Archetype Analysis:
The bruiser archetype is essentially a sponge for damage. It cannot dodge, with successful hits being easy to score, but high armor reduces even elementally maximized damage taken. While your companions are chipping mere slivers from its mighty health bar, the bruiser is dishing out pain with unwelcome generosity.

Keep the bruiser occupied by one defendable, healable tank character, and use any functional freezing or halting spell to slow its attack rate and grant breathing space. Petrify can halt any enemy, but also acts as further armor on the target.

Settling in for the long haul against any creature with a large health bar, first remove all lesser ranks from the battlefield to prevent interruptions.

Commander

Archetype Traits:

- Immune to Silence
- High armor
- High fortitude

Archetype Analysis:
The commander archetype not only presents a tough fight individually, but also plays a supporting role that greatly increases the peril posed by an opposing force. Commanders extend an aura over the battlefield, healing and conferring specific benefits on their allies. This archetype is also capable of self-defensive abilities and boasts a powerful medium-to-long range debilitation spell or Area of Effect artillery.

A commander's aura appears as a halo around its supported allies' ground rings, though it may be lifted temporarily if the commander is stunned or incapacitated. As they can take time to defeat, this is one way to turn off the buffs they provide for their subordinate ranks. Have one character stun the commander and be ready to remove those enemies closest to death.

Devastator

Archetype Traits:

- Very weak health
- Very weak armor
- Immense spellcasting damage

Archetype Analysis:
Devastators are magical artillery units, possessing a strong "nuke" spell that will swiftly explain the archetype's name unless interrupted. Devastators deploy a ranged Area of Effect spell, a defensive spell and a teleport. The status effects and elemental affinities vary with the devastator's group or faction.

Such enemies are a top priority for elimination and, despite their weaknesses, they often maintain a stiff challenge for any party seeking speedy removal. Once the devastator has used its teleport (which can take it to a number of pre-determined points on the map), it cannot do so again until the Cooldown period expires.

Boss

Archetype Traits:

- Immune to Knockdown
- Immune to Immobilized
- Immune to Paralyzed
- Immune to Enslavement
- Weak attack

Archetype Analysis:
This archetype offers no special abilities beyond additional toughness, resistance and immunity. Of course, that's enough to scupper many standard combat tactics.

- Critical hits can play a useful role in the later game, with many skills and items ready to enhance them.
- Build Anders as a healer and unlock his advanced regenerative powers to create a more resilient party. Otherwise, be prepared to gulp down a few Potions and slap on a few Injury Kits along the way.
- Bosses will still be forced to pick a target, and can be led on a merry chase by a mobile tank while their companions unleash ranged attacks.

Archboss

Archetype Traits:

- Immune to Knockback
- Immune to Knockdown
- Immune to Immobile
- Immune to Stun
- Immune to Paralyzed
- Immune to Enslavement
- Immune to Sleep
- Immune to Inevitable Death
- Immune to Explosive Death

Archetype Analysis:
The toughest bosses test your staying power and party management. Consult the individual entries and walkthrough for tactics and contextual information.

RANKS

After the assignment of archetype, it is rank that determines the exact level of toughness of an enemy on an internal scale – **critter < normal < lieutenant < leader**. Thus, a guard detachment composed entirely of troopers may contain a tougher lieutenant trooper and some critter troopers of much weaker stock. Look for visual indicators in the size of the health bar and the color of the name above the enemy's head (with bright red text for higher ranks).

Higher rank confers the following bonuses:

- Increased resistances to elemental attacks.
- Increased health, attack and damage ratings.
- Lower susceptibility to Knockdown and cross-class combos, while spells won't hold them for so long.
- Increased amount of items dropped.

Leader ranks are immune to certain attacks, such as Crushing Prison and Brittle status. Leader ranks can also offset player attack and defense ratings, reducing player resistances to the leader's attacks.

Note the Vanguard ability of Deathblow: this warrior advantage automatically removes normal ranks below 20% health and lieutenants below 10% health, and is most effective in the latter case against an enemy with high health or armor.

Critter rank

Normal rank

Lieutenant rank and higher

ENEMY IDENTIFICATION

The extraordinary opponents you meet in Dragon Age II will often have their own names or titles, but many of them are instances of a standard core creature in terms of attributes and behavior. So whenever you encounter an enemy whose name is unfamiliar, use the following directory to identify the core creature type on which they are based (note that we haven't included main bosses in this directory to avoid spoilers). You can then consult the corresponding entry in this chapter to find out all about their respective strengths and weaknesses.

Take Brekker, for instance. From his name alone, you cannot know what type of enemy he is. Look up his on-screen title in this directory, though, and you will see he is based on the Coterie Member. A complete analysis of that opponent is available in the Coterie group section of this Bestiary.

Enemy In-Game Name	Core Creature in the Bestiary
Amaranthine Conspirator	Mercenary
Antivan Assassin	Raider Assassin
Athenril	Dalish Assassin
Bancroft	Blood Mage
Bandit Leader	Coterie Member
Bartrand	Carta Assassin
Beacon	Revenant
Blood Mage Controller	Blood Mage
Blood Mage Hypnotist	Blood Mage
Blood Mage Leader	Blood Mage
Bloodrager	Blood Mage
Bounty Hunter Assassin	Coterie Member
Bounty Hunter Commander	Templar Captain
Brekker	Coterie Member
Bysmor	Corpse
"Captain" Qerth	Kirkwall Commander
Captain Reiner	Raider Assassin
Carta Lieutenant	Carta Assassin
Castillon	Raider Reaver
Cor "The Bastard" Blimey	Mercenary Archer
Coterie Assassin	Coterie Member
Coterie Leader	Coterie Member
Coterie Lieutenant	Coterie Thug
Coterie Rogue	Coterie Member
Crazed Commander	Kirkwall Commander
Crazed Guard	Mercenary Warrior
Crazed Loner	Apostate
Cutthroat	Coterie Member
Danzig	Coterie Alchemist
Decimus	Blood Mage
Denerim Avenger	Mercenary Warrior
Dougal Gavorn	Carta Assassin
Dwarven Bodyguard	Mercenary Warrior
Elven Fanatic	Mercenary Warrior
Enchanter	Circle High Mage
Enforcer	Raider Assassin
Ethereal Golem	Stone Golem
Evelina	Abomination
Evets	Raider Reaver
Fenarel	Shadow Warrior Captain
Feynriel	Abomination
Follower of She	Carta Assassin
Frost Horror	Arcane Horror
Frost Skeleton	Skeleton Archer
Gifre	Revenant
Ginnis	Mercenary Warrior
Grace	Blood Mage
"Gracious" Gillian Winger	Coterie Archer
Guard Captain	Kirkwall Commander
Guard Commander	Kirkwall Commander
Guardsman Donnic	Kirkwall Guard
Hahren Paivel	Dalish Warrior
Hanker	Desire Demon
Hayder	Raider Reaver
Heborah de Soliere	Blood Mage
Hunter Spider	Corrupted Spider
Huon	Blood Mage
Hybris	Pride Demon (Poison)
Ignacio Strand	Raider Assassin
Ineria	Dalish Assassin
Innley of Starkhaven	Blood Mage
Invisible Sister (1)	Raider Assassin
Invisible Sister (2)	Raider Warrior
Jake the Black	Blood Mage
Jakeson "The Bleeder" Hall	Blood Mage
Jess "Leashmaster" Varvel	Slaver Mage
Jeven	Assassin
"Kanky" Hammertoe	Carta Assassin
Knight-Captain Cullen	Templar Captain
Knight-Lieutenant Barsus	Templar Captain
Leech	Blood Mage
Lord Renvil Harrowmont	Mercenary Warrior
Lyrium Smuggler Foreman	Mercenary Warrior
Magister Hadriana	Slaver Mage
Magistrate Vanard	Street Thug
Master Ilen	Shadow Warrior Captain
Master Slaver	Slaver Mage
Medan	Arcane Horror
Meeran	Coterie Member
Mercenary Assassin	Coterie Member
Mercenary Captain	Templar Captain
Mercenary Commander	Mercenary Captain
Mercenary Officer	Templar Captain
Mob Leader	Templar Captain
Nathaniel Howe	Mercenary Archer
Nuncio	Coterie Alchemist
Nuncio's Guard	Coterie Member
Orwald the Braggart	Kirkwall Guard
Patron	Mercenary Archer
Pit Boss	Carta Assassin
Possession of Alessa	Desire Demon
Possession of Leandra	Desire Demon
Possession of Ninette	Desire Demon
Pride Abomination	Abomination
Progenitor	Blood Mage
Quentin	Blood Mage
Qunari Death Squad	Qunari Warrior
Qunari Delegate	Qunari General
Raider Ambusher	Raider Reaver
Redwater Raider	Raider Reaver
Rivaini Legendary Beard	Street Thug
Rock Wraith Abomination	Profane
Senestra	Coterie Member
Ser Agatha	Templar Captain
Ser Alrik	Templar Captain
Ser Karras	Templar Captain
Ser Mettin	Templar Captain
Ser Varnell	Templar Captain
Shadow Assassin	Dalish Assassin
Shadow Warrior	Shadow Warrior Captain
Ship Captain	Coterie Member or Carta Assassin
Sophia Dryden	Kirkwall Commander
Swindler	Carta Assassin
Tal-Vashoth Leader	Qunari General
Tal-Vashoth Officer	Qunari General
Tal-Vashoth Saarebas	Saarebas
Tarohne	Circle High Mage
Templar Hunter	Templar Seeker
Templar Lieutenant	Templar Captain
Tevinter Enchanter	Circle High Mage
Tevinter Magister	Slaver Mage
Tevinter Mercenary	Slaver Warrior
Thief Leader	Raider Assassin
Thrask	Templar Warrior
Torpor	Shade
Undercut Thrifter	Carta Assassin
Varian Ilithis	Templar Captain
Veld	Mercenary Captain
Wasp Spider	Poison Spider
Wilmod	Shade
Wryme	Pride Demon (Poison)
Xebenkeck	Desire Demon
Zevran	Dalish Assassin

DARKSPAWN

Now believed to be born of corrupted broodmothers in the foulest recesses of the subterrain, the darkspawn rose up from the Deep Roads to lay waste to Ferelden. Even with the passing of the Blight, small raiding parties still make forays to the surface to kill and scavenge. Their numbers will multiply in time and the Deep Roads will not remain quiet for long.

Group Traits:

- Immune to Slow
- Very weak to spirit
- Very weak to nature

Group Analysis:

- Hurlocks serve as an introduction to the trooper, the use of Area of Effect attacks and crowd control. When they reappear in the Deep Roads, they may be tougher than you expect and bolstered by Emissary support. Keep looking for those on low health to drive down the number of attackers.
- Do not underestimate the Hurlock Bolter, even when of low rank. A volley of shots can incapacitate a weaker companion with repeated Knockback or accumulate considerable damage.

Standard Darkspawn:

- Hurlock Grunt (Trooper – Weapon and Shield)
- Hurlock (Trooper – Weapon and Shield)
- Hurlock Bolter (Trooper – Archery)
- Emissary Apprentice (Trooper – Staff)

Elite Darkspawn:

- Darkspawn Emissary
- Ogre

Ogre

Elemental Resistances				
Normal	Normal	Normal	Very Weak	Very Weak

Loot Category	Archetype
Darkspawn	Bruiser

Notable Abilities	Special Traits
• Hurls boulders • Rush attack looks for line through enemies • Ground Slam shockwave tests Fortitude for Knockdown • Basic punch attack inflicts Knockback	• Immune to Slow • Very high damage • Medium attack bonus • Moderate armor bonus • Very weak defense

- The Ogre's moves are telegraphed by a brief build-up animation and may be dodged at medium to long range.
- Can be frozen, outflanked, confused or redirected by threat generation. You can even outrun an Ogre, leading it on a chase while your companions loose ranged attacks.
- Hurl and Rush have a 20-second Cooldown period before they can be used again.
- Petrify can stop many enemies briefly but also acts as further armor, reducing damage inflicted.
- Abilities that aid the probability and efficacy of critical hits often pay off during a long fight.

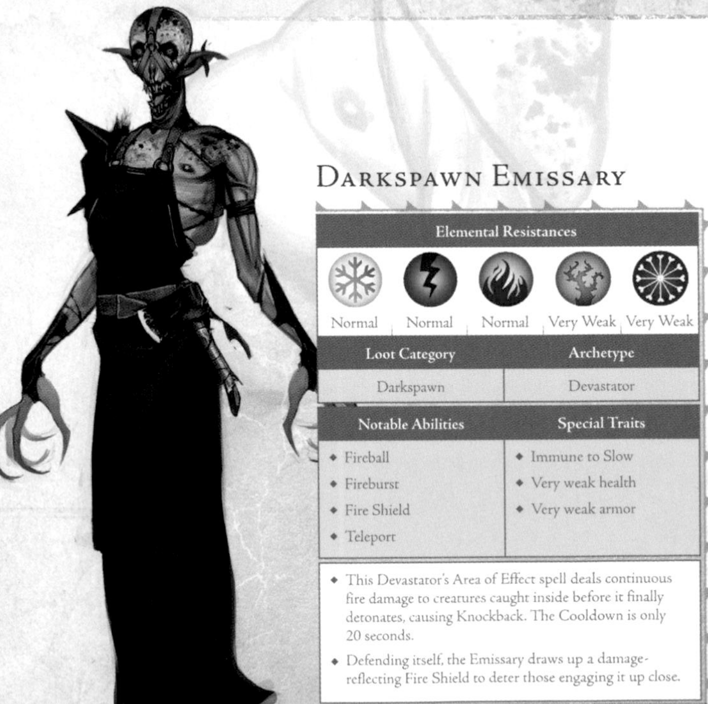

Darkspawn Emissary

Elemental Resistances				
Normal	Normal	Normal	Very Weak	Very Weak

Loot Category	Archetype
Darkspawn	Devastator

Notable Abilities	Special Traits
• Fireball • Fireburst • Fire Shield • Teleport	• Immune to Slow • Very weak health • Very weak armor

- This Devastator's Area of Effect spell deals continuous fire damage to creatures caught inside before it finally detonates, causing Knockback. The Cooldown is only 20 seconds.
- Defending itself, the Emissary draws up a damage-reflecting Fire Shield to deter those engaging it up close.

MABARI

Beasts of renown, these loyal war hounds bind to their masters for life and are prized for their intelligence as well as their ferocity. The duration of that lifelong bond may be tested frequently, as trained mabari show no fear in tackling much larger opponents or leaping into the fray against overwhelming numbers. Sadly, mabari aren't treated as respectfully in Kirkwall as in Ferelden – perhaps because of the urban profusion of sidewalks, and the absence of trees.

Group Traits:

- Immune to fire*
- Very weak to cold

Group Analysis:

- No special abilities
- Easy to freeze, confuse or stun

Standard Mabari:

- Mabari (Trooper)

DRAGONS

Female dragons give birth to vast numbers of offspring in a single clutch, though only a few hatchlings ever survive to adulthood. Mature dragonbone, fangs and scale have long been prized as raw materials in parts of Thedas, and dragons can live for many hundreds of years, so there is more than usual opportunity for misfortune.

Group Traits:

- Immune to fire*
- Immune to Knockdown
- Immune to Sleep
- Very weak to cold

Group Analysis:

- Even Dragonlings are capable of repeated Knockdown if your rogues and mages haven't gained some Fortitude or equivalent by the time you attempt the Bone Pit quest. Protect them with your fighters.
- Runes of Fire Warding and other resistances can assist if you can stack them to a reasonable degree, favoring your tank character's equipment.
- Dragonlings can be frozen, petrified or tagged with a Walking Bomb.
- The first Dragon sub-boss has the attacks of a Mature Dragon but is considerably weaker and easier to slay.

Standard Dragons:

- Dragonling (Trooper)
- Dragon (Trooper)

Elite Dragons:

- Mature Dragon
- High Dragon

Mature Dragon

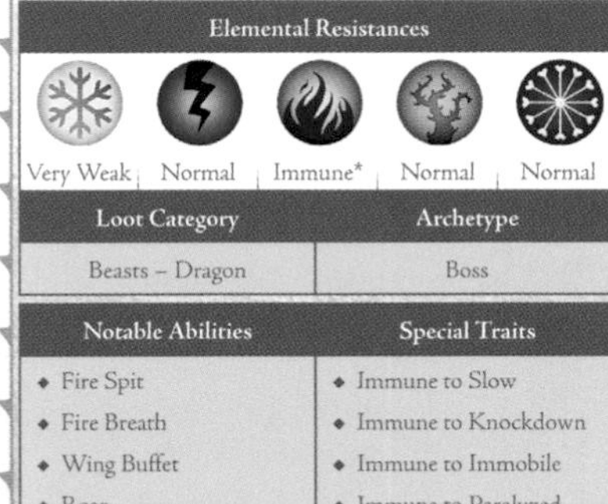

Elemental Resistances				
Very Weak	Normal	Immune*	Normal	Normal

Loot Category	Archetype
Beasts – Dragon	Boss

Notable Abilities	Special Traits
Fire Spit	Immune to Slow
Fire Breath	Immune to Knockdown
Wing Buffet	Immune to Immobile
Roar	Immune to Paralyzed
Tail Swipe	Immune to Enslavement
Summons Dragonlings	Very high health
	Medium damage bonus
	Weak attack

- The Fire Spit is a homing shot, harder to avoid than normal projectiles. It's distinct from the Dragon's Fire Breath, which moves side to side to create a cone of flame.
- Without Fortitude, Wing Buffet draws all enemies toward the Dragon for close attacks. It's a set-up for the Tail Swipe's Knockdown, activated when the beast is outflanked. If you're not holding a melee weapon, keep a sensible distance.
- The Dragon's Roar is a group stun with a surprisingly effective range. If your tank Taunts the beast to a far corner, it buys enough space for your mages and archers to stay out of reach.
- A long battle demands a slight shift in preparation. You should look to recruiting a healer or packing Potions, which should include Stamina Drafts for your tank. They will need to keep Taunting and possibly Stonewalling or maintaining an Aegis for the survival of themselves and others.
- Arcane Shield and a Barrier on your tank can help everyone survive for longer.
- Don't settle for your mages' upgraded cold attacks alone: have your warriors and Bianca follow up with damage multipliers against Brittle opponents.

High Dragon

Elemental Resistances				
Very Weak	Normal	Immune*	Normal	Normal

Loot Category	Archetype
Beasts – Dragon	Archboss

Notable Abilities	Special Traits
Fire Spit	Immune to Knockback
Fire Breath	Immune to Knockdown
Wing Buffet	Immune to Immobile
Roar	Immune to Slow
Tail Swipe	Immune to Stun
Stomp	Immune to Paralyzed
Summons Dragonlings	Immune to Enslavement
	Immune to Sleep
	Immune to Inevitable Death
	Immune to Explosive Death
	Very high health

- The huge size of the battlefield can work both ways, with the High Dragon using its power of flight to dominate. Don't let your characters run off on their own, and draw together for healing.
- Waves of Dragonlings spawn out of nowhere to annoy warriors and trouble mages. Leave one character to deal with these using Area of Effect spells. Merrill, with her nature spells, can be especially useful in this battle.
- Melee fighters will see the High Dragon's own attack is a powerful bite and toss. Otherwise, this is a tougher version of earlier Dragon encounters demanding similar tactics.
- The beast's roasting flame can be anticipated as soon as you see it drawing a deep breath. You won't be so lucky with the spit, which homes in on its enemy. This is where having armor or magical substitutes with fire resistance helps.
- The High Dragon can't be frozen and is immune to Brittle.
- The length of this battle and the damage often inflicted means a healer is a necessity. The Cooldown time on potions leaves too much to chance, though you might use Life Ward or Mythal's Favor for a second wind.

* Only on Nightmare difficulty.

SPIDERS

Scholars have speculated that the unprecedented size of these arachnids is down to the proximity of contaminating magical energies, or leaks from the Fade warping the physical laws governing their growth. The Corrupted Spider is a different matter altogether: it has fed on the darkspawn, absorbing their corruption, and its abnormal development now passes to its ravenous, twisted offspring.

Group Traits:

- Immune to nature*
- Medium attack bonus
- Immune to Immobile
- Weak armor
- Very weak to electricity

Group Analysis:

- Spiders frequently ambush their prey, dropping from webs above. Outside, you'll see them well in advance and can peel them off one by one if necessary. In either instance, you should prepare for a trooper rush and use a choke point to manage numbers while protecting weaker and ranged companions.
- The Poison Spider has a ranged attack that inflicts continuous nature damage over time. Unlike an archer, it tends to use this before closing in.
- Chain Lightning and electricity bonuses work well against web-spinners.

Standard Spiders:

- Giant Spider (Trooper)
- Corrupted Spider (Trooper)
- Poison Spider (Trooper)

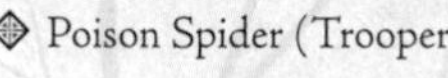

Elite Spiders:

- Varterral
- Monstrous Spider

Varterral

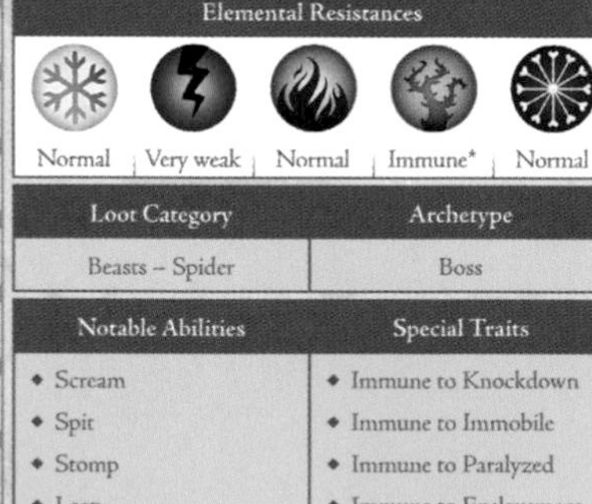

Elemental Resistances				
Normal	Very weak	Normal	Immune*	Normal

Loot Category	Archetype
Beasts – Spider	Boss

Notable Abilities	Special Traits
• Scream • Spit • Stomp • Leap • Ground Pound	• Immune to Knockdown • Immune to Immobile • Immune to Paralyzed • Immune to Enslavement • Very high health • Medium bonus to attack, defense & damage • Moderate magic resistance bonus • Weak armor

- The Primal tree is the mage's friend here.
- This creature has an elven name of Varterral, a guardian associated with the lost culture of Arlathan. Its spitting attack inflicts a corrosive poison, causing nature damage over time.
- High boss health means a long battle and demands solid party management: keeping the enemy distracted with your tank, applying buffs and shields and healing as you go. Consider a Life Ward potion for your weakest companion.
- The agility with which it can leap onto its prey should remind players that it is impossible to immobilize, knock off-balance or paralyze.

Monstrous Spider

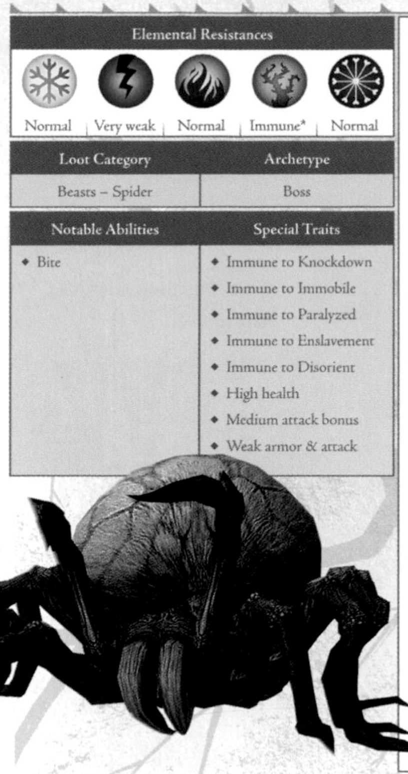

Elemental Resistances				
Normal	Very weak	Normal	Immune*	Normal

Loot Category	Archetype
Beasts – Spider	Boss

Notable Abilities	Special Traits
• Bite	• Immune to Knockdown • Immune to Immobile • Immune to Paralyzed • Immune to Enslavement • Immune to Disorient • High health • Medium attack bonus • Weak armor & attack

- You won't have trouble spotting this spider among the others. It's the big one. It summons more little ones at 50% health.
- In the Deep Roads encounter, there is a spot at the top of the steps where the boss cannot reach. It is effectively a prisoner of its arena. The battle can be won easily with one ranged attacker standing there.
- Unlike its little ones, the Monstrous Spider can't be frozen and is immune to Brittle status.
- Its basic bite attack means it is really an oversized Trooper, but with overwhelming knockback.
- As with the Varterral, keeping the enemy distracted with your tank and healing as soon as it is needed will keep you on top of the situation. But its armor is weak so high physical damage and critical hits (from stealth or directed with Brand) will make the battle shorter, reducing the risk to your party.
- Galvanism maxes the Primal tree for 125% pain. It's possible for an effective mage with electricity damage buffs, staff and upgraded spells to pull threat from your tank by doing much greater damage. In general, threat redirection and transfer (such as Goad and Armistice from the Scoundrel tree or the Swashbuckler's abilities) can save a weak character and keep the boss busy.

THE CARTA

For those who fall foul of the dwarven caste system and lose their status, there is always the Carta – often, only the Carta. The casteless must get by in any way they can, even if it means getting their hands dirty, and some dusters end up enjoying their tasks a little too much. Since the unfortunate secession of business in Orzammar, the Carta has seen a need to expand operations topside.

Group Traits:

- High magic resistance
- Immune to Dispel
- Very weak to cold

Group Analysis:

- The Dwarves are renowned for their magic resistance, so Sleep and other effects cannot be reliably employed.
- Physical stuns are still possible, and you may find it advantageous to avoid a magic-centered party altogether.
- That said, cold attacks remain among the strongest for both damage and crowd control. Just be sure to cross-class combo Scythes and Punishing Lance for damage multipliers against Brittle enemies.

Standard Carta:

- Carta Thug (Trooper – Weapon and Shield)

Elite Carta:

- Carta Assassin

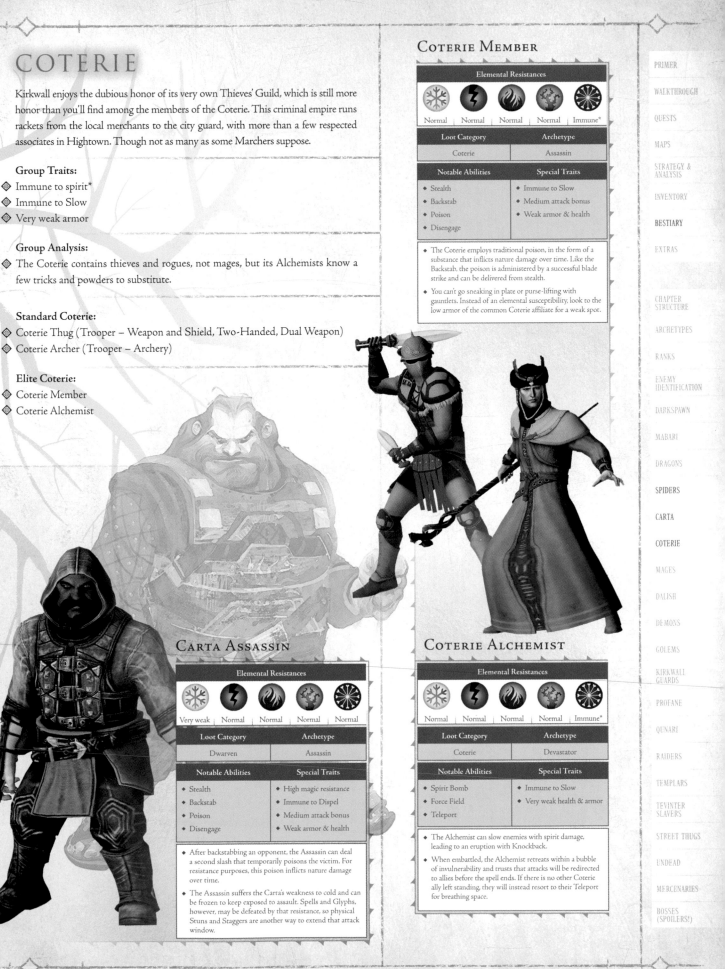

COTERIE

Kirkwall enjoys the dubious honor of its very own Thieves' Guild, which is still more honor than you'll find among the members of the Coterie. This criminal empire runs rackets from the local merchants to the city guard, with more than a few respected associates in Hightown. Though not as many as some Marchers suppose.

Group Traits:

- Immune to spirit*
- Immune to Slow
- Very weak armor

Group Analysis:

- The Coterie contains thieves and rogues, not mages, but its Alchemists know a few tricks and powders to substitute.

Standard Coterie:

- Coterie Thug (Trooper – Weapon and Shield, Two-Handed, Dual Weapon)
- Coterie Archer (Trooper – Archery)

Elite Coterie:

- Coterie Member
- Coterie Alchemist

Coterie Member

Elemental Resistances				

Normal	Normal	Normal	Normal	Immune*

Loot Category	Archetype
Coterie	Assassin

Notable Abilities	Special Traits
• Stealth	• Immune to Slow
• Backstab	• Medium attack bonus
• Poison	• Weak armor & health
• Disengage	

- The Coterie employs traditional poison, in the form of a substance that inflicts nature damage over time. Like the Backstab, the poison is administered by a successful blade strike and can be delivered from stealth.
- You can't go sneaking in plate or purse-lifting with gauntlets. Instead of an elemental susceptibility, look to the low armor of the common Coterie affiliate for a weak spot.

Carta Assassin

Elemental Resistances				

Very weak	Normal	Normal	Normal	Normal

Loot Category	Archetype
Dwarven	Assassin

Notable Abilities	Special Traits
• Stealth	• High magic resistance
• Backstab	• Immune to Dispel
• Poison	• Medium attack bonus
• Disengage	• Weak armor & health

- After backstabbing an opponent, the Assassin can deal a second slash that temporarily poisons the victim. For resistance purposes, this poison inflicts nature damage over time.
- The Assassin suffers the Carta's weakness to cold and can be frozen to keep exposed to assault. Spells and Glyphs, however, may be defeated by that resistance, so physical Stuns and Staggers are another way to extend that attack window.

Coterie Alchemist

Elemental Resistances				

Normal	Normal	Normal	Normal	Immune*

Loot Category	Archetype
Coterie	Devastator

Notable Abilities	Special Traits
• Spirit Bomb	• Immune to Slow
• Force Field	• Very weak health & armor
• Teleport	

- The Alchemist can slow enemies with spirit damage, leading to an eruption with Knockback.
- When embattled, the Alchemist retreats within a bubble of invulnerability and trusts that attacks will be redirected to allies before the spell ends. If there is no other Coterie ally left standing, they will instead resort to their Teleport for breathing space.

* Only on Nightmare difficulty.

MAGES

Though it may often seem that Kirkwall has no shortage of Apostates, the large majority of the city's talented mages reside within the Circle of Magi and remain under the vigilant gaze of the templars.

Group Traits:

- High magic resistance
- Immune to Paralyzed
- Very weak armor
- Very weak to spirit

Group Analysis:

- Both Spirit and Entropy trees can deliver spirit damage abilities. Aiming for the 25% bonus of Spirit Mastery isn't a bad idea in the long run for maximum efficiency against mages.
- Dispel Magic interrupts enemy spellcasting, with spirit damage.
- Mages are always a priority target, and can swiftly undo painstaking work by revealing a Heal spell at less than 25% health. Finish what you start, as the Apostate can possess a teleport.
- With a maxed-out Tevinter Fugitive tree, Fenris can acquire 45% magic resistance before any other buffs or accessories. If you intend to slay plenty of staff-wielders, build him with this in mind.

Standard Mages:

- Circle Mage (Trooper – Staff)
- Apostate (Trooper – Staff)

Elite Mages:

- Blood Mage
- Circle High Mage

Circle High Mage

Elemental Resistances				
Normal	Normal	Normal	Normal	Very Weak

Loot Category	Archetype
Circle of Magi	Devastator

Notable Abilities	Special Traits
• Spirit Orb	• High magic resistance
• Bolt	• Immune to Paralyzed
• Force Field	• Very weak health & armor
• Teleport	

- The Spirit Orb slows its victims to a crawl with a field of spirit damage, building up to an explosion with serious Knockback.
- Once under attack, the High Mage may choose to withdraw within a sphere of temporary invulnerability. Alternatively, they will use a Teleport spell to retreat and recover.
- The Circle High Mage shares abilities with the Slaver Mage and Coterie Alchemist.

Blood Mage

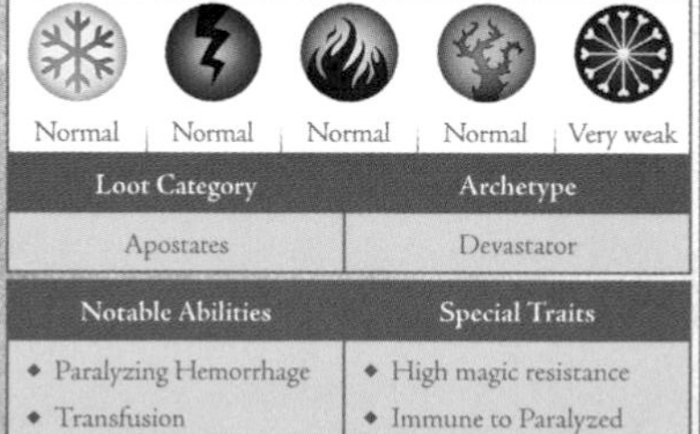

Elemental Resistances				
Normal	Normal	Normal	Normal	Very weak

Loot Category	Archetype
Apostates	Devastator

Notable Abilities	Special Traits
• Paralyzing Hemorrhage	• High magic resistance
• Transfusion	• Immune to Paralyzed
• Teleport	• Very weak health & armor

- For its magnum opus, the mage invokes Blood Magic to sap the life of all enemies caught in the Area of Effect. A continuous slowing effect culminates in total paralysis, which often leaves the victim prone when they most need to heal.
- Doing little to undo the popular perception of their trade, the Blood Mage's defensive ability drains life from surrounding enemies and transfers it to the caster.
- Although weak against spirit magic, the Blood Mage's ability to teleport and replenish health from others can prolong a battle unless they are prioritized for swift cauterization.

THE DALISH

Having chosen to live by the old ways, the Dalish are a tougher breed than the city elves of the alienage. Dalish hunters are known to be talented in archery – a common *shemlen* stereotype – but they are no less dangerous when swinging a longsword with a 1,000 years of seething hatred weighting the blow.

Group Traits:

- Immune to nature*
- Immune to Paralyzed
- Very weak to electricity

Group Analysis:

- Despite their affinity for magic, this is very much a straight opponent, albeit with potential trouble from an Assassin.
- Unless you take a certain decision in Merrill's story, there are limited encounters with the Dalish.

Standard Dalish:

- Dalish Warrior (Trooper – Weapon and Shield, Two-Handed, Dual Weapon)
- Dalish Archer (Trooper – Archery)

Elite Dalish:

- Dalish Assassin

Dalish Assassin

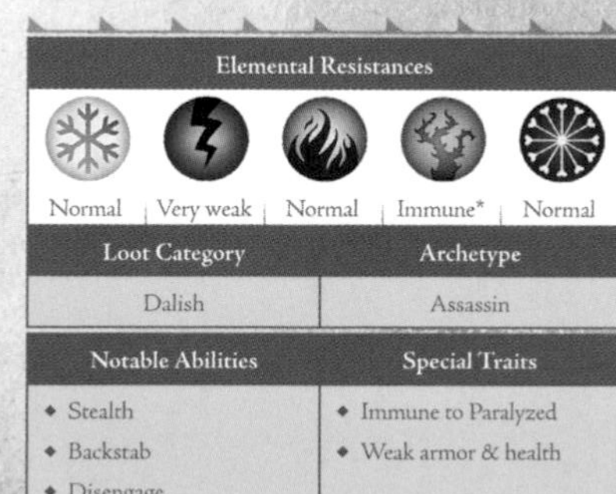

Elemental Resistances				
Normal	Very weak	Normal	Immune*	Normal

Loot Category	Archetype
Dalish	Assassin

Notable Abilities	Special Traits
• Stealth	• Immune to Paralyzed
• Backstab	• Weak armor & health
• Disengage	

- The Dalish do not deal in the more familiar toxins and poisons of the shemlen. Their enchanted blades strike at the very soul of a creature, leaving a wound that continues to bleed with spirit damage.
- An innate immunity to Paralysis prevents the technique of protecting oneself against Assassins with a Glyph.

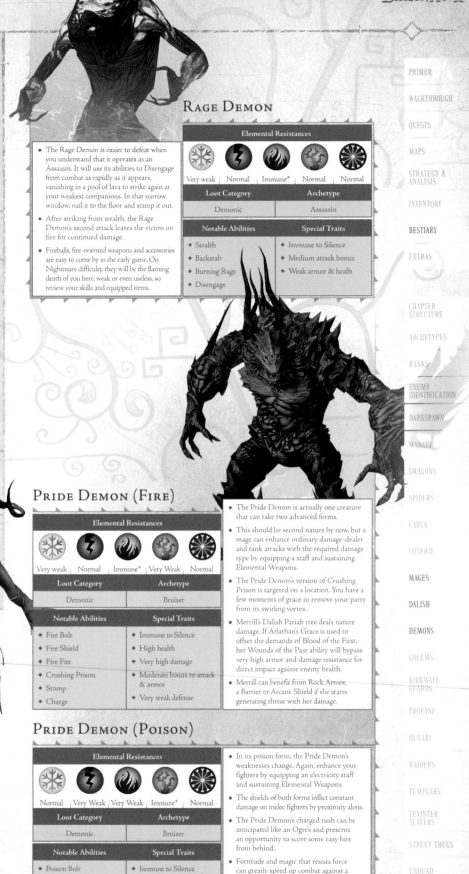

DEMONS

The most dangerous entities beyond the Veil look for sustenance in mortal emotions, seeking to feed on them. The most menacing creatures arise when a mage is possessed, which is the reason why the Circle of Magi was first established. See the encyclopedia entries on demons and the Fade on page 254 of the Extras chapter.

Group Traits:

- Immune to Silence

Group Analysis:

- Demons can ambush at any time and place, rising out of the ground or even possessing and transforming an existing creature. If you place your weak companions too far back from the fight, you may return to find them under attack with no nearby assistance. A rogue's Back to Back skill can aid stranded mages.
- Merrill's Dalish Pariah tree works great to exploit a demon's weakness to nature damage.
- Shades can be put to sleep effectively when grouped.

Standard Demons:

- Shade (Trooper)
- Abomination (Trooper)

Elite Demons:

- Desire Demon
- Rage Demon
- Pride Demon (Fire)
- Pride Demon (Poison)

Rage Demon

Elemental Resistances				
Very weak	Normal	Immune*	Normal	Normal

Loot Category	Archetype
Demonic	Assassin

Notable Abilities	Special Traits
• Stealth • Backstab • Burning Rage • Disengage	• Immune to Silence • Medium attack bonus • Weak armor & health

- The Rage Demon is easier to defeat when you understand that it operates as an Assassin. It will use its abilities to Disengage from combat as rapidly as it appears, vanishing in a pool of lava to strike again at your weakest companions. In that narrow window, nail it to the floor and stamp it out.
- After striking from stealth, the Rage Demon's second attack leaves the victim on fire for continued damage.
- Fireballs, fire-oriented weapons and accessories are easy to come by in the early game. On Nightmare difficulty, they will be the flaming death of you here, weak or even useless, so review your skills and equipped items.

Pride Demon (Fire)

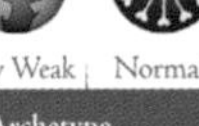

Elemental Resistances				
Very weak	Normal	Immune*	Very Weak	Normal

Loot Category	Archetype
Demonic	Bruiser

Notable Abilities	Special Traits
• Fire Bolt • Fire Shield • Fire Fist • Crushing Prison • Stomp • Charge	• Immune to Silence • High health • Very high damage • Moderate bonus to attack & armor • Very weak defense

- The Pride Demon is actually one creature that can take two advanced forms.
- This should be second nature by now, but a mage can enhance ordinary damage-dealer and tank attacks with the required damage type by equipping a staff and sustaining Elemental Weapons.
- The Pride Demon's version of Crushing Prison is targeted on a location. You have a few moments of grace to remove your party from its swirling vortex.
- Merrill's Dalish Pariah tree deals nature damage. If Arlathan's Grace is used to offset the demands of Blood of the First, her Wounds of the Past ability will bypass very high armor and damage resistance for direct impact against enemy health.
- Merrill can benefit from Rock Armor, a Barrier or Arcane Shield if she starts generating threat with her damage.

Desire Demon

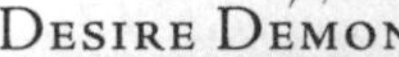

Elemental Resistances				
Normal	Very weak	Normal	Very weak	Immune*

Loot Category	Archetype
Demonic	Commander

Notable Abilities	Special Traits
• Vulnerability Hex • Aura of Magic Resistance	• Immune to Silence • High armor • High Fortitude

- The Desire Demon avoids melee combat, favoring the moderate damage of her ranged attack while her Shades advance.
- Her commander's aura imbues others with greater magic resistance.
- The Desire Demon actually possesses a weak defense, relying on her armor rating to withstand repeated attacks. On Nightmare difficulty, make sure your mages aren't equipped with spirit staves for their ranged retaliation.

Pride Demon (Poison)

Elemental Resistances				
Normal	Very Weak	Very Weak	Immune*	Normal

Loot Category	Archetype
Demonic	Bruiser

Notable Abilities	Special Traits
• Poison Bolt • Poison Shield • Crushing Prison • Stomp • Charge	• Immune to Silence • High damage • Moderate bonus to attack & armor • Very weak defense

- In its poison form, the Pride Demon's weaknesses change. Again, enhance your fighters by equipping an electricity staff and sustaining Elemental Weapons.
- The shields of both forms inflict constant damage on melee fighters by proximity alone.
- The Pride Demon's charged rush can be anticipated like an Ogre's and presents an opportunity to score some easy hits from behind.
- Fortitude and magic that resists force can greatly speed up combat against a Pride Demon, overcoming its capacity for knockdowns with many moves.
- High boss damage can suddenly claim a party member and throw tactics off-balance. Besides protective Arcane Shields and Barriers, another way to keep a unified party is through a warrior with the Battlemaster tree.

* Only on Nightmare difficulty.

GOLEMS

Living war machines of immense strength and resilience, the Golems were once proudly manufactured to order by their dwarven inventors. Though the secret of their creation and animation has been lost, some remain sufficiently intact and operational to inspire fear and awe. The achievement suggests the grand scale on which the ancient wars were once fought and, more poignantly, reminds the dwarves of how much they have been forced to yield to the darkspawn.

Group Traits:

- Immune to nature*
- Immune to Stun
- Immune to critical hits
- Very weak to cold
- Very weak to electricity

Group Analysis:

- The Stone Golem has a charged Knockdown punch that can reach enemies who try to move clear.
- Immunity to critical hits can disable the rogue's advantage, but sufficient damage of any kind inflicted at an early stage can still interrupt their charged stun and boulder-grabbing moves.
- Freezing remains a good option against the Golem, especially if it sets up a Brittle status for cross-class combos. All Golems may be slowed by a barrage of cold and electricity damage.

Standard Golems:

- Slave Statue (Trooper)
- Stone Golem (Trooper)

Elite Golems:

- Gate Guardian

Gate Guardian

Elemental Resistances				

Very weak	Very weak	Normal	Immune*	Normal

Loot Category	Archetype
Generic – Accessories	Boss

Notable Abilities	Special Traits
• Three attack modes • Dual wielding Mode: Flurry • Spear mode: Whirlwind • Spider mode: Fireball and Flame Blast	• Immune to Stun • Immune to critical hits • Immune to Knockdown • Immune to Immobile • Immune to Paralyzed • Immune to Enslavement • Extremely high health • High damage • Moderate armor bonus

- Upgraded cold spells can do extreme damage and will slow the Guardian's attack rate.
- Spider mode enables the Guardian to attack close melee enemies on all sides, though it's possible to withdraw from the wheeling blades.
- In Spear mode, the weapon sweep has an enormous reach.
- The Guardian is slow to move and can be stalled further by manipulating threat generation to switch its targets.
- If you're having trouble targeting, look up!

KIRKWALL GUARDS

Answerable to the viscount, whose authority they enforce, the city guard is ultimately responsible for law and order in Kirkwall. While the templars concern themselves with apostasy and demonic possession, matters of crime and contraband fall to the guardsmen who walk the patrols and undertake the investigations.

Group Traits:

- Immune to cold*
- Immune to Movement Speed effects
- Very weak to fire

Group Analysis:

- Weakness to fire means that Firestorm gets a chance to shine.
- Rogue skills of Confusion and Fog excel at disorienting the enemy. Useful in itself for stalling enemies, this is better exploited by attacks such as Assault, Disperse, Spirit Strike and Golem's Fist for damage multipliers.

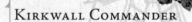

Standard Kirkwall Guards:

- Kirkwall Guard (Trooper – Weapon and Shield)
- Kirkwall Guard (Trooper – Two-Handed)
- Kirkwall Guard Archer (Trooper – Archery)

Elite Kirkwall Guards:

- Kirkwall Commander

Kirkwall Commander

Elemental Resistances				

Immune*	Normal	Very weak	Normal	Normal

Loot Category	Archetype
Kirkwall	Commander

Notable Abilities	Special Traits
• Arresting Field • Aura of Protection	• High armor • High Fortitude • Immune to Silence

- The commander's ranged power inflicts minor damage over the Area of Effect while slowing those who attempt to escape the long arm of the law.
- Protecting and serving, the aura emanating from Kirkwall's finest increases the armor rating of friendly units.

PROFANE

Subjects of dwarven legend, the profane are said to be cursed souls –dwarves so corrupted that, in death, even the Stone refused to take them back. Forced to wander the Deep without rest, they fed upon the energy of the lyrium veins and their hunger grew.

Group Traits:

- Immune to electricity*
- Immune to Movement Speed effects
- Very weak to cold
- Very weak to spirit

Group Analysis:

- The profane boast strong electricity affinities in ranged attack, causing continuous damage over time. Runes of Lightning Warding may assist.
- Spirit spells and freezes from the Elemental tree can drain, hold and weaken the profane.
- Immunity to Movement Speed effects doesn't prevent you slowing their Attack Speed.

Standard Profane:

- Rubble Golems (Trooper)

Elite Profane:

- Ancient Rock Wraith

Ancient Rock Wraith

Elemental Resistances				

Very weak	Immune*	Normal	Normal	Very weak

Loot Category	Archetype
Profane	Archboss

Notable Abilities	Special Traits
• Dust Storm • Arcane Blast • Earth Teleport • Spike Ball • Rock Stab • Rock Roll • Summons low rank Profane	• Immune to Knockback • Immune to Knockdown • Immune to Immobile • Immune to Stun • Immune to Paralyzed • Immune to Enslavement • Immune to Sleep • Immune to Movement Speed effects • Immune to Inevitable Death • Immune to Explosive Death • Very high health • High magic resistance • Medium damage bonus

- Exploit the four cavern columns throughout this battle. They block the Wraith's Rock Roll, the outpouring of energy from its Arcane Blast and the pull of the Dust Storm, while hiding you from its ranged Spike Ball flail arm. You can begin to dodge its roll attack when it forms into a ball in mid-air.
- The Blast and Storm attacks that expose the Wraith's core also mark the time when it is most vulnerable. Have one character ready to step out and deliver damage while another protects them with Barrier or an ability such as Hero's Synergy.
- While fighting, the Wraith frequently summons waves of lesser profane to.interrupt your plans. This is the time to roll out an AoE attack that wipes them out incidentally while maintaining damage on the Wraith. Otherwise, conserve your mana and stamina reserves for single-target damage.
- If you don't have a heal spell, expect to burn a few Potions. The Wraith is a regular dealer of Knockdown effects, so maintain distance if you aren't resistant.
- Hex of Torment makes it slightly more susceptible to damage. Corrosive Walking Bomb is an effective minor drain spell, even without the detonation.
- Following the Wraith's teleport, you can re-target and reposition companions as soon as it starts to emerge from the earth.

* Only on Nightmare difficulty.

QUNARI

The Qunari encountered in the Lowtown compound are all soldiers, having been (supposedly) marooned by the sinking of their dreadnought. This also means they are all male, by the way of the Qun.

Although they have rejected the Qun religion, the Tal-Vashoth also fall under this group in terms of strengths and weaknesses.

Group Traits:

- Immune to fire*
- Immune to electricity*
- Immune to flanking
- Very weak to cold
- Very weak to nature

Group Analysis:

- Winter's Grasp and Cone of Cold can hold Qunari at bay, especially when upgraded. Follow up on Brittle opponents with Shattering Blows and Shattering Arrows.
- Although the Qunari regard magic with suspicion, their Saarebas thrall remains a rare but significant devastator menace in any group. In the company of a commander, the threat multiplies. Use Dispel Magic to interrupt spellcasting and freeze the devastator first – if it starts to use its teleport, it can lead you on a less-than-merry chase.

Standard Qunari:

- Karashok (Trooper – Two-Handed)
- Ashaad (Trooper – Archery)
- Qunari General (Commander)

Elite Qunari:

- Saarebas
- Sten

STEN

Elemental Resistances				
Very weak	Immune*	Immune*	Very weak	Normal

Loot Category	Archetype
Qunari	Commander

Notable Abilities	Special Traits
• Aura of Healing and Armor • Stun Magic	• Immune to Flanking • Immune to Silence • High armor • High Fortitude

- The Sten's ranged capacity is the ability to stun. Though short-lived, it has sufficient distance and Area of Effect to incapacitate an entire party while his warriors advance.
- The Sten's presence confers greater combat protection and restores health to the troops under his command.

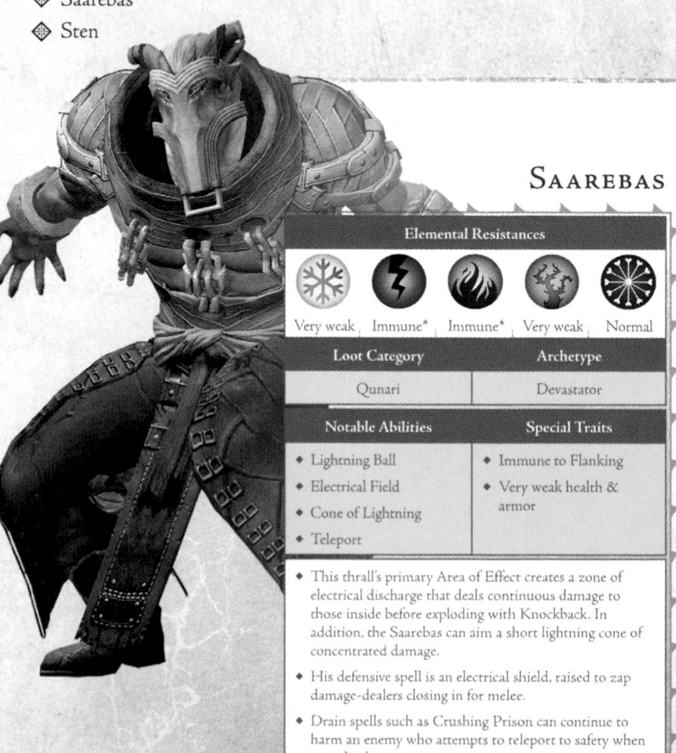

SAAREBAS

Elemental Resistances				
Very weak	Immune*	Immune*	Very weak	Normal

Loot Category	Archetype
Qunari	Devastator

Notable Abilities	Special Traits
• Lightning Ball • Electrical Field • Cone of Lightning • Teleport	• Immune to Flanking • Very weak health & armor

- This thrall's primary Area of Effect creates a zone of electrical discharge that deals continuous damage to those inside before exploding with Knockback. In addition, the Saarebas can aim a short lightning cone of concentrated damage.
- His defensive spell is an electrical shield, raised to zap damage-dealers closing in for melee.
- Drain spells such as Crushing Prison can continue to harm an enemy who attempts to teleport to safety when near death.

RAIDERS

The Raiders of the Waking Sea is a title that recalls the more flamboyant tales of the Felicisima Armada, as told by bards and Orlesian novelists. Pirates they are, to the merchant ships out of Antiva. Smugglers and tide-scum, more often than not, when encountered in the flesh. If you have any business on the Docks, conduct it at night if you're looking for trouble.

Group Traits:

- Immune to nature*
- Immune to Knockdown
- Very weak to electricity

Group Analysis:

- Storms, the bane of every seafarer. Chain Lightning is intensified if set up against Staggered enemies.
- Still, any salt who can learn to stay upright on deck isn't going to be phased by Knockdown from a Fireball or similar. Instead, Shackling Hex and Sleep can slow or stall enemies who appear in waves.

Standard Raiders:

- Raider Warrior (Trooper – Weapon and Shield)
- Raider Warrior (Trooper – Dual Weapon)
- Raider Reaver (Trooper – Two-Handed)
- Raider Archer (Trooper – Archery)

Elite Raiders:

- Raider Assassin

Raider Assassin

Elemental Resistances				

Normal	Very weak	Normal	Immune*	Normal

Loot Category	Archetype
Raiders	Assassin

Notable Abilities	Special Traits
• Stealth	• Immune to Knockdown
• Backstab	• Medium attack bonus
• Poison	• Weak armor & health
• Disengage	

- Potentially one of the first Assassins you will meet, this practiced killer has a second attack from stealth that slashes the victim with a venom-coated blade. Visually, you'll be alerted to the duration of the poison's effect by puffs of green fog.
- The venom causes nature damage over time. There is no antidote but it is short-lived and offers an opportunity to cure victims low on health.

TEMPLARS

Bearing the blazon of a flaming sword, the militarized arm of the Chantry is a focal point for the later events of the game. To a minor extent, your opinion of magic will sometimes determine whether you fight against the templars or alongside them, but there will be inevitable encounters before that time.

Group Traits:

- Immune to Silence
- High magic resistance
- Very weak to spirit
- Very weak to cold

Group Analysis:

- The combination of mixed-rank troopers, assassins and even a commander can present an extremely tough skirmish against a trained and well-equipped army.
- Despair inflicts continous spirit damage on enemies that another player has stunned.
- The templars are resistant to a mage-heavy party. Think about swapping in another fighter and using physical stuns and disorientation to set up auto-critical cross-class combos between rogues and warriors.

Standard Templars:

- Templar Warrior (Trooper – Weapon and Shield)
- Templar Warrior (Trooper – Two-Handed)
- Templar Archer (Trooper – Archery)

Elite Templars:

- Templar Captain
- Templar Seeker

Templar Captain

Elemental Resistances				

Very weak	Normal	Normal	Normal	Very weak

Loot Category	Archetype
Templars	Commander

Notable Abilities	Special Traits
• Captive Field	• Immune to Silence
• Anti-Magic Aura	• High armor
	• High Fortitude
	• High magic resistance

- To assist in the apprehension of Apostates, a Captain can invoke a ranged ability resembling that of the Kirkwall Commander – an Area of Effect that slows its victims while inflicting minor damage over time.
- Countering the mage threat, the Captain's resolute leadership increases the magic resistance of fellow templars on the battlefield.

Templar Seeker

Elemental Resistances				
Very weak	Normal	Normal	Normal	Very weak

Loot Category	Archetype
Templars	Assassin

Notable Abilities	Special Traits
• Stealth	• Immune to Silence
• Backstab	• High magic resistance
• Spirit Drain	• Medium attack bonus
• Disengage	• Weak armor & health

- Exploiting a known weakness of their quarry, the Templar Seeker employs blessed blades. When the blow is delivered from stealth, the attack can inflict spirit damage that continues to burn like poison for a brief period.
- To move stealthily, the Seeker must forego the polished plate and rattling mail of the Order and opt instead for lighter formal garb. The armor absorbs less damage following a successful hit, so the Seeker must rely on dodging blows or staying hidden.

* Only on Nightmare difficulty.

TEVINTER SLAVERS

There are historical and geographical ties that bring the slavers to Kirkwall. But the Tevinters often work to a contract, seeking specific purchases on behalf of their clientele or tracing lost merchandise. You will come to know them by their distinctive armor, redolent of the old empire.

Group Traits:

- Immune to cold*
- Immune to Silence
- Very weak to fire

Group Analysis:

- A welcome chance to stack those fire damage enhancements by Rune or accessory in early encounters.
- The difficulty climbs once the devastator joins in for later battles.

Standard Tevinter Slavers:

- Slaver Warrior (Trooper – Weapon and Shield)
- Slaver Warrior (Trooper – Two-Handed)
- Slaver Warrior (Trooper – Dual Weapon)

Elite Tevinter Slavers:

- Slaver Mage

Slaver Mage

Elemental Resistances

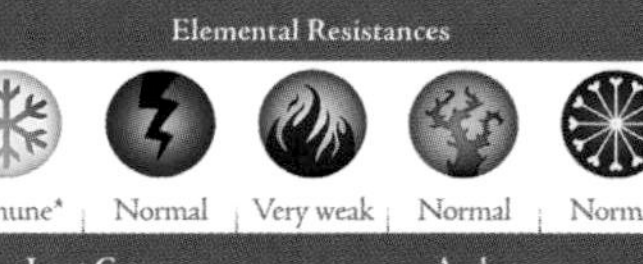

Immune*	Normal	Very weak	Normal	Normal

Loot Category	Archetype
Slavers	Devastator

Notable Abilities	Special Traits
• Spirit Orb • Force Field • Teleport	• Immune to Silence • Very weak health & armor

- In the flavor of old Tevinter, the Slaver Mage's cruel ranged ability is a sphere of spirit that slows those within before subjecting them to a punishing Knockback explosion.
- The Slaver Mage would rather teleport away from danger than face it alone, but while they have allies around to distract enemies, they can activate a personal bubble of invulnerability to buy themselves some recovery time.
- Devastators are always priority targets, and this one is susceptible to common fire damage and weapon buffs.

STREET THUGS

Common villains, muggers, cutpurses and footpads also make their home in the city. The streets of Lowtown won't be safe after dark until somebody deals with them.

Group Traits:

- Immune to fire*
- Very weak to cold

Group Analysis:

- A chance to flex your muscles. You shouldn't find too much to test you here, but it will teach you something about positioning your party to engage greater numbers.
- In particular, note how the game spawns secondary waves of enemies when the first is reduced to a trigger threshold; don't let your companions run off into the streets.

Standard Street Thugs:

- Street Thug (Trooper – Two-Handed)
- Street Thug (Trooper – Dual Weapon)

UNDEAD

Always seeking to find a path across, some demons are drawn to the weakest of traces in this world and fix upon the unresisting remains of the dead. Assuming the martial skills or spellcasting abilities of their deceased hosts, these undead terrors present a much greater challenge than the shambling enemies often found in their company.

Group Traits:

- Immune to nature*
- Immune to Sleep
- Very weak to spirit
- Very weak to electricity

Group Analysis:

- Chain Reaction does additional damage against Staggered enemies. Multiply an existing weakness by shooting lightning after your warriors have Pummeled and Sundered the enemy.
- Despair inflicts continous spirit damage on enemies that another player has stunned.

Standard Undead:

- Corpse (Trooper)
- Skeleton Archer (Trooper – Archery)

Elite Undead:

- Shadow Warrior Captain
- Arcane Horror
- Revenant

Shadow Warrior Captain

Elemental Resistances				
Normal	Very weak	Normal	Immune*	Very weak

Loot Category	Archetype
Demonic	Commander

Notable Abilities	Special Traits
• Shadow Field • Shadow Aura	• Immune to Sleep • Immune to Silence • High armor • High Fortitude • Medium resistance to Movement Speed effects

- The resilience of this enemy makes it advisable to kill its companions first.
- This commander radiates a supporting healing aura to its brethren from the Fade, so that first task will be more difficult.
- Because of its high armor, it is something of an immovable tank enemy and a damage soak that takes effort to remove.
- Fortunately, it is not especially harmful and can be managed effectively with attention to its weaknesses.

Arcane Horror

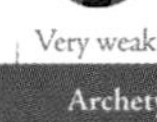

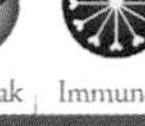

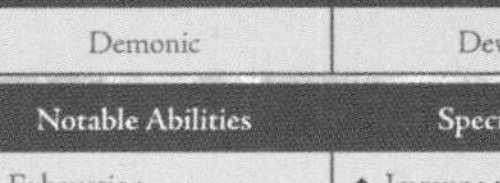

Elemental Resistances				
Very weak	Very weak	Normal	Very weak	Immune*

Loot Category	Archetype
Demonic	Devastator

Notable Abilities	Special Traits
• Exhaustion • Spirit Shield • Spirit Bolt • Teleport	• Immune to Sleep • Very weak health & armor

- The Arcane Horror launches a field magic that saps health, mana and stamina while slowing those attempting to flee or attack. It defends itself with a much closer field that inflicts continuous spirit damage.
- Having a strong spirit affinity, the Horror shrugs off Arcane Magic, but its own Spirit Bolt delivers a blasting Knockdown against even the steadfast.
- Nature magic, cold damage and electricity buffs exploit the Arcane Horror's weaknesses. However, it is a cautious combatant and will always use its teleport to escape, advancing when ready to launch another assault.

Revenant

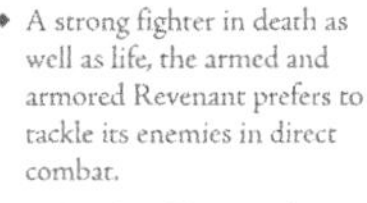

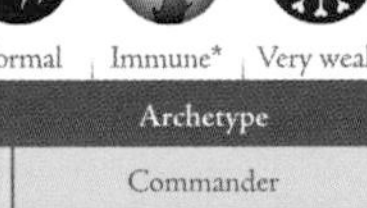

Elemental Resistances				
Immune*	Very weak	Normal	Immune*	Very weak

Loot Category	Archetype
Demonic	Commander

Notable Abilities	Special Traits
• Aura of Defense • Gravity Pull	• Immune to Sleep • Immune to Silence • High armor • High Fortitude

- A strong fighter in death as well as life, the armed and armored Revenant prefers to tackle its enemies in direct combat.
- It doesn't suffer cowards, either. The undead commander's ranged ability exerts a pulling force, used on ranged targets or rogues seeking to disengage after a stealth strike.
- The presence of a Revenant empowers its possessed cohorts with similar advantages of increased armor and defense.

* Only on Nightmare difficulty.

MERCENARIES

Kirkwall has never known a shortage of individuals willing to kill for money, so any distinction is more often one of skill, accomplishment and business acumen. This group covers some of the more capable sell-swords and shooters available for hire.

Group Traits:

- Immune to cold*
- Immune to Enslavement
- Very weak to nature

Group Analysis:

- Your Cone of Cold upgrade will be busy here, so remember Two-Handed attacks and Varric's Bianca versus Brittle opponents.
- When waves of mercenaries spring from all sides, an upgraded Glyph of Paralysis will halt enemies on one flank while you concentrate on the other flank.
- Bellow, the upgraded Taunt, will draw enemies from both flanks to one tank target.
- Crushing Prison and Walking Bomb can get to work on low-ranking Archers when there's no way to fight through the mercenary vanguard.

Standard Mercenaries:

- Mercenary Warrior (Trooper – Weapon and Shield)
- Mercenary Warrior (Trooper – Two-Handed)
- Mercenary Warrior (Trooper – Dual Weapon)
- Mercenary Archer (Trooper – Archery)

Elite Mercenaries:

- Mercenary Captain

Mercenary Captain

Elemental Resistances				

Immune*	Normal	Normal	Very weak	Normal

Loot Category	Archetype
Generic	Commander

Notable Abilities	Special Traits
• Aura of Healing	• Immune to Enslavement • Immune to Silence • High armor • High Fortitude

- This commander is weak to one of the rarer elemental attack forms, so you may find it easier to stick with your character's strongest attack.
- Aim for physical stuns and Staggers that can be followed by cross-class combo damage. While he is stunned, his Mercenary colleagues lose the advantage of the commander's aura.

BOSSES & UNIQUE ENEMIES

Arishok

Elemental Resistances				

Very weak	Immune*	Immune*	Very weak	Normal

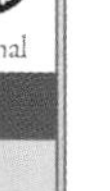

Loot Category	Archetype
Qunari	Boss

Notable Abilities	Special Traits
• Impale • Rush • Slice	• Immune to Flanking • Immune to Knockdown • Immune to Immobile • Immune to Paralyzed • Immune to Enslavement • Very high defense • High health & Fortitude • Medium bonus to damage • Weak attack

- The Rush attack is telegraphed and can be dodged, leaving the Arishok wide open to attacks while he recovers.
- He can be glyphed, frozen, mind-blasted and petrified to earn time. Gravitic Ring, AoE abilities, spells like Entropic Cloud and more generally all buffs/debuffs will also help. It's most important for characters with low fortitude to keep their distance, as those blade moves have Knockdown effects powerful enough to chain without a Force Mage's Unshakable passive resistance. (See page 179 for an introduction to "kiting".)
- Watch for Impale, which raises the victim on a sword and holds for continuous damage.
- Stock up on Potions for this battle.
- The Arishok is not above using Potions to restore health himself.

Meredith

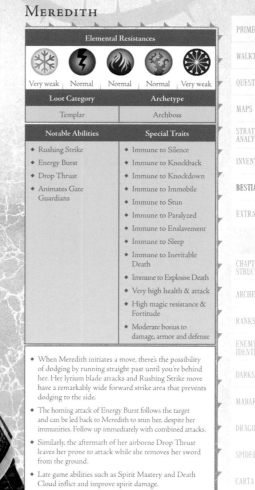

Elemental Resistances				
 Very weak	 Normal	 Normal	 Normal	Very weak

Loot Category	Archetype
Templar	Archboss

Notable Abilities	Special Traits
• Rushing Strike • Energy Burst • Drop Thrust • Animates Gate Guardians	• Immune to Silence • Immune to Knockback • Immune to Knockdown • Immune to Immobile • Immune to Stun • Immune to Paralyzed • Immune to Enslavement • Immune to Sleep • Immune to Inevitable Death • Immune to Explosive Death • Very high health & attack • High magic resistance & Fortitude • Moderate bonus to damage, armor and defense

- When Meredith initiates a move, there's the possibility of dodging by running straight past until you're behind her. Her lyrium blade attacks and Rushing Strike move have a remarkably wide forward strike area that prevents dodging to the side.
- The homing attack of Energy Burst follows the target and can be led back to Meredith to stun her, despite her immunities. Follow up immediately with combined attacks.
- Similarly, the aftermath of her airborne Drop Thrust leaves her prone to attack while she removes her sword from the ground.
- Late game abilities such as Spirit Mastery and Death Cloud inflict and improve spirit damage.
- At 75% health, Meredith uses the lyrium blade to animate the first Gate Guardian. At 50% health she will awaken the other Statues in the Gallows courtyard.

Orsino

Elemental Resistances				
Normal	Very weak	Normal	Immune*	Very weak

Loot Category	Archetype
Circle of Magi	Boss

Notable Abilities	Special Traits
• Ground Slam • Blood Drain • Gut Throw • Blood Spurt • Wet End • Summons Corpses	• Immune to Knockdown • Immune to Immobile • Immune to Paralyzed • Immune to Enslavement • Immune to Sleep • Medium bonus to health • Moderate bonus to damage • Weak attack

- Orsino's most devastating attack is his blood-draining hold, which paralyzes the victim while transferring health. Be ready to heal weaker companions before the attack concludes. It can be interrupted by a powerful attack, the window is small – one trick is to pack Combustion Grenades that can be used by any party member.
- When Orsino is flanked, he punches the ground to stun enemies close by. He also has a melee punch with knockdown that can be rebounded with Stonewall.
- Hulking Orsino has two stages, completely regenerating his health by reforming. After reforming he can remove one arm and bludgeon opponents with the "wet end". In this form, he may also remove his innards to hurl them like a boulder (in an equally telegraphed animation, to help you dodge), or spray the contents of his guts as a ranged attack.
- Scuttling Orsino detaches itself from the main corpse construct and changes the pace of the battle. It will regenerate the hulk form after taking sufficient damage.
- The Corpses summoned are low rank distractions, easily dispatched.
- Although he cannot be frozen or made Brittle, upgraded cold spells can slow hulk Orsino's rate of attack as well as dedicated talents.

Fenris, Anders & Merrill

When you must confront previous companions as enemies on the battlefield, your influence over their development is spurned. The skills and equipment you gave them will have no bearing on the opponents you face anew, though, as before, their level of experience will be in tune with yours.

Fenris

In opposition, the branded elf returns with no other talents but his Two-Handed and Tevinter Fugitive talent trees maxed out. That includes all upgrades to Mighty Blow, Scythe, Whirlwind and Spirit Pulse.

Anders

The dangerous insurrectionist possesses most of his Vengeance talent tree and the fully upgraded forms of Mind Blast, Heal, Winter's Grasp, Cone of Cold, Crushing Prison and Arcane Shield.

Merrill

With only some of her Dalish Pariah talent tree retained, the outcast mage keeps Wrath of the Elven, Stone's Throw and Ensnare fully upgraded. She spreads her other abilities by gaining Spirit Strike, Death Hex, Despair, Shackling Hex, Golem's Fist, Petrify, Rock Armor and Galvanism.

* Only on Nightmare difficulty.

EXTRAS

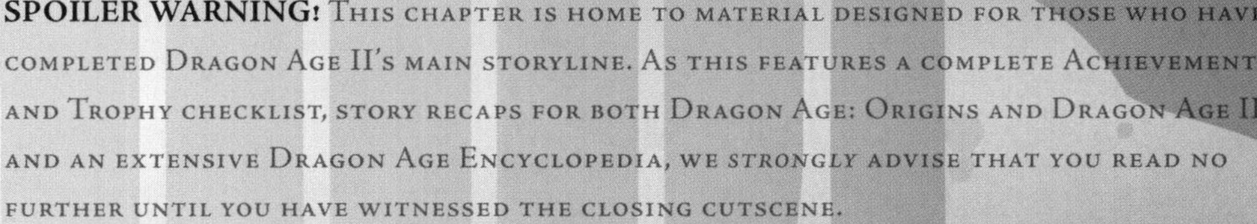

SPOILER WARNING! This chapter is home to material designed for those who have completed Dragon Age II's main storyline. As this features a complete Achievement and Trophy checklist, story recaps for both Dragon Age: Origins and Dragon Age II, and an extensive Dragon Age Encyclopedia, we *strongly* advise that you read no further until you have witnessed the closing cutscene.

ACHIEVEMENTS & TROPHIES

Dragon Age II has a sizable, wide-ranging selection of Achievements and Trophies, many of which are designed to reward players who invest time and effort into truly mastering the game – and especially those who embark on at least one additional playthrough.

Story Milestones

These accomplishments are all unlocked by completing main plot quests and cannot be missed.

Icon	Name	G	Trophy	Unlock Conditions
	Tale Within a Tale	5	Bronze	Defeat the Ogre during the opening section of the Prologue.
	Immigrant	5	Bronze	Complete the Prologue.
	Full House	10	Bronze	Recruit four companions. This will unlock once you complete the Tranquility or Long Way Home quests during Act 1.
	Stone Cold	5	Bronze	Defeat the Rock Wraith during the Deep Roads Expedition in Act 1.
	Delver of the Deep	10	Bronze	Leave the Deep Roads area during the final quest of Act 1.
	Friends in High Places	15	Bronze	Unlocked late in Act 2 when you meet the final member of Kirkwall's ruling elite.
	Conqueror	15	Bronze	Defeat Meredith at the end of Act 3.
	Champion of Kirkwall	20	Silver	Complete Dragon Age II; the narrative conclusion isn't important.

Optional Story Accomplishments

This selection of Achievements and Trophies can only be obtained by completing certain optional quests or by making specific decisions at critical points in the main storyline.

Icon	Name	G	Trophy	Unlock Conditions
	Nefarious	10	Bronze	Choose to work for Athenril at the conclusion of the Prologue.
	Mercenary	10	Bronze	Choose to work for Meeran at the conclusion of the Prologue.
	Birthright	15	Bronze	Complete the Birthright companion quest. This must be completed before you set off for the Deep Roads during Act 1.
	Financier	10	Bronze	Pay Bartrand to join the Deep Roads expedition. This does not unlock if you accept a loan from Dougal.
	That Thing Has Legs	25	Bronze	Kill a Varterral. You can encounter this creature during the Mirror Image companion quest during Act 2 (see page 83).
	A Worthy Rival	25	Silver	Earn the respect of the Arishok before the conclusion of the Demands of the Qun main plot quest in Act 2 (see page 72).
	King of the Hill	10	Bronze	During the Demands of the Qun quest (see page 75), you must engineer an outcome where Hawke defeats the Arishok in open combat (either in a duel, or alongside his fellow warriors). This will not unlock if you choose the "diplomatic" solution whereby Isabela is taken back to Par Vollen as a prisoner.

Icon	Name	G	Trophy	Unlock Conditions
	Exorcist	25	Bronze	Find and kill the undying Xebenkeck. This enemy is encountered during the Forbidden Knowledge quest in Act 2 (see page 88).
	Spelunker	25	Bronze	Visit any 10 caves in and around Kirkwall while completing quests. If you finish most secondary and companion quests, you should unlock this during Act 2.
	Arcane Defender	25	Silver	Side with mages in five separate quests from the following list: Wayward Son, Act of Mercy, Enemies Among Us, Night Terrors, Best Served Cold, On the Loose and Showdown.
	Mage Hunter	25	Silver	Support the templars in five individual quests – consult the list above for details. Naturally, it is only possible to unlock Mage Hunter or Arcane Defender during a single playthrough.
	Dragon Slayer	25	Silver	Complete the Mine Massacre secondary quest in Act 3 (see page 97).
	Demon Slayer	25	Silver	Kill the ancient demon Hybris after completing steps in a very special quest: see page 105.
	Crowning Achievement	25	Silver	Side with the templars in the climax of Act 3. See page 94 for details.
	Epic	50	Gold	Complete Dragon Age II twice, or finish a single playthrough where you import a Dragon Age: Origins save during the character creation process.
	Mass Exodus	25	Bronze	Complete the Prologue with all three classes on separate playthroughs. You do not need to finish the entire game, just the opening section up to and including the transition to Act 1.

Gameplay Milestones

Players will obtain these minor gameplay accomplishments during the course of a standard playthrough.

Icon	Name	G	Trophy	Unlock Conditions
	Talented	5	Bronze	Select a talent upgrade while leveling up.
	Darkness Falls	5	Bronze	On the World Map screen, toggle the Kirkwall map display from day to night.
	Explorer	5	Bronze	Leave Kirkwall to visit a location in the Free Marches for the first time.
	Craftsman	5	Bronze	Acquire your first crafting recipe. Effectively impossible to miss as you'll pick one up early in Act 1.
	Specialized	25	Bronze	Acquire two specializations for Hawke. These are awarded at levels 7 and 14, so you should unlock this during Act 3 at the latest.
	Dedicated	15	Bronze	Reach level 10. Even on a sprint through main plot quests only, ignoring all optional asides, you should unlock this during Act 2.

Special Accomplishments

These Achievements and Trophies all reward very specific feats and, as such, require at least a little effort to obtain.

Icon	Name	G	Trophy	Unlock Conditions
	Legendary	50	Silver	Reach level 20. Players taking a fairly comprehensive path through the story and all optional quests should unlock this during Act 3.
	A Friend in Need	5	Bronze	Collect or purchase an armor upgrade for a companion. The first one that you can acquire for free is found at the end of the Birthright quest (see page 63).
	Enchanter	5	Bronze	Use a rune on a piece of equipment with an available rune slot. See page 214 for details.
	Master Craftsman	25	Silver	Find all available recipes for one of the three crafting "disciplines" (runes, potions or poisons and bombs), then create every item within that category. See page 213 for details.
	I Got Your Back	25	Bronze	Upgrade a single companion's armor to its maximum level. See page 211 for further details.
	Weapon Master	25	Bronze	Unlock all abilities and upgrades in a single weapon-specific talent tree: Weapon and Shield, Two-Handed, Dual Weapon or Archery.
	Tag Team	5	Bronze	Perform a cross-class combo by switching between party members. See page 174.
	Unstoppable	50	Silver	Complete an entire Act without a party member being knocked out. Possible (though tricky) on Normal difficulty level, we'd suggest that players obtain this by completing the shorter Act 3 on Casual.
	Mogul	25	Bronze	Accumulate a total of 100 sovereigns in your purse. If you can bear to ignore the lure of shopping opportunities, this is easily accomplished if you complete the majority of quests in Act 1 and refrain from paying Bartrand until the very last minute.
	Gift Giver	5	Bronze	Give a gift to a companion. See page 161.
	Flirtatious	5	Bronze	Flirt with a companion to initiate a romance. See page 161.
	Romantic	25	Bronze	See a romance with a companion through to its conclusion. See page 161.
	Friend	25	Bronze	Earn the friendship of a companion. See page 161.
	Rival	25	Bronze	Establish a rivalry with a companion. See page 161.
	Great Minds Think Alike	50	Silver	Have four companions in a state of simultaneous friendship or four active rivalries. This requires a little forward planning and management. See page 182 for further details.
	Treasure Hunter	25	Silver	Open 50 containers.
	Knowledgeable	25	Bronze	Unlock 100 codex entries. You should receive this during Act 1 on a completionist-grade playthrough.
	Supplier	25	Silver	Find all possible crafting ingredients during your travels. See page 213 for further details.
	Archeologist	50	Silver	There are four "special" Codex collectibles per Act signed by the "Band of Three". Collect three out of four of these in each Act to unlock this. • Act 1: The Bone Pit, The Gallows, Viscount's Keep, Lowtown (Night). • Act 2: Chantry, Darktown, Gallows Dungeon (during the Dissent quest), Docks (Qunari Compound). • Act 3: These are all found during quests: two during Justice, one during Gamlen's Greatest Treasure, and the final one at the Docks during the Last Straw.
	Chantry Historian	25	Silver	Collect all four chapters of "The History of the Chantry" by Brother Genitivi. Three of these are found in the Chantry during a daylight visit, one per Act. Chapter 3, however, can only be collected during the Following the Qun quest: see page 74.
	The Ultimate Reward (PS3 only)	-	Platinum	Unlock all the other Trophies.

The Exiled Prince

You must purchase and install The Exiled Prince (see dragonage.com/da2/addons for details) to access storyline elements related to these accomplishments.

Icon	Name	G	Trophy	Unlock Conditions
	Retribution	25	Bronze	Complete the Duty companion quest in Act 1 or 2.
	Avenged	25	Bronze	Complete the Repentance companion quest in Act 2.
	Cloak and Dagger	25	Bronze	Complete the Faith companion quest in Act 3.
	Memento	25	Bronze	Find the Starkhaven Longbow during the Repentance quest and present it to the prince (see page 81).
	Loyalty of the Prince	30	Bronze	Establish complete friendship or rivalry with Sebastian.

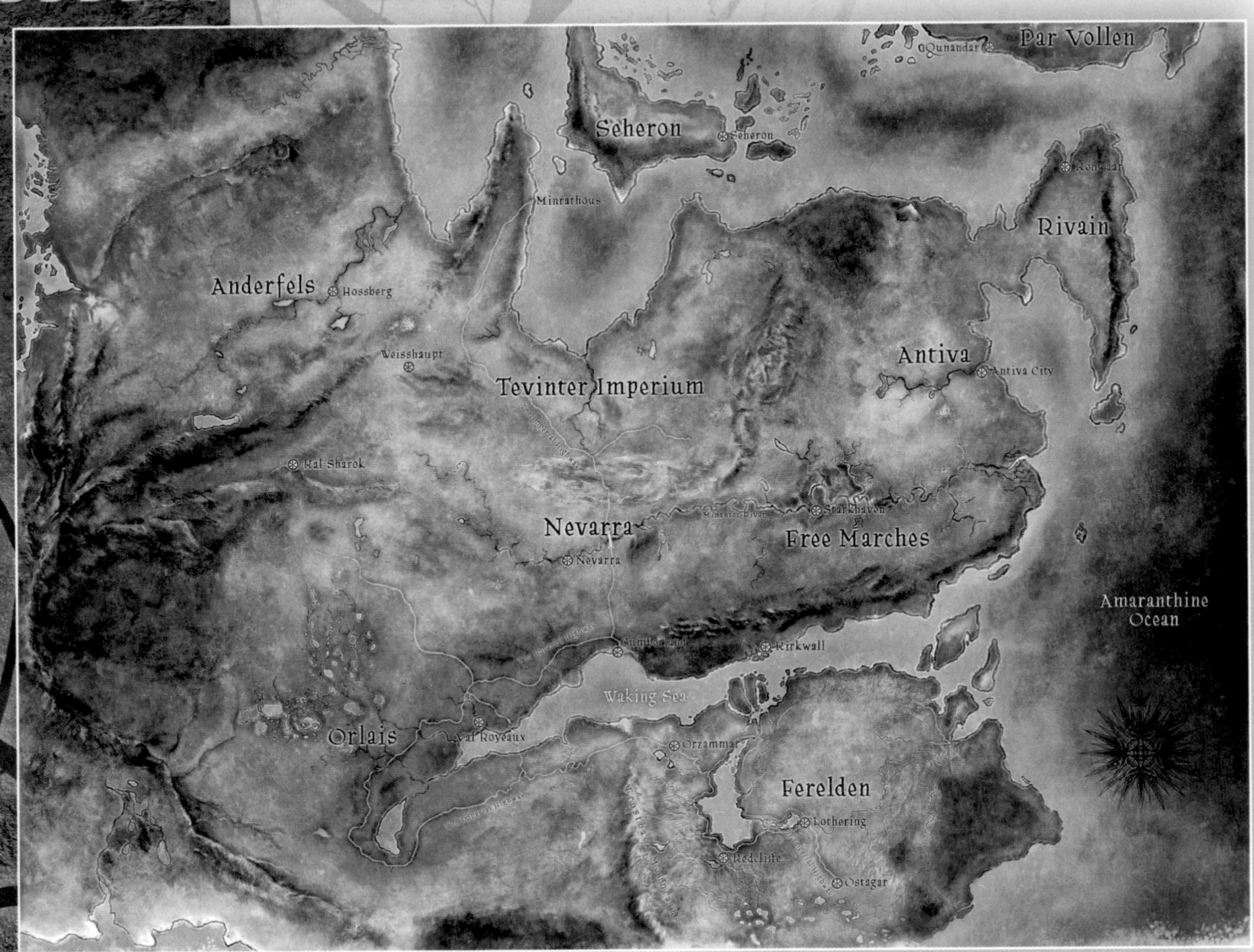

THE CONTINENT OF THEDAS

Orlais

Ambitious and wealthy Orlais is the most powerful single human nation in Thedas. Under its current ruler, Empress Celene I, Orlais has a large aristocracy famed for its culture and extravagance. Celene shares the expansionist dream of Orlais' founder, Kordilius Drakon, that the nation's borders should stretch to the edges of the continent.

Many Orlesian nobles belong to its renowned knightly order, the Chevaliers. The martial training of the Chevaliers is legendarily harsh, instilling in the knights a fierce discipline and code of honor that takes precedence over the value of their own lives. The Chevaliers know no fear and their loyalty is absolute. The penalty for dishonor is death, something that a Chevalier welcomes if he or she has failed their lord.

Another characteristic of the noble class is their penchant for high fashion, often copied in other lands such as Nevarra and the Free Marches but always at its most extreme within Orlais. Both men and women wear cosmetics of various kinds, with subtle differences that indicate social standing. In public, they are also prone to wearing very elaborate masks. These are hereditary and identify one's family almost as uniquely as the heraldry on a crest.

The capital city is Val Royeaux, which boasts the University of Orlais: a major center of learning that attracts young nobles from all over Thedas with the best education one can buy. The University is a relatively modern institution, whose liberal-minded professors have already clashed with religious conservatives over the content of their classes. This is likely to become a much larger issue in the future.

Tevinter Imperium

Formerly an empire that stretched the entirety of Thedas, all that survives of Tevinter is a decadent remnant, centered around Minrathous in the north. This fabled city, once the jewel of the entire continent, is governed by powerful magic users through a form of magocracy.

Tevinter is almost universally reviled by other nations. Its nobility is famously debauched and slavery is still practiced. The Imperium is the center of the black market, smuggling (including the harboring of mage fugitives from other lands), and slave trade. While it might seem in decline, the Imperium is still a very powerful nation with considerable military might. Without a doubt, it would turn on the nations to the south if its attention were not diverted by the constant wars with the Qunari, in Seheron and Par Vollen.

The ancient magister lords ruled the Imperium as a group, maintaining a tight hold over the people through the power to infiltrate their dreams. These lords are no more, but even today some mages are quietly acknowledged as the most proficient dream-walkers and diviners.

The Imperium draws a variety of soldiers from its territories to form its impressive army. Two features of the Tevinter military, however, are considered legendary and are known throughout Thedas. One is the use of elephant mounts, these huge creatures having been imported into Tevinter for centuries through the coastal colonies near the northwestern jungles. The other is equally impressive: a trio of gigantic war golems purchased from the dwarves, which are known as the juggernauts.

The Tevinters have left their mark all over Thedas, still felt in the ruins and roads of the fallen empire. Though the tales are now told to scare children, the truth of their excesses could still shock the hardest heart.

Ferelden

Ferelden is a relatively temperate nation in the far southeast of Thedas populated by a barbarian, militaristic culture that has only begun to civilize in the last few centuries. Still considered a backwater by other nations – especially the Orlesians, who controlled and occupied the Ferelden valley for centuries – the Fereldans have made great strides in recent years. A proud and independent people, they resent being considered "primitive" and are well on their way to becoming a power on the continent.

Ferelden borders the Orlesian Empire to the west, with whom it continues to have a very tense relationship. The Frostback Mountain range divides the two nations and prevents hostilities from being more frequent. Orzammar, the last kingdom of the dwarves, rests in the Frostbacks.

Fereldan cities are considered anarchic by most standards. The Fereldan desire for freedom has engendered a laissez-faire cultural attitude towards law enforcement and behavior in general. While the worst offenses are quickly put down, many others are ignored and citizens are often left to make their own justice. Petty theft is common, as guardsmen will only go out of their way to deal with major crimes. Commerce is largely unregulated as long as taxes are paid: businesses such as brothels and gambling halls are not only tolerated, but expected.

Lothering and the Imperial Highway

The Hawkes made their home in Lothering, a village north of the ancient fortress of Ostagar. The settlement arose on a crossroads of the Imperial Highway, starting out as a trading post and supplying goods to Redcliffe and the merchants of Orzammar. In time, the settlers became self-sufficient through mills and farmland.

The Imperial Highway is an ancient architectural wonder that was originally built by the Tevinter Imperium. Constructed from stone quarried by slaves in Kirkwall, this elevated road ran from Minrathous down to Orlais and then east to Ferelden. The intended project was never finished, and many sections have fallen into disrepair over the centuries. Nevertheless, it remains useful to many travelers fearful of wolves.

The Free Marches

The Free Marches is a collective name given to the group of wealthy city-states in the central part of the continent. The "Marchers" are independent descendants from tough barbarians, their cities standing in a loose confederation that rarely unites on any matter unless one of their larger neighbors becomes aggressive. In this event, the Marchers assemble a united military front that even the greatest power cannot ignore.

The Free Marches is best known as the breadbasket of Thedas, its farms along the banks of the great Minanter River being the source of much of the continent's food. Starkhaven is the largest of the cities, welcoming visitors on the waterway to its regal central square.

Kirkwall

The last of the great Imperium cities, Kirkwall was founded in 620 Ancient by archmage Emerius Krayvan. Elven slaves were shipped in by the thousand to quarry the stone, enduring brutality that would first mark Kirkwall's bloody reputation. Built on this foundation of suffering, the "City of Chains" became the center of the Imperial slave trade and the destination of those taken captive by conquest. It is now one of the larger Free Marches cities.

Approaching by sea, it is impossible to miss the imposing black wall that gives the city its name. Leering from the cliff face are the carvings of the Old Gods, a pantheon of profane idols smugly provoking the waves. Despite the best efforts of both the Chantry and the weather to eradicate them, the continued presence of these vile guardians seems assured for centuries to come.

Marine access to the harbor is via a narrow channel, also carved into the cliff, and flanked by colossal bronze statues – the Twins of Kirkwall. By extending a chain net from the lighthouse to the Twins, the city is able to close off the only navigable sea lane and extort duties from passing ships.

The Gallows

Petrified in anguish, the many statues of tortured slaves pay no tribute to those sold into bondage. Instead, this city entrance and its high-walled courtyard are legacies of Kirkwall's cruel past. The magisters intended the Gallows to crush the spirit of new arrivals, allowing no hope of escape or emancipation to enter the city. Daily executions furnished the gibbets with corpses as a visceral reminder of the only way a slave might one day find release. Stepping from the pitch-black hold of a galley to be corralled along the docks toward the Gallows, today's Fereldan refugees might feel the same enfeebling sense of utter hopelessness.

Lowtown

In the days of the Imperium, this area was an enclosure for the slaves. Living conditions may have improved – slightly – but there's no mistaking Kirkwall's geographical divisions of social class. An endless labyrinth of shantytowns, alleyways and makeshift buildings, Lowtown is home to characters both colorful and occasionally pungent. The elven alienage is the largest of many ghettos, where despair at the squalid conditions is occasionally swept away by the evident pride of the close-knit communities.

The residents can at least take heart that they are not at the bottom of the social ladder: the poorest of all resort to making their beds in the sewers below, and in such numbers that Kirkwall's underground tunnel network has earned the nickname of "Darktown".

Hightown

Constructed for the local elite at the height of the Imperium's fortunes, the mansions and plazas of Hightown still have the power to impress. Ascending the narrow staircase, visitors in the past would have entered a more decadent, extravagant playground than the refinement that greets them today.

Both the Keep and the Chantry now stand proud as symbols of Kirkwall's respectability. Both are converted from the lavish residences of magister lords who accrued wealth from the slave trade. The original masters imagined that Hightown's elevation could isolate them from events below: when the uprising came, they were unprepared for the self-sacrificing determination of those who had absolutely nothing to lose.

Nevarra

Originally one of the larger Free Marches city-states, Nevarra benefited from its position and has aggressively expanded over the last two centuries, becoming a power to rival Orlais itself. When a long war with the Orlesians wrested control of the mineral-rich hills to the west, the victory earned Nevarra considerable prestige in addition to the wealth.

While the capital lies in the original city of Nevarra, the city of Cumberland's location on the Minanter River makes it a natural and busy point of trade with the rest of the Free Marches and beyond.

The Nevarrans can boast many legendary heroes in their past, with names that are still worshipped by the modern populace. Statues of these men and women are common, their bodies preserved in palatial tombs. Ancestors of the ruling Pentaghast family were once famed as dragon hunters, driving the beasts to near-extinction.

The Anderfels

The Anders people were the first humans to fight the darkspawn, and it is from their language that hurlocks and genlocks received their names. In this desolate landscape, centuries of Blight have so devastated expanses of the steppes that it is said the corpses of the fallen never decay: no beast or insect survives there to feed on them. Nevertheless, a history of repelling darkspawn incursions has hardened the proud inhabitants of this poor, remote nation with a steel spirit and grim determination. Their priests are the most devout, their warriors the most feared throughout Thedas.

The order of the Grey Wardens was founded in the Anderfels to drive back the first Blight, and it retains its headquarters at Weisshaupt fortress with a strong military force. Though a king sits in the capital of Hossberg, the Wardens are also treated as lords and banns. While their political power has waned elsewhere, the old order can still wield influence wherever the people are beset by the constant menace of invasion.

Antiva

Enjoying a warm north-eastern climate, Antiva is a nation of prodigious vineyards and good living. It possesses a respected noble lineage that can be traced back over millennia, though it is unofficially a private plutocracy. In reality, the authority of the existing monarchy has long been eclipsed by the true power of the bankers and the affluent classes. Money controls power in Antiva, possessing sufficient capital to resolve any external diplomatic quandaries with a well-aimed purse or threat of withdrawn trade.

Despite the lack of a strong military tradition, there is another reason why Antiva has rarely feared invasion: the infamous House of Crows. Contemporary Antivans may not boast a distinguished reputation on the battlefield, but they produce some of the deadliest assassins in Thedas. Were a conquering general to make this land his own, how long would he enjoy it before death arrived in the form of a wine glass, a loose balcony or a delicious cake? Such is the reputation of the Crows, to have kept whole armies at bay. Should you ever do something to regret in docile Antiva, understand that you have entered a land of daggers.

Deep Roads

Any dwarf today can tell you tales of the Deep Roads as they once were – a grand network of tunnels that joined the thaigs, the caverns where settlements were built in honor of the Paragons. These subterranean highways were works of unparalleled artisan achievement, with centuries of planning and engineering demonstrated in the geometry of their walls. Statues of the Paragons watched over passing travelers, and channels carried a flow of lava that kept the Deep Roads lit and warm.

This once-proud creation is now the source of much lament for what they have lost. Today, only two thaigs even remain inhabited: Kal-Sharok and Orzammar in the Frostback Mountains. When the darkspawn first appeared, the dwarves sealed off the entrances to their cherished roads, abandoning everything that lay beyond, and retreated. With each passing year, the foulness spreads a little further.

Par Vollen

Some scholars believe that the first humans in Thedas came from the rainforests of Par Vollen many thousands of years ago, migrating south from the archipelago. The pyramids they built still stand to this day and are regarded by travelers to the region as true wonders.

Three hundred years ago, circa 6:30 Steel, the first Qunari warships landed. Clad in armor and bearing cannons, the invading force swiftly overwhelmed the native people in a brief but decisive bloodbath. A colony was established and the settlers built a strategic base on the southern coast. Qunandar is now a glittering capital city, famous for its great domes and aqueducts.

Though they were ousted from the Thedas mainland by the Exalted Marches, the Qunari held Par Vollen and regard it as part of their empire. It remains their strongest foothold in the region. Contact with their homeland has been intermittent at best across the turbulent northern oceans and there is doubt as to whether a ship has made contact in many years.

It is said that another people known as the Fex also inhabit Par Vollen, though little is known of them.

Rivain

The Rivaini are unique among the humans of Thedas in regard to their appearance and their culture. They are olive-skinned or darker and often distinguish themselves further with tattoos and body piercings – the more elaborate the decorations, the higher one's social standing or rank. They have a cordial relation with the elves, from whom the practice may have been adopted. They are not commonly followers of Andraste, and some have even converted to the Qun, the Qunari religion.

Another front for the great war when the Qunari invaded the mainland, there are many tales of massacres and war crimes on both sides of Rivain's history. The Qunari forces were eventually driven back to the north, which they retained when the peace treaty known as the Llomeryn Accords was negotiated. In the centuries since, the city of Kont-aar has existed relatively peacefully within the rest of Rivain – nowhere else in Thedas is there as much interaction between the two cultures.

Despite prohibitions on magic, the Rivaini revere their seers as a matter of tradition. These apostates are wise women, local hedge witches who converse with spirits and even allow themselves to be possessed, though they supposedly do so for the benefit of their villages.

Seheron

While Par Vollen remains comfortably in the grip of the Qunari, Seheron is an island in dispute. It was part of the Tevinter Imperium until it was claimed by the Qunari sixty years ago, though the battle for domination continues. Adding to the turmoil is the significant presence of the Tal-Vashoth, bands of the horned race (known as the kossith) who have rejected the Qun.

Seheron's most impressive features date back to the glory days of the ancient Imperium, but its legacy has turned against it. Many elven slaves have willingly converted to the Qun and now hold office within the Qunari ranks, helping the invaders to oust their old Tevinter masters. Some humans who remain also feel abandoned by the Imperium. Because the Tevinters never signed the Llomeryn Accords, it is here that the Qunari invasion continues to be fought. Seheron is still kabethari in Qunari eyes – a land to be conquered and converted, literally "those who need to be taught".

RACES AND RELIGION

Humans

The most numerous, yet the most divided of all the races. Only four times have they ever united under a single cause, and it has been many centuries since the last. Religion and the Chantry play a large part in human society. It distinguishes them culturally from elves and dwarves more than anything else. While the other races dwindle, humanity has thrived and continues to spread.

Humans in times past worshipped a draconic pantheon of Old Gods, dragonlords that supposedly once ruled over Thedas and now slumber beneath the earth. But the people would come to suffer instead under the yoke of the Tevinter Imperium, a vast empire famously ruled by lords of dark magic, the magisters. Eventually, the Imperium was challenged from the south by a barbarian uprising, the armies led by Maferath and his wife, the prophet Andraste.

Andraste brought the teachings of a new god, the Maker, and her word spread quickly. The oppressed masses of the Imperium rose up in rebellion to support the invading barbarians and eventually most of the south fell to their might. Andraste was not stopped in her Exalted March until she was betrayed by her husband: jealous of her power, Maferath turned Andraste over to the Tevinter archon and she was burned at the stake.

The Chant of Light would say that the Maker turned his back on humanity when she died. He would only return and make the world into a paradise when the Chant of Light was sung from all corners of the world, and so the Chantry began to spread. The clerics of the Chantry were oppressed until the legendary emperor Drakon of Orlais converted and took up their cause, spreading the Chantry throughout all the lands that he conquered in its name. In modern times, the Chantry has spread throughout the known world, its power unquestioned even as it begins to give way to internal strife.

Elves

When they were the first and only race, the elves are said to have been immortals who lived in harmony with nature. Then came the "shemlen", human migrants from the north, and before long the great forests were making way for towns and cities. These quicklings, whose lives blinked by in an instant, were considered no more than a pest. But too late did the elves discover that contact with humans brought disease and even caused the immortal races to "quicken" – to age, and finally to die. Horrified at this, they withdrew to their home of Elvhenan before humanity's relentless expansion and broke off all contact.

In 981 Ancient, the Tevinter Imperium took the act of isolation as hostility and declared war. The fabled elven city of Arlathan was besieged but held out for six grim years. Eventually, the magisters resorted to an unprecedented blood ritual that dragged the entire city beneath the earth, obliterating it. The few survivors were enslaved and all evidence of their ancient culture was lost.

Despite being freed upon the Imperium's collapse, the damage was done: the elves had lost their immortality, much language and history, and they blamed humanity for it. They attempted to rebuild a homeland in the Dales, but their pagan practices caused the Chantry to declare an Exalted March against them. Defeated again, the elves themselves were divided. The proud nobility became homeless wanderers known as the Dalish, traveling in groups and stubbornly continuing to worship their gods and maintain their traditions. The other elves became bitterly resigned to their fate and now live amongst humankind as "city elves": second-class citizens, servants, and laborers who have all but forgotten the proud folk they once were.

Dwarves

It is well known that dwarves are a stout, bearded race, often making up in width what they lack in height. The stereotype also suggests a hardy constitution, as sickness is thought to be rare among the dwarven folk. But their proximity to the darkspawn means their numbers are dwindling – a low fertility rate, combined with the steady rate of fatalities in battle, means the population of dwarves has been falling steadily for nearly a thousand years.

Their steadfast nature has been a blessing and a curse. It has granted them the mental fortitude to survive in conditions that would kill any other race, and the patience to develop their engineering to a level of technology that surpasses everyone but the Qunari (the dwarves have mastered clockwork and limited steam power). They have also developed some immunity to lyrium. However, their refusal to accept change over tradition has stultified their society with a rigid caste system, in which everything a dwarf can expect from life is determined at birth. The worst victims of this system are the casteless, dwarves who lost their legal standing by committing a crime, are descendant of criminals, or who have relinquished caste to live on the surface. Eventually they may end up running with the Carta, the criminal organization whose gangs can always find unpleasant work for the desperate.

The dwarves don't have a religion, per se, nor do they believe in gods. Instead, their philosophy promotes excellence and an almost intimate tie to the rock that houses them. Referring reverentially to the Stone, the dwarves speak of it as being alive. They are the Stone's children: they respect her, they fear her, they cherish her, and they give thanks to her for protecting them and providing them with her bounty.

Worship is reserved for ancestors. The greatest dwarves form the stuff of legend, their achievements earning the status of Paragon. In death, a Paragon is said to become one with the densest stone at the base of all mountains – quite literally, a part of the foundation upon which all dwarven society rests. In the thaig of Orzammar, enormous statues of past Paragons hold up the cavernous ceiling. This honor isn't restricted solely to warriors: some of the greatest Paragons have been smiths and artisans, commoners as well as kings.

Qunari

Bronze-skinned giants who sailed from a land far beyond the Boeric Ocean, the Qunari are a mystery to most. Technologically advanced, they reached the shores of Par Vollen in fabulous ships and immediately embarked on a conquest of human territory. The cannons of their dreadnaughts laid waste to the mainland, striking first into Rivain and then Seheron. On land, the glitter of their steel armor accentuated their physical superiority. Surprised by an unknown enemy, the defenders were no match for regimented Qunari discipline. Human history books may call this the First Qunari War, but there was little resistance to record as they marched deep into Tevinter for ten years.

They were finally repelled by an Exalted March, a crusade declared in 7:25 Storm that united the human forces on a scale unseen since the previous Blight. Its secret weapon was the Circle of Magi: the Qunari disdain for magic had not prepared them for its advanced potential, and their artillery was countered with volleys of fireballs. By 7:84 Storm, the invading army had withered and was ready to make a truce. All sides gathered in Rivain to sign a peace treaty, the Llomeryn Accords, with the exception of the Tevinters.

The Qun

The horned race formerly called the *kossith* only became known as the Qunari after the prophet Koslun bestowed upon them the Qun philosophy and religion. The teachings of the Qun turned their society into a model of efficiency and order. That order rested on unity, so no deviant beliefs would be tolerated again.

Rigorously structured, Qunari society has dispensed with the family unit. Couples are paired for breeding purely to reproduce, and all children are handed to the Tamassran to be raised. Priests and teachers, the Tamassran evaluate the talents of their wards and assign them a station in life at the age of twelve. Gender precludes certain roles, so only men may become warriors while women are favored for administrative tasks. Not all Qunari are born with horns, and those without can be assigned envoy roles as a Ben-Hassrath.

The Qun philosophy regards magic as a corrupting influence, at odds with self-discipline: the more you attempt to master it, the more it masters you. But everyone must have a role to play, so those saarebas born with magical talent are placed on a lead and entrusted to a handler or arvaarad. If found practicing forbidden magic, their tongues are cut out to prevent them corrupting others.

To the Qunari, humanity is a lesser race that still practices forbidden magic and would benefit from the higher order that the Qun brings. To humans, the Qunari are tyrannical zealots with an unfathomable disregard for individual rights. Though a delicate peace exists currently between the Qunari and humanity, future aggression is almost assured: the Qun is an implacable doctrine that will not be denied.

Darkspawn & Blight

Darkspawn is the collective name for the corrupted creatures that dwell underground, infesting the Deep Roads and occasionally finding their way to the surface. Wild and savage, these marauders have presented a threat ever since they were first discovered by the dwarves.

In times of Blight, an archdemon arises that can marshal the bestial darkspawn into an organized army. Thousands swarm from the deep, destroying all life and spreading their taint across the world.

The horde's presence brings the Blight disease, a plague that can leave the land twisted and blackened. Even when slain, the darkspawn's poisonous blood defiles the soil and the animals that feed upon it. Madness and physical deformity commonly afflicts those exposed to the corruption. The Blight disease is ultimately fatal.

Slumbering beneath the earth, the beings known as Old Gods call out in their dreams. The darkspawn hear them, searching and digging in the hope of finding one. But they bring their corruption to the Old Gods they disturb just as they do to all else, and so spawn an archdemon. This draconic entity communicates directly to the mind of the horde.

In the events of Dragon Age: Origins – Awakening, The Architect proposed that the darkspawn capture females to create broodmothers. Though few survive the transmutation, it explains why the different types resemble monstrous imitations of the surface races. Corrupted human mothers produce hurlock broods; genlocks originate from dwarves; the shriek from elves; while the ogre echoes the Qunari.

The Chantry teaches that darkspawn are the Maker's curse for the arrogance of men and that the Magisters of old Tevinter used their magic to open portals to the Golden City of the Maker, believing they could step into heaven itself. But their presence in this holiest of places instantly corrupted it with their sin. In His anger, the Maker transformed them into vile monstrosities and cast them down to the sunless depths of the earth, thereafter turning his back on his creation. Only when the Chant of Light is sung from all four corners of the world will the Maker return.

Magic

Magic is hard work, demanding training and discipline to achieve specific, supernatural effects that are often usefully formalized as spells. A mage cannot simply make a wish and point a finger.

As a matter of fact, not everyone can cast magic, and mana is the latent ability that defines a mage. Often inherited, it is a potential that may lay hidden and unknown in the mage unless drawn out by another. But those who possess such a potential have a special connection to the Fade – the spirit plane – and may draw upon its power. Mana is a measurement of one's ability to channel energy from the Fade, and this energy is expended in the practice of magic. Just as the Fade can be reshaped by those who have grasped its nature, so this world can be manipulated by magic.

Lyrium

The most precious of substances, lyrium is a catalyst for enchantment and magical activities. Hazardous in its raw form. lyrium is safer when processed, becoming a shimmering silver liquid – though no less potent. The ore occurs naturally in veins and deep natural deposits: the dwarves' resistance to lyrium and their unparalleled expertise in mining underpins a trade more lucrative than silverite or veridium. Nevertheless, tales of madness, side-effects and death continue to plague those who deal in it.

The legendary reputation of dwarven weapons and armor rests on their Smith Caste's talent for working lyrium into steel. It is used in the production of enchantments, and by the Formari branch of the Circle of Magi. Lyrium consumption strengthens a mage's relation to the Fade, thereby boosting mana. Even the templars are said to indulge its use for the purpose of anti-magic.

Forbidden Magic

Blood magic is the art of fueling spells with life force, specifically in the form of blood, instead of mana. It was common practice, at one time, for a magister to keep a number of slaves on hand so that he could use their blood to bolster the casting of spells that were physically beyond his abilities.

Over time, however, the Imperium discovered types of spells that could only be worked by blood. Although lyrium will allow a mage to send his conscious mind into the Fade, blood would allow him to find the sleeping minds of others; to view their dreams, and even influence or dominate their thoughts. Just as treacherous, blood magic can also be used to allow demons physical entry into the real world.

The use of blood magic was criminalized with the inception of the Circle of Magi, as common wisdom holds that there is no way to use blood magic with good intentions. Inevitably, even blood mages who tap their own blood find a need for the power of others, or find a need to control minds or summon demons.

Maleficar and Apostates

While maleficarum practice forbidden magic, apostates, by contrast, are those practicing normal magic outside the sanction of the Circle of Magi. All mages outside the Circle's control, even those not practicing the forbidden arts, are considered dangerous as they can fall prey to a demon and become an abomination. They are hunted by the martial arm of the Chantry – the templars – to be placed safely in the custody of the Circle. Ironically, this hunt sometimes forces errant mages into blood magic or demon-summoning in order to escape.

There are still, however, many remote places where maleficarum and apostates exist quietly or in disguise. In some remote areas, ancient folk-magic traditions persist: the shamans in barbarian villages, the local alchemist who makes love charms, the hermit witch who casts curses on intruders, and the Dalish Keepers are all technically mages without Circle training. Most of these magic users are aware that they are apostates or maleficarum in the eyes of the Chantry and thus tend to be circumspect and reclusive. Because these individuals are subject to demonic possession, tales of witches and shamans going mad are quite common.

The Fade

Where do we go when we dream? The Fade is the spirit plane, the realm of thought and the source of all magic, only separated from this world by the metaphysical Veil. It is the domain of the Maker, whose once-golden city sits at the center. Shifting and impermanent, its puzzling architecture is familiar to us from our dreams. Unable to create for themselves, the spirits endlessly re-shape their world from whatever they glimpse in ours. Only a mage, with the aid of lyrium, may learn to explore the dreamworld consciously – and at risk of permanent disconnection from their body. While most mortals forget their time in the Fade upon waking, mages are cursed to recall it.

From any point in the Fade you might look up to catch sight of the Black City, the corrupted palace of the absent Maker. An approaching traveler will find it remains at a constant distance, always beyond reach.

Spirits and Demons

Sleeping visitors of the Fade realm find their most comforting thoughts under the watchful presence of its benign inhabitants. Spirits of fortitude and compassion weave dreams that strengthen the soul of the waking, while more powerful spirits of justice, faith and hope can elicit visions and promote divine epiphanies in their mortal wards.

For each of the five groups of benevolent spirits, it is their counterparts, the demons, who are the source of the fear regarding mages and forbidden magic. Common lore says the spirits were the Maker's first children, beautiful but flawed, and that some grew jealous of the creatures he subsequently created and imbued with the divine spark of life.

In times past, the Tevinter lords summoned demons to do their bidding against their enemies. Such pacts now count as forbidden magic, but it is not necessary to invite a demon willingly. By their nature, mages are constantly at risk of becoming the conduit for a demon's appearance.

Demons can possess the bodies of any susceptible creature, both the living and the dead, if the Veil between this world and the Fade is thin enough for them to cross between the two. It is enough merely to dream, for that is when mortal minds wander the Fade and may be lured by their whispers. But demons are most empowered when they can feed on emotions – rage, sloth, hunger, desire, pride – and these determine the form of demonic manifestation.

The abomination is the most powerful and destructive force of all, occurring when a demon possesses a living being with magical ability. It is the fear of unleashing such a terror that prompted the establishment of the Circle of Magi, where mages could be contained and monitored – culled, if necessary – to prevent an outbreak.

Economy and Money

Although the names and appearance of coins vary from nation to nation, they follow the same system. One hundred copper pieces are worth one silver piece, and one hundred silver pieces are worth one gold piece. At one time, the size and purity of these coins differed from one land to the next, which meant that some regions would not accept another's coinage in trade, so the dwarven merchant guilds developed a standard and refused to accept currency that did not meet their specifications. Most nations quickly converted. Particularly expensive transactions may be completed in "bars" (solid bricks) and "strands" (stacked groups), but those are the province of merchant guilds and government, rarely seen in day-to-day commerce.

Piece	Fereldan Name	Orlesian Name	Equivalence
1 gold	1 sovereign	1 royal	100 silvers
1 silver	1 silver	1 crown	100 coppers
1 copper	1 bit	1 penny	-

The Landsmeet

When Ferelden was divided among barbaric tribes, the banns (or barons) recognized that issues affecting them all required a common decision. The Landsmeet was the solution, during which each bann was guaranteed safe passage and a truce throughout the meeting.

In the Landsmeet, the banns have chosen to fight against the occupation of the Imperium; to repel the werewolves; and to follow Maferath and Andraste into history. Since then, the Landsmeet has been an official legislative body, and it can override the king on any matter of law, although the Landsmeet tends not to exercise its power if the king is strong.

Originally, the location changed with each Landsmeet, but since the crowning of the first king, they have taken place exclusively in Denerim. The Landsmeet occurs at least once a year, although since King Maric acceded to the throne, it has begun to meet once per season. Most noble families thus maintain an estate in Denerim to house themselves and their entourages when they are in the Fereldan capital.

The Timeline

Dragon Age II takes its name from the Chantry calendar, adopted to replace those of Tevinter and the individual races. The year is 9:30 Dragon, or the thirtieth year of the ninth age. Each age spans one hundred years, and it is during the ninety-ninth year that the clerics of Val Royeaux watch for portents and omens of the future. They advise the Divine on a new name for the following age, one that will foretell the century to come: the sighting of a mature dragon, believed extinct, was said to herald a time of violence and upheaval.

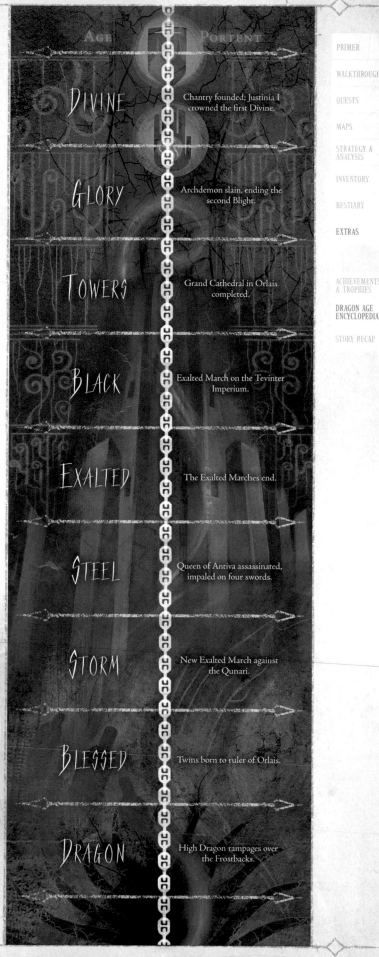

Age	Portent
Divine	Chantry founded; Justinia I crowned the first Divine.
Glory	Archdemon slain, ending the second Blight.
Towers	Grand Cathedral in Orlais completed.
Black	Exalted March on the Tevinter Imperium.
Exalted	The Exalted Marches end.
Steel	Queen of Antiva assassinated, impaled on four swords.
Storm	New Exalted March against the Qunari.
Blessed	Twins born to ruler of Orlais.
Dragon	High Dragon rampages over the Frostbacks.

MAJOR GROUPS & ORGANIZATIONS

The Chantry and the Templars

The Chantry is the church of the dominant religion in Thedas. Predominantly human in its following, it was established by those followers of the prophet Andraste who refused to abandon their faith after her death. Andrastians worship the Maker, the creator of all things, in the hope that they can one day be forgiven. The primary text of the religion is the Chant of Light, a collection of prayers and parables that spring from the prophet's teachings.

The first person converted to the cause was supposedly Hessarian, the archon who ordered Andraste's execution. The Chant tells that Hessarian felt such remorse as he watched Andraste burn that he ran her through with his sword to save her from a slow and painful death. The sword thus became an emblem of mercy in Chantry symbolism, and Hessarian allowed worship of the Maker to flourish in his own search for redemption. But it was emperor Kordilius Drakon I of Orlais who formalized the cult into a religion and created the first Chantry.

The central belief of the Chantry is that mankind has sinned against the Maker, namely through the worship of Old Gods; through the practice of forbidden magic; and the final transgression of the magisters, to trespass in heaven itself, imagining they could usurp Him from his Golden City. Since then, he has forsaken us and left us to face our punishment in the form of the darkspawn. But if the Chant of Light should ring out from the four corners of the world, the Maker will hear and return to restore order.

That act of redemption has been interpreted evangelically as a need to preach, to proselytize, to carry the message and convert followers – by force, when all else fails. And so the Chantry established their military arm – the Order of the Templars – to enforce the prohibitions on apostasy and heretical crimes. The templars have adopted the flaming sword as their insignia.

All Chantry priestesses are female, on the basis that Andraste was a woman. Men can be brothers, serving as academics and initiates, but it is a junior position and non-ordained. Those who have received religious and martial instruction while being raised in the Chantry may become templars. At the head of the Chantry is the Divine, who leads from her seat in the Grand Cathedral of Val Royeaux. Below her are the grand clerics, some of whom administer the chantries of major cities.

The Chantry permeates human society in every nation: at least one temple can be found in every village. It delivers practical services to the community, caring for the sick and collecting alms for the poor. The Chantry provides hospitality to travelers and a public network of communications. Should an illiterate commoner need to send word to another town, the Chantry's educated priests write and send the letter for him.

With so much influence over the people, the Chantry can also exert considerable political pressure on the ruling classes in many areas of concern. In extraordinary times, and in deference to Andraste, the Divine may also be moved to declare an Exalted March. These religious crusades have mobilized armies of thousands to destroy the heretical enemies of the Maker, the most recent being led against the Qunari.

The Circle of Magi

The Chantry does not forbid magic completely. The commandment of the Maker states that magic should serve man rather than rule him. The Circle of Magi was thus created as a way of legitimately and safely using magic. It keeps close tabs on those with magical ability. Affinity for magic usually surfaces by adolescence, and those found to have significant magical ability are required to join the nearest Circle of Magi and act under its supervision. To practice magic and not join a Circle is a capital offense, and mages who do so are hunted as apostates. Mages practicing the forbidden arts such as blood magic, by contrast, are labeled maleficarum, and are hunted mercilessly.

The mages of today's Circle of Magi do their best to avoid the appearance of corruption, fearing a return to the days of persecution and the loss of some rather fragile rights. Templars are ostensibly present by the invitation of the Circle; though in truth they are stationed as watchdogs in every tower, conducting investigations at the slightest whiff of dangerous magic use. The Circle suffers this indignity as a necessity.

A first enchanter, who oversees the numerous mages and their apprentices, heads each Circle. He or she assumes this position for life and retains the right to choose his successor, taking into consideration the "strong suggestions" of the templars, which, until recent years, were rarely contravened. When required, the first enchanters will congregate in the city of Cumberland, at their college, to elect a grand enchanter. This grand enchanter is the Circle of Magi's direct representative to the Chantry who also attends the Grand Cathedral in Val Royeaux and acts as an advisor to the Divine and as an observer.

The Tranquil

Apprentices in the Circle of Magi must pass the secretive trial of the Harrowing to prove their resistance to demonic possession. Conducted in co-operation with the templars, who keep an executioner on hand, the test exposes those who are too great a risk to be allowed to live. But if there is already doubt about an apprentice's chances then, alternatively, they may be put forward for the Rite of Tranquility, or even request it themselves.

The Rite severs the apprentice's connection to the Fade, thereby eliminating their potential to attract demons across the Veil. The more contentious side-effect is that it removes all capacity for both magic and emotion. No longer distracted by dreams or desires, or feelings of any kind, the coldly detached Tranquil demonstrate a superior faculty of concentration. They commonly put this to use in the painstaking and fastidious creation of magical items, and the Circle's Formari branch of enchanters is exclusively Tranquil.

Grey Wardens

A renowned group of fearless warriors, mages, and rangers, the Grey Wardens dedicate themselves to the eradication of the darkspawn. They are said to sense the presence of the horde and have greater knowledge of the tactics required to fight them. Theirs are the only records that contain details of forays into the underground caverns, telling of the broodmothers and detailing the archdemons that have risen so far, to be destroyed at the Grey Wardens' hands. The nations of humanity once gladly tithed to the Grey Wardens and sent them not only food and equipment, but also a steady stream of new recruits.

In better days, the fabled fortress of Weisshaupt once housed thousands of men and a fleet of griffons ready for battle. However, the organization has fallen into obscurity for many. Although they are still respected and sometimes even feared for their martial prowess, they are still largely thought irrelevant in lands where the darkspawn have not appeared for centuries. Only in the Anderfels, the victim of continual invasions, do the Grey Wardens retain some semblance of the influence they once had. Here the Order was formed by ex-soldiers of the Imperium, battle-hardened veterans who renounced their oaths of fealty and swore instead to reclaim the land from the darkspawn curse.

Candidates for the Grey Wardens are usually selected for a specific talent, perhaps their superior will, stamina, or combat prowess (whether physical or magical). If necessary, a Warden Commander can invoke powers of conscription to recruit from other organizations. But there is also mercy shown to those with the Blight disease, as the Wardens share a terrible secret.

New candidates are compelled to undergo the Joining, an initiation ritual that involves drinking a carefully prepared mixture containing darkspawn blood. Some are killed instantly. But not all, and those that survive receive the darkspawn corruption. They develop a deep connection with the darkspawn, sensing their presence and hearing the archdemon when it calls out to the horde. They develop immunity to the Blight disease, for which there is no other cure. They become Grey Wardens, carrying a darkness within their light. And they will likely die within thirty years as the poison claims them. As such, they often spend their last days foraging into the Deep Roads to take as many of the darkspawn down with them, an honorable fate that earns them great respect among the dwarves.

The forfeiture does not end there. An archdemon cannot be killed conventionally because its spirit simply passes to the nearest soulless darkspawn to be reborn whenever its body is destroyed. But the Grey Warden, a tainted being, may also draw the archdemon's spirit. The Warden who delivers the deathblow thus tricks the creature's soul into their own body – ending the Blight, but with fatal results for both.

The motto of the Grey Wardens? In war, victory. In peace, vigilance. In death, sacrifice.

The Crows

When a love rival vanishes or a young man drops dead in the prime of life, it is normally regarded a mystery. But not in Antiva, where fingers will always point to the House of Crows. As the most feared guild of assassins, spies and thieves ever to offer their services to the rich and powerful, the Crows thrive as profitably on their infamy as on the cruel efficiency of the dark agents they train from youth.

Hence, no treasure in Antiva is guarded so fiercely as that of the Crows' reputation. Their code of honor, if it does not sully the word, demands that contracts are met and agreements are kept. Failure to eliminate a mark means the life of the operative is also forfeit – though one has been rumored to elude his unhappy Guildmasters through skill or fate.

The Felicisima Armada

Operating out of the coastal city of Llomerryn, the pirate captains of the Rialto Bay are as numerous as the tales told of them – if not always as tall. They were commonly known as the Raiders of the Waking Sea, making brazen incursions along the coastal trade routes all the way down to Orlais. But when the Qunari invasion threatened the future of their lucrative merchant bounties, the Raiders agreed to an unusual contract. Granted privateer status under a single flag, the Felicisima Armada gathered together the largest fleet of scoundrels, smugglers and corsairs the world has ever seen. Having outwitted and outmaneuvered the authorities for years, the Raiders turned their dirty tricks on the fearsome Qunari dreadnaughts and even launched assaults on Par Vollen. Today's merchants must now regret that the Armada remains loosely intact, its leaders having seen the profit of working together.

MAJOR CHARACTERS

Spoiler Alert!

The following pages contain character profiles that reveal the personal secrets and motivations held by the main characters of Dragon Age II. Because these facts are normally revealed through companion quests and conversations, it is strongly recommended that you do not consult this section until you have played the game and explored the possibilities for yourself.

Hawke

The one certain fact about Hawke is that he or she ends up as the Champion of Kirkwall. Players opting for a female lead will become Marian Hawke by default, otherwise taking the male default of Garrett Hawke. The rest of the aspects of Hawke's personality, appearance, actions and interactions with others are freely determined by the player. Whether Hawke is merciful and generous or ruthless and mean; supportive, dismissive, or always looking for the humorous response; in favor of the mages or the templars; all of these choices are entirely up to the player and determine the outcome of most of the events that occur throughout the storyline.

Hawke's Lineage

Hawke's father was no less than a Fereldan mage, a practitioner whose apostasy forced the family to relocate to the quiet outskirts of rural Lothering. Keeping a low profile and always looking to stay one step ahead of the authorities, Malcolm Hawke was able to keep the family together and raise his offspring in a manner that nurtured their individual talents. Malcolm died three years before the events of the game's prologue, leaving the future Champion as head of the household.

The Champion can also cite a noble bloodline, if a discredited one, from his mother, Leandra Amell. Leandra was supposed to marry a noble in Kirkwall, one Comte de Launcet, but she fell in love with Malcolm Hawke – a Fereldan apostate – and moved away with him. It is Leandra who was meant to inherit her parents' estate when they died, but as she was in Ferelden, Gamlen took it and eventually squandered it away with his gambling habit.

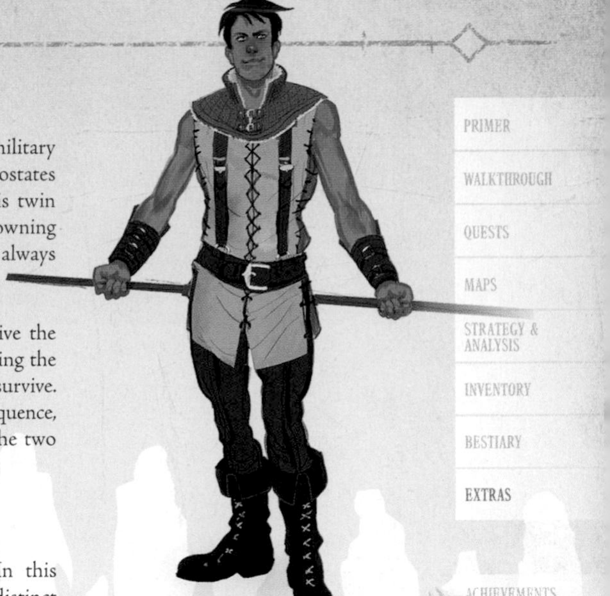

Carver

The Champion's brash younger brother, Carver signed up for military service immediately after his father died. Raised in a family of apostates but never showing any sign of the magical talent that made his twin sister Bethany special, he hid his feelings of inferiority behind clowning and risk-taking. Worse, any attempt to prove his own worth was always eclipsed by Hawke.

If your Champion is a rogue or warrior, Carver will not survive the Prologue. His life is also in peril if he catches Blight disease during the Deep Roads expedition, and he must become a Grey Warden to survive. Otherwise, his future rests with the templars. He will distance himself from the family as a consequence, but with the passing of years it is possible to develop a mutual respect that will again find the two brothers fighting side by side in times of crisis.

Bethany

Bethany is the Champion's sister and also Carver's twin. In this generation, be it gift or curse, Bethany inherited the bloodline's distinct aptitude for magic. She can turn her skill to any mystical discipline, given the right opportunities, but the Hawkes have chosen to keep Bethany's latent talents hidden away from the prying eyes of the templars and the Circle of Magi.

If your Champion is a mage, Bethany will not survive the Prologue. Her life is also forfeit if she accompanies Hawke to the Deep Roads unless she joins the Grey Wardens, thereafter becoming a distant figure who patrols the far reaches of civilization. Otherwise, she is outed by templars in the Champion's absence and inducted into the Circle of Magi.

Varric Tethras

Born into a merchant family, Varric is the youngest child of the noble House Tethras. While his brother Bartrand is old enough to remember life in Orzammar, Varric was raised on the surface after the family was exiled. A "skyer" by birth, and a city-dweller to boot, he has never belonged to a dwarven homeland and wouldn't know how to work the Stone if his ancestors were standing over him.

Outwardly, Varric gives the impression of a flamboyant dilettante, all mouth and chest hair; a rascal son from a wealthy family whose accidental inheritance now sustains many a tavern. True enough, he does enjoy spinning a fanciful yarn and expects a full tankard to keep the vocal chords moist throughout the telling. But Varric has found the perfect cover for a shrewd spymaster, his network of contacts feeding him inside knowledge of everything happening in the city.

In time, even Varric must come to terms with taking on his brother's responsibilities. Everyone involved with the Champion's rise to power finds their lives unexpectedly altered in some way.

Aveline Vallen

Aveline's father was a proud Chevalier, forced to flee Orlais when his patron became a victim of court intrigue. Reduced to running a Ferelden farmstead, he named his daughter after the legendary first female knight and invested far more in her than the gift of his training in chivalrous combat. But on seeing her king fall at Ostagar, then her husband Wesley claimed by Blight, Aveline would form her own opinions of loyalty, honor and sacrifice.

Aveline puts her talents to good use in defending Kirkwall as an officer of the city guard, eliminating the corruption of her superiors and asserting the viscount's authority to maintain the peace. Her idea of duty extends to protective feelings about Hawke, though it is solely in a sisterly sense.

In time, Aveline can forgive herself for Wesley's death and even come to love another in guardsman Donnic Hendyr, though this is one area in which Aveline feels less than adept. It will take the Champion's involvement to ensure that she doesn't make an entire mess of things, as Aveline's knowledge of matters of the heart has too long focused on how to run a blade through one.

Isabela

Rivaini by birth, pirate by profession, trouble by nature: Isabela has the kind of reputation that doesn't simply precede but also chases her, hurriedly, from port to port. Marooned in Kirkwall, the swashbuckling scoundrel has instead been making waves on land in pursuit of treasure and kicks. But her stories of shipwreck prove to have as much veracity as Varric's yarns after a fifth tankard of Garbolg's quaffing ale, and she may come to play a crucial role in the city's Qunari affair.

Her vessel was actually scuttled by cannon fire while fleeing the Qunari dreadnought – the accepted international greeting for someone who has just stolen the Tome of Koslun from the Arishok. Isabela imagined that the relic could pay off her debt to the scheming Antivan merchant, Castillon – not that it would cause a crisis with the Qunari.

Dragon Age: Origins players who previously 'encountered' Isabela in the Denerim brothel, The Pearl, will know that she's always interested in a profitable dalliance. Those who disappoint her eventually feel the coldness of either her twin blades or her tongue, with some dispute over which can cut the deepest.

Merrill

Dry tradition was certainly never enough for Merrill. We first met her in the Dalish Elf path of Dragon Age: Origins, where her apprenticeship to the Dalish Keeper versed her in the old ways. Merrill has come to believe that the elves hold themselves back by refusing to reclaim the magical powers they once commanded. She believes passionately in what she is now doing, even if it leaves her branded an outcast by the very people she seeks to protect.

If the player chooses to become involved in her plight, even romantically, they will discover that Merrill walks a tightrope. She has made a demonic pact to acquire powers of forbidden magic, hoping that she can restore an arcane eluvian mirror and learn more from its study.

Anders

As a gifted adolescent, Anders was captured by the templars many times but always managed to escape. Persecution planted in him a seed of rebellion that has since grown into a consuming political activism.

Becoming a Grey Warden during the events of the Awakening expansion, the idealistic Anders appealed to the spirit of Justice not to ignore the plight of the world's mages. Torn from the Fade and lost on the wrong side of the Veil, this wandering spirit warrior agreed to merge with Anders in his pursuit of a noble cause.

But the bargain was also a curse, twisted by the Grey Warden's zeal and anger once invoked. When Hawke chances upon him in Kirkwall, Anders appears to be leading a life of charity and atonement that gives little hint of the alter-ego that is Vengeance. He has fallen in with the mage underground movement and his beliefs are propelling him along a dangerous path, finding no solution without violence. Healer or killer? Anders is able to unleash a terrible rage that is just as likely to claim innocent lives.

Fenris

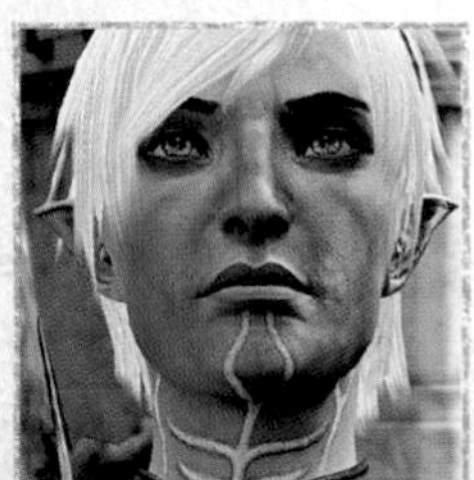

Indentured to the Tevinter Magister Danarius while still a child, this elven slave was destined for a lifetime of servitude. Luminescent lyrium tattoos were agonizingly burnt into his skin through a painstaking process, wiping his memory and forging him into a magical weapon as if he were living, malleable metal to be shaped and enchanted with runes. Fenris was kept as a bodyguard, a killing machine, a hound on the leash of his owner – until his escape.

The tragedy of his condition is that Fenris chose it for himself, fought for it, in sacrifice for a family he has since forgotten. Fenris is eventually led to face his old master and discover a betrayal; if the Champion intervenes to spare the sister, Varania, then Fenris may learn the truth of his past – but it cannot prevent him feeling alone in the world.

Sebastian Vael

Gambling, drinking and womanizing were Sebastian's first salvation: if his family hadn't committed him to the Chantry in an effort to clean up his act, he would have been killed alongside them. Sebastian was once the playboy prince of Starkhaven, a neighboring Free Marches state, but he has been forced to endure exile since the ruling Vaels were assassinated in a bloody coup d'etat.

The Champion was Sebastian's second salvation, taking up his cause and tracking down the mercenaries who deposed his family. Realizing they were no more than hired hands, Sebastian confronted the power behind the coup – the Harimanns of Kirkwall – and discovered a desire demon at the root.

Sebastian's third salvation was the Maker Himself, as he now finds a strength of faith in the vows he once took half-heartedly. He's still at liberty to assist the Champion whenever called on, though: Grand Cleric Elthina isn't entirely convinced that the exiled prince is ready to re-enter the Chantry, and she appreciates his somewhat earthier view of the secular world.

Bartrand Tethras

On first meeting, Bartrand shows little interest in granting the Champion a place on his Deep Roads expedition. It takes Varric to explain that the fastest way to his brother's heart is with a sound cash investment.

Unlike his sibling, Bartrand was born in Orzammar and vaguely remembers his childhood in a noble dwarven household. The shame that led to his family's exile only robbed him of his birthright, but Bartrand's wistful longing for that privileged existence has turned to bitterness. Resentful of the human society he must now endure, Bartrand's passion is for money and the relief it can bring. He has established many lucrative enterprises and useful contacts through the old dwarf network of the kalnas and has set about creating a small empire as if the ceiling of Orzammar were still above him. If it will make surface living more bearable, anything that can buy a taste of the old days is worth the sacrifice.

Following the expedition, possession of the lyrium statue begins to warp Bartrand's mind even further. Exposure leads to madness, though it is the Champion's involvement that determines whether Varric takes pity or revenge.

Knight-Commander Meredith

The Order of Templars exerts considerable influence in Kirkwall, though its warriors are merely the steel gauntlet that sheathes the knight-commander's political grip. A crusader to her core, Meredith's strength springs from her belief that what she does is right and just. If left uncontrolled, magic would throw the world into chaos or expose it to demonic invasion. Harsh actions are thus justified if it protects the people from the corrupting influence of forbidden powers.

In the end sequences of the game, it is revealed that Meredith was the purchaser of the lyrium statue found during the Deep Roads expedition. She has had it reshaped, forged into a weapon with which to smite magic. Knowing Bartrand's fate, the player can surmise that Meredith's erratic behavior isn't entirely down to her conviction.

First Enchanter Orsino

As the first enchanter, Orsino holds the unenviable position of being in command of the Circle of Magi – in reality, and certainly in Kirkwall, a title granting little more power than that of prisoners' representative. It is a testament to his sense of duty that he tirelessly defends his quarantined wards against templar accusations, even while some regard him as a traitor and apologist.

Orsino is determined to make life better for his charges by standing up to Meredith and demonstrating that the Circle can act for the good of the people. As both a mage and an elf – still a slave race in this part of the world – he understands how fear leads to oppression. But he is also quick to overlook the threat posed by the knight-commander's enshrined Rights of Annulment, and is perhaps too willing to excuse the transgressions of his initiates as a consequence.

Grand Cleric Elthina

Perched in Kirkwall's Hightown, the Chantry looks down on the city with the lofty distance of the Maker himself. A similar sense of permanence surrounds Elthina, the grand cleric in charge, whose mollifying presence has often resolved the city's power struggles. Many squabbles between templars and the Circle have been pacified by Elthina's interventions down the years, and it's testament to her earnest good nature that she has managed to retain the utmost respect of all concerned while holding the post for as long as anyone can remember. But while she is loved by the people, Elthina is not always strong or decisive on their behalf. Ultimately, the grand cleric bears a responsibility for relinquishing too much authority to the more aggressive knight-commander.

Cassandra Pentaghast

Cassandra belongs to an exclusive order within the templars called the Seekers of Truth, as indicated by her uniform's insignia of an all-seeing eye. While ordinary templars are the Chantry's martial enforcers, policing the realm for magical apostasy, the Seekers are its investigators and inspectors. They uncover the hidden practice of magic and seek to stamp out its corruption, even within their own ranks.

As her surname reveals, Cassandra is a member of the royal family of Nevarra. She can trace her ancestry back to the figures of legend who, hundreds of years ago, nearly exterminated the dragons once and for all. Introduced in this game as the skeptical audience for Varric's oft-unreliable account, Cassandra is likely destined to play a much greater role in the future.

The Arishok

A Qunari dreadnought ran aground near Kirkwall after a fierce storm, stranding an entire crew of warriors and their general, the Arishok. They quickly established a makeshift camp in Lowtown, supposedly waiting for ships from the main fleet to collect them. Under the peace treaty with the Qunari, the city could hardly ask them to leave: but it is fair to say that their presence has been difficult and undesirable.

In truth, the Arishok cannot leave. He has lost a holy relic, the Tome of Koslun, and returning home without it would bring a dishonor worse than death. But the discord and unruliness of human society offends his Qunari sense of harmony, testing his patience and his tolerance of the heathen races.

"Arishok" is actually a title for a military leader, not a name, and it is an aspect of Qunari culture to define self-identity by one's assigned station or purpose. Qunari generals are also warriors rather than tacticians, leading from the front, so the Arishok outranks his troops by a measure of strength, physique and prowess. Supremely confident, he elicits total obedience from his men.

Flemeth

Many tales are told about the Witch of the Wilds, a very old and powerful sorceress. Some of the tastier ones are even true, as Flemeth has lived long enough to make them happen. Hawke may not realize he has cut a deal with a shapeshifter whose guile is more dangerous than her dragon form, but the fates are hard to defy when your life is saved by a figure of legend.

In Dragon Age: Origins, Morrigan recovered Flemeth's black grimoire and learned the dread secret of her mother's longevity. For centuries, the Witch had seduced and slain the menfolk of the Chasind tribes until she produced a suitable girl. She would dutifully raise the child until it came of age. But when the time was right, Flemeth would steal the daughter's body as a vessel for her own spirit, extending her life through successive generations.

King Cailan Theirin & Queen Anora

Son of the respected King Maric, Cailan was the first of his line to oversee a land free of foreign rule for two generations. At peace with Orlais, Ferelden began to consolidate and prosper as an independent nation. But peacetime did not always sit so agreeably with Cailan: a good man, but one who longed to make his name by heroic deeds. Sensible governance and diplomacy were more the forte of his shrewd consort, Queen Anora. The young king thus jumped at the chance to quash a Fifth Blight, marshalling his own regiment at Ostagar in his eagerness to fight darkspawn alongside the Grey Wardens.

Cailan was betrayed by his general and Anora's father, Teyrn Loghain, who withdrew the support of the main army. Hawke, Carver, Aveline and Wesley were among the few survivors to make it out of the massacre in Ostagar that night. Their king did not.

Alistair Theirin

Alistair was enlisted by the Grey Wardens before taking his templar vows, though it's uncertain that he fully possessed the requisite mindset for a dedicated mage-hunter. As the companion of the Hero of Ferelden, and one of the main characters in Origins, he was disposed to see the good and the bad in all of the factions united against the darkspawn by the ancient treaties.

Several canonical versions of the storyline reveal that Alistair was the bastard son of King Maric, granting him a stronger claim to the crown than Loghain's daughter, Anora. King Alistair accedes to the throne of Ferelden following his part in the defeat of the archdemon and the repulsion of the Fifth Blight. Other versions find him still a Grey Warden, or even a washed-up drunkard.

STORY RECAP

You do not need to have played any previous Dragon Age games to understand and enjoy Dragon Age II and its story. Although they are set in the same richly developed universe, each episode stands alone. But if you are intrigued by the setting, it's worth noting that there is a continuity of incidents and characters. Some of the same events are covered from different perspectives. The games are broadly contemporaneous, taking place during and after the Fifth Blight, though Dragon Age II covers ten years rather than the two to three years of Origins and its Awakening expansion.

DRAGON AGE: ORIGINS

Origins opens in Year 30 of the Dragon Age, when Ferelden was threatened by the Fifth Blight. Our protagonist, later known as the Hero of Ferelden, was plucked from their place of birth under Right of Conscription and recruited by Duncan, a senior Grey Warden on his way to join King Cailan's forces. Reaching the historic stronghold of Ostagar, the new recruits were sent out on their first rookie mission to retrieve some old paperwork from a Warden outpost before the darkspawn advanced. Deep in the Korcari Wilds they encountered Morrigan and her mother Flemeth, an old Witch of the Wilds, who handed over the scrolls they were seeking.

On returning to Ostagar, the new recruits were put through an initiation ceremony known as The Joining. Only by drinking a preparation of the poisonous blood of the darkspawn can one become a Warden. Not all survive the test, and those that do are forever marked by the Taint.

As the darkspawn horde gathered, the Hero of Ferelden was assigned to light the beacon that would signal Teyrn Loghain's forces to launch a flanking assault. The King's regiment stood proudly before Ostagar, drawing the horde into a trap. But when the attack began, Loghain treacherously retired from battle and left Ostagar to perish. Both the King and Duncan were slain. The hero and fellow Warden Alistair were both rescued from the beacon tower by the old Witch, Flemeth.

Fearing that the world was lost, the survivors – now joined by Morrigan – resolved to invoke the invested authority of the Grey Wardens. Under the venerable law of Thedas, the scrolls of Ancient Treaties they had collected could revive age-old allegiances in days of Blight.

And so the hero's party swiftly set out to invoke the Treaties. After many quests and adventures, they enlisted the armies of Arl Eamon of Redcliffe; the clans of the Dalish Elves; the Dwarves of deep Orzammar; and even the Circle of Magi, whose members had been quarantined under the vigilant gaze of the Order of Templars. In a time of peril, the races and factions of Ferelden had always been compelled to forget their differences in confronting a common foe.

A Landsmeet was called in which the assembled forces rallied and the usurper Loghain's authority was challenged. They learned that only a Grey Warden may slay the archdemon leading the Blight – an act of sacrifice that would claim both lives. The demon's life essence would be reborn in the nearest darkspawn host, rendering it immortal, unless it could be drawn to the Warden instead – or to the Warden's unborn child if the player decided to perform a specific ritual with Morrigan.

Many endgame choices were open to the player, and it's worth noting that no one Dragon Age: Origins ending is considered the 'canon' or proper version of events by the developers.

Dragon Age: Origins – Awakening

The Awakening expansion picked up the story six months after the conclusion of Origins. The player then assumed the role of a Warden-Commander, commissioned to take charge of the Grey Wardens at Vigil's Keep. Traveling from the city of Amaranthine, the Warden arrived to find the Keep had been attacked by darkspawn. With the end of the Fifth Blight, and no archdemon to control these darkspawn, such an organized assault should have been impossible.

Cleaning the tower led to the discovery of a new form of darkspawn, known as the "disciples", that were not only intelligent but capable of speech, hitherto thought impossible. With admirable regard for the empirical method, the Warden-Commander went on to establish that disciples could still bleed and die like any other darkspawn.

An encounter with the enigmatic Architect (the "father" of the disciples) revealed the existence of even stranger creatures. The player learned of the Mother – a sentient broodmother – and was quested to track it down. Only later was it revealed that the Fifth Blight was brought about by The Architect's sincere but botched experiment to create independent, free-thinking disciples.

Awakening concluded with a typically difficult choice. A darkspawn band had gathered to besiege the city of Amaranthine, while another was advancing on Vigil's Keep. Duties conflicted, the Warden-Commander was forced to choose between the two in lending support and saving lives.

Familiar Faces

Origins players may be able to spot the return of both major and minor characters while playing Dragon Age II. Although these are mostly cameos, it's a reminder that the Fifth Blight was only one chapter in the turbulent history of Thedas – and that life goes on, thanks to the Hero of Ferelden.

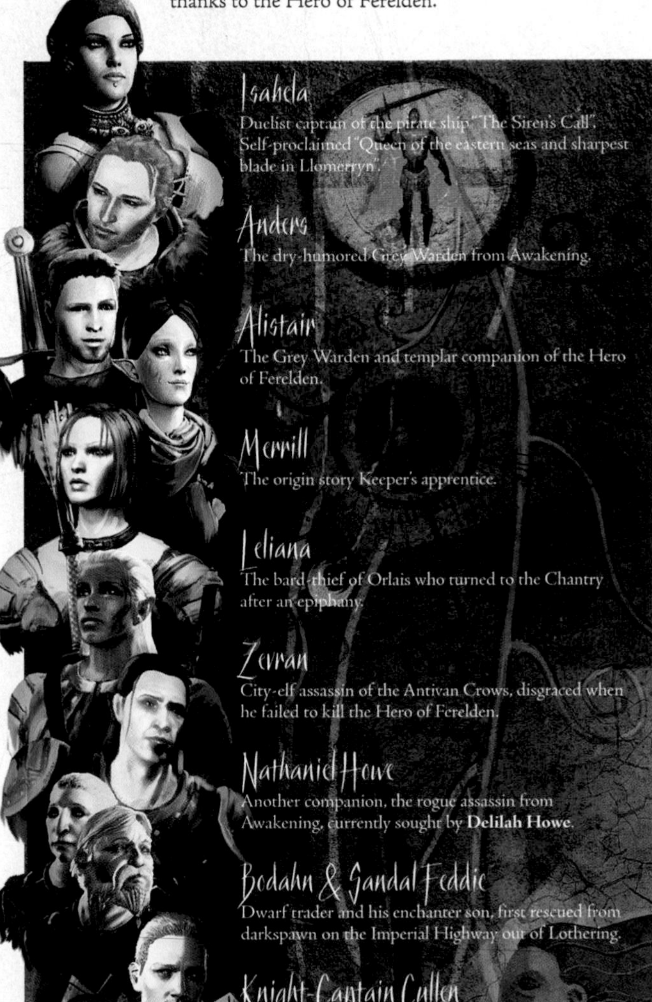

Isabela
Duelist captain of the pirate ship "The Siren's Call". Self-proclaimed "Queen of the eastern seas and sharpest blade in Llomerryn".
Anders
The dry-humored Grey Warden from Awakening.
Alistair
The Grey Warden and templar companion of the Hero of Ferelden.
Merrill
The origin story Keeper's apprentice.
Leliana
The bard-thief of Orlais who turned to the Chantry after an epiphany.
Zevran
City-elf assassin of the Antivan Crows, disgraced when he failed to kill the Hero of Ferelden.
Nathaniel Howe
Another companion, the rogue assassin from Awakening, currently sought by **Delilah Howe**.
Bodahn & Sandal Feddic
Dwarf trader and his enchanter son, first rescued from darkspawn on the Imperial Highway out of Lothering.
Knight-Captain Cullen
The templar imprisoned by Uldred in the Broken Circle quest, now enjoying a promotion.
Justice
A spirit from the Fade who has now fused with Anders, much as a spirit bound itself to Wynne.
Sketch
The bookish city elf from Leliana's Song (downloadable content).
Bonny Lem
A merchant spy in the service of Marjolaine.
Sophia Dryden
Warden-Commander from Warden's Keep (downloadable content) who became involved in blood magic.

Spoiler Alert!

The following overview of events in Dragon Age II reveals the challenges that lay ahead for the Champion and gives away the culmination of each Act. It should be clear that first-time players ought to avoid this section and return to our earlier walkthrough chapters until they have completed the game.

The Storyteller's Conceit

Dragon Age II tells its tale through a "framed narrative", a story within a story. In the opening scenes, the picaresque frame placed around our tale is that of Varric being interrogated by Cassandra Pentaghast as she pursues the truth about the rise to power of the Champion of Kirkwall. The world is on the brink of ruin, and Cassandra believes that Hawke has a key role to play in the future. But the Champion is nowhere to be found. If there's to be any hope of resolution, she needs to understand the target of her investigation. Chronologically, then, the events of Hawke's life in Dragon Age II are now also history.

As Varric recounts what he knows of Hawke's adventures, it is down to the player to write those adventures by reliving them. Each Act of the game's plot focuses on a crucial period in a ten year history, leaping forward through time at the end of each chronicle, such that the consequences of your decisions are all the more apparent.

Prologue: The Escape to Kirkwall

Overlapping the events of Origins, the prologue begins around the year 9:30 Dragon in the Dragon Age calendar, as the Fifth Blight is spreading with nothing to stem the tide of darkspawn.

Ahead of that surge came a deluge of human migrants, overwhelming the village of Lothering. Leaving almost too late, the Hawke family was among the last to make it out alive. Hawke's mother Leandra suggests that they flee to Kirkwall, where her younger brother Gamlen holds the Amell estate.

On the road they stumble into Aveline and her husband, Wesley, also survivors of the massacre. During their escape, they run into further bands of darkspawn. Though the party defeats many of these creatures, victory comes at a cruel price: Aveline's husband and Hawke's sibling are both slain.

The battle only really ends when a dragon swoops from the clouds and blasts the encroaching horde. The beast then transforms into Flemeth, the shapeshifting Witch of the Wilds. She rescues Hawke just as she recently rescued the Warden from the Tower of Ishal (covered in Origins). Having seen them defeat an ogre, Flemeth knows they cannot be peasants, and that means they may be of use. She is intrigued and asks them to perform a favor in return for safe passage past the horde.

They board a ship from Gwaren to Kirkwall, the towering city port. There is no welcome here: the authorities are unwilling to accept the influx of immigrants. All refugees are being held at the gates by the harbor guard, ready to be sent back to Ferelden. The bad news continues when they chance upon their uncle, only to find the family fortune gone and the estate sold. Gamlen explains that he can get them inside if they agree to work for a contact who can be convinced to vouch for them with hard cash. If Hawke will choose a sponsor, they can begin working off the considerable debt...

Act 1: From Rags to Riches

Over a year has passed, in which the player has made friends but little money. Brothers Varric and Bartrand plan an expedition into the Deep Roads. The end of the Fifth Blight makes this the safest time to venture into the abandoned dwarven network in search of antiquities. Though Bartrand dismisses the need for Hawke's services, Varric persuades the hero to become a business partner.

Principally, partnership means stumping up fifty sovereigns to 'co-invest' in the expedition on the promise of being repaid many times over with great treasures from the depths. Hawke simply needs to raise some capital, taking on whatever work can be found.

Hawke recruits a number of characters to aid him in future ventures, including Varric, as well as Aveline who has joined the city guard and offers some contract work to get started. Hawke also encounters Isabela, the pirate captain without a ship; Sebastian, the Exiled Prince; and is hired by Fenris, a fugitive slave. Bartrand believes that no venture into the Deep Roads would be safe without a Grey Warden to scan for darkspawn, so Hawke also tracks down the highly charged Anders. Later, completing Flemeth's errand introduces Merrill.

The expedition into the Deep Roads leads to an ancient dwarven thaig. Greed gets the better of Bartrand when they uncover a small but priceless statue fashioned from pure lyrium. Double crossing his own brother, Bartrand seals the tomb and leaves his partners to die. The party must tread a more dangerous path to escape.

Act 2: The Champion of Kirkwall

Three years pass. Hawke's status in Kirkwall has improved, the Deep Roads expedition delivering fame, fortune, and the accompanying opportunities and prestige. When people have problems that need solving in a very particular way, they come to Hawke.

The situation with the Qunari – stranded after their dreadnought ran aground near Kirkwall – is deteriorating. Instead of repairing their ship to return home, they have dismantled it to create a permanent camp within Kirkwall. Despite their leader, the Arishok, claiming to have contacted Par Vollen, no vessel has arrived to ship out his crew. And though the treaty grants them peaceful passage, their continued presence makes the citizens uneasy. Minor incidents between locals and Qunari threaten to ignite the situation.

If the Arishok were to find his holy relic, he could return home. Only a death-deserving dishonor awaits him without it. But Kirkwall is running out of time as the tension with the Qunari rises. When Aveline's city guard attempts to arrest some elves claiming religious sanctuary within the Qunari camp, the Arishok takes umbrage. Marshalling his forces, he demonstrates the disciplined effectiveness of his fighting force with an audacious counterattack. The streets of Kirkwall play host to running battles. Brooking no blasphemy, he declares that the city will be converted to the Qun or suffer the consequences – consequences that are clearly established when the Arishok throws the viscount's body before the crowd in the main hall.

Hawke decides upon a course of action – peaceful if the relic is retrieved, or bloody otherwise – that saves the city and earns him the title of the Champion of Kirkwall.

Act 3: The Circle is Broken

Another three years pass. Knight-Commander Meredith has taken stewardship of the city at the request of the Chantry, seizing power in what they considered the only way of keeping order following the viscount's death. Hawke's title of Champion is also endorsed by the Chantry, and has earned him more than an estate in Hightown...

The templars are controlling the city like a police state, imagining maleficar under every bed. Since the escape of several mages from the Circle, Meredith has been seeing conspiracies in every action. She orders raids and crackdowns, immediately incarcerating all suspects. There are also tales of insurrection against the templars that could only be the work of magic, so it appears neither faction is blameless. Riots in the slums tell of the fear and anger of the people, who look to their Champion to deliver them true justice and salvation.

Over time, it becomes clear that Hawke will have to choose to support First Enchanter Orsino and the mage cause, or the knight-commander and her templars.

Events reach a tipping point when an arrest warrant arrives for Anders. He claims he is no blood mage but believes the persecution has gone too far. Anders intends to send a message to the world and the Kirkwall Chantry explodes with the fury of that message.

Meredith immediately seeks the Right of Annulment for the safety of the city, which would entitle her to kill all mages. Without Elthina's mediation, war between mages and templars begins. In desperation, and with no way out, Orsino initiates a blood ritual by harvesting the bodies of sacrificed mages. Immediately possessed, he becomes an abomination in order to defeat the knight-commander's forces. Even if the Champion wishes to protect the Circle, this creature cannot be allowed to run rampant.

The final reckoning is with Meredith, whose exposure to lyrium has also made her a monster of sorts. She believes the Champion has become a threat, and she can no longer ignore such transgressions.

The showdown calls on the Champion to choose between friends and bear the consequences. If the player sides with the mages, those who escape spread the news. Despite being liberated by the Champion and surviving a massacre, Kirkwall is to become a byword for injustice and brutality once again.

Alternatively, the Champion sides with the templars and shows determination in exterminating the mage threat. Gaining the respect of the Order, Hawke is appointed the new Viscount of Kirkwall.

Epilogue: The Dark Times

In closing Hawke's story, Varric reflects on his friend's legacy. We learn that the Champion has since vanished or else the dwarf has no desire to let on what he knows.

So what does the future hold? The mage/templar crisis has drawn the battle lines, setting the scene for rebellion and persecution. Religious purges and expurgation can be expected from the Chantry, but news of Kirkwall may incite other Circles to rise up in revolt.

Perhaps more intriguing, is there a reason why Hawke is now "gone, like the Warden", as revealed by Cassandra in the final scenes? Do the Champion and the Hero of Ferelden have more in common than we know? And what do the mysterious Seekers of Truth have to do with this? Will some kind of inquisition be at the heart of the events of the next Dragon Age title?

Finally, is it safe to speculate that Morrigan may play a major role in future events? Flemeth's cryptic explanation for her journey to Sundermount ("A bit of security, should the inevitable occur. And if I know my Morrigan, it already has.") may refer to the Warden's battle with the Witch of the Wilds – or, perhaps, an artfully conjured facsimile – at her furious daughter's behest. Flemeth, lest we forget, was discovered to have achieved a form of immortality by periodically appropriating the bodies of numerous "daughters" throughout her history. Then again, with Morrigan carrying a child infused with the spirit of the archdemon in one likely narrative eventuality, it could mean so much more...

INDEX

If you are looking for specific information, this alphabetical listing is just what you need. In compiling this Index, we have chosen not to invert the definite/indefinite articles where these exist within established in-game terminology. To avoid any potential spoilers, note that all entries that link to sensitive content are written in red.

Quick Glossary

- **AoE:** "Area of Effect". Used to describe abilities that cover a designated patch of ground rather than a specific target.
- **Buff:** A beneficial **status effect** – that is, one that enhances the capabilities or durability of the individual in question.
- **Debuff:** A **status effect** that has an injurious or debilitating consequence for the victim.
- **DPS:** The average amount of damage per second that a character or weapon can potentially inflict.
- **Kiting:** A combat strategy where a character outruns their opponent and leads them around the battlefield as if "flying a kite", while other party members pile on ranged damage.
- **Micromanagement:** A combat strategy where you pause the action and manually control the positioning and actions of party members. This can be employed briefly for critical moments in battles that otherwise take place in real time or for the entire course of a tough encounter.
- **Nuke:** A damage dealer who speeds up the process of dispatching the opposition by inflicting massive amounts of damage in very little time.
- **Loot:** Any collectible that can be pillaged from containers or enemy drops. There are broadly three categories: equipment (weapons, armor and accessories), raw currency and junk.
- **Status Effect:** A temporary condition that increases an individual's combat prowess (**buff**), or impedes his or her performance or mobility (**debuff**).
- **Tank:** A sturdy, highly resilient fighter whose purpose is to draw dangerous enemies away from weaker party members. Also known as a "meat shield".
- **Threat:** The system that governs which party member enemies will target. Characters generate threat in a variety of ways but do so most commonly by inflicting damage.

CREDITS

The Complete Official Guide to **Dragon Age™ II** is a Piggyback Interactive Limited production.

PIGGYBACK

Managing Directors:	Louie Beatty, Vincent Pargney
Project Manager:	Matthias Loges
Creative Manager:	Carsten Ostermann
Editorial Director:	Mathieu Daujam
Authors:	James Price, Zy Nicholson
Research:	Nicolas Decerf, Klaus-Dieter Hartwig, Markus Bösebeck
Logistics:	Kristin Rüther
Art Directors:	Jeanette Killmann, Martin-Christoph Schneider (Glorienschein)
Designers:	Cathrin Queins, Arnie Medel, Wolfgang Bundschuh, Christian Runkel

ENGLISH VERSION

Sub-Editing:	Maura Sutton

FRENCH VERSION

Editors:	Mathieu Daujam, Claude-Olivier Eliçabe

GERMAN VERSION

Editor:	Klaus-Dieter Hartwig
Review:	Barbara Bode

ITALIAN VERSION

Editor:	Synthesis International srl
Localisation Managers:	Emanuele Scichilone, Marco Auletta

SPANISH VERSION

Editor:	Synthesis Iberia SL
Localisation Manager:	Gus Díaz

PRODUCTION

Preprint:	Uli Banse, Katharina Börner, Nicole Hannowsky, Ilse Hüttner, Anke Mattke, Petra Reidath, Arwed Scibba, Stefan Soltau, Torsten Wedemeier (AlsterWerk)

Special Thanks to:

Frank Adler, Beatriz Esteban Agustí, Thomas Altemeier, Antoine Bailly, Daniela Bartels, Marion Daujam, Oscar del Moral, Simone Dorn, Oliver Dorn, Jürgen Endres, Simone Fuller, John Holder, Martin Holder, Rishi Kartaram, Anskje Kirschner, Patricia López, Marco Nuzzi, Cristina Herraiz Olivas, Alberto Morán Roa, Stephanie Sanchez, Wolfgang Schallert, Marcel Sommer.

The Complete Official Guide to **Dragon Age™ II** is co-published in North America by Piggyback Interactive Limited and Prima Games, a division of Random House, Inc.

PRIMA GAMES

President:	Debra Kempker
Publishing Director:	Julie Asbury
Sales Director:	Mark Hughes
Senior Licensing Manager:	Aaron Lockhart

BIOWARE **DRAGON AGE™ II** GUIDE TEAM

LEADS SUPPORT

Executive Producer and Project Director:	Mark Darrah
Art Director:	Matthew Goldman
Lead Designer:	Mike Laidlaw
Strategy Guide Project Manager:	Chris Corfe

ART SUPPORT

Art:	Ben Carriere, Warren Heise, Nate LaMartina, Tyler Lee, Shane Hawco, Geordie Moffatt, Sheila Nash
Concept Artists:	Ben Huen, Ville Kinnunen, Steve Klit, Casper Konefal, Matt Rhodes, Ramil Sunga, Nick Thornborrow

DESIGN SUPPORT

Cinematic Design:	John Epler, Frank Gordon, Jonathan Perry
Editing:	Carlo Lynch, Karin Weekes
Systems Design:	Josh Stiksma, Peter Thomas
Technical Design:	Mark Barazzuol, Ferret Baudoin, Tony Evans, Craig Graff, Jason Hill, Yaron Jakobs, Kaelin Lavallee, Antony Lynch, Grant Mackay, Cori May, David Sims, Keith Warner
Writing:	Sheryl Chee, Dave Gaider, Jennifer Hepler, Mary Kirby, Luke Kristjanson

AUDIO, LOCALIZATION AND EXTERNAL RESOURCES SUPPORT:	Jason Barlow, Melanie Faulknor
PRODUCTION SUPPORT:	Rob Bartel (DLC Team), Dan Lazin, Colleen Perman, Aidan Scanlan, Ryan Warden
PROGRAMMING SUPPORT:	Bryan Derksen, Jacques Lebrun, Curtis Onuczko, Jon Thompson, Mika Uusnakki
QUALITY ASSURANCE & BUILD SUPPORT:	Gary Conrad, Andrew Crowe, Kristin Czarny, Chad De Wolfe, Patrick Irwin, Cody Ouimet, Edward Pollard, Matt Powell, Mark Ramsden, Tim Rideout, Joel Roy, Corey Runnals, Colin Steedman, Stanley Woo
BUSINESS DEVELOPMENT:	Chris Bain, Richard Iwaniuk, Jim Stadelman
FACILITIES SUPPORT:	Kelly Wambold

INFORMATION SYSTEMS SUPPORT

Assistant Director of Information Systems:	Lee Evanochko
Desktop Support:	Dave McGruther, Shane Gaudry

MARKETING SUPPORT

Worldwide Director of Marketing:	David S. Silverman
Additional Marketing:	Matthew Villeneuve Deeka Macdonald, Maria Sayans (EA Global Publishing)

Important:
Piggyback Interactive Limited has made every effort to determine that the information contained in this book is accurate. However, the publisher makes no warranty, either expressed or implied, as to the accuracy, effectiveness, or completeness of the material in this book; nor does the publisher assume liability for damages, either incidental or consequential, that may result from using the information in this book. The publisher cannot provide information regarding game play, hints and strategies, or problems with hardware or software. Questions should be directed to the support numbers provided by the game and device manufacturers in their documentation. Some game tricks require precise timing and may require repeated attempts before the desired result is achieved.

© 2011 Electronic Arts Inc. BioWare, BioWare logo and Dragon Age are trademarks of EA International (Studio and Publishing) Ltd. EA and the EA logo are trademarks of Electronic Arts Inc.

Xbox and Xbox 360 are trademarks of the Microsoft group of companies and are used under license from Microsoft.

"PlayStation" is a registered trademark of Sony Computer Entertainment Inc.

All other trademarks are the property of their respective owners.

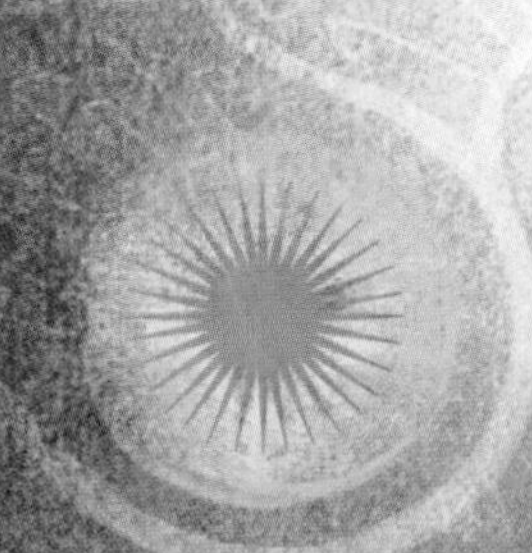